Managing Institutional Complexity

D1607719

A Core Research Project of the International Human Dimensions Programme on Global Environmental Change (IHDP)

Oran R. Young, Leslie A. King, and Heike Schroeder, eds., *Institutions and Environmental Change: Principal Findings, Applications, and Research Frontiers* (2008)

Frank Biermann and Bernd Siebenhüner, eds., *Managers of Global Change: The Influence of International Environmental Bureaucracies* (2009)

Sebastian Oberthür and Olav Schram Stokke, eds., *Managing Institutional Complexity: Regime Interplay and Global Environmental Change* (2011)

Managing Institutional Complexity
Regime Interplay and Global Environmental Change

edited by Sebastian Oberthür and Olav Schram Stokke

Institutional Dimensions of Global Environmental Change
A Core Research Project of the International Human Dimensions
Programme on Global Environmental Change (IHDP)

The MIT Press
Cambridge, Massachusetts
London, England

© 2011 Massachusetts Institute of Technology

All rights reserved. No part of this book may be reproduced in any form by any electronic or mechanical means (including photocopying, recording, or information storage and retrieval) without permission in writing from the publisher.

For information about special quantity discounts, please email special_sales@mitpress.mit .edu

This book was set in Sabon by Toppan Best-set Premedia Limited. Printed and bound in the United States of America.

Library of Congress Cataloging-in-Publication Data

Managing institutional complexity : regime interplay and global environmental change / edited by Sebastian Oberthür and Olav Schram Stokke.
    p. cm.—(Institutional dimensions of global environmental change)
Includes bibliographical references and index.
ISBN 978-0-262-01591-2 (hardcover : alk. paper)—ISBN 978-0-262-51624-2 (pbk. : alk. paper)
1. Environmental policy–International cooperation. 2. Climatic changes–International cooperation. 3. Global warming–International cooperation. 4. Environmental law, International. I. Oberthür, Sebastian. II. Stokke, Olav Schram, 1961–
GE170.M36   2011
363.738′74561—dc22

                                                                    2010054079

10   9   8   7   6   5   4   3   2   1

Contents

Foreword

Oran R. Young

During the preparation of the Science Plan for the long-term project on the Institutional Dimensions of Global Environmental Change (IDGEC) in 1997 and 1998, we spent a lot of time discussing what emerged as the project's analytical themes, or the set of topics we deemed ripe for a major research push over a period of five to ten years. The themes we selected became known in the research community as the problems of fit, interplay, and scale (Young et al. 1999/2005). The problem of fit is a matter of compatibility between the features of institutional arrangements or governance systems and the character of the socioecological systems they are designed to manage. The problem of interplay concerns interactions between and among regimes created to address specific issues, such as climate and trade, that belong to separate issue areas. The problem of scale is a matter of the generalizability of findings relating to governance systems in the dimensions of space, time, and authority. As the synthesis volume we produced to record the most important results of IDGEC research makes clear, the project played a significant role in advancing knowledge regarding all three of these analytical themes (Young, King, and Schroeder 2008).

The stream of research that IDGEC triggered relating to institutional interplay or interactions among governance systems has proved particularly robust. In the IDGEC Science Plan, we drew simple distinctions between horizontal and vertical interplay and between functional and political interplay. This yielded a 2 × 2 matrix pointing to four different types of interplay. The matrix proved sufficient to trigger a growing and increasingly sophisticated body of research on institutional interplay. I am happy to report that it also led a number of researchers, including the editors of this volume, to raise probing questions about the formulation included in the IDGEC Science Plan and to experiment with new and improved ways to frame some of the important research questions pertaining to interplay. This sort of critical but constructive analysis exemplifies the best traditions in scientific research, and the results have broadened and deepened our understanding of this important subject.

One major finding of the stream of recent research on institutional interplay is that interactions between regimes can produce mutually beneficial and even synergistic results (Oberthür and Gehring 2006). Although intuitively this may not seem surprising, it is worth noting that much of the initial interest in interplay arose from a concern that the rapid growth in the number of international regimes would trigger a substantial increase in conflicts in this realm. The prospect of tensions and even open conflict between the global trade regime and various multilateral environmental agreements undoubtedly fueled this concern. But as the work of scholars such as Thomas Gehring and Sebastian Oberthür has made clear, conflict is by no means inevitable in this realm. Others have shown that regimes often occupy distinct niches, performing tasks such as building knowledge, creating norms, enhancing capacity, and enforcing compliance (Stokke 2007). This means that, at least in some cases, distinct regimes may develop in a manner that is complementary rather than conflictual.

This book, which is one of the last of the scientific products directly attributable to the IDGEC project, carries this stream of research forward with chapters that report on the latest findings of cutting-edge research regarding institutional interplay. Although each of the chapters has its own story to tell, the editors have done an excellent job in showing how, in aggregate, they shed substantial light on two prominent themes, interplay management and institutional complexes. Interplay management refers to conscious efforts on the part of those associated with distinct regimes or those approaching these matters in more synoptic terms to enhance positive interactions and minimize interference between and among regimes. This theme will surely increase in prominence in the near future. Institutional complexes arise when two or more distinct regimes generate interlocking governance structures relating to broad issue areas (e.g., climate, biodiversity) and coevolve in such a way as to produce emergent properties. The emergence of such complexes, whether they represent planned developments or reflect de facto trends, is another phenomenon that is of growing significance in a world in which both the number and the variety of international regimes are on the increase.

The importance of institutional interplay is destined to grow as more and more issues appear requiring governance systems that are transboundary, international, or global in scope. There is nothing surprising about this. It is a matter that has long been familiar to policymakers and researchers studying political institutions in domestic settings, who have introduced concepts such as conflict of laws to organize thinking about institutional interplay and have developed judicial procedures to sort out complications that arise when two or more sets of rules or regulatory arrangements address the same issue area. At the international level, where there is no government or public authority in the ordinary sense of the term, there is a need to make use of procedures that focus more on the role of negotiation to minimize conflict and encourage synergy among interacting regimes. This will put a premium on the conduct of policy-relevant research designed to provide the knowledge needed by those responsible for such negotiations. The quality of the chapters in this book provides grounds for optimism regarding the capacity of the research community to rise to this challenge. The best tribute to the success of this volume will be its ability to stimulate an ongoing stream of research on institutional interplay that will not only extend some of the findings reported in these chapters but will also open up new questions that will provide opportunities for contributions from the next generation of analysts interested in institutional interplay.

References

Oberthür, Sebastian, and Thomas Gehring, eds. 2006. *Institutional Interaction in Global Environmental Governance: Synergy and Conflict among International and EU Policies*. Cambridge, Mass.: MIT Press.

Stokke, Olav Schram. 2007. Examining the Consequences of Arctic Institutions. In *International Cooperation and Arctic Governance: Regime Effectiveness and Northern Region Building*, ed. Olav Schram Stokke and Geir Honneland, 13–26. London: Routledge.

Young, Oran R., with contributions from Arun Agrawal, Leslie A. King, Peter H. Sand, Arild Underdal, and Merrilyn Wasson. 1999/2005. *Institutional Dimensions of Global Environmental Change (IDGEC) Science Plan*. Report No. 9/16. Bonn: International Human Dimensions Programme on Global Environmental Change.

Young, Oran R., Leslie A. King, and Heike Schroeder, eds. 2008. *Institutions and Environmental Change: Principal Findings, Applications, and Research Frontiers*. Cambridge, Mass.: MIT Press.

Acknowledgments

This book is the youngest offspring of the Institutional Dimensions of Global Environmental Change (IDGEC) project. IDGEC was a core project of the International Human Dimensions Programme of Global Environmental Change (IHDP) from 1998 to 2007. It has since been succeeded by the Earth System Governance Project, launched in 2009 (http://www.earthsystemgovernance.org), so this volume may also be seen as a bridge to this new core IHDP program.

Work on this book took off in Bali in December 2006, at the final IDGEC Synthesis Conference, held to harvest the results of nearly ten years of research. As one of the analytical themes of the IDGEC project, institutional interaction or interplay also formed one of the core themes of the Bali conference. The contributors to this book were able to present and discuss first drafts of their chapters at the conference, and later further developed their work in several rounds. Without the Bali conference, this book could not have been realized, so we owe many thanks to the conference sponsors. In particular, we wish to acknowledge the support of the United Nations University Institute of Advanced Studies for work on the analytical theme of institutional interplay.

Over the years, many people have contributed to the progress and success of this book project. We owe particular thanks to Oran R. Young, who skillfully directed the IDGEC project and commented on parts of the manuscript with his usual combination of stern criticism and amiable support. We are also grateful for the support of many members of the IDGEC and Earth System Governance Project community, among others Frank Biermann and Arild Underdal. Our thanks also go to the three anonymous reviewers who offered constructive comments on individual chapters as well as on the overall structure of the book.

We wish to acknowledge financial support from our own institutions, the Institute for European Studies at the Vrije Universiteit Brussels and the Fridtjof Nansen Institute in Lysaker, Norway. Alexander Daniel, Ashley Hennekam, Melanie Jung, and Lawrence Steenstra all provided valuable technical and logistical assistance at various stages. Claire Dupont deserves our special thanks for diligently and patiently guiding and organizing the editing of the various versions of the manuscript. In this process, Susan Høivik provided excellent—indeed, invaluable—language assistance.

Finally, we thank Clay Morgan at the MIT Press for a smooth review process and for helpful advice and continuous support of our project.

List of Abbreviations

ABS	Access and benefit sharing
ACAP	Arctic Contaminants Action Program
AEPS	Arctic Environmental Protection Strategy
AMAP	Arctic Monitoring and Assessment Program
APP	Asia-Pacific Partnership for Clean Development and Climate
CBD	Convention on Biological Diversity
CDM	Clean Development Mechanism
CER	Certified Emission Reduction
CFC	Chlorofluorocarbon
CGIAR	Consultative Group on International Agricultural Research
CITES	Convention on International Trade in Endangered Species of Wild Fauna and Flora
CLRTAP	Convention on Long-Range Transboundary Air Pollution
COP	Conference of the Parties
CSD	Commission on Sustainable Development
CTE	Committee on Trade and Environment of the World Trade Organization
DWFN	Distant-water fishing nation
ECE	UN Economic Commission for Europe
ECOSOC	Economic and Social Council
EEZ	Exclusive economic zone
EU	European Union
FAO	Food and Agriculture Organization of the United Nations
GATT	General Agreement on Tariffs and Trade
GDP	Gross Domestic Product

GEA	Global Energy Assessment
GEF	Global Environment Facility
GHG	Greenhouse gas
GMO	Genetically modified organism
HCFC	Hydrochlorofluorocarbon
HFC	Hydrofluorocarbon
ICCAT	International Convention for the Conservation of Atlantic Tunas
ICES	International Council for the Exploration of the Sea
ICTSD	International Center for Trade and Sustainable Development
IDGEC	Institutional Dimensions of Global Environmental Change
IEA	International Energy Agency
IEA database	International Environmental Agreements database
IFQ	Individual fishing quota
IGO	Intergovernmental organization
IHDP	International Human Dimensions Programme of Global Environmental Change
IISD	International Institute for Sustainable Development
ILO	International Labor Organization
IMF	International Monetary Fund
IMO	International Maritime Organization
IPCC	Intergovernmental Panel on Climate Change
IPR	Intellectual property right
IRENA	International Renewable Energy Agency
ISF	International Seed Federation
ITPGR	International Treaty on Plant Genetic Resources for Food and Agriculture
ITQ	Individual transferable quota
IUCN	International Union for the Conservation of Nature
IUU	Illegal, unreported, unregulated
JLG	Joint Liaison Group
MA	Millennium Ecosystem Assessment
MDG	Millennium Development Goal
MEA	Multilateral environmental agreement
MFN	Most-favored nation (principle)

MOP	Meeting of the Parties
NAFO	Northwest Atlantic Fisheries Organization
NATO	North Atlantic Treaty Organization
NEAFC	North-East Atlantic Fisheries Commission
NGO	Nongovernmental organization
OECD	Organisation for Economic Co-operation and Development
OPEC	Organization of Petroleum Exporting Countries
OSPAR Convention	Convention for the Protection of the Marine Environment of the North-East Atlantic
PAMs	Policies and measures
PCB	Polychlorinated biphenyl
PGRFA	Plant Genetic Resources for Food and Agriculture
POP	Persistent organic pollutant
RFMO	Regional fisheries management organization
SBSTA	Subsidiary Body for Scientific and Technological Advice
SPS Agreement	Agreement on Sanitary and Phytosanitary Measures
TEAP	Technology and Economic Assessment Panel of the Montreal Protocol
TRIPS Agreement	Agreement on Trade-Related Aspects of Intellectual Property Rights
TURFs	Territorial use rights in fisheries
UN	United Nations
UNCCD	United Nations Convention to Combat Desertification
UNCLOS	United Nations Convention on the Law of the Sea
UNDP	United Nations Development Programme
UNEP	United Nations Environment Programme
UNFCCC	United Nations Framework Convention on Climate Change
UNIDO	United Nations Industrial Development Organization
UNTS	United Nations Treaty Series
UPOV	International Union for the Protection of New Varieties of Plants
VCLT	Vienna Convention on the Law of Treaties
WEHAB	Water, energy, health, agriculture, and biodiversity

WEO	World Environment Organization
WHO	World Health Organization
WMO	World Meteorological Organization
WSSD	World Summit on Sustainable Development
WTO	World Trade Organization

1

Introduction

Institutional Interaction in Global Environmental Change

Olav Schram Stokke and Sebastian Oberthür

The Institutional Dimensions of Global Environmental Change (IDGEC) project was of central importance for research on the role of institutional interaction or interplay in global environmental change.[1] From 1998 to 2007, IDGEC formed one of the core projects of the International Human Dimensions Programme of Global Environmental Change (IHDP). Its 1998 Science Plan (Young et al. 1999/2005) put institutional interplay on the agenda of global change research after a few scholars pointed to the risk of "treaty congestion" (Brown Weiss 1993, 679) and to an increasing "regime density" (Young 1996, 1) in the international system. Since then, research on institutional interplay has made important progress, both conceptually and empirically. However, there remain some important areas of the research agenda on institutional interaction that promise high returns on investment in further research (Gehring and Oberthür 2008).

As one of the main legacies of IDGEC, the present volume aims to advance our understanding of interinstitutional influence and its consequences by focusing on two areas in particular need of further research. First, the contributors investigate how states and other actors, individually and collectively, go about improving interinstitutional synergy or avoiding disruption, and what factors condition their success. They thus examine the crucial issue of the management of institutional interaction (*interplay management*). Second, the book asks what forces drive the emergence and change of so-called *institutional complexes*—complex interaction situations in which two or more international institutions interact to cogovern issue areas in international relations (Raustiala and Victor 2004) and form interlocking structures (Underdal and Young 2004, 374–375) of global governance. This exploration of institutional complexes includes an investigation of how competing concerns are balanced and what factors account for stability and change.

This introduction lays the conceptual foundations for the book and provides an overview of its structure and contents. First we introduce four core concepts that inform the individual contributions and allow investigation of the two central themes of the volume. In this way we establish our understanding of international institutions, institutional interaction, interplay management, and institutional complexes. We then outline the structure of the book and offer a brief overview of the content of each chapter.

International Institutions

Institutions are "persistent and connected sets of rules and practices that prescribe behavioral roles, constrain activity, and shape expectations" (Keohane 1989, 3). They include "negotiated" arrangements that governments and others deliberately establish in order to shape policy outcomes and behavior, as well as "spontaneous" institutions (Young 1982) that emerge, much as customary law does, from practice and interaction. From a governance perspective, negotiated institutions are of particular interest because they may be employed instrumentally to bring about change and influence outcomes. Consequently, they have been the major focus of the literature on international institutions in global environmental governance (see, e.g., Haas, Keohane, and Levy 1993; Victor, Raustiala, and Skolnikoff 1998; Miles et al. 2002; Oberthür and Gehring 2006a). The essays in this book mainly deal with negotiated institutions.

Negotiated international institutions have two components. First, they comprise substantive rules and obligations that indicate socially desirable behavior. These norms are the principal instruments of governance that may affect addressee behavior and have an impact on the issue in question. Second, unlike spontaneous institutions, negotiated institutions typically set out procedural rules for how participants are to make and implement decisions or change substantive provisions (Young 1980; Gehring 1994). Decision rules and other parts of an institution's procedural component can be vital for its ability to adapt and respond to changes in the issue area it regulates, or in the state of knowledge on that area. And in environmental governance, such changes can be frequent and rapid (Young et al. 1999/2005).

We consider both international regimes and international organizations as international institutions. International regimes are the subset of institutions that involve states and concern behavior within specific issue areas (Levy, Young, and Zürn 1995). International organizations may also govern specific issue areas, but their distinctive features are the actor qualities that contracting states have endowed them with, such as a physical location, a staff of employees, and usually a legal personality (Young 1986, 110). Accordingly, an international organization is a possible but not a necessary part of the procedural components of an international regime. For example, the World Trade Organization (WTO) serves as an instrument for operating the global trade regime, and the International Maritime Organization (IMO) and the United Nations Environment Programme (UNEP) provide a range of services to numerous international regimes within their respective functional remits. Unlike these, the climate change regime has established a specialized administrative structure, located in Bonn, Germany. Like the IMO and UNEP, it forms part of the UN system of organizations.

Clarifying the use of these terms should help facilitate communication among scholars and practitioners from various disciplines, as well as those who use different conceptual frameworks. Beyond the common denominator of regimes and organizations both being international institutions (see also Martin and Simmons 1998; Simmons and Martin 2002), organizations are regarded by some (including some of the contributors to this volume) primarily as procedural and administrative frameworks for decision making, guided by a shared objective, whereas others emphasize that some organizations also include substantive rules and norms governing a particular area of international relations. Hence, in this book we do not draw a sharp distinction between international regimes or institutions and international organizations, as some other segments of relevant research do (e.g., Biermann and Siebenhüner 2007; Young 2008).

International regimes and international organizations both form part of our research agenda on institutional interplay. Up until the 1970s, international organizations such as the UN Food and Agriculture Organization (FAO), the UN Industrial Development Organization, and the IMO were the major subjects of research on international institutions (Martin and Simmons 1998). Then the focus shifted to international regimes and their formation, development, and effectiveness (e.g., Krasner 1982; Keohane 1984; Gehring 1994; Young 1999; Miles et al. 2002). More recently, international administrations and bureaucracies have attracted increasing research attention (Biermann and Siebenhüner 2009; Young 2010). Since international regimes and international organizations often complement each other, it is useful to take both into account in exploring the institutional framework of global governance.

There is nothing sacrosanct about our way of conceptualizing the field. However, the clarifications above should assist the reader in better grasping the research agenda that underlies this volume. This agenda includes the full range of interaction across institutional boundaries, whether it concerns substantive international rules, decision-making processes, or related administrative structures (secretariats, other bodies). We refer to all these phenomena as "institutional interaction" or "interplay."

Institutional Interaction: The Starting Point

Institutional interaction or interplay arises in situations in which one institution affects the development or performance of another institution. For example, WTO rules and procedures on free trade have constrained the willingness and ability of parties to multilateral environmental agreements (MEAs) to design and implement trade restrictions that can support their collective environmental protection goals (see Axelrod in this volume; Gehring in this volume). In the field of environmental governance, the 1997 Kyoto Protocol to the UN Framework Convention on Climate Change created incentives for establishing fast-growing monocultural tree plantations in order to maximize carbon sequestration from the atmosphere, but this works against the goal of the 1992 Convention on Biological Diversity (CBD) to preserve the biological diversity of forest ecosystems (Pontecorvo 1999). In contrast to such disruptive interplay, the global regime on the transboundary movement of hazardous wastes has been strengthened as a result of numerous regional regimes that address the same environmental problem in complementary ways (Meinke 2002). Synergetic relationships can also be based in contingency relationships between institutions. For instance, the effectiveness of restrictions on trade in ozone-depleting substances under the Montreal Protocol was contingent on adaptation of the World Customs Organization's harmonized system of customs codes, which were poorly equipped to single out products containing such substances (Oberthür 2001). Institutional interaction may involve institutions at the same level of governance (horizontal interplay) or at different levels, as with the relationship between international and national institutions (vertical interplay).

The mere coexistence or parallel but unrelated evolution of two or more institutions is less relevant to the study of institutional interaction: institutional interplay requires actual interinstitutional influence (see, e.g., King 1997; Stokke 2000; Oberthür and Gehring 2006a; Young et al. 1999/2005). Such influence may concern regime dynamics—that is, the creation or maintenance of institutions, which may include normative development—or their consequences in various domains, including their effectiveness in addressing and resolving the problems that led to their creation in the first place.

The rise of institutional interplay as a subject of research in global governance is due to the growing density of the international institutional landscape, as is now well documented. The number of international treaties has increased steadily, from less than 15,000 in 1960 to more than 55,000 in 1997 (Zürn et al. 2007). Mitchell (2007) lists more than 900 multilateral agreements in the environmental area; hence, international environmental governance is one of the institutionally most fragmented areas of international law and policy (Beisheim et al. 1999). New agreements further expand the scope of international environmental regulation, in the 2000s covering additional issues such as trade in genetically modified organisms and persistent organic pollutants. States are continually entering into new treaties and elaborating or expanding existing ones, as illustrated by the regulatory expansion of the international climate change regime (Yamin and Depledge 2004) and the growing specificity of high-seas fisheries law (Stokke 2001a). With this growing number of institutions, any new arrangement enters an institutional setting that is already densely populated, so the scope for institutional interaction thus increases.

Institutional interplay has become a ubiquitous phenomenon in, and an important determinant of, international environmental governance (Oberthür and Gehring 2006c). Indeed, it is hardly surprising that research on institutional interplay has come to the fore of the institutional research agenda early in the twenty-first century. In the 1980s, research on international institutions focused on the formation and development of international regimes (Krasner 1982; Hasenclever, Mayer, and Rittberger 1997). It turned to the issue of institutional effectiveness in the 1990s, concentrating heavily on international environmental governance (Haas, Keohane, and Levy 1993; Stokke and Vidas 1996; Victor, Raustiala, and Skolnikoff 1998; Young 1999; Miles et al. 2002). Along with contributions by legal scholars (e.g., Leebron 2002; Wolfrum and Matz 2003; Vranes 2006), this work on institutional effectiveness forms the basis for ongoing research on institutional interplay and institutional complexes. Whereas effectiveness studies highlight the impacts individual institutions have within their own governance domain, institutional interaction revolves around the effects institutions have on each other.

As such, institutional interplay forms part of the broader consequences that institutions may have beyond their own domains (Underdal and Young 2004).

As Sebastian Oberthür and Thomas Gehring show in chapter 2, both conceptual and empirical research on institutional interaction has advanced tremendously since the second half of the 1990s. In particular, many empirical studies have shed light on the various facets of the relationship between the governance of trade and the environment, on ocean governance, and on climate change governance. These studies provide a rich array of empirical material that future work may further exploit and supplement. On this stronger empirical basis, conceptual progress has helped clarify several analytic categories that are now regularly employed in the study of institutional interplay. And, quite important, research has identified a range of causal mechanisms that can help us understand the driving forces and governance conditions that structure the realm of institutional interaction. These advances constitute promising first steps and a sound basis for further explorations of the field of institutional interplay and for advancing our understanding of global governance. They also provide the starting point of this volume.

Interplay Management

Interplay management refers to conscious efforts by any relevant actor or group of actors, in whatever form or forum, to address and improve institutional interaction and its effects (see also Stokke 2001b; Oberthür 2009). It usually involves the pursuit of collective objectives as enshrined in the institutions in question. The possibility for such management is inherent in the concept of institutional interplay. As regards negotiated institutions, interaction originates in political decisions made within one institution and can be influenced by decisions in an affected institution (Oberthür and Gehring 2006a). Furthermore, individual actors are often able to respond to such interaction and may shape its effects when implementing decisions. Whereas institutional interplay as such may occur even without the knowledge of the actors concerned, interplay *management* requires awareness of and reflection on the interaction.

The concept of interplay management differs from other closely related notions in the literature on institutional interaction. The IDGEC Science Plan introduced the concept of political linkages (in contrast to functional linkages), which "arise when actors decide to consider two or more arrangements as parts of a larger institutional complex" (Young et al. 1999/2005, 62). This concept builds on Young's (1996) earlier notion of "clustering" as something that occurs when actors combine different governance arrangements in institutional packages even when there is no compelling functional need to do so. For example, the UN Convention on the Law of the Sea (UNCLOS) joins under one umbrella international regimes concerning navigation, fisheries, marine pollution, scientific research, and numerous more specific activities. Political linkage differs from interplay management by not requiring any preceding or anticipated interplay. States could decide, for instance, to integrate the Basel Convention on hazardous waste and the climate change regime within a World Environment Organization, even though institutional interaction between those first two regimes has been minimal so far. In such a case, interplay would result from clustering, rather than driving it. Furthermore, especially the notion of clustering but also the wider concept of political linkages connotes a predilection for institutional aggregation. In contrast, the notion of interplay management also encompasses, as will become clearer below, approaches with little or no cross-institutional coordination.

Interplay management differs also from the concept of policy response to interaction. A policy response is additional to the original institutional interplay: it occurs as a reaction to the effects of interaction (Gehring and Oberthür 2006, 314–316). In contrast, interplay management may also occur in anticipation of such effects, thereby co-constituting the original interaction. To illustrate, those who negotiated the compliance system of the Kyoto Protocol on climate change were anxious to avoid substantive or procedural elements that might contradict the international trade regime (Stokke 2004). Similarly, while the WTO significantly influenced the trade-related provisions of the Cartagena Protocol on Biosafety, parties to that protocol retained some room for maneuver, which they used for consciously managing the interplay with the global trade regime (Oberthür and Gehring 2006c). In some cases, members of an institution may even decide to reject pressure from another institution and deliberately opt for noninteraction as a means of interplay management (see Gehring in this volume). Policy responses to interaction thus form part of interplay management, but the latter is broader because it includes activities beyond policy responses.

Interplay management, moreover, implies a standard of evaluation. In contrast to concepts like political linkage, clustering, and policy response, "managing" something implicitly requires a goal or objective. Various standards may be applied. In research on global environmental change, enhancing the effectiveness of global environmental governance is a prominent candidate (see, e.g., Stokke 2001b; Oberthür 2009), given the extensive research on this phenomenon (e.g., Haas, Keohane, and Levy 1993; Young 1999; Miles et al. 2002). In this volume, the contributions by Sebastian Oberthür, Claire Dupont, and Yasuko Matsumoto (chapter 5) as well as Olav Schram Stokke (chapter 6) explicitly apply this standard. Other standards may also prove fruitful. For example, institutional management may generally aim to enhance synergy and mitigate disrup-⁣tion among the institutions involved, without giving priority to environmental objectives. We may note the use of such a standard in the chapters by Harro van Asselt, Mark Axelrod, Stefan Jungcurt, Fariborz Zelli, and Thomas Gehring in this volume. Yet other standards applied in the evaluation of public policy or environmental institutions in particular reflect various notions of social justice and equity (international, intranational, or intergenerational), efficiency, or "good governance" (Young 1994; Mitchell 2008). On the basis of these general criteria, one may also develop multidimensional standards. Notably, Sylvia I. Karlsson-Vinkhuyzen and Marcel T. J. Kok (chapter 11) apply sustainable development as their standard. As with the wider field of research on the performance of environmental institutions, scope remains for expanding the criteria in use (Mitchell 2008). While any study of interplay management must be clear about the standard it applies, comparison of findings across interplay management studies is more powerful if the same standard has been applied.

A further dimension of interplay management concerns the instruments or means actors use to avoid or deal with disruptive interplay or to maximize synergy. In the literature on international and European governance, several categorizations of instruments have emerged, in particular with a view to distinguishing hierarchical regulatory approaches from "new modes" of governance that emphasize, among other things, participatory and informational means (Jordan, Wurzel, and Zito 2003; von Homeyer 2006). Similarly, distinctions between command-and-control regulation, market-based approaches, and information measures are common in debates about public policy instruments at the national level (Vedung 1998). These categories can also serve as a starting point for thinking about means of interplay management. For example, Oberthür (2009, 377–378) differentiates between regulatory interplay management and enabling interplay management (learning and capacity building), and Stokke in this volume makes a distinction between cognitional, normative, and utilitarian interplay management (see also Stokke 2001b).

Relevant actors may advance interplay management at various levels of coordination among those involved (Oberthür 2009, 375–377). At the first and highest level, interplay management could rely on *overarching institutional frameworks*, which requires decision making beyond the interacting institutions. In the absence of a hierarchical political authority ("world government") at the international level, institutions that span sectoral governance systems may specialize in one particular policy field, as UNEP does. Such overarching institutions may also be more comprehensive and cut across policy fields, as evident in the UN itself and in the general rules of international law, including those laid out in the 1969 Vienna Convention on the Law of Treaties. Proposals for a World Environment Organization aim at establishing a new, specialized overarching institution intended, inter alia, as a means for interplay management (Biermann and Bauer 2005).

At the second level, *joint interplay management* of the institutions concerned involves targeted efforts to coordinate the activities of interacting institutions, possibly even to create joint rules governing the interaction. Coordination requires a communication process across the interacting institutions, for example in the form of an exchange of information between the relevant secretariats, representation at each other's meetings, or the creation of special bodies at scientific, administrative, or political levels to take up issues of common concern. Joint management thus involves horizontal structures for coordination between the sectoral regimes that characterize international environmental governance. This level of interplay management has received considerable attention, as reflected in the chapters by van Asselt and Zelli in this volume (see also Chambers 2008 and the discussion on clustering and political linkages above). Where joint management evolves into the establishment of a permanent interinstitutional body, the level of coordination approaches that of an overarching institutional framework.

At a third level, *unilateral management by individual institutions* involves collective decision making and action within one or more of the interacting institutions, without any coordination *between* them. For instance, the interaction between the WTO and the MEAs that employ environmental trade restrictions has been shaped largely through independent decision making within the respective institutions (Gehring in this volume). By not involving interinstitutional coordination of decision making, unilateral management plays with the existing repertoire of international environmental governance.

At the fourth and lowest level of coordination, governments and other actors, such as civil society organizations and businesses, may engage in *autonomous management* efforts at national and regional levels. Individual actors constantly have to make decisions on the implementation of international rules and norms. Some of them are also involved in the decision-making processes in international institutions, also concerning collective interplay management. In this regard, individual actors face obvious choices that affect the overall interaction situation. For example, a state may implement environmental trade restrictions mandated by an MEA but in tension with WTO rules, with a view to provoking either tacit acceptance by other actors or a decision under the WTO dispute settlement procedure that would explicitly permit such restrictions under WTO law. Relevant activities of individual actors or groups of actors may either be in line with the objectives of the institutions involved or focus on realizing narrow self-interest. In our view, research on autonomous interplay management should differentiate clearly between these different orientations. It may even be useful to reserve the term "interplay management" for those activities that aim to pursue, maximize, or reconcile the collectively agreed-upon objectives of the interacting institutions. The contributions to this volume generally employ the concept of interplay management in this perspective.

These conceptual clarifications provide the basis and starting point for the investigation of interplay management in this volume. Interplay management is a topic that has generally been underresearched (see Gehring and Oberthür 2008, 221–222). Given the necessarily limited scope of our endeavor, we may not expect final answers, but the intention with this volume is to advance our understanding of interplay management by taking up some central questions, including the following: To what extent, with what means, and at what levels of coordination do states and other actors pursue interplay management? What are the achievements of interplay management so far? What factors have shaped its success or failure? And how might interplay management be improved in the future?

Institutional Complexes

Individual international institutions not only interact with each other, they also form parts of broader institutional complexes, and their interaction generates interlocking governance structures (Raustiala and Victor 2004; Underdal and Young 2004, 374–375; Biermann et al. 2009) that frequently extend beyond the environmental realm (see Karlsson-Vinkhuyzen and Kok in this volume). Institutions may interact concurrently in several ways, and may influence and feed back to each other over time (Oberthür and Gehring 2006b, 29–30; see also Young 2002, 83–138). For instance, at least four international institutions—the WTO, the International Union for the Protection of New Varieties of Plants (UPOV), and the regimes based on the CBD and the International Treaty on Plant Genetic Resources for Food and Agriculture (ITPGR)—cogovern the provision and use of plant genetic resources and thereby influence each other's development and effectiveness (Jungcurt 2008 and in this volume; see also Raustiala and Victor 2004). Understanding each dyadic institutional relationship requires attention to the larger institutional complex as well.

Such complex interaction settings may produce new properties that are not inherent in the individual components but derive from their coexistence and coevolution, much as the emergent properties of a forest derive from the mutual influences among the trees and plants it comprises, influences that one cannot grasp by examining individual trees and plants (Gehring and Oberthür 2009). Exploring systematically the nature, evolution, and consequences of sets of institutions that cogovern particular issue areas, and the broader governance structures they form, therefore promises to advance a more integrated understanding of the dynamics and effectiveness of global governance (Raustiala and Victor 2004) and "global governance architectures" (Biermann et al. 2009). It requires moving from an analysis of the effects international institutions have on each other to an exploration of how these institutions cogovern their overlapping area of governance.

A basic question when exploring an institutional complex is to delimit the issue area in focus. In a first variant, issue areas may be determined functionally by examining certain sectors of governance. Thus, Jungcurt in this volume investigates the institutional complex for the management of plant genetic resources, Gehring examines the relationship between the WTO and several MEAs, and Karlsson-Vinkhuyzen and Kok explore the nexus of climate, energy, and development. Stokke presents a spatial variant by starting out from one particular region, the Arctic, and examining the interplay of Arctic-specific institutions and those with a broader ambit. The various possibilities for defining the borders of an institutional complex call to mind the discussion on the most suitable delimitation of the issue areas of individual international regimes (see Potter 1980; Haas 1975). In contrast to international regimes, institutional complexes are rarely "negotiated," and policymakers do thus not regularly define the boundaries of institutional complexes by "political linkages" or "clustering." As a practical guide for implementing a functional or spatial delimitation, the density and strength of institutional interplay may serve as a prime criterion. However, it may be difficult to reach a common understanding of the exact set of institutions among which interplay is dense and strong. It may thus be advisable to employ issue area delimitations that are widely shared by other researchers or policymakers as an additional criterion. Accordingly, all contributions to this volume investigate institutional complexes that combine relatively dense and strong interaction with high political and scholarly salience.

To further structure our thinking about institutional complexes, it may be useful to distinguish causal chains and clusters as two principal patterns of more complex interaction situations (Gehring and Oberthür 2009). In a causal chain, one case of interplay gives rise to a subsequent case that feeds back on the original source institution or influences a third institution. For example, the failure of parties to the global Basel Convention on hazardous wastes to adopt a ban of waste exports from members of the Organisation for Economic Co-operation and Development (OECD) to developing countries encouraged several developing countries to devise regional agreements barring imports of hazardous wastes from OECD countries. These agreements subsequently facilitated the adoption of a global export ban, which in turn affected the world trading system (Meinke 2002). Cases of interplay may also "cluster" around certain issues and institutions, forming more or less dense networks of institutional interaction. While causal chains refer to sequential interaction cases, clusters involve concurrent cases in which several institutions address an issue in complementary or competitive ways. Accordingly, we may find competitive clusters like the interaction of the WTO and MEAs (see Gehring in this volume), complementary interaction clusters like those affecting air pollution or fisheries management in the Arctic (see Stokke in this volume), or mixed clusters like the complex governing the provision and use of plant genetic resources (see Jungcurt in this volume).

Understanding institutional complexes and not only individual interactions is crucial for designing adequate interplay management strategies in global environmental governance. When sets of institutions interlock into larger complexes, sound analysis requires attention to broader interaction effects beyond the immediate interplay in focus. An improved understanding of such broader effects should permit more effective interplay management strategies and is therefore highly relevant to the debate about reforming and developing global environmental governance. Proposals for such reform, including the creation of a World Environment Organization (Biermann and Bauer 2005), aim precisely at improving interinstitutional relationships and shaping the institutional structure of global environmental governance (see also Chambers and Green 2005; Najam, Papa, and Taiyab 2006). A better understanding of the dynamics and effects of institutional complexes contributes to this debate by allowing broader assessment of the effects of various forms of interplay management and proposed grand architectures of global environmental governance (see also Biermann et al. 2009). It is exactly from this perspective—one that sees institutional complexes as both a challenge and an opportunity for interplay management—that most of the contributions to this book approach the issue.

As one of the key areas of institutional interaction research in need of more attention, along with interplay management (Gehring and Oberthür 2008, 222), institutional complexes provide the second main theme of this volume. Starting from the conceptual foundation laid out above, we examine the structure, dynamics, emergent properties, and effects of institutional complexes, in particular by focusing on the following questions: What forces drive the emergence of institutional complexes? How are competing concerns and interests balanced within them? What factors determine any division of labor among the institutions involved or any prevalence of one institution over another? Finally, what factors account for stability and change within institutional complexes?

Organization of the Book

This book aims at advancing the research frontier on institutional interaction, and global environmental governance more broadly, by focusing on the two central themes highlighted above, *interplay management* and *institutional complexes*. Individual contributions address one or both of these issues by exploring various fields of international environmental governance. They may concentrate on specific institutional complexes (such as that concerning the interface of trade and the environment), the interplay management of particular interinstitutional relationships (such as the one between the regimes for the protection of the ozone layer and climate change), or relevant cross-cutting issues (such as the use of savings clauses in treaty making or relations between regional and global institutions). Of note, several of the contributions include a time dimension by investigating changes over time.

In accordance with the state of research on institutional interplay, the book adopts an explorative and inductive approach. Taken as a whole, the cases and examples of interplay management and institutional complexes under study here constitute a broad sample that promises important insights across the field of global environmental governance. The contributions span a wide range of prominent areas of international environmental governance, including fisheries management, climate change, protection of the ozone layer, governance of the Arctic, relationships between trade and the environment, the conservation of biodiversity and the management of genetic resources, and sustainable development and energy. As editors, we are not aware of any particular selection bias, for instance in terms of successful or failed interplay management. While the varying substantive and theoretical foci required adaptations in the structure of individual chapters, the authors were asked to investigate and bring out how the analyses of their particular focus areas can illuminate the overall guiding questions regarding interplay management and institutional complexes. At the same time, we wish to acknowledge that the contributions do not necessarily constitute representative empirical samples of cases of institutional management and institutional complexes, even in the environmental and resource management domains, and that may of course limit the generalizability of our findings as they are synthesized in the final chapter of this volume.

The structure of this volume and the order of the individual contributions follow from the focus on interplay management and institutional complexes. The next chapter lays the foundation by providing a comprehensive overview of the status of research on institutional interaction. The subsequent three chapters focus on interplay management, shedding light on different types, levels, and consequences of such management. Thereafter the following six chapters turn increasingly toward institutional complexes. It would have been artificial, perhaps impossible, to establish a clear dividing line between the contributions focusing on interplay management and those dealing with institutional complexes, since interplay management is an important activity within institutional complexes. Consequently, the contributions on institutional complexes also speak to the theme of interplay management to varying degrees. Finally, in the concluding chapter we attempt to aggregate the findings of the volume with respect to its two main themes.

In chapter 2, Sebastian Oberthür and Thomas Gehring give an overview of major scholarly contributions to our understanding of institutional interaction. The authors first review the empirical focus of studies of horizontal interplay among international institutions and their major findings. With respect to conceptual advances, they highlight progress in the understanding of several causal mechanisms that underlie and drive institutional interplay. They further set out certain principal strategies that scholars use when exploring institutional interaction, and discuss how attention to this phenomenon changes the way we understand international institutions and global environmental governance, and the policy relevance of existing research findings. Their review of progress in research on institutional interaction leads them to identify interplay management and institutional complexes as two priority research areas.

In chapter 3, Harro van Asselt assesses various different means of interplay management with a view to enhancing synergy and mitigating conflict between regimes relevant to global climate governance. Since climate change interlinks in both cause and effect with many areas of human activity, van Asselt is addressing an inevitably complex and institutionally highly fragmented governance area. He identifies various ways of managing interplay between formalized multilateral regimes, distinguishing between "legal" and "political" approaches and examining their potential and limitations in reaping synergies and addressing conflicts between multilateral regimes relevant to climate change.

In chapter 4, Mark Axelrod argues that established techniques of interplay management in international law tend to be biased toward preserving the status quo and against institutional change. He examines the hypothesis that concern about potential conflict with international trade rules has the effect of "chilling" environmental treaties by discouraging or weakening ambitious proposals. Analyzing a new data set that codes deference to existing international law in more than two hundred multilateral agreements, he finds that a clear majority of multilateral agreements at least acknowledge the importance of some existing international law, with nearly 40 percent of them explicitly deferring to existing international law. Although MEAs are no more likely to defer to existing treaties than multilateral agreements in other issue areas, Axelrod sees evidence of a chilling effect in the finding that MEAs are significantly more likely than other treaties to take account of existing international agreements outside their own policy field.

In chapter 5, Sebastian Oberthür, Claire Dupont, and Yasuko Matsumoto examine the management of the interaction between the international regimes for protection of the ozone layer and on climate change with respect to fluorinated greenhouse gases. In focus are projects supported under the climate change regime that may promote higher production and use of some ozone-depleting substances. Exploring the interplay management activities that have occurred largely separately within each regime, the authors report mixed results so far. Interplay management has not prevented the execution of a significant number of climate change projects with problematic interinstitutional effects, but eligibility constraints have limited the damage. Moreover, stricter hydrochlorofluorocarbon controls under the Montreal Protocol have brought additional benefits to both the ozone layer and the global climate, and ongoing initiatives have the potential to further strengthen synergy between both regimes.

Chapter 6 marks the transition to institutional complexes and their management. Olav Schram Stokke examines institutional complexes of regional and broader regimes relevant to Arctic resources and the environment, and argues that divisions of labor between the institutions of those complexes reflect interplay management efforts by those operating the institutions, who aim to exploit the specific capacities of their institutions. He identifies certain governance niches, or tasks that an institution may concentrate on amid existing efforts to solve the problem in hand: building knowledge, creating norms, enhancing capacity, and enforcing compliance. On the basis of general causal mechanisms that may connect institutions and environmental problem solving, Stokke pinpoints conditions for occupying those niches effectively, and explores for each governance niche distinctive features that equip an institution for meeting them. This framework for analyzing interplay management within an institutional complex is then applied to four cases of niche selection in Arctic environmental governance.

In chapter 7, Stefan Jungcurt focuses on interplay management in the institutional complex for international governance of conservation and use of plant genetic resources. Four international treaties regulate property rights to such resources. Two of them, the CBD and the ITPGR, deal mainly with the concerns of suppliers of genetic resources, whereas the WTO and UPOV primarily address resource user concerns, notably the protection of intellectual property regarding innovations. Jungcurt finds through "cross-dyadic" analysis of interinstitutional relationships that interactions between agreements with similar objectives tend to be synergistic, whereas those between supplier- and user-focused agreements are prone to disruption. Moreover, while management of the interplay between the ITPGR and UPOV has been quite successful, such management has so far failed to mitigate disruptive interplay between the CBD and the WTO. Jungcurt explores various possible explanations for this, including the existence of a network of experts that evolved into an influential epistemic community in the success case.

In chapter 8, Fariborz Zelli relates the core themes of this book—institutional complexes and interplay management—to certain causal factors that loom large in the broader analysis of international regimes. He draws attention to causal factors and processes that can explain which regimes prevail in conflictive institutional complexes, and why. The author argues that dimensions of the power structure and the knowledge structure—two core determinants derived from general theories of international relations—may account for cross-case variation of regime prevalence. Zelli suggests that interplay management can significantly affect this dependent variable, and that employing core variables of social theories is helpful for identifying the conditions for successful interplay management.

In chapter 9, Thomas Gehring examines the dynamics of the institutional complex of trade and environment. He decomposes the difficult relationship between the world trade system and the numerous MEAs that include restrictions on trade, and examines the influence of the WTO on the normative development and effectiveness of environmental regimes, and vice versa. Gehring argues that, as a result of those influences, a division of labor has emerged in the trade–environment interface: the WTO defines the general standards that states must observe when considering environmental trade measures, while MEAs provide arenas for adopting and implementing such measures. By perpetuating a specific form of interaction among the functionally specialized component institutions, an interlocking governance structure of remarkable coherence is gradually evolving in the institutional complex of trade and environment.

Frank Alcock in chapter 10 explores the dynamics of vertical interplay in the institutional complex of international, national, and subnational property rights institutions in fisheries in the postwar era. The negotiation of UNCLOS redistributed the division of competences between coastal states and others by converting vast areas of oceanic space from a global commons to national exclusive economic zones. Whereas most chapters in this book deal with horizontal interplay, Alcock focuses on the vertical dimension. He shows how institutional changes at the international level have led to adaptations of national and subnational fisheries arrangements, and that follow-on effects continue to unfold. Experimentation with innovative fisheries management arrangements, such as tradable quotas at national and local levels, may feed back to the international level through the adoption of new approaches to property rights delineation in regional fisheries management organizations.

Sylvia I. Karlsson-Vinkhuyzen and Marcel T. J. Kok in chapter 11 explore the integration of policy concerns in the nexus of the three broad policy domains of energy, development, and climate change and the associated institutional complex. In particular, they examine how such integration can be achieved through improved interplay management. The authors specify functional interdependencies among those domains and explore some options for interplay management, dyadically and within the nexus as a whole. Karlsson-Vinkhuyzen and Kok find that the prevailing unilateral interplay management in the nexus has so far proved inadequate, although the resultant institutional complex appears relatively stable. They argue that a forum with the necessary clout to advance a more integrated, joint management of the interfaces between the three domains and related interinstitutional coordination is lacking, not least because of variation in the levels of "legalization" and the strength of political status quo interests in the energy sector.

In chapter 12, we provide a synopsis of the major findings of the overall volume with respect to the two central themes, interplay management and institutional complexes. We highlight the pervasiveness and remarkable, if insufficient, effectiveness of decentralized interplay management in global environmental governance. The contributions to this volume furthermore demonstrate the emergence of divisions of labor among the elemental regimes of institutional complexes over time, which form meta-institutional interlocking structures. We also discuss the relative stability of such interlocking structures, which are reproduced by the mutual expectations they generate among relevant actors. Finally, we point out some areas for future research that promise particular returns on investment.

Acknowledgments

We would like to thank Mark Axelrod, Thomas Gehring, Sylvia Karlsson-Vinkhuyzen, Marcel Kok, Harro van Asselt, Fariborz Zelli, and three anonymous reviewers for very helpful comments on an earlier version of this chapter.

Note

1. The terms "institutional interaction" and "institutional interplay" are used interchangeably throughout this chapter and throughout much of the book.

References

Beisheim, Marianne, Sabine Dreher, Gregor Walter, Bernard Zangl, and Michael Zürn. 1999. *Im Zeitalter der Globalisierung? Thesen und Daten zur gesell-schaftlichen und politischen Denationalisierung.* Baden-Baden: Nomos.

Biermann, Frank, and Steffen Bauer, eds. 2005. *A World Environment Organization: Solution or Threat for International Environmental Governance?* Aldershot, UK: Ashgate.

Biermann, Frank, and Bernd Siebenhüner. 2007. *Managers of Global Change: The Core Findings of the MANUS Project on the Influence of International Bureaucracies.* Global Governance Working Paper 25. Amsterdam: Global Governance Project.

Biermann, Frank, and Bernd Siebenhüner. 2009. *Managers of Global Change: The Influence of International Environmental Bureaucracies.* Cambridge, Mass.: MIT Press.

Biermann, Frank, Philipp Pattberg, Harro van Asselt, and Fariborz Zelli. 2009. The Fragmentation of Global Governance Architectures: A Framework for Analysis. *Global Environmental Politics* 9 (4): 14–40.

Brown Weiss, Edith. 1993. International Environmental Issues and the Emergence of a New World Order. *Georgetown Law Journal* 81 (3): 675–710.

Chambers, W. Bradnee. 2008. *Interlinkages and the Effectiveness of Multilateral Environmental Agreements.* Tokyo: United Nations University Press.

Chambers, W. Bradnee, and Jessica F. Green. 2005. Toward an Effective Framework for Sustainable Development. In *Reforming International Environmental Governance: from Institutional Limits to Innovative Reforms,* ed. W. Bradnee Chambers and Jessica F. Green, 1–12. Tokyo: United Nations University Press.

Gehring, Thomas. 1994. *Dynamic International Regimes: Institutions for International Environmental Governance.* Frankfurt: Peter Lang.

Gehring, Thomas, and Sebastian Oberthür. 2006. Comparative Empirical Analysis and Ideal Types of Institutional Interaction. In *Institutional Interaction in Global Environmental Governance: Synergy and Conflict among International and EU Policies,* ed. Sebastian Oberthür and Thomas Gehring, 307–371. Cambridge, Mass.: MIT Press.

Gehring, Thomas, and Sebastian Oberthür. 2008. Interplay: Exploring Institutional Interaction. In *Institutions and Environmental Change: Principal Findings, Applications, and Research Frontiers,* ed. Oran R. Young, Leslie A. King, and Heike Schroeder, 187–223. Cambridge, Mass.: MIT Press.

Gehring, Thomas, and Sebastian Oberthür. 2009. The Causal Mechanisms of Interaction between International Institutions. *European Journal of International Relations* 15 (1): 125–156.

Haas, Ernst B. 1975. Is There a Hole in the Whole? Knowledge, Technology, Interdependence, and the Construction of International Regimes. *International Organization* 29:827–876.

Haas, Peter M., Robert O. Keohane, and Marc A. Levy, eds. 1993. *Institutions for the Earth: Sources of Effective International Environmental Protection*. Cambridge, Mass.: MIT Press.

Hasenclever, Andreas, Peter Mayer, and Volker Rittberger. 1997. *Theories of International Regimes*. Cambridge: Cambridge University Press.

Jordan, Andrew, Rüdiger K. W. Wurzel, and Anthony R. Zito. 2003. "New" Environmental Policy Instruments: An Evolution or a Revolution in Environmental Policy? *Environmental Politics* 12 (1): 201–224.

Jungcurt, Stefan. 2008. *Institutional Interplay in International Environmental Governance: Policy Interdependence and Strategic Interaction in the Regime Complex on Plant Genetic Resources for Food and Agriculture*. Aachen: Schaken Verlag.

Keohane, Robert O. 1984. *After Hegemony: Cooperation and Discord in the World Political Economy*. Princeton, N.J.: Princeton University Press.

Keohane, Robert O. 1989. Neoliberal Institutionalism. A Perspective on World Politics. In *International Institutions and State Power: Essays in International Relations Theory*, ed. Robert Keohane, 1–20. Boulder, Col.: Westview.

King, Leslie A. 1997. Institutional Interplay: Research Questions. Background paper prepared for the IDGEC project. School of Natural Resources, University of Vermont, Burlington.

Krasner, Stephen D. 1982. Structural Causes and Regime Consequences: Regimes as Intervening Variables. *International Organization* 36 (2): 185–206.

Leebron, David W. 2002. Linkages. *American Journal of International Law* 96 (1): 5–27.

Levy, Marc A., Oran R. Young, and Michael Zürn. 1995. The Study of International Regimes. *European Journal of International Relations* 1:267–330.

Martin, Lisa L., and Beth A. Simmons. 1998. Theories and Empirical Studies of International Institutions. *International Organization* 52 (4): 687–727.

Meinke, Britta. 2002. *Multi-Regime-Regulierung: Wechselwirkungen zwischen globalen und regionalen Umweltregimen*. Wiesbaden: Deutscher Universitäts-Verlag.

Miles, Edward L., Arild Underdal, Steinar Andresen, Jørgen Wettestad, Jon Birger Skjærseth, and Elaine M. Carlin, eds. 2002. *Environmental Regime Effectiveness: Confronting Theory with Evidence*. Cambridge, Mass.: MIT Press.

Mitchell, Ronald B. 2007. International Environmental Agreements Database Project (Version 2007.1). http://iea.uoregon.edu/ (accessed 28 January 2008).

Mitchell, Ronald B. 2008. Evaluating the Performance of Environmental Institutions: What to Evaluate and How to Evaluate It? In *Institutions and Environmental Change: Principal Findings, Applications, and Research Frontiers*, ed. Oran R. Young, Leslie A. King, and Heike Schroeder, 79–114. Cambridge, Mass.: MIT Press.

Najam, Adil, Mihaela Papa, and Nadaa Taiyab. 2006. *Global Environmental Governance: A Reform Agenda*. Winnipeg: International Institute for Sustainable Development.

Oberthür, Sebastian. 2001. Linkages between the Montreal and Kyoto Protocols: Enhancing Synergies between Protecting the Ozone Layer and the Global Climate. *International Environmental Agreements: Politics, Law and Economics* 1 (3): 357–377.

Oberthür, Sebastian. 2009. Interplay Management: Enhancing Environmental Policy Integration among International Institutions. *International Environmental Agreements: Politics, Law and Economics* 9 (4): 371–391.

Oberthür, Sebastian, and Thomas Gehring. 2006a. Conceptual Foundations of Institutional Interaction. In *Institutional Interaction in Global Environmental Governance: Synergy and Conflict among International and EU Policies*, ed. Sebastian Oberthür and Thomas Gehring, 19–51. Cambridge, Mass.: MIT Press.

Oberthür, Sebastian, and Thomas Gehring. 2006b. Institutional Interaction in Global Environmental Governance: The Case of the Cartagena Protocol and the World Trade Organization. *Global Environmental Politics* 6 (2):1–31.

Oberthür, Sebastian, and Thomas Gehring, eds. 2006c. *Institutional Interaction in Global Environmental Governance: Synergy and Conflict among International and EU Policies*. Cambridge, Mass.: MIT Press.

Pontecorvo, Concetta Maria. 1999. Interdependence between Global Environmental Regimes: The Kyoto Protocol on Climate Change and Forest Protection. *Zeitschrift für ausländisches öffentiches Recht und Völkerrecht* 59 (3): 709–749.

Potter, William C. 1980. Issue Area and Foreign Policy Analysis. *International Organization* 34 (3): 405–428.

Raustiala, Kal, and David G. Victor. 2004. The Regime Complex for Plant Genetic Resources. *International Organization* 55:277–309.

Simmons, Beth A., and Lisa L. Martin. 2002. International Organizations and Institutions. In *Handbook of International Relations*, ed. Walter Carlsnaes, Thomas Risse, and Beth Simmons, 192–211. London: Sage.

Stokke, Olav Schram. 2000. Managing Straddling Stocks: The Interplay of Global and Regional Regimes. *Ocean and Coastal Management* 43:205–234.

Stokke, Olav Schram, ed. 2001a. *Governing High Seas Fisheries: The Interplay of Global and Regional Regimes*. Oxford: Oxford University Press.

Stokke, Olav Schram. 2001b. *The Interplay of International Regimes: Putting Effectiveness Theory to Work*. Report No. 14. Oslo: Fridtjof Nansen Institute.

Stokke, Olav Schram. 2004. Trade Measures and Climate Compliance: Interplay Between WTO and the Marrakesh Accords. *International Environmental Agreements: Politics, Law and Economics* 4 (4): 339–357.

Stokke, Olav Schram, and Davor Vidas, eds. 1996. *Governing the Antarctic: The Effectiveness and Legitimacy of the Antarctic Treaty System.* Cambridge: Cambridge University Press.

Underdal, Arild, and Oran R. Young, eds. 2004. *Regime Consequences: Methodological Challenges and Research Strategies.* Dordrecht: Kluwer Academic.

Vedung, Evert. 1998. Policy Instruments: Typologies and Theories. In *Carrots, Sticks, and Sermons: Policy Instruments and Their Evaluation*, ed. Marie-Louise Bemelmans-Videc, Ray C. Rist, and Evert Vedung, 21–58. New Brunswick, N.J.: Transaction.

Victor, David G., Kal Raustiala, and Eugene B. Skolnikoff, eds. 1998. *The Implementation and Effectiveness of International Environmental Commitments: Theory and Practice.* Cambridge, Mass.: MIT Press.

von Homeyer, Ingmar. 2006. The EU Deliberate Release Directive: Environmental Precaution versus Trade and Product Regulation. In *Institutional Interaction in Global Environmental Governance: Synergy and Conflict among International and EU Policies*, ed. Sebastian Oberthür and Thomas Gehring, 259–283. Cambridge, Mass.: MIT Press.

Vranes, Erich. 2006. The Definition of "Norm Conflict" in International Law and Legal Theory. *European Journal of International Law* 17 (2): 395–418.

Wolfrum, Rüdiger, and Nele Matz. 2003. *Conflicts in International Environmental Law.* Berlin: Springer-Verlag.

Yamin, Farhana, and Joanna Depledge. 2004. *The International Climate Change Regime: A Guide to Rules, Institutions and Procedures.* Cambridge: Cambridge University Press.

Young, Oran R. 1980. International Regimes: Problems of Concept Formation. *World Politics* 32:331–356.

Young, Oran R. 1982. Regime Dynamics: The Rise and Fall of International Regimes. *International Organization* 36:277–297.

Young, Oran R. 1986. International Regimes: Toward a New Theory of Institutions. *World Politics* 39:104–122.

Young, Oran R. 1994. *International Governance: Protecting the Environment in a Stateless Society.* Ithaca, N.Y.: Cornell University Press.

Young, Oran R. 1996. Institutional Linkages in International Society: Polar Perspectives. *Global Governance* 2 (1): 1–24.

Young, Oran R. 1999. *The Effectiveness of International Environmental Regimes: Causal Connections and Behavioral Mechanisms.* Cambridge, Mass.: MIT Press.

Young, Oran R. 2002. *The Institutional Dimensions of Environmental Change: Fit, Interplay, and Scale.* Cambridge, Mass.: MIT Press.

Young, Oran R., with contributions from Arun Agrawal, Leslie A. King, Peter H. Sand, Arild Underdal, and Merrilyn Wasson. 1999/2005. *Institutional Dimensions of Global Environmental Change (IDGEC) Science Plan.* IHDP Report No. 9/16. Bonn: International Human Dimensions Programme on Global Environmental Change.

Young, Oran R. 2008. Institutions and Environmental Change: The Scientific Legacy of a Decade of IDGEC Research. In *Institutions and Environmental Change: Principal Findings, Applications, and Research Frontiers*, ed. Oran R. Young, Leslie A. King, and Heike Schroeder, 3–45. Cambridge, Mass.: MIT Press.

Young, Oran R. 2010. *Institutional Dynamics: Emergent Patterns in International Environmental Governance.* Cambridge, Mass.: MIT Press.

Zürn, Michael, Martin Binder, Matthias Ecker-Ehrhardt, and Katrin Radtke. 2007. Politische Ordnungsbildung wider Willen. *Zeitschrift für Internationale Beziehungen* 14 (1): 129–164.

2

Institutional Interaction

Ten Years of Scholarly Development

Sebastian Oberthür and Thomas Gehring

Since the development of the Institutional Dimensions of Global Environmental Change (IDGEC) Science Plan in 1998 (Young et al. 1999/2005), institutional interaction has become an important subject of inquiry. The Science Plan served to put institutional interaction on the agenda of global change research at a time when only a handful of scholars had raised the general issue. Their work drew attention to the risk of "treaty congestion" (Brown Weiss 1993, 679) and to an increasing "regime density" (Young 1996, 1) in the international system. Today it is widely recognized that "the effectiveness of specific institutions often depends not only on their own features but also on their interactions with other institutions" (Young et al. 1999/2005, 60). Many environmental issue areas are cogoverned by several international institutions, with governance also involving institutions at lower levels of societal and administrative organization (regional, national, local) (Young 2002, 83–138).[1]

Although research on institutional interaction is closely related to the study of the effectiveness of international institutions, it employs a distinct perspective and transcends the focus on individual institutions. Institutional interaction is part of the broader consequences that international institutions may have beyond their own domains (Underdal and Young 2004). Exploration of such interaction supplements the traditional inquiry into the establishment, development, and effectiveness of individual international institutions. The focus is on the relationship among institutions, whereas traditional institutional research deals with the relationship between actors and institutions. In this chapter we review the important advances made in knowledge about institutional interaction since the inception of IDGEC. Our discussion of institutional interaction starts with a review of the empirical progress achieved through the study of horizontal interaction among international institutions. Subsequently we examine the theoretical development, arguing that significant progress has been made toward developing a theory of institutional interaction through the identification of a limited number of relevant causal mechanisms and ideal types. Next we introduce four principal strategies that have been employed in the exploration of institutional interaction. We then analyze the implications of institutional interaction for an understanding of international institutions and global environmental governance, before concluding by highlighting the need for further research on the themes of interplay management and institutional complexes.

The Growth of Empirical Analyses

The number of empirical analyses of institutional interaction by both social scientists and lawyers has grown tremendously over the past decade. This work has confirmed that interinstitutional influence significantly affects the development and performance of virtually all institutions. Generally, this empirical research has focused on a limited number of "hot spots," so considerable potential exists for broadening the overall empirical coverage. Here we review progress in the most prominent areas of research.

The World Trade Organization and Multilateral Environmental Agreements

Trade-environment interactions are one of the oldest areas of relevant scientific inquiry. Several trade-related multilateral environmental agreements (MEAs) have been found to interact with the World Trade Organization (WTO). Some MEAs concern the regulation of international trade, such as the Convention on International Trade in Endangered Species of Wild Fauna and Flora (CITES), the Basel Convention on the Control of Transboundary Movement of Hazardous Wastes and Their Disposal, the Rotterdam Convention on the Prior Informed Consent Procedure for Certain Hazardous Chemicals and Pesticides in International Trade, and the Cartagena Protocol on Biosafety. Other MEAs, such as various fisheries agreements and the Montreal Protocol on Substances That Deplete the Ozone Layer, employ trade restrictions as an enforcement measure (see, e.g., Brack 2002; Eckersley 2004; Palmer, Chaytor, and Werksman 2006). Driven by the expansion of the world trade regime to cover, among other things, intellectual property rights and sanitary/phytosanitary measures, and by the emergence of further MEAs, the scope of trade–environment interactions has also expanded (see, e.g., Rosendal 2001, 2006; Andersen 2002; Oberthür and Gehring 2006c; Young et al. 2008).

Studies by social scientists and legal scholars alike have highlighted the potential for conflict between the WTO and trade-related MEAs, and have offered possible solutions. In particular, attention has been drawn to the ways in which the WTO, backed by its comparatively strong dispute settlement mechanism, works against effective global environmental governance. Existing obligations under the WTO serve to "chill" negotiations on MEAs by constituting obstacles to agreement on environmental trade restrictions or limiting the effectiveness of such restrictions (Brack 2002; Eckersley 2004). WTO obligations also undermine the effective implementation of MEAs by protecting free trade in goods, irrespective of the environmental consequences of the underlying production processes. Identification of such conflicting areas has generated analyses of various possible solutions, including mechanisms available in international law (Pauwelyn 2003) and options for institutional reform of the WTO (Tarasofsky 1997; Biermann 2001).

More recent studies have found that MEAs have proved surprisingly robust in influencing the WTO. Despite the chilling effect of the WTO, more than twenty MEAs have included trade measures to date. Their proponents have found, and made use of, room for maneuver to adapt to the WTO requirements while still pursuing their objectives with trade measures. Among other things, this has led to specific efforts to avoid discrimination against non-parties (Palmer, Chaytor, and Werksman 2006). In turn, the introduction of trade-restrictive measures adapted in this way has restricted the WTO's regulatory scope and authority (see e.g., Oberthür and Gehring 2006b) and has triggered adaptations on the side of the WTO to allow for resulting multilateral trade measures. This has produced increasing acceptance of appropriately designed MEA trade measures, as reflected in the interpretation of the WTO regulations by the WTO Appellate Body and in the proceedings of the WTO Committee on Trade and Environment. As a result, no dispute concerning the implementation of an MEA has yet been brought before the dispute settlement mechanism of the WTO (Charnovitz 1998; Palmer, Chaytor, and Werksman 2006, 187).

On the whole, these results indicate that the interaction between the WTO and MEAs is more balanced than some early analyses might have suggested. The emerging picture is one of an increasingly institutionalized (and thus recognized) division of competences and labor between MEAs and the WTO (see Gehring in this volume). Certainly the current balance may not be sufficient or satisfactory, and tensions may worsen in the future owing to the persisting societal conflict between free trade and environmental objectives. However, the latent interinstitutional conflict between the WTO and MEAs highlighted in many early analyses appears to have been managed relatively successfully so far, as it has not become acute. If further confirmed, this observation would provide an indication that the current decentralized management of institutional interaction has been more successful than traditionally assumed (see "Implications for Policymaking," below).

Climate Governance

The growing literature on institutional interaction in climate governance illustrates the particular multi-institutional nature of this area of governance. The international climate regime based on the UN Framework Convention on Climate Change and its Kyoto Protocol has an enormous scope, overlapping and interacting with a multitude of other issue areas and institutions in various ways (van Asselt in this volume). In addition to the multifaceted and multi-institutional nature of international climate governance, the paramount importance of climate change on the international (environmental) agenda has contributed to the emergence of a rich literature on the wide-ranging interactions with various other environmental institutions as well as with institutions not primarily oriented toward the environment.

Several studies of interactions among the international climate change regime and other MEAs have highlighted the potential hegemony of climate governance over other environmental concerns. For instance, the objective of maximizing carbon uptake by monocultural forest plantations may, as reinforced by the economic incentives built into the Kyoto Protocol, defeat the competing objective of preserving natural biodiversity-rich ecosystems under the Convention on Biological Diversity (Pontecorvo 1999; Jacquemont and Caparrós 2002; van Asselt, Sindico, and Mehling 2008). Also, the climate change regime drove the adoption, in 2006, of an amendment to the London dumping convention that allows carbon sequestration in deep-sea deposits (International Maritime Organization 2006). Similarly, activities under the Kyoto Protocol's Clean Development Mechanism (CDM), which helps fund climate protection projects in developing countries, might clash with efforts to phase out ozone-depleting substances under the Montreal Protocol to protect the ozone layer (Oberthür, Dupont, and Matsumoto in this volume). At the same time, the Montreal Protocol has itself affected the Kyoto Protocol in various ways. On the positive side, the Montreal Protocol has informed the design of several aspects of the Kyoto Protocol and has contributed to climate protection by phasing out ozone-depleting substances (such as chlorofluorocarbons, CFCs) that are also powerful greenhouse gases. On the negative side, it has led to growing consumption of certain fluorinated greenhouse gases that are regulated under the Kyoto Protocol (Oberthür 2001). Interactions with further MEAs, such as the Convention to Combat Desertification and the Ramsar Convention on Wetlands, have been identified but not analyzed in detail (Oberthür 2006; van Asselt, Biermann, and Gupta 2004).

With respect to nonenvironmental institutions, most analyses have focused on interactions with economic institutions, in particular the WTO. In line with the traditional trade–environment debate, there have been explorations of the WTO compatibility of multilateral or unilateral trade measures as a means of climate protection (e.g., Charnovitz 2003; Biermann and Brohm 2005). In addition, the market mechanisms of the Kyoto Protocol, most notably emissions trading, provide a particular angle for the trade–environment debate. Furthermore, the relevance of international trade and investment rules and financial institutions has become an issue, particularly with respect to the implementation of climate protection projects under the CDM and Joint Implementation schemes of the Kyoto Protocol (Chambers 1998, 2001). Beyond the core economic and financial institutions, analyses of the interaction of the climate change regime with the International Civil Aviation Organization (ICAO) and the International Maritime Organization (IMO) in regard to greenhouse gas emissions from international transport have highlighted the difficulties that can arise from regulatory competition and a lack of coordination among international institutions (Oberthür 2003, 2006). Further interactions of the climate regime with nonenvironmental institutions, such as the World Health Organization, have received less attention (van Asselt, Biermann, and Gupta 2004).

Ocean Governance
Ocean governance is a third area that has attracted considerable scientific attention. The prominence of relevant research is evident from the aforementioned discussion of both the interplay between the WTO and MEAs and institutional interaction in climate governance, because ocean-related issues play an important role in both areas (e.g., WTO and fisheries agreements; IMO and climate protection). In addition, studies have focused on various subsets of the many institutions that interact in

manifold ways in this area of governance. Particularly striking is the large number of studies exploring fisheries governance (see, e.g., Stokke 2001a; DeSombre 2005; Stokke and Coffey 2006).

Research has examined a range of pertinent issues. A prime focus has been exploring the interplay of various institutions' geographic areas of ocean governance in particular. Related studies have shed light on the interplay of various functionally differentiated institutions in the governance of particular regions such as the North Sea (e.g., Skjærseth 2000, 2006), the Arctic (e.g., Stokke 2007; Stokke and Hønneland 2007; Stokke in this volume), and the Antarctic (e.g., Stokke and Vidas 1996). Such studies have frequently also looked into the effects of the nesting of regional arrangements or functionally specialized institutions (e.g., fisheries agreements) into broader global institutions, in particular the UN Convention on the Law of the Sea (Vidas 2000a, 2000b) and the UN Fish Stocks Agreement (e.g., Boyle 1999; Stokke 2000, 2001a). Yet another important research area has been the governance of particularly vulnerable marine species, such as whales. Here it has been shown that the existence of numerous functionally specialized institutions creates opportunities for forum shopping that could be exploited by other interested actors. For example, the protection of whales, usually pursued within the International Whaling Commission, might also be addressed under CITES (Gillespie 2002).

Other Areas of Empirical Research
The field of legal scholarship has made two noteworthy contributions in particular. First, there have been investigations of the relationship and mutual influence of various courts and quasi-judicial procedures (e.g., Schiffman 1999; Boyle 1999; Shany 2003). The dispute between Ireland and the United Kingdom concerning the UK's MOX plant in Sellafield has, for example, been addressed by procedures under the UN Convention on the Law of the Sea, the OSPAR Convention, and the European Court of Justice (Lavranos 2006). To some extent, there exist formal rules on jurisdictional delimitation and more informal mechanisms (e.g., regarding information exchange) that minimize the risk of contradictory judgments and jurisdictional competition. These could be further advanced to tackle such issues. Second, legal scholars have analyzed the consequences that norm conflicts may have in general for the system of international law, as well as the means available in international law for resolving such conflicts (Pauwelyn 2003; Wolfrum and Matz 2003). The resulting legal analyses have shown how existing constitutional rules of

international law, such as the *lex posterior* and the *lex specialis* rules reflected in the Vienna Convention on the Law of Treaties, are insufficient. Resolution of norm conflicts frequently has to resort to a case-by-case approach for clarifying the situation. As one result, many international treaties in international environmental governance explicitly take up the question of the relationship with other treaties (Axelrod in this volume). Jurisdictional norm interpretation has also played an important role with respect to managing the tensions between the WTO and MEAs. In other cases, resolution may have to rely on the political rather than the jurisdictional process of norm development and interpretation (see van Asselt in this volume).

Other areas of environmental governance with possible interaction effects have received far less scholarly attention. Only rarely have studies touched on aspects such as the regional-global interactions concerning the north-south transfer of hazardous wastes (Meinke 2002) or addressed European air pollution as an empirical field (Selin and VanDeveer 2003). Since virtually all areas of environmental governance are cogoverned by several institutions, there is further room for many more empirical analyses of institutional interaction to shed light on, for instance, the governance of chemicals or the protection of species and biodiversity. Even with respect to the WTO-MEA relationship, global climate governance, and ocean governance, there is substantial scope for further interplay analyses. In none of these areas have studies yet provided a comprehensive picture of the problems and promises of interaction. Moreover, there have been few studies of large numbers of cases that could provide a basis for comparative analyses. To our knowledge, our own research (Oberthür and Gehring 2006c) is the only example of such a large-*n* study to date, although other scholars have begun to investigate specific aspects of interaction by employing quantitative means (see, e.g., Axelrod in this volume).

Synergy and Conflict

One of the most noteworthy results of recent empirical research concerns the relationship of synergy and conflict in the realm of institutional interaction. Whereas Keohane, Haas, and Levy (1993, 15–16) identified more interinstitutional synergy than they had expected, early analyses of individual cases, such as the relationship among the WTO and MEAs, focused on conflict, and supported the view that institutional interaction is inherently problematic. Evaluating 163 cases of environmentally relevant interaction, we found in our own study that synergy is in fact at least as common among international and EU environmental governance institutions as is disruption (Gehring and Oberthür 2006, 316–325). The majority of our cases of institutional interaction led to synergy, whereas only about a quarter resulted in clear disruption. Furthermore, disruption and conflict tend to occur as unintended side effects rather than deliberate results. Undoubtedly, conflict is not negligible: it poses severe problems, especially in interactions among environmental and nonenvironmental regimes; however, synergy dominates overall. Hence, the larger-*n* study points to a selection bias toward the conflictive, more politically salient cases.

Moreover, collective action is taken much more frequently in response to disruptive than to synergistic interaction. Positive effects of institutional interaction are commonly "consumed" without further action, irrespective of the potential for further improvement that may exist. This phenomenon appears to be widespread, and was identified in about 30 percent of our cases. Potentials for improvement are much more frequently neglected in cases involving positive effects than in disruptive cases. The higher salience so far of problematic cases of interaction may be explained by the fact that people generally react more strongly to the risk of losses entailed in conflict than to the advantage of additional benefits (Tversky and Kahnemann 1981, 1984) and by the presence of aggrieved actors struggling for change. Thus, it may be worth investing effort in identifying potentials for improvement, irrespective of whether the original effect of an interaction was synergistic or disruptive, and placing more emphasis on preserving and enhancing synergistic institutional interaction as compared to minimizing interinstitutional conflict.

Conceptual Progress: From Classification to Causal Mechanisms

Sound concepts are a prerequisite for more systematic research on institutional interaction. Since the mid-1990s, the search for a reliable conceptual foundation for institutional interaction has moved from classification efforts to more general propositions about the driving forces of institutional interaction and the deductive identification of causal mechanisms, elucidating both the pathways through which influence can travel from one institution to another and the consequences of interaction.

Categories for Classification of Institutional Interaction

The search for analytical concepts began with several categories for classification. These classifications are useful for a first-cut exploration of the field of institutional interaction and establish valuable distinctions. They do not, however, capture the forces that drive the interaction.

Prior to the IDGEC Science Plan, Young (1996) put forward four types of institutional interaction and began to explore their inherent dynamics. He observed that issue-specific regimes are usually *embedded* in overarching principles and practices, such as sovereignty, and that they may trigger long-term processes of change in these overarching structures. A second type, institutional *nesting*, concerns interactions in which specific arrangements are folded into broader institutional frameworks that deal with the same general issue area but are less detailed. An example is the nesting of the Multi-Fiber Agreement within the General Agreement on Tariffs and Trade (GATT)/WTO (Aggarwal 1983). In cases of institutional *clustering*, actors combine different governance arrangements in institutional packages even when there is no compelling functional need to do so, as occurred with the UN Convention on the Law of the Sea. Finally, *overlap* involves linkages in which individual regimes formed for different purposes and largely without reference to one another intersect on a de facto basis, producing substantial impacts on each other in the process. Young drew attention to the fact that nesting and clustering are typically the result of intentional attempts to redesign the institutional landscape, whereas embeddedness and overlap regularly reflect unintentional consequences of human action. In the preparatory stages of the Science Plan, King (1997) developed a taxonomy of different types of institutional interaction, which included possible political responses to institutional interaction. Rosendal (2001) conjectured that interaction will create synergy if the specific rules of the institutions involved are compatible and will create conflict if they prove to be incompatible, whereas the broader norms of institutions will be less relevant. Later, however, the development of general causal mechanisms of institutional interaction showed that the broader norms reflecting the policy direction of two or more institutions may have a tremendous impact on the quality of effects (see below).

The IDGEC Science Plan proposed a distinction between horizontal and vertical interaction (Young et al. 1999/2005; see also Young 2002, 83–138). Horizontal interaction occurs among institutions located at the same level of social organization or at the same point on the administrative scale. At the international level, this kind of interaction originates in the high degree of fragmentation of the international system, where actors frequently choose to pursue their common interests by establishing new institutions rather than expanding existing ones. By contrast, vertical interaction addresses the influence of institutions across different levels of social organization or administration. For example, the institutional design of domestic political systems shapes state interests and thus exerts influence on the design of international and European institutional arrangements (Héritier 1999). And global or regional environmental governance requires appropriate institutional underpinnings at the national and local levels (see Galaz et al. 2008).

Most important, the Science Plan articulated a distinction between political and functional linkages among institutions (Young et al. 1999/2005, 50; see also Young 2002, 23). Juxtaposing political and functional linkages provides an initial idea of some of the fundamental forces that drive institutional interaction: deliberate political action, and the underlying properties of the governance targets for international institutions that escape human control. A functional linkage was seen as a fact of life "in the sense that the operation of one institution directly influences the effectiveness of another through some substantive connection of the activities involved" (Young et al. 1999/2005, 50). It would exist "when substantive problems that two or more institutions address are linked in biogeophysical or socioeconomic terms" (Young 2002, 23; see also 83–109). For example, action taken within the ozone regime on CFCs is immediately relevant for the climate change regime because CFCs have ozone-depleting properties and are also potent greenhouse gases. Political linkages, on the other hand, involve the deliberate design of a relationship between or among different institutions. They were believed to "arise when actors decide to consider two or more arrangements as parts of a larger institutional complex" (Young et al. 1999/2005, 50). For example, member states of the climate change regime assigned the operation of the financial mechanism of this institution to the Global Environment Facility, thereby establishing a permanent working relationship between the two institutions (Yamin and Depledge 2004, chap. 10). The distinction between functional and political linkages adapts the concepts of functional and political spillover from neofunctionalist integration theory (Rosamond 2000, 59–68).

This approach, however, is burdened with considerable analytical difficulties (see also Stokke 2001a). It underspecifies the realm of institutional interaction because not all instances of institutional interaction fit either type and arise from either unavoidable fact of life or deliberate political design. For instance, the difficult relationship between trade-restricting MEAs and the WTO has not been deliberately designed by the member states of either of the institutions involved, nor is it an unavoidable fact of life, because it originates in intended political action. The distinction also overspecifies the realm of institutional interaction because the two categories do not denote mutually exclusive types. Young et al. (1999/2005, 53) cite the protocols on SO_2, NO_X, and volatile organic compounds of the international regime on transboundary air pollution as an example of a functional linkage, even though all these protocols belong to one convention managed under the UN Economic Commission for Europe and are thus undoubtedly parts of a larger institutional complex.

In addition to functional and political linkages, other types of interaction can be identified if various key factors believed crucial for the identification of causal pathways are systematically varied (Gehring and Oberthür 2004, 253–267). Interaction may occur not only because institutions are functionally or politically linked but also because they comprise different memberships, so that there is interaction, for example, between a regional and a global institution operating in the same issue area. Interaction patterns can be expected to differ profoundly depending on whether or not a regime whose actors wish to affect the development of another regime can do so unilaterally, causing the interaction to occur without the consent (or even awareness) of actors operating within the target regime. Moreover, political action in response to observed or anticipated interaction can occur within either or all institutions involved.

Altogether, the classifications of interaction illustrate the wide variety of possible paths of inquiry and serve as useful initial distinctions for structuring the field. The distinction between horizontal and vertical interaction is now well established, as is that between synergistic and conflictual qualities of effect among institutions. Young's four classes of institutional interaction provide an analytical framework for more specific inquiries; however, they have not been employed to analyze theoretically the causal factors behind institutional interaction.

Causal Mechanisms of Institutional Interaction

Several scholars have set out to investigate the forces that drive institutional interaction and to identify general pathways clarifying how the institutions involved are related to each other. These attempts have yielded insights into how and under what conditions an international institution can influence another institution. Indicating factors that might be important for causal analysis, these insights constitute a promising foundation for the search for theoretical models to elucidate the causes and effects of interplay between or among institutions.

In a series of studies on international resource management, Stokke (2001a; see also 2000, 2001b, and in this volume) has proposed a set of three causal pathways through which institutional interaction may influence the effectiveness of the regimes involved. These pathways are derived from the major theoretical approaches of international relations. Hence, "ideational" interaction (originally referred to as "diffusive" interaction) relates to "processes of learning" (Stokke 2001a, 10) and implies that the substantive or operational rules of one institution serve as models for those negotiating another regime. This may help in understanding, for example, the rapid spread of general normative principles such as sustainability, precaution, and ecosystem management. "Normative" interaction refers to situations where the substantive or operational norms of one institution either contradict or validate those of another institution (as in the case of the relationship of the WTO and MEAs). "Utilitarian" interaction relates to situations where decisions made within one institution alter the costs and benefits of options available in another institution. Stokke (2001b) then introduced the term "interplay management" to denote deliberate efforts by states or other regime participants to alter the effects of interaction through one or another of those three mechanisms (see also Stokke and Oberthür in this volume).

Against this backdrop, a group of European scholars has developed several theoretically derived models of causal mechanisms and more specific ideal types of interaction that demonstrate how influence can travel from one institution to another (see Oberthür and Gehring 2006a). These models provide an account of how one institution (the source institution) exerts influence through a particular pathway on the normative development or effectiveness of another institution (the target institution). Causal mechanisms open the black box of the cause-and-effect relationship between or among the institutions involved and provide a microfoundation for the analysis of institutional interaction.

One specification of the causal mechanism approach to institutional interaction distinguishes among four mutually exclusive general mechanisms covering three levels of effectiveness of governance institutions. These three levels are *output* (collective knowledge or norms prescribing, proscribing, or permitting behavior); *outcome* (behavioral change of relevant actors); and *impact* (the ultimate target of governance) (Underdal 2004, 34; 2008). Two causal mechanisms are located at the output level and exert influence on the decision-making process of the target institution. A third causal mechanism is located at the outcome level, involving changes in the behavior of relevant actors, while the fourth causal mechanism occurs at the impact level. The latter two mechanisms do not modify the decision making of the target institution but affect its effectiveness within its issue area. The four causal mechanisms are held to cover the full range of fundamental rationales that may drive institutional interaction. More specific ideal types are needed, however, to derive hypotheses about the conditions under which institutional interaction can be expected to occur and the consequences for environmental governance.

Cognitive Interaction   Institutional interaction can be driven by the power of knowledge and ideas. The causal mechanism of cognitive interaction is based purely on persuasion and may be conceived of as a particular form of interinstitutional learning (see also Stokke 2001a, 10). If the rationality of actors is "bounded" because their information-processing capacity is limited (Simon 1972; Keohane 1984, 100–115), or if relevant information is not readily available, such actors will be prepared to adapt their preferences to new information. The decision-making process of an international institution will be influenced if information, knowledge, or ideas produced within the source institution modify the perception of decision makers operating within the target institution. For cognitive interaction to occur, the source institution must generate some new information (such as a report), revealing, for example, new scientific or technological insights or an institutional arrangement solving a particular regulatory problem, which is subsequently fed into the decision-making process of the target institution by an actor. The information must change the order of preferences of actors relevant to the target institution, in this way affecting the collective negotiation process and the output of the target institution. Depending on whether an interaction was triggered intentionally or not, we can distinguish two ideal types of cognitive interaction.

If cognitive interaction is unintentionally triggered by the source institution, members of the target institution voluntarily use some aspect of the source institution as a policy model. For example, the compliance system under the Montreal Protocol on Substances that Deplete the Ozone Layer influenced the negotiations on the compliance system under the Kyoto Protocol on climate change because it provided a model of how to supervise implementation and deal with cases of possible non-compliance (Oberthür and Ott 1999, 215–222). This type of cognitive interaction can occur between any two institutions because international institutions share various functional challenges related to monitoring, verification, enforcement, and decision making. Also, various different types of actors may pick up the information or idea and feed it into the decision-making process of another institution. Learning from a policy model can generally be expected to strengthen the effectiveness of the target institution, because it presupposes that the members and subjects of the target institution collectively consider the model to be useful. Policy models, however, are frequently modified or adapted to ensure their fit with the particular needs of the target ("complex learning"—see Haas 1990). The policy model type of interaction highlights how members of an institution can improve the effectiveness of their governance efforts through learning from other institutions.

If cognitive interaction is intentionally triggered by the source institution, it takes the form of a request by the source institution for assistance from the target institution. For example, the World Customs Organization adapted its customs codes in response to a request by CITES, thus supporting the implementation and enforcement of the latter's trade restrictions (Lanchbery 2006). A request for assistance requires that the issue areas in question overlap; otherwise adaptation by the target institution would be meaningless for the source institution. Moreover, it will usually be successful only if the requested adaptation is either beneficial for, or at least neutral to, the effectiveness of the target institution. Members of an institution cannot be expected to act on external requests that would harm their own institution. Since a request for assistance is intended to create a positive feedback effect on the source institution, it enables an institution to draw on other institutions in order to enhance its own effectiveness, even if it cannot force the target institution to adapt its rules.

Interaction through Commitment   Normative commitments may also provide the driver of interaction, based on the premise that international obligations create at least some binding force on those they address. For this form of interaction to occur, a prescription or proscription adopted under one institution must affect the preferences and negotiating behavior of members in another institution (the target institution), in ways that influence that institution's collective decision-making process and output. For example, the WTO commitment not to discriminate against imported goods renders it difficult for WTO members to adopt trade sanctions within MEAs that would reinforce the effectiveness of these institutions (Brack 2002). Activation of this causal mechanism requires that both memberships and issue areas overlap at least partially. Without overlapping memberships, no member state of the target institution would be committed to obligations established under the source institution. And without overlapping issue areas, commitments established under one institution could not redefine preferences related to issues dealt with under the other institution.

If the membership of one institution forms part of the membership of another formally independent institution with similar objectives and governance instruments, interaction through commitment creates synergies among the institutions nested in this way. Such "interaction between nested institutions" constitutes a mechanism for policy diffusion within the same policy field. It is typically easier to reach agreement within a smaller institution (e.g., a regional one) than in a larger (e.g., global) one (Snidal 1994). States committed within the smaller institution may develop a common interest in transferring their obligations to the larger institution that governs the same issue area. For example, the ban on trade in hazardous wastes was more easily reached in a number of regional agreements than in the global Basel Convention on the Control of Transboundary Movement of Hazardous Wastes and Their Disposal, but the latter was subsequently heavily influenced by the regional agreements governing the same issue area (Clapp 1994). Interaction between nested institutions provides opportunities for "forum shopping"—actors exploring the opportunities offered by different institutions to pursue their own interests. The matching objectives of the institutions generate compatible priorities and render disruptive effects highly improbable, if not impossible.

If a group of states addresses the same issues within two institutions pursuing different objectives, interaction through commitment creates mutual disruption of the institutions involved and, therefore, a demand for the delimitation of jurisdictions. Typically, institutions with differing objectives will appraise a policy measure differently, so that disputes about the appropriate regulation arise. Environmentally motivated trade restrictions may be seen either as undesirable obstacles to free trade or as desirable instruments that support environmental cooperation. In situations of this type, the members of the institutions in question possess a general interest in some sort of separation of jurisdictions in order to avoid fruitless regulatory competition; however, conflicting preferences regarding the appropriate solution make it notoriously difficult to solve such problems. Jurisdictional delimitation cases pose the governance challenge of identifying measures that honor the basic objectives of both institutions involved. This does not necessarily require an overarching institutional structure: it may be achieved through mutual adjustment of institutional structures, or even through careful implementation of obligations by the addressees.

If a group of actors pursues the same objectives within institutions controlling different governance instruments, interaction through commitment will produce synergistic effects because it activates an additional means. Such interaction occurs in two stages. First, actors committed under one institution transfer an obligation to another institution. Second, incorporation of the transferred obligation must mobilize an additional governance instrument, such as a particular form of law or a specific enforcement or assistance mechanism, that provides an additional incentive to implement the obligation. For example, political agreement achieved at the high-level International North Sea Conferences paved the way for the acceptance of identical obligations enshrined in hard law within the regime for the protection of the North-East Atlantic (OSPAR) (Skjærseth 2006). Such interaction will boost the effectiveness of both institutions involved because the additional governance instrument benefits the implementation of both institutions simultaneously.

Behavioral Interaction   Institutional interaction may also be based on the interconnectedness of behavior across the domains of institutions. Behavioral interaction will occur if behavioral changes triggered by the source institution become relevant for the implementation of the target institution. This form of interaction is located at the outcome level and affects the performance of an international institution within its own domain. If relevant states or non-state actors adapt their behavior in response to the output produced by the source institution, such behavioral changes may be relevant for the effectiveness of the target institution. If, for example, the Kyoto Protocol creates incentives to plant fast-growing trees in ways that encroach on biodiversity, this will undermine the performance of the Convention on Biological Diversity (Jacquemont and Caparrós 2002; van Asselt, Sindico, and Mehling 2008). Behavioral interaction requires that the issue areas governed by the institutions involved as well as the direct and indirect addressees of institutional obligations be close enough to matter to each other. It does not depend on a collective decision within the target institution because it occurs as the aggregate result of the behavior of actors operating within the two issue areas involved.

Implications of behavioral interaction for global governance depend, again, on whether the institutions involved differ notably in their objectives. If different (usually overlapping) groups of actors address a given set of issues within institutions with similar objectives, behavioral interaction will, because of the matching objectives, always create synergy. If a group of actors addresses a set of issues within two institutions that pursue different objectives, interaction will tend to result in disruption of the target institution, because behavioral changes triggered by the source institution are likely to be at odds with the objectives of the target institution and may thus undermine the latter's performance.

Impact-Level Interaction   Institutional interaction may also rest on the interdependence of the ultimate governance targets of the institutions involved. In impact-level interaction, the ultimate governance target of one institution—such as economic growth or the ozone layer—is directly influenced by side effects that originate in the ultimate governance target of another institution. Consider a stylized example: since cod eat herring, successful protection of cod by one institution, resulting in a growing population of this species, will unintentionally decrease the population of herring protected by another institution. In contrast to behavioral interaction, interinstitutional influence in this case does not depend on any action within the target institution or its domain but rests on the "functional linkage" (Young 2002, 23, see also 83–109) of the ultimate governance targets of the institutions involved at the impact level. It is the increased population of cod, not human behavior, that leads directly to a decreasing population of herring. While impact-level interaction may rely on stable interdependencies of the biophysical environment, as with cod and herring, functional linkages may themselves be subject to possible long-term change. For example, economic growth promoted by the WTO and the resultant growth in international transport has led to increased emissions of greenhouse gases, thereby undermining the effectiveness of the global climate regime. This kind of functional interdependence, however, might one day be overcome by technical progress or changes in production methods.

The value added by the general causal mechanisms and their subtypes is twofold. First, the models provide a promising foundation for developing an elaborated theory of institutional interaction. They allow the formulation of meaningful hypotheses about the preconditions for institutional interaction and regarding the effects of interaction for global environmental governance. Second, they provide analytical tools for use in structured analysis of empirical interaction cases, to help explain how influence travels from one institution to another, as well as which groups of actors might be involved in this process. However, such models cannot replace the empirical exploration of existing interaction cases. They do not release the researcher from the need to establish the causal relationship between the (potentially) interacting institutions, in part by exploring alternative causal pathways. Nor can they provide precise descriptions of all properties of relevant cases of interaction. Being deductively derived, they cannot be empirically right or wrong (Snidal 1985). Like game-theoretic models, they reflect the relevant components of the different causal pathways that a case of interaction may follow, and in that way assist the empirical analysis of real-world situations.

Principal Research Strategies on Institutional Interaction

Research on institutional interaction has adopted a range of different perspectives; the new field of inquiry has not yet produced one or more standard approaches. However, meaningful studies on institutional interaction, like research on any other subject of the social sciences, have to be founded on some basic assumptions about the dependent and independent variables and their relationship. Choices made in this respect influence the research questions that can be pursued in a particular study.

Explicitly or implicitly, the design of research on institutional interaction has to be based on decisions about the role of actors and institutions. Systemic approaches focus on the causal relationship among institutions, so that both the dependent and the independent variables are located at the macrolevel of institutions rather than at the microlevel of actors. Studies of institutional interaction, including many legal analyses of overlapping and conflicting jurisdictions, often concentrate entirely on the systemic level and bracket the activities of actors. In contrast, actor-centered research strategies see actors as either the independent variable or the dependent variable, locating other variables at the macrolevel of institutions. Relevant research may start from a given interest of one or more relevant actors and explore the opportunities to exploit institutional interaction as an instrument for pursuing these interests effectively (forum shopping). Alternatively, research may focus on the undesired side effects of institutional interaction that actors must take into account when establishing or redesigning a given institution. Explorations of the effects originating in institutional interaction, regime complexes (Raustiala and Victor 2004), and "regime complexity" (Alter and Meunier 2009) on the behavior of relevant states and non-state actors also reflect an actor-centered strategy.

Research on institutional interaction may also focus on different units of analysis. It may single out specific dyadic cases of interinstitutional influence in which one institution affects the normative development or performance of another institution (Oberthür and Gehring 2006a, 26–31). This perspective may require the decomposition of complex interaction situations. Even a comparatively narrow situation, such as the interplay between the WTO and MEAs with trade restrictions, may prove to be composed of several component cases running in different directions and passing through different causal mechanisms (Palmer, Chaytor, and Werksman 2006). Or research may take as its unit of analysis the overall patterns emerging from complex interaction situations, perhaps involving several institutions and many individual cases of interaction (see, e.g., Alter and Meunier 2009). It will then seek to develop an integrated view on a complex phenomenon like the relationship between MEAs and the WTO, or the institutional setting affecting the Antarctic environment (Young 1996). This approach has been called "integrationist" (Young 2008, 152–154).

Squaring these two dimensions, we get four different research strategies. Each of them is particularly well suited for dealing with certain research questions but ignores others. Table 2.1 shows the four strategies and indicates their core research questions.

Inquiries located at the system level and focusing on one or more specific cases of interaction (cell I) address the core question of how, and with what effects, an international institution can and does influence another international institution. The focus is on institutional interaction effects rather than on actors' behavioral changes (even if actor behavior forms part of the causal chain explored). The combination of a systemic or macro perspective with a case-oriented approach is particularly suited for rigorous analysis of the causal mechanisms and effects of specific incidents of institutional interaction. Causal analysis requires identifying a clear direction of causal influence running from one institution to another, which is difficult in complex situations where the origins and targets of influence are not readily discernible or where feedback effects occur. This research strategy has proved especially popular and has supported significant theoretical development, as reflected in the

Table 2.1
Key research questions of different perspectives on institutional interaction

| | | Unit of analysis | |
		Case of interaction	Complex interaction setting
Level of analysis	Systemic	**I** How, and with what effects, does an international institution influence another international institution?	**II** How, and with what effects, does an institutional interaction affect the institutional structure of the international system?
	Actor-centered	**III** How can and do actors exploit opportunities arising from institutional interaction or avoid undesired interaction effects? How does institutional interaction frame the policy choices of actors?	**IV** How, and with what effects, do actors change the institutional structure of the international system through institutional interaction?

determination of causal mechanisms and more specific ideal types driving cases of interaction (see above). Empirical studies of institutional interaction (as explored above) have also (implicitly) employed this strategy. Likewise, studies analyzing the specific legal implications of one sectoral legal system for the *interpretation* of another one usually follow this research strategy (Wolfrum and Matz 2003).

Systemic inquiries exploring complex interaction settings (cell II) tackle the core question of how, and with what effects, institutional interaction affects the institutional structure of the international system. Because of the complexity of the empirical subject of inquiry, this research strategy will frequently start from empirical observation and description of complex settings or with a classification of interaction patterns. In contrast to case-specific research, it stays closer to the actual appearances of real-world interaction patterns, but it may be limited in its analytical grip on the forces generating the observed effects. The taxonomy of four different types of interaction put forward by Oran Young (1996; see also "Categories for the Classification of Institutional Interaction," above), the exploration of the political consequences of "international regime complexity" (Alter and Meunier 2009), and analysis of the emerging division of labor between the WTO and MEAs with trade restrictions (Gehring in this volume) or between different institutions for governing a specific region (Stokke in this volume) provide some examples of this approach.

The study of specific cases of institutional interaction using an actor-centered approach (cell III) examines how interested actors can and do seek to exploit opportunities arising from institutional interaction, or seek to avoid undesired interaction effects. Of note, a key part of this line of research is "interplay management," which is a major focus of this volume. In contrast to research falling into cells I and II, this strategy allows the researcher to apply existing theoretical and methodological tools for the analysis of collective action problems to the issue of institutional interaction. Interaction effects are treated like any other effects originating from an international institution. This research strategy is particularly suited for exploring how actors deal strategically with expected or anticipated institutional interaction in specific situations and how they exploit related opportunities for forum shopping. For example, Skjærseth, Stokke, and Wettestad (2006) examine how actors wishing to enhance the effectiveness of North Sea pollution control established the North Sea Conferences, in order to exert influence on the Oslo-Paris Commission. Likewise, studies assessing the options for improving an interaction situation generally follow this research strategy (e.g., Biermann 2001; Oberthür 2001; see also various contributions to this volume). Studies may also investigate how institutional interaction frames the policy choices of individual actors at the outcome level when international agreements are implemented.

Actor-centered studies focusing on more complex interaction patterns (cell IV) seek to investigate how the efforts of actors to employ institutional interaction change the institutional structure of the international system. They reflect the fact that all institutional structures originate in interdependent human action and affect human behavior. However, studies following this research strategy have to bridge a particularly wide gap between actors and institutions. The institutional structures of the international system emerging from institutional interaction are only an indirect consequence of human action that feeds into institutional interaction. Thus, cell IV research almost inevitably includes aspects of cell III and cell I research as well. Raustiala and Victor (2004) partially adopted this strategy in their study of the regime complex for plant

genetic resources when examining the overall implications of postnego-
tiation implementation of decisions adopted within international institutions dealing with legal inconsistencies of the normative systems involved.
Their study demonstrates that this research strategy may entail going
beyond the traditional understanding of institutions as resulting from the
rational design of actors attempting to realize a common interest.
Expanding traditional research on the effectiveness of institutions, and
studies exploring the combined effects of institutional complexes on the
behavior of relevant states and non-state actors, also belong to this
research strategy (Andersen 2008; see also Alter and Meunier 2009).

The choice among these research strategies depends primarily on the
particular research interest. Although two or even more strategies may
be combined in a single project, that renders the construction of a reliable
research concept more ambitious. Unless the different components are
convincingly integrated, conceptual broadness may restrict analytical
and theoretical depth. However, the four strategies are neither mutually
exclusive nor diametrically opposed. For example, research focusing on
the exploration of individual cases of interaction (cells I and III) may
well provide a sound basis for exploring complex interaction settings
(cells II and IV). Likewise, cell III research will usually include insights
from cell I inquiries. The various research strategies therefore may well
be employed in complementary ways.

Implications for Our Understanding of International Institutions

The study of international governance institutions has been dominated by
the collective action approach. This approach focuses almost exclusively
on formal international institutions (Keohane 1993) and their rational
design against the backdrop of well-defined preferences and constellations
of interests of relevant actors (Koremenos, Lipson, and Snidal 2001).
These institutions fulfill auxiliary functions depending on the characteristics of the underlying socially problematic situation (Oye 1985). In
prisoner's dilemma situations, for example, institutions serve to define
what is collectively considered cooperation and defection, to produce
transparency about the cooperators' behavior, and—possibly—to organize sanctions in order to preclude free riding and stabilize cooperation
(Martin 1993). The collective action approach implies a top-down perspective in which actors implement valid regime rules (unless free riding
occurs). Research on the effectiveness of international environmental
governance adopts a stimulus-response perspective (Miles et al. 2002).

By comparison, from the social practices perspective, institutions are seen as reflecting social expectations of appropriate behavior and as shaping actors' preferences and identities (Young 2002, 31–32). Institutions constitute social practices that are not collectively decided on or formally established but are produced, reproduced, and changed in a permanent interaction process of relevant actors (Wendt 1987). If actors behave in line with existing practices, they will reproduce them. If actors deviate from these practices, they will contribute to their modification or breakdown. Hence, social practices reflect "spontaneous" institutions that emerge from action (Young 1982), whereas formal institutions and their "rational design" constitute but one among several ways to change an established social practice.

With the social practices approach to institutions we can more readily grasp important aspects of institutional interaction. The influence of one institution on the normative structure of other institutions cannot simply be traced back to the existing preferences of relevant actors and the resultant constellation of interests. Two of the causal mechanisms uncovered above, cognitive interaction and interaction through commitment, demonstrate how an institution can affect actor preferences regarding issues dealt with by another institution. In many cases, they will be driven more by the unintended side effects of an institution than by the deliberate efforts of actors. Similarly, Raustiala and Victor (2004, 296) have pointed out that power, interests, and ideas do not map directly onto institutional decisions because other institutions also shape them. At a minimum, institutional interaction, in addition to exogenous interests, thus significantly affects and shapes the preferences of actors. Accordingly, preference formation cannot easily be separated from institutional analysis.

Institutional interaction also affects broader institutional structures in international society that are difficult to design rationally. To date, these broader institutional or "interlocking" structures (Underdal and Young 2004, 374–375) have not arisen from collective bargaining or institutionalized decision making at the aggregate level but rather have gradually evolved from, and are continuously shaped and reshaped by, the numerous decentralized decisions made within individual institutions and the interaction effects thereby arising. Interaction may lead to a particular division of labor of the institutions involved or to the mutual reinforcement of their effectiveness, as an emergent effect that is not reflected in either of these institutions. Whereas virtually all institutions in international environmental governance have their own permanent decision-making centers, if only in the form of a conference of the parties, no overarching decision-making body governing interaction between international institutions exists. The EU and domestic political systems possess unitary institutional frameworks that can address related issues, but the international system lacks a similar capacity. Overarching arrangements like the Vienna Convention on the Law of Treaties or the International Court of Justice play a limited role at best. Under these circumstances, interaction emerges from, and is influenced by, decentralized decisions made within any of the institutions involved and the behavior of individual actors. Far from being designed, interaction thus evolves and is produced and reproduced through the practices of relevant actors. To be sure, there is nothing to indicate that institutional interaction could not, in principle, be made subject to rational design and political governance. However, the current realities of international governance do not provide sufficient structures or means for doing so.

If institutional interaction affects the implementation of obligations established under international institutions, it will modify the meaning of these obligations. The causal mechanism of behavioral interaction demonstrates how an institution can affect the effectiveness of another institution at the outcome level. Even if the formal rules of the target institution remain unchanged, their effects and their meaning as reflected in the social practices of relevant actors may change significantly. Similarly, Raustiala and Victor (2004, 302) suggest that interacting institutions may deal with legal inconsistencies by means of mutual adaptation during implementation. Whereas the collective action approach assumes from a top-down perspective that actors implement fixed regime rules (unless there is free riding), institutional interaction highlights how the social practices emerging in the implementation of one institution may also be shaped by other institutions. The top-down implementation perspective may thus provide a valuable first cut, but it does not encompass the effects of institutional interaction at the outcome level and would need to be significantly adapted, and further developed, to do so.

Implications for Policymaking

The progress of research on institutional interaction achieved so far has several implications for policymaking. First, institutional interaction requires that policymaking take into account the broader policy implications of particular governance projects. Research of the past decade has shown the importance of interinstitutional effects at all three levels of effectiveness: output, outcome, and impact. It is now established that environmental governance is frequently the result of several institutions, and that an institution will often have implications for other institutions. Skillful policymaking will need to consider the existence of several institutions cogoverning an issue area. Accordingly, the institutional environment of the institution in which a policy initiative is launched is likely to have repercussions for its prospects of success regarding acceptance by other actors and effective implementation. The converse is also true: assessment of the impact of a policy initiative on an institution should take into account various "side effects" on and from other institutions (see also Alter and Meunier 2009).

While to some extent constraining policymaking, institutional interaction also offers a wealth of new opportunities. Actors can develop integrated "cross-institutional political strategies" (Alter and Meunier 2009, 17) for the pursuit of their preferences that take into consideration the potential of the various institutions affecting an issue area for both norm making and implementation. Since the normative development of an institution can be influenced not only from within that institution but also by other institutions, actors may engage in forum shopping (Gillespie 2002; Raustiala and Victor 2004, 299–300). To the extent that issue areas overlap, actors can choose the most suitable institution for a policy initiative. Interested actors might even establish a new institution with the sole purpose of influencing an existing one, as the North Sea coastal states did with the establishment of the International North Sea Conferences directed at strengthening the existing OSPAR Commission (Skjærseth 2006). Moreover, they may create "strategic inconsistency" (Raustiala and Victor 2004, 301), causing disruption of an unwanted institution or regulation in order to increase the pressure for its revision or cancellation.

The research results have important implications for discussions of the reform of international environmental governance and the political management of institutional interaction, be it through the creation of a World Environment Organization (see, e.g., Biermann and Bauer 2005) or a more cautious strengthening of coherence and environmental policy integration in global environmental governance (e.g., Chambers and Green 2005; Najam, Papa, and Taiyab 2006). First, synergy among institutions has been found to be at least as common as disruption (see "Synergy and Conflict," above). This finding contradicts the assumption held by most contributions to the debate on reforming international environmental governance, that conflict is the prevailing feature of institutional interaction. It indicates a need for greater emphasis on preserving and enhancing synergistic institutional interaction as compared to minimizing interinstitutional conflict. Accordingly, both the rationale for reform proposals and the yardstick for assessing their effectiveness will need to be adapted. In particular, institutional reform proposals will have to demonstrate that, in addition to mitigating conflict, they can preserve and enhance synergy among institutions.

Second, institutional interaction research indicates that the institutional fragmentation of international environmental governance may constitute a strength rather than a weakness. Institutions with large regulatory overlaps appear to create substantial added benefit if they employ complementary governance instruments, represent different memberships, or provide for significantly different decision-making procedures. What may at first sight appear as "duplication of work" or "redundancy" arising from institutional fragmentation, commonly deplored by policymakers and in the relevant literature, is in fact frequently a sign of effective governance. Slight differences in the instruments or procedures employed or the memberships of the institutions can make two (or more) institutions contribute in complementary ways to effective governance, as illustrated in the ideal type of interaction activating an "additional means." Regulatory competition among different forums can help prevent institutional sclerosis and serve as an important driver of overall progress. Before pursuing the reduction of "duplication of work"— for instance, through a World Environment Organization or through clustering functionally related institutions or elements of institutions in global environmental governance (Oberthür 2002; von Moltke 2005)— policymakers and analysts would be well advised to check carefully for any "hidden" added value of the currently fragmented arrangements.

Third, research indicates that disruption among international institutions is mainly rooted in competing institutional objectives, as is apparent in the jurisdictional delimitation type of interaction through commitment and the corollary type of behavioral interaction. Accordingly, reform proposals would have to show how they promise to reconcile diverging objectives of the institutions involved. For example, constructing a unitary institutional framework in the form of a World Environment Organization does not as such promise to resolve the trade-off between the competing environmental objectives of climate change and the protection of biodiversity regarding forest management. It would also require further clarification of how a World Environment Organization or other reform proposal(s) could help in mediating trade-offs with the nonenvironmental objectives pursued by institutions such as the WTO.

These findings present important challenges for current debates about reforming global environmental governance. While they do not eliminate the shortcomings of the current system of global environmental governance, they do question the rationale of current reform discussions, which have focused mainly on the potential for institutional coordination and integration at the international level. The findings of research on institutional interaction indicate the need to rethink this rationale and focus.

The Research Frontier: Interplay Management and Institutional Complexes

There is a good reason why the central themes of this volume, interplay management and institutional complexes, have been mentioned only in passing in our review of the state of the art of research on institutional interaction: these themes are at the research frontier and have so far remained underresearched. Surprisingly little is known about the extent to which, how, and with what effect relevant actors or groups of actors have dealt with and improved institutional interaction and its effects. More empirical research into existing interplay management efforts and their performance over time may help in advancing our knowledge about the most promising strategies and the conditions for their successful implementation. The focus of this volume on interplay management makes a welcome contribution to this end.

Similarly, the systematic investigation of institutional complexes and broader governance structures is still at an early stage. Systematic exploration of the nature, evolution, and consequences of sets of institutions that cogovern particular issue areas promises more integrated understanding (Raustiala and Victor 2004). Although academic interest in institutional complexes and complexity appears to be growing (see, e.g., Alter and Meunier 2009; Keohane and Victor 2010), we need to understand better the particular division of labor that develops over time among several institutions cogoverning an issue area and the resulting governance effects. Such governance effects may include "emergent" properties that arise from complex interaction situations but cannot be traced back to any concrete relationships and effects of the component parts. Only on the basis of a better understanding of the nature, evolution, and consequences of institutional complexes that have so far emerged spontaneously rather than as a product of rational design may we be able to advance toward designing and actively shaping institutional complexes.

Notes

This chapter is a shortened, adapted, and updated version of Gehring and Oberthür 2008.

1. Various terms have been used to denote the various phenomena subsumed here under "institutional interaction," including *interplay, linkage, interlinkage, overlap,* and *interconnection* (see, e.g., Herr and Chia 1995; Stokke 2000; Young et al. 1999/2005, 2008; Young 2002; Raustiala and Victor 2004). We use the term *interaction* in this chapter.

References

Aggarwal, Vinod K. 1983. The Unraveling of the Multi-Fiber Arrangement, 1981: An Examination of International Regime Change. *International Organization* 37 (4): 617–646.

Alter, Karen J., and Sophie Meunier. 2009. The Politics of International Regime Complexity. *Perspectives on Politics* 7 (1): 13–24.

Andersen, Regine. 2002. The Time Dimension in International Regime Interplay. *Global Environmental Politics* 2 (3): 98–117.

Andersen, Regine. 2008. *Governing Agrobiodiversity: Plant Genetics and Developing Countries.* Aldershot, UK: Ashgate.

Biermann, Frank. 2001. The Rising Tide of Green Unilateralism in World Trade Law: Options for Reconciling the Emerging North-South Conflict. *Journal of World Trade* 35 (3): 421–448.

Biermann, Frank, and Steffen Bauer, eds. 2005. *A World Environment Organization: Solution or Threat for International Environmental Governance?* Aldershot, UK: Ashgate.

Biermann, Frank, and Rainer Brohm. 2005. Implementing the Kyoto Protocol without the United States: The Strategic Role of Energy Tax Adjustments at the Border. *Climate Policy* 4 (3): 289–302.

Boyle, Alan E. 1999. Problems of Compulsory Jurisdiction and the Settlement of Disputes Relating to Straddling Fish Stocks. *International Journal of Marine and Coastal Law* 14 (1): 1–26.

Brack, Duncan. 2002. Environmental Treaties and Trade: Multilateral Environmental Agreements and the Multilateral Trading System. In *Trade, Environment, and the Millennium*, 2nd ed., ed. Gary P. Sampson and W. Bradnee Chambers, 321–352. Tokyo: United Nations University Press.

Brown Weiss, Edith. 1993. International Environmental Issues and the Emergence of a New World Order. *Georgetown Law Journal* 81 (3): 675–710.

Chambers, W. Bradnee, ed. 1998. *Global Climate Governance: Inter-linkages between the Kyoto Protocol and Other Multilateral Regimes*. Tokyo: United Nations University Press.

Chambers, W. Bradnee, ed. 2001. *Inter-linkages: The Kyoto Protocol and the International Trade and Investment Regimes*. Tokyo: United Nations University Press.

Chambers, W. Bradnee, and Jessica F. Green, eds. 2005. *Reforming International Environmental Governance: From Institutional Limits to Innovative Reforms*. Tokyo: United Nations University Press.

Charnovitz, Steve. 1998. The World Trade Organization and the Environment. *Yearbook of International Environmental Law* 8: 98–116.

Charnovitz, Steve. 2003. *Trade and Climate: Potential Conflict and Synergies*. Washington, D.C.: Pew Center on Global Climate Change.

Clapp, Jennifer. 1994. Africa, NGOs, and the International Toxic Waste Trade. *Journal of Environment & Development* 2 (1): 17–46.

DeSombre, Elizabeth R. 2005. Fishing under Flags of Convenience: Using Market Power to Increase Participation in International Regulation. *Global Environmental Politics* 5 (4): 73–94.

Eckersley, Robyn. 2004. The Big Chill: The WTO and Multilateral Environmental Agreements. *Global Environmental Politics* 4 (2): 24–50.

Galaz, Victor, Per Olsson, Thomas Hahn, Carl Folke, and Uno Svedin. 2008. The Problem of Fit among Biophysical Systems, Environment and Resource Regimes, and Broader Governance Systems: Insights and Emerging Challenges. In *Institutions and Environmental Change: Principal Findings, Applications, and Research Frontiers*, ed. Oran R. Young, Leslie A. King, and Heike Schroeder, 147–186. Cambridge, Mass.: MIT Press.

Gehring, Thomas, and Sebastian Oberthür. 2004. Exploring Regime Interaction: A Framework of Analysis. In *Regime Consequences: Methodological Challenges and Research Strategies*, ed. Arild Underdal and Oran R. Young, 247–269. Dordrecht: Kluwer-Academic.

Gehring, Thomas, and Sebastian Oberthür. 2006. Comparative Empirical Analysis and Ideal Types of Institutional Interaction. In *Institutional Interaction in Global Environmental Governance: Synergy and Conflict among International and EU Policies*, ed. Sebastian Oberthür and Thomas Gehring, 307–371. Cambridge, Mass.: MIT Press.

Gehring, Thomas, and Sebastian Oberthür. 2008. Interplay: Exploring Institutional Interaction. In *Institutions and Environmental Change: Principal Findings, Applications, and Research Frontiers*, ed. Oran R. Young, Leslie A. King, and Heike Schroeder, 187–223. Cambridge, Mass.: MIT Press.

Gillespie, Alexander. 2002. Forum Shopping in International Environmental Law: The IWC, CITES, and the Management of Cetaceans. *Ocean Development and International Law* 33 (1): 17–56.

Haas, Ernst B. 1990. *When Knowledge Is Power: Three Models of Change in International Organizations*. Berkeley and Los Angeles: University of California Press.

Héritier, Adrienne. 1999. *Policy-making and Diversity in Europe: Escaping Deadlock*. Cambridge: Cambridge University Press.

Herr, Richard A., and Edmund Chia. 1995. The Concept of Regime Overlap: Toward Identification and Assessment. In *Overlapping Maritime Regimes: An Initial Reconnaissance*, ed. Bruce W. Davis, 11–26. Hobart, Tasmania, Australia: Antarctic CRC and Institute of Antarctic and Southern Ocean Studies.

International Maritime Organization. 2006. New International Rules to Allow Storage of CO_2 in Seabed Adopted. IMO Press Briefing 43/2006, November 8. London: International Maritime Organization.

Jacquemont, Frédéric, and Alejandro Caparrós. 2002. The Convention on Biological Diversity and the Climate Change Convention 10 Years after Rio: Towards a Synergy of the Two Regimes? *Review of European Community & International Environmental Law* 11 (2): 139–180.

Keohane, Robert O. 1984. *After Hegemony: Cooperation and Discord in the World Political Economy*. Princeton, N.J.: Princeton University Press.

Keohane, Robert O. 1993. The Analysis of International Regimes: Towards a European–American Research Programme. In *Regime Theory and International Relations*, ed. Volker Rittberger, 23–45. Oxford: Clarendon Press.

Keohane, Robert O., Peter M. Haas, and Marc A. Levy. 1993. The Effectiveness of International Environmental Institutions. In *Institutions for the Earth*, ed. Peter M. Haas, Robert O. Keohane, and Marc A. Levy, 3–24. Cambridge, Mass.: MIT Press.

Keohane, Robert O., and David G. Victor. 2010. The Regime Complex for Climate Change. The Harvard Project on International Climate Agreements, Discussion Paper 10–33 (January 2010). John F. Kennedy School of Government, Harvard University, Cambridge, Mass.

King, Leslie A. 1997. Institutional Interplay: Research Questions. Background paper prepared for the IDGEC project. School of Natural Resources, University of Vermont, Burlington.

Koremenos, Barbara, Charles Lipson, and Duncan Snidal. 2001. The Rational Design of International Institutions. *International Organization* 55 (4): 761–799.

Lanchbery, John. 2006. The Convention on International Trade in Endangered Species of Wild Fauna and Flora (CITES): Responding to Calls for Action from Other Nature Conservation Regimes. In *Institutional Interaction in Global Environmental Governance: Synergy and Conflict among International and EU Policies*, ed. Sebastian Oberthür and Thomas Gehring, 157–179. Cambridge, Mass.: MIT Press.

Lavranos, Nikolaos. 2006. The MOX Plant and Ijzeren Rijn Disputes: Which Court Is the Supreme Arbiter? *Leiden Journal of International Law* 19 (1): 223–246.

Martin, Lisa L. 1993. The Rational State Choice of Multilateralism. In *Multilateralism Matters: The Theory and Praxis of an Institutional Form*, ed. John G. Ruggie, 91–121. New York: Columbia University Press.

Meinke, Britta. 2002. *Multi-Regime-Regulierung: Wechselwirkungen zwischen globalen und regionalen Umweltregimen*. Wiesbaden: Deutscher Universitäts-Verlag.

Miles, Edward. L., Arild Underdal, Steinar Andresen, Jørgen Wettestad, Jon Birger Skjærseth, and Elaine M. Carlin, eds. 2002. *Environmental Regime Effectiveness: Confronting Theory with Evidence*. Cambridge, Mass.: MIT Press.

Najam, Adil, Mihaela Papa, and Nadaa Taiyab. 2006. *Global Environmental Governance: A Reform Agenda*. Winnipeg, MB: International Institute for Sustainable Development.

Oberthür, Sebastian. 2001. Linkages between the Montreal and Kyoto Protocols: Enhancing Synergies between Protecting the Ozone Layer and the Global Climate. *International Environmental Agreements: Politics, Law and Economics* 1 (3): 357–377.

Oberthür, Sebastian. 2002. Clustering of Multilateral Environmental Agreements: Potentials and Limitations. *International Environmental Agreements: Politics, Law and Economics* 2 (4): 317–340.

Oberthür, Sebastian. 2003. Institutional Interaction to Address Greenhouse Gas Emissions from International Transport: ICAO, IMO and the Kyoto Protocol. *Climate Policy* 3 (3): 191–205.

Oberthür, Sebastian. 2006. The Climate Change Regime: Interactions with ICAO, IMO, and the EU Burden-Sharing Agreement. In *Institutional Interaction in Global Environmental Governance: Synergy and Conflict among International and EU Policies*, ed. Sebastian Oberthür and Thomas Gehring, 53–77. Cambridge, Mass.: MIT Press.

Oberthür, Sebastian, and Hermann E. Ott. 1999. *The Kyoto Protocol: International Climate Policy for the 21st Century*. Berlin: Springer-Verlag.

Oberthür, Sebastian, and Thomas Gehring. 2006a. Conceptual Foundations of Institutional Interaction. In *Institutional Interaction in Global Environmental Governance: Synergy and Conflict among International and EU Policies*, ed. Sebastian Oberthür and Thomas Gehring, 19–51. Cambridge, Mass.: MIT Press.

Oberthür, Sebastian, and Thomas Gehring. 2006b. Institutional Interaction in Global Environmental Governance: The Case of the Cartagena Protocol and the World Trade Organization. *Global Environmental Politics* 6 (2): 1–31.

Oberthür, Sebastian, and Thomas Gehring, eds. 2006c. *Institutional Interaction in Global Environmental Governance: Synergy and Conflict among International and EU Policies*. Cambridge, Mass.: MIT Press.

Oye, Kenneth A. 1985. Explaining Cooperation under Anarchy: Hypotheses and Strategies. *World Politics* 38 (1): 1–24.

Palmer, Alice, Beatrice Chaytor, and Jacob Werksman. 2006. Interaction between the World Trade Organization and International Environmental Regimes. In *Institutional Interaction in Global Environmental Governance: Synergy and*

Conflict among International and EU Policies, ed. Sebastian Oberthür and Thomas Gehring, 181–204. Cambridge, Mass.: MIT Press.

Pauwelyn, Joost. 2003. *Conflict of Norms in Public International Law: How WTO Law Relates to Other Rules of International Law.* Cambridge: Cambridge University Press.

Pontecorvo, Concetta M. 1999. Interdependence between Global Environmental Regimes: The Kyoto Protocol on Climate Change and Forest Protection. *Zeitschrift für ausländisches öffentliches Recht und Völkerrecht* 59 (3): 709–749.

Raustiala, Kal, and David G. Victor. 2004. The Regime Complex for Plant Genetic Resources. *International Organization* 55:277–309.

Rosamond, Ben. 2000. *Theories of European Integration.* Basingstoke, UK: Palgrave Macmillan.

Rosendal, Kristin. 2001. Impacts of Overlapping International Regimes: The Case of Biodiversity. *Global Governance* 7 (1): 95–117.

Rosendal, Kristin. 2006. The Convention on Biological Diversity: Tensions with the WTO TRIPS Agreement over Access to Genetic Resources and the Sharing of Benefits. In *Institutional Interaction in Global Environmental Governance: Synergy and Conflict among International and EU Policies,* ed. Sebastian Oberthür and Thomas Gehring, 79–102. Cambridge, Mass.: MIT Press.

Schiffman, Howard. 1999. The Southern Bluefin Tuna Case: ITLOS Hears Its First Fishery Dispute. *Journal of International Wildlife Law and Policy* 2 (3): 1–15.

Selin, Henrik, and Stacey D. VanDeveer. 2003. Mapping Institutional Linkages in European Air Pollution Politics. *Global Environmental Politics* 3 (3): 14–46.

Shany, Yuval. 2003. *The Competing Jurisdictions of International Courts and Tribunals.* Oxford: Oxford University Press.

Simon, Herbert A. 1972. Theories of Bounded Rationality. In *Decision and Organization,* ed. Charles B. McGuire and Roy Radner, 161–176. Amsterdam: North-Holland.

Skjærseth, Jon Birger. 2000. *North Sea Cooperation: Linking International and Domestic Pollution Control.* Manchester: Manchester University Press.

Skjærseth, Jon Birger. 2006. Protecting the Northeast Atlantic: One Problem, Three Institutions. In *Institutional Interaction in Global Environmental Governance: Synergy and Conflict among International and EU Policies,* ed. Sebastian Oberthür and Thomas Gehring, 102–125. Cambridge, Mass.: MIT Press.

Skjærseth, Jon Birger, Olav Schram Stokke, and Jørgen Wettestad. 2006. Soft Law, Hard Law, and Effective Implementation of International Environmental Norms. *Global Environmental Politics* 6 (3): 104–120.

Snidal, Duncan. 1985. The Game Theory of International Politics. *World Politics* 38 (1): 25–57.

Snidal, Duncan. 1994. The Politics of Scope: Endogenous Actors, Heterogeneity and Institutions. *Journal of Theoretical Politics* 6 (4): 449–472.

Stokke, Olav Schram. 2000. Managing Straddling Stocks: The Interplay of Global and Regional Regimes. *Ocean and Coastal Management* 43 (2/3): 205–234.

Stokke, Olav Schram, ed. 2001a. *Governing High Seas Fisheries: The Interplay of Global and Regional Regimes*. Oxford: Oxford University Press.

Stokke, Olav Schram. 2001b. *The Interplay of International Regimes: Putting Effectiveness Theory to Work*. Report No. 14. Lysaker, Norway: Fridtjof Nansen Institute.

Stokke, Olav Schram. 2007. A Legal Regime for the Arctic? Interplay with the Law of the Sea Convention. *Marine Policy* 31 (4): 402–408.

Stokke, Olav Schram, and Claire Coffey. 2006. Institutional Interplay and Responsible Fisheries: Combating Subsidies, Developing Precaution. In *Institutional Interaction in Global Environmental Governance: Synergy and Conflict among International and EU Policies*, ed. Sebastian Oberthür and Thomas Gehring, 127–155. Cambridge, Mass.: MIT Press.

Stokke, Olav Schram, and Davor Vidas. 1996. *Governing the Antarctic: The Effectiveness and Legitimacy of the Antarctic Treaty System*. Cambridge: Cambridge University Press.

Stokke, Olav Schram, and Geir Hønneland, eds. 2007. *International Cooperation and Arctic Governance: Regime Effectiveness and Northern Region Building*. London: Routledge.

Tarasofsky, Richard G. 1997. Ensuring Compatibility between Multilateral Environmental Agreements and GATT/WTO. *Yearbook of International Environmental Law* 7:52–74.

Tversky, Amos, and Daniel Kahnemann. 1981. The Framing of Decision and Rational Choice. *Science* 211:453–458.

Tversky, Amos, and Daniel Kahnemann. 1984. Choices, Values, and Frames. *American Psychologist* 39 (4): 341–350.

Underdal, Arild. 2004. Methodological Challenges in the Study of Regime Effectiveness. In *Regime Consequences: Methodological Challenges and Research Strategies*, ed. Arild Underdal and Oran R. Young, 27–48. Dordrecht: Kluwer.

Underdal, Arild. 2008. Determining the Causal Significance of Institutions: Accomplishments and Challenges. In *Institutions and Environmental Change: Principal Findings, Applications, and Research Frontiers*, ed. Oran R. Young, Leslie A. King, and Heike Schroeder, 49–78. Cambridge, Mass.: MIT Press.

Underdal, Arild, and Oran R. Young, eds. 2004. *Regime Consequences: Methodological Challenges and Research Strategies*. Dordrecht: Kluwer-Academic.

van Asselt, Harro, Frank Biermann, and Joyeeta Gupta. 2004. Interlinkages of Global Climate Governance. In *Beyond Climate: Options for Broadening Climate Policy*, ed. Marcel Kok and Heleen de Coninck, 221–246. Netherlands Research Programme on Climate Change, Report 500036001. Bilthoven: RIVM.

van Asselt, Harro, Francesco Sindico, and Michael A. Mehling. 2008. Global Climate Change and the Fragmentation of International Law. *Law & Policy* 30 (4): 423–449.

Vidas, Davor. 2000a. Emerging Law of the Sea Issues in the Antarctic Maritime Area: A Heritage for the New Century? *Ocean Development and International Law* 31 (1/2): 197–222.

Vidas, Davor, ed. 2000b. *Protecting the Polar Marine Environment: Law and Policy for Pollution Prevention.* Cambridge: Cambridge University Press.

von Moltke, Konrad. 2005. Clustering International Environmental Agreements as an Alternative to a World Environment Organization. In *A World Environment Organization: Solution or Threat for Effective International Environmental Governance?*, ed. Frank Biermann and Steffen Bauer, 175–204. Aldershot, UK: Ashgate.

Wendt, Alexander. 1987. The Agent-Structure Problem in International Relations Theory. *International Organization* 41 (3): 335–370.

Wolfrum, Rüdiger, and Nele Matz. 2003. *Conflicts in International Environmental Law.* Berlin: Springer-Verlag.

Yamin, Farhana, and Joanna Depledge. 2004. *The International Climate Change Regime: A Guide to Rules, Institutions and Procedures.* Cambridge: Cambridge University Press.

Young, Oran R. 1982. Regime Dynamics: The Rise and Fall of International Regimes. *International Organization* 36 (2): 277–297.

Young, Oran R. 1996. Institutional Linkages in International Society: Polar Perspectives. *Global Governance* 2 (1): 1–24.

Young, Oran R. 2002. *The Institutional Dimensions of Environmental Change: Fit, Interplay, and Scale.* Cambridge, Mass.: MIT Press.

Young, Oran R. 2008. Deriving Insights from the Case of the WTO and the Cartagena Protocol. In *Institutional Interplay: Biosafety and Trade*, ed. Oran R. Young, W. Bradnee Chambers, Joy A. Kim, and Claudia ten Have, 131–158. Tokyo: United Nations University Press.

Young, Oran R., with contributions from Arun Agrawal, Leslie A. King, Peter H. Sand, Arild Underdal, and Merrilyn Wasson. 1999/2005. *Institutional Dimensions of Global Environmental Change (IDGEC) Science Plan.* IHDP Report Nos. 9 and 16. Bonn: International Human Dimensions Programme on Global Environmental Change.

Young, Oran R., W. Bradnee Chambers, Joy A. Kim, and Claudia ten Have, eds. 2008. *Institutional Interplay: Biosafety and Trade.* Tokyo: United Nations University Press.

3

Legal and Political Approaches in Interplay Management

Dealing with the Fragmentation of Global Climate Governance

Harro van Asselt

This chapter focuses on ways of dealing with the fragmentation of international regimes on climate change and the subsequent interactions among them. It assesses various means of interplay management with a view to enhancing synergy and mitigating conflict between regimes in this issue area. Whereas other authors have focused mainly on the political aspects of interplay management (e.g., Stokke 2001; Gehring and Oberthür 2006), I employ a slightly wider angle by including the role of international law. Although international law by itself cannot deal comprehensively with the fragmentation of global climate governance, it offers some relevant avenues for addressing conflicts between environmental and nonenvironmental treaties. However, there is a need to complement these approaches with political efforts aimed at enhancing coordination and cooperation between environmental regimes.

Anthropogenic climate change has many wide-ranging impacts on the natural environment and society, and various human activities and sectors of society contribute to increased concentrations of greenhouse gases in the atmosphere. Because of the intricate connections between climate change and other issue areas, there are interrelationships between the global climate regime and other areas of international law. Notwithstanding the relevance of these other areas, the lion's share of international law on climate change is still to be found in the 1992 United Nations Framework Convention on Climate Change (UNFCCC) and its 1997 Kyoto Protocol, and in decisions made by the Conference of the Parties (COP) to the UNFCCC and the Conference of the Parties serving as the Meeting of the Parties (COP/MOP) to the Kyoto Protocol. Issue coverage of the treaties in question frequently overlaps, sometimes to a large extent, causing "treaty congestion" (Brown Weiss 1993, 679; Hicks 1999), with potential consequences for their effectiveness. To give but a few examples: climate change is affecting and will continue to affect flora and fauna protected under various biodiversity-related treaties (IPCC 2002; SCBD 2003); substitutes for ozone-depleting substances promoted under the Montreal Protocol may increase greenhouse gas emissions (Oberthür 2001; Oberthür, Dupont, and Matsumoto in this volume); certain forms of oceanic carbon sequestration, a potential form of climate change mitigation, may be in violation of the law of the sea (Scott 2005); bilateral or regional investment agreements may prohibit the kind of conditioning of investments promoted by the Kyoto Protocol's flexibility mechanisms (Werksman, Baumert, and Dubash 2003); and so on. In short, the very nature of climate change as an issue of sustainable development makes it almost impossible to capture all relevant aspects under a single legal regime, necessitating the consideration of interactions with other regimes (van Asselt, Gupta, and Biermann 2005).

This fragmentation of global climate governance poses a significant challenge, as different international norms may have a bearing on any given situation. By "fragmentation" I refer to the increased specialization and diversification in international governance arrangements, including the overlap of substantive rules and jurisdictions. The implications of this fragmentation may take the form of conflicts between treaties, but they may also take the form of synergies. These conflicts and synergies between regimes are not always apparent from the rules agreed on at the international level. Tensions below the surface could lead to divergences in the implementation of different treaties. Similarly, it is not always necessary for two treaties to state their mutual supportiveness in order for states to implement them in a synergetic fashion.

One might argue that fragmentation "reflects the high political salience of environmental issues and their particular problem structure" and should be regarded as "a strength rather than a weakness of environmental co-operation" (Oberthür and Gehring 2004, 369). However, the multiplicity of institutional arrangements, and consequently the overlapping of regimes, could also pose a threat to the coherence of international environmental governance. For interplay management, it is therefore important to strengthen the overall coherence of international cooperation by exploiting synergies between different agreements while minimizing potential or actual conflicts.

The scope of this chapter is limited to horizontal interactions between the climate regime and other multilateral regimes. It does not examine vertical interactions between, for instance, the climate regime and EU policies (see Oberthür 2006). Nor does the chapter deal with all political approaches in interplay management: it focuses on cooperation and coordination among regime bodies and does not deal with autonomous adaptation within one or several regimes, or actions by individual states or groups of states (see Oberthür 2009; Stokke and Oberthür in this volume). Furthermore, I discuss interactions between treaty-based regimes in particular issue areas only. Interactions between the climate regime and international organizations are not analyzed, although, where appropriate, the role of international organizations in addressing interactions is brought into the discussion.

The chapter is structured as follows. The next section explains how international law forms a means of interplay management, arguing that there are limitations to its use, as it deals primarily with avoiding and resolving conflicts. I then examine what approaches are possible beyond international law, focusing more on exploiting synergies. The final section offers some concluding thoughts.

Limits and Merits of International Law

In dealing with relations between treaties, international lawyers have shown a heavy preoccupation with conflicting instances (e.g., Jenks 1953; Pauwelyn 2003; Wolfrum and Matz 2003; Borgen 2005; ILC 2006; Vranes 2006).[1] This emphasis on avoiding and resolving conflicts can be explained by a desire to establish legal certainty as to which norm applies in a particular situation.

The main questions for international lawyers are (1) can a conflict be established? and (2) if so, which treaty prevails? This section provides an overview of traditional legal techniques for establishing and resolving conflicts, followed by an examination of more forward-looking approaches. It also discusses to what extent these legal techniques could be useful in addressing climate-related interactions.

Traditional Approaches to Conflict Resolution

Before arguing whether international law can take on a role in addressing conflicts, we must first establish whether a conflict—in the legal sense—actually exists. According to the classic definition of Jenks (1953, 426), a "conflict in the strict sense of direct incompatibility arises only where a party to the two treaties cannot simultaneously comply with its obligations under both treaties." This definition does not include conflicts involving permissive norms, and would thus deny the existence of a conflict, for example, if the climate regime should permit its parties to use trade-restrictive measures that would violate the General Agreement on Tariffs and Trade (GATT). Pauwelyn (2003) takes a slightly broader approach to the concept of "conflict of norms," dealing with conflicts of legally binding norms—which can consist of obligations and rights—in international law. However, especially in international environmental law, this construction of conflicts still does not cover all the divergences and inconsistencies between treaties that may have negative effects (Wolfrum and Matz 2003), as treaty provisions may provide indirect incentives for behavior inconsistent with other treaties. Therefore, conceptualizing conflict more broadly, "as a situation where two rules or principles suggest different ways of dealing with a problem" (ILC 2006, 19), would appear better suited to cover all climate-related interactions. However, such a definition would be overly broad, as "different ways of dealing with a problem" might also lead to mutually supportive and complementary outcomes. It should thus be added that these "different ways" lead to contradictory behavior. That definition seems at least broad enough to cover conflicts between international legal instruments with diverging objectives, and could also be useful in dealing with conflicts between multilateral environmental agreements (MEAs).

An additional challenge is posed by possibly inconsistent decision making by different treaty bodies, which are increasingly involved in rule development that comes close to de facto lawmaking (Brunnée 2002). As a result, discrepancies between two different issue areas could result not only from the treaties but also from subsequent rules agreed upon by their treaty bodies. However, a definition of conflicts as described above does not cover these inconsistencies.

"Conflict Clauses"

The starting point in addressing conflicts is to examine whether states have sought to regulate these through "conflict clauses" (Pauwelyn 2003). The purpose of these clauses is to clarify the relation between treaties, thus preventing contradictions. This can be achieved by, for example, stipulating that existing treaties shall prevail, or that a new agreement shall prevail over existing ones (Wolfrum and Matz 2003; see also Axelrod in this volume). Not all treaties contain such clauses. The agreement establishing the World Trade Organization (WTO), for example, does not set out how it relates to existing or future treaties, nor does the Montreal Protocol. However, various agreements under the auspices of the WTO include an environmental exception clause. The best-known clause in this regard is Article XX(b) and (g) of GATT, which makes an exception for trade measures "necessary to protect human, animal or plant life or health" and "relating to the conservation of exhaustible natural resources," respectively.

In contrast, the climate agreements contain several clauses that regulate their relation with other multilateral treaties. With regard to the Montreal Protocol, the UNFCCC and the Kyoto Protocol delimit their scope by covering only "greenhouse gases not controlled by the Montreal Protocol." These agreements thereby express awareness of the substantive interlinkages between the problems of climate change and ozone layer depletion, as some ozone-depleting substances are also greenhouse gases. However, such awareness cannot in itself prevent or resolve conflicts (Oberthür 2001).

Another clause concerns the use of carbon sinks in the Kyoto Protocol's Clean Development Mechanism (CDM). Forestry projects are to a limited extent eligible for emission reduction credits under the CDM rules. However, fears have been expressed that these rules fail to ensure the protection of biodiversity and the prevention of land degradation, and hence could conflict with obligations under other environmental treaties (Pontecorvo 1999; Jacquemont and Caparrós 2002). One key concern is that the rules enable projects resulting in destructive large-scale monoculture plantations rather than providing protection for existing old-growth forests. Plantations are cost-effective, given that they involve fast-growing trees (such as eucalyptus) that would result in more carbon dioxide being sequestered and hence more credits being generated; however, such projects may have negative impacts on local biodiversity or landscape. The Kyoto Protocol calls on its parties to implement policies and measures, including the protection and enhancement of sinks and reservoirs, "taking into account its commitments under relevant international environmental agreements" (Article 2.1(a)(ii) of the Kyoto Protocol). Although this provision does not state *which* agreements need to be taken into account, it is reasonable to assume that the role of forests and wetlands as sinks renders the Convention on Biological Diversity (CBD), the UN Convention to Combat Desertification (UNCCD), and the Ramsar Convention on Wetlands "relevant." Additionally, the membership of these agreements should be taken into account: an agreement can hardly be "relevant" for a party that has not signed or ratified it. However, the precise meaning of "taking into account" remains unclear, leaving open the question of which treaty would prevail in case of conflict (Pontecorvo 1999).

Article 3.5 of the UNFCCC, on coherence with the trade regime, is also arguably a "conflict clause," using language lifted straight from the

GATT environmental exception and thus at least implicitly acknowledging the relation between the climate agreements and the WTO agreements. Furthermore, Article 2.3 of the Kyoto Protocol provides a clear statement supporting the objectives of the WTO agreements. These provisions do not establish a hierarchy between the two regimes beyond this acknowledgment. Nevertheless, there are strong arguments for the priority of WTO law over the climate agreements: these agreements do not explicitly state they are not subordinate to the WTO agreements, in contrast to the Cartagena Protocol on Biosafety; and trade measures against non-parties or noncompliers are not explicitly allowed by the rules elaborated under the Kyoto Protocol (Stokke 2004).

Other treaties also contain conflict clauses on the relation with relevant international agreements, which include the UNFCCC and the Kyoto Protocol. The CBD contains a clause that aims to give priority to existing agreements. This clause seems to put a limit on climate change mitigation measures that threaten biodiversity: CBD Article 22.1 does not give priority to existing agreements in cases "where the exercise of those rights and obligations would cause a serious damage or threat to biological diversity." Besides the question of how this clause would apply when a country is not a party to one of the treaties, the CBD clause applies only to existing treaties, and thus not to the subsequent Kyoto Protocol. Doelle (2004, 86) argues that this nonapplication to the Kyoto Protocol makes this avenue for addressing the CBD/Kyoto Protocol conflict "legally minimal and practically nonexistent."

There are various difficulties with the use of conflict clauses: their wording is often unclear and open to diverging interpretations (what would establish "a serious damage or threat to biological diversity"?); they are not dynamic enough to reflect new developments (such as changes in scientific insights); it is not always clear at what point a treaty comes into existence (Vierdag 1988); and chances are that such clauses may never be applied "in the absence of a single, unifying dispute settlement system" (Werksman 1999, 2). From the perspective of international law, however, they provide the primary means of addressing the relation between treaties. Therefore, it is important that whenever a new agreement or amendment is negotiated, either within the UNFCCC context or outside it, conflict clauses are drafted in a way that fully considers the implications for other treaties, and preferably in an unambiguous manner (Wolfrum and Matz 2003; Borgen 2005). Hence, it makes sense to draw up a list of all international legal instruments that may have an impact on the treaty under negotiation (Wolfrum and Matz 2003). This is also the crux of Hicks's (1999) proposal for a "stop and think approach" in which the impacts of a new treaty or a treaty amendment are carefully assessed, where appropriate, in cooperation with the relevant states, secretariats, and international organizations.

Treaty Interpretation

Treaty interpretation is a technique that diplomats and dispute settlement bodies may apply to harmonize two norms that seem to be in conflict. It cannot, however, resolve "genuine conflicts"—cases in which compliance with one norm leads to breach of another (Pauwelyn 2003). The main rules on how to interpret treaties are found in the Vienna Convention on the Law of Treaties (VCLT).

Article 31 of the VCLT provides basic interpretation rules, stipulating that the ordinary meaning, context, and the object and purpose of a treaty are to be taken into consideration. The convention also gives more dynamic interpretation rules, specifying that interpretation should take into account (1) any subsequent agreement between the parties on the interpretation of the treaty, (2) any subsequent practice in the application of the treaty, and (3) "any relevant rules of international law applicable in the relations between the parties" (Article 31.3). The first part of this provision refers to a possible "authentic interpretation" that parties may adopt. WTO members, for example, could adopt an interpretative statement concerning the scope of the GATT environmental exception, enabling compatibility between the trade and climate agreements (Stokke 2004). Although this may clarify aspects of the relation between the agreements, adopting such an interpretation could prove politically infeasible if some states are party to only one of the treaties in question.

This caveat holds also for "any subsequent practice" (Wolfrum and Matz 2003). Subsequent practice by states could indicate a tacit agreement on how to interpret certain provisions. However, verifying the existence of such an agreement would be difficult, as "the tacit agreement must also be documented by equally tacit concerted action in regard to the implementation of the agreement" (ibid., 143).

The third rule of Article 31.1(c) is the most interesting one. It includes a principle of "systemic integration" (McLachlan 2005), permitting interpretation of treaties in light of the broader system of international law. Given the relatively young age of international environmental law, the lack of references to environmental considerations, linkages between environmental and nonenvironmental issue areas, and continuous changes in scientific insights (French 2006), it seems attractive to apply this interpretative tool in disputes between, for example, climate and trade. Pontecorvo (1999) argues that the provision supports a "harmonizing approach" to the conflict between the CBD and the Kyoto Protocol on the matter of sinks. More generally, Chambers (2008) finds that Article 31.1(c) provides a window for applying a "principle of interlinkages" that could ensure consistency between two treaties. The main question here is whether the relevant law must be in place at the time of the adoption of a new treaty or at the time of interpretation. The latter allows a more evolutionary approach to treaty interpretation and is arguably appropriate when interpreting terms that are likely to change over time (Pauwelyn 2003).

However, even more dynamic treaty interpretation cannot remove the general limitations of this legal technique. First, interpretation always intends to give meaning to treaty terms that are insufficiently clear (Wolfrum and Matz 2003). Hence, any rule from another treaty to be used in the interpretation must relate to the ambiguous provision. Simply put, interpretation cannot result in a rule of one treaty replacing a rule of another. Second, and relevant especially for interactions between the trade and climate regimes, international environmental law lacks a strong system for dispute settlement. As the WTO has a particularly strong dispute settlement mechanism, most trade-environment disputes would be adjudicated through a "trade lens," resulting in a bias against international environmental rules (Voigt 2009).

Conflict Resolution Rules

Article 30 of the VCLT provides rules for the resolution of conflicts. An apparent limitation of this provision is that it applies only to treaties relating to the same subject matter (Article 30.1). If the "subject matter" is broadly seen as "environmental protection," Article 30 could theoretically apply to conflicts between the UNFCCC and the CBD. However, Jacquemont and Caparrós (2002) argue that the issues of climate change and biodiversity cannot reasonably be seen as related to the same subject matter. Similarly, McCabe (2007, 453) states that in the case of conflict between the Montreal and Kyoto Protocols, "both treaties would have to govern climate change or both would have to govern ozone depletion." However, the ILC (2006, 130) argues that whenever "the fulfillment of the obligation under one treaty affects the fulfillment of the obligation of another," the two treaties should be seen as relating to the same subject matter. This would mean that not only conflicts between environmental regimes but also trade-environment conflicts are potentially resolvable through the VCLT. Borgen (2005, 603) applies a more stringent interpretation and concludes that "the [VCLT] is not applicable to the thornier issues of what happens when treaties have different foci but overlapping issue areas."

Whether or not Article 30 of the VCLT is applicable, the general rules on treaty conflicts, including *lex posterior* and *lex specialis*, may still be applied. However, the relevance of the *lex posterior* rule—that the newer treaty prevails over the older one—faces severe limitations when the parties to the treaties are not identical (Wolfrum and Matz 2003). Furthermore, there are general legal uncertainties about when a treaty comes into existence (Vierdag 1988). This is particularly pertinent in the case of the Rio conventions (UNFCCC, CBD, and UNCCD), which were negotiated in parallel but were adopted and entered into force on different dates. The usefulness of the *lex specialis* maxim—that the more specific treaty prevails over the more general one—is also limited by applying only to treaties that relate to the same subject matter. Furthermore, it is difficult to show that a treaty is "more specialized" than another (McCabe 2007).

Alternative Legal Approaches to Conflict Resolution

Even if the conflict rules of the law of treaties do not provide for clear-cut solutions to addressing interactions, there may still be a role for general international law in interplay management. Besides treaties, general international law comprises customary international (environmental) law and general principles of law. As the precise contents of general principles of law and customary international law are not entirely clear, there is an opportunity to inject principles and rules of international environmental law into the law applicable to a certain conflict, thereby balancing the interests of different regimes. The application of general international law is different from treaty interpretation, although the two can be used side by side as tools in a dispute. Addressing a conflict by applying general international law assumes a more important role of the norms outside the treaty, as they are directly applicable.

Voigt (2009, 186) argues that sustainable development can be considered an applicable general principle of law because of "[i]ts normative force, broad scope and support in the international community." The application of such general principles could indeed entail a more balanced appraisal of environmental and nonenvironmental considerations in the case of a dispute related to trade measures taken pursuant to the climate treaties.

A related question is whether international environmental law can constitute *jus cogens*—norms of general international law from which no derogation is possible—and to what extent this can assist in dealing with fragmentation and interactions (Paulus 2005). Although international norms must fulfill strict criteria to qualify, some norms of international environmental law might possibly constitute *jus cogens* in the future (cf. Kornicker Uhlmann 1998). This approach seems pertinent in dealing with conflicts between nonenvironmental regimes and the climate regime. However, it would be helpful only to a limited extent in cases involving conflict between the climate agreements and other environmental treaties, as it is difficult to apply general international law if the conflict concerns not the black-letter rules but only the practical execution of these rules. Furthermore, the introduction of *jus cogens* into relations between environmental treaties implies establishing a hierarchy among them. That would run counter to the idea of creating synergies, where the aim is instead to harmonize treaties.

Finally, international law allows parties to amend treaties in order to address conflicts or to enhance synergies, essentially by creating new conflict clauses. Thus, for example, the GATT could be amended so as to allow certain climate-friendly processes and production methods (Stokke 2004), or the parties to the UNFCCC could adopt a protocol on climate change and biodiversity (Wolfrum and Matz 2003). Such a protocol could address the interactions between the Kyoto Protocol's flexibility mechanisms and other environmental regimes in a more comprehensive manner—by specifying that they should provide incentives for achieving the goals of other environmental treaties, for example by giving preference to CDM projects that also contribute to restoring and preserving wetlands. However, given the nature of international environmental negotiation processes, changing a treaty is more a question of political will than one of international law, and it is likely that the status quo will be maintained (Axelrod in this volume). In addition, owing to the potential implications of treaty amendments, the rules for amending a treaty are generally cumbersome. Furthermore, given the elaborate rule development in, for example, the climate and biodiversity regimes through their respective treaty bodies, interaction questions are likely to be dealt with by COP decisions rather than by amendment.

Implications of Legal Approaches to Interplay Management

Several inferences can be drawn on the basis of the foregoing. First, the role of international law in interplay management is aimed primarily at preventing and resolving conflicts rather than enhancing synergies.

International law does not provide an incentive to exploit synergies when the objectives or specific provisions of two treaties are overlapping. The VCLT, for example, does not deal with the procedural aspects of overlapping treaties, such as different reporting requirements (Hicks 1999). Ultimately, international law plays a role primarily in the delimitation of issue areas, which "tends to be a matter of conflict and of the distribution of power between the institutions involved, rather than of amicable problem solving" (Gehring and Oberthür 2006, 337).

Second, the VCLT does not seem to be the proper instrument for dealing with conflicts between treaty norms in practice. As Borgen (2005, 605) notes, "When instances of treaty conflicts are mentioned it is usually by academics or other observers. Further, when such conflicts do attract the attention of decision makers, they tend to be resolved in ad hoc political bargains rather than by an application of black-letter principles." In particular, the conflict rules of the VCLT appear to lack the subtlety needed for dealing with complex interactions between MEAs, where establishing hierarchical relationships between treaties is neither possible nor desirable (Pontecorvo 1999).

Third, international law fails to deal with conflicts arising from decisions of treaty bodies. The climate treaties leave many issues up to their respective treaty bodies, and at times the treaty language remains ambiguous. This could mean—as with the sinks issue—that the texts of two treaties may be perfectly compatible, and it is subsequent decisions of the treaty body that trigger the conflict. Since the VCLT applies only to *treaties* as such, that further limits its usefulness.

Finally, international law does offer some relevant avenues for addressing conflicts with nonenvironmental regimes, such as the trade regime. First, these include ways to avoid conflicts or enhance synergies from the negotiation stages onward, through more careful and unambiguous drafting of conflict clauses before a treaty comes into existence, through amending an existing treaty, or perhaps through negotiating a new one. Second, there is room for more creative use of dynamic treaty interpretation. That could include the use of emerging principles of international law concerning sustainable development and the provisions of environmental agreements, and the use of these principles and rules in the law applicable to a conflict.

From Conflicts to Synergies? Beyond International Law

The previous section has shown that legal techniques aim primarily to address conflicts, a finding seemingly at odds with the observation that cases of synergy are at least as common as conflicts in international environmental governance (Gehring and Oberthür 2006). That observation calls for attention to ongoing activities and further options for enhancing these synergies. In this section the focus is on coordination and cooperation between treaty bodies; I do not deal with other political approaches to interplay management, such as autonomous adaptation by one regime, or unilateral action by one or multiple actors (see Oberthür 2009). Stokke (2001) has noted the relevance of institutional coordination and cooperation in dealing with interactions. This could take place simply through information exchange between treaty bodies, or in the "more ambitious form of comprising joint planning of programmes or even the coordination of substantive decision-making or implementation activities" (Stokke 2001, 12).

This section first discusses existing efforts to enhance synergies and mitigate conflicts between the climate regime and other regimes. It then reviews various options for strengthening such efforts, followed by a discussion of the usefulness of these political approaches in dealing with climate-related interactions.

Ongoing Coordination and Cooperation

The decision-making bodies of the climate regime have increasingly sought coordination and cooperation with other regimes. In particular, they have sought to address interactions in five ways: (1) by promoting coherence of rules, (2) by promoting coherence of national implementation, (3) by supporting implementation through cooperation, (4) through joint or coordinated scientific research and assessment, and (5) through information exchange (Yamin and Depledge 2004). However, these activities as such do not necessarily enhance synergies or address conflicts (Zelli in this volume): indeed, excessive coordination might even make matters worse by overburdening the administrative bodies of the regimes. For the UNFCCC, coordination requires additional efforts from the UNFCCC secretariat, and the question is whether this body is capable of coordinating all interactions between the climate regime and other regimes. Furthermore, there are limits to coordination and cooperation, especially in cases of interactions across policy areas.

Coordination and Cooperation with Other Environmental Regimes

The potential for enhancing synergies is greatest when the objectives of treaties already overlap or share similar key concepts, such as sustainable development or the ecosystem approach. As that is the case for most

MEAs, it is not surprising that we find various ongoing coordination and cooperation efforts between the climate regime and other environmental regimes.

The three Rio conventions all aim to contribute to the overarching goal of sustainable development. More specifically, the UNFCCC is cognizant of the potential synergies with biodiversity protection. Its objective of stabilizing atmospheric greenhouse gas concentrations at nondangerous levels is to be achieved "within a time-frame sufficient to allow ecosystems to adapt naturally to climate change" (Article 2). Furthermore, parties to the UNFCCC are committed to promoting and cooperating "in the conservation and enhancement . . . of sinks and reservoirs . . . , including biomass, forests and oceans as well as other terrestrial, coastal and marine ecosystems" (Article 4.1(d)). The UNFCCC explicitly acknowledges the need to protect areas prone to desertification and droughts (Article 4.1(e)) and implies the protection of wetlands. The goals of the CBD and UNCCD are also arguably in line with the UNFCCC objective.

The Rio conventions all encourage cooperation with other relevant treaty bodies and international organizations.[2] The Ramsar Convention for the Protection of Wetlands, adopted long before the Rio conventions, does not call for cooperation, but its aim, which is to ensure the conservation and wise use of wetlands (Article 3.1), has over the years been defined in the context of sustainable development.

The provisions of the climate and ozone treaties are in principle synergetic, as the Montreal Protocol intends to phase out certain ozone-depleting substances that are also greenhouse gases. In practice, however, the relation between the two agreements is in part conflictive, since some substitutes for ozone-depleting substances promoted by the Montreal Protocol (e.g., hydrofluorocarbons, HFCs) are also potent greenhouse gases (Oberthür 2001). A more recent case of conflictive interaction concerns destruction projects for the powerful greenhouse gas HFC-23, which is a by-product of the ozone-depleting substance HCFC-22. Large revenues can be earned by reducing HFC-23 emissions in developing countries through CDM projects. Such prospects could actually lead to the construction of new plants that produce HCFC-22—with consequent adverse impacts on the ozone layer (Oberthür, Dupont, and Matsumoto in this volume). The mandate of the UNFCCC secretariat includes coordination with other secretariats, including the ozone secretariat (Article 8.2(e) of the UNFCCC; Article 14.2 of the Kyoto Protocol). Similarly, the ozone secretariat is charged with coordination (Article 7.1(e) of the

Vienna Convention for the Protection of the Ozone Layer). However, interinstitutional coordination remains largely limited to mutual attendance at meetings, scientific cooperation, and information exchange, as linking abatement action in the area of climate change to ozone depletion has proved difficult for political reasons. Yamin and Depledge (2004) note that the United States, given its nonratification of the Kyoto Protocol and its early conversion from chlorofluorocarbons (CFCs) to HFCs, has been reluctant to address the issues together. Furthermore, there is resistance from developing countries that already use HFCs.

Institutional cooperation between the UNFCCC and other MEAs occurs mainly in response to activities under other treaties. Although cooperation has been an item on the agenda of the Subsidiary Body for Scientific and Technological Advice (SBSTA) for some time, interactions among the Rio conventions began only in 1999 (UNFCCC 1999). In 2002, the COP called for enhanced cooperation between the Rio conventions "with the aim of ensuring the environmental integrity of the conventions and promoting synergies under the common objective of sustainable development, in order to avoid duplication of efforts, strengthen joint efforts and use available resources more efficiently" (UNFCCC 2003a, para. 1).

The COP of the CBD has been particularly active in addressing interactions with the climate regime and has repeatedly urged the CBD secretariat to develop closer ties with the UNFCCC. With regard to forest biological diversity, for example, the CBD has requested the UNFCCC to ensure that future activities "are consistent with and supportive of the conservation and sustainable use of biological diversity" (CBD 2000, para. 16). The main purpose of these decisions is apparently to avoid conflicts related to forestry and biodiversity questions, and they have been instrumental in highlighting biodiversity concerns in UNFCCC COP decisions (Yamin and Depledge 2004). There have also been several decisions aimed at promoting synergies. In 2004, for instance, the CBD adopted a decision on biodiversity and climate change, noting the opportunities to implement climate change mitigation and adaptation activities in ways that would contribute to fulfilling the objectives of several environmental treaties at the same time (CBD 2004). Another decision on biodiversity was adopted in 2008, with an indicative list of activities to promote synergies among the Rio conventions (CBD 2008).

The UNCCD has also actively sought cooperation with the other Rio conventions. The activities it promotes and discusses primarily concern enhancing synergies, such as the parallel development of climate change adaptation plans and action programs to combat desertification, or the use of the CDM as an incentive (UNCCD 1999, 2005).

In 2001, a Joint Liaison Group (JLG) was formed among the secretariats of the three Rio conventions, at the initiative of the parties to the CBD. The UNFCCC parties asked the JLG to enhance coordination between the three conventions, and to explore options for further cooperation (UNFCCC 2001). The group has met ten times (as of November 2010), focusing on cross-cutting issues such as research and monitoring, information exchange, technology transfer, capacity building, financial resources, education and public awareness, and adaptation. In 2004 the JLG prepared a report on enhanced cooperation among the Rio conventions (UNFCCC 2004). Options in focus were further collaboration among national focal points; further collaboration between secretariats and convention bodies, including more systematic cross-participation, joint thematic workshops, and coordinated requests for scientific advice from external bodies; and cooperation in specific cross-cutting areas. In addition to the JLG, the secretariats of the conventions attend each other's COPs and have organized joint workshops to enhance synergies.

The Ramsar Convention has increasingly been seeking cooperation with the UNFCCC. Specifically, the Ramsar Bureau (responsible for administrative activities of the convention) has shown its willingness to work together with secretariats of other MEAs. The bureau has concluded a set of memoranda on cooperation with several secretariats and international organizations, including the CBD and UNCCD secretariats—but not with the UNFCCC secretariat. Still, the Ramsar Bureau has yet to become a full member of the JLG. In 2002 the Ramsar COP adopted a resolution on climate change and wetlands calling for, among other things, wetland management to increase wetland resilience to climate change, and action to minimize the degradation and promote restoration of wetlands with significant carbon storage or sequestration ability. Of importance, the resolution urges parties to the UNFCCC and the Kyoto Protocol to ensure that climate change mitigation activities do not "lead to serious damage to the ecological character of their wetlands" (Ramsar 2002, para. 17).

Coordination and Cooperation with Nonenvironmental Regimes

Attention to coordination with nonenvironmental regimes focuses mainly on the interactions with the multilateral trading system. One notable exception is the coordination that the climate regime seeks with the International Maritime Organization (IMO), which negotiates and oversees various treaties on maritime safety and vessel-source pollution. Article 2.2 of the Kyoto Protocol calls on parties to address emissions from vessels by working through the IMO (bunker fuels). However, this provision has not yet resulted in any real action to reduce emissions (Oberthür 2003, 2006).[3]

Given the many (potential) interactions between climate and trade (Chambers 2001; Charnovitz 2003; UNEP/WTO 2009), the scant attention shown by the UNFCCC regime to institutional relations with the WTO is perhaps surprising. Not until 2003 did the UNFCCC secretariat summarize the state of the negotiations in the WTO relevant for the climate regime (UNFCCC 2003b), and the issue received concerted political attention only at the COP in Bali, Indonesia, in 2007, where trade ministers emphasized the need for increased high-level engagement with a view to improving the mutual supportiveness of the climate and trade regimes. In contrast, relations with a range of MEAs—not the climate treaties specifically—have been a longstanding issue in the WTO, mostly within the WTO's Committee on Trade and Environment (CTE) (see also Gehring in this volume). Although the CTE mandate is to address trade-related environmental measures pursuant to MEAs, no substantive outcomes have emerged from its discussions (Yamin and Depledge 2004). The UNFCCC secretariat has observer status (on an ad hoc basis) in the CTE, but not in the CTE's Special Sessions, which constitute the discussion forum for most environmental aspects of the Doha round of trade negotiations that started in 2001. In May 2006, the Special Sessions decided to move away from discussing an "environmental window" for the UNFCCC and other environmental treaties, thereby lowering hopes that the WTO will deal satisfactorily with interactions between trade and climate. The question is whether it is at all desirable to use the WTO to address the interactions between the climate and trade regimes: it is uncertain whether the WTO will work to promote the goals of the UNFCCC or will undermine them (Linnér 2006, 285).

Options for Enhanced Coordination and Cooperation

Despite the several initiatives undertaken by various treaty bodies, interactions between the climate regime and other regimes have not yet been addressed in a comprehensive manner. The literature on international environmental governance includes many proposals on how to achieve this, some of which are discussed below. A common thread is to move beyond "ad hoc-ism," and to address interactions in a more structured fashion that can do justice to the complex interconnections among and between different issue areas.

Enhanced Coordination and Cooperation with Other Environmental Regimes

A first step toward reducing conflicts and enhancing synergies would be to enhance coordination and cooperation between environmental regimes beyond the initiatives already taken by actors in the various regimes (information exchange, joint assessments, etc.). I do not suggest completely replacing existing initiatives, as there is still much to learn from them (see, e.g., UNFCCC 2004). For instance, one of the tools for addressing interactions, the memorandum of understanding, could be applied to interactions between the Montreal and Kyoto Protocols (Oberthür 2001). Such a memorandum could state that funding for substitutes for ozone-depleting substances should not lead to increased greenhouse gas emissions, or that projects for reducing greenhouse gas emissions under the CDM should not be approved if they lead to an increase in ozone-depleting substances.

The United Nations Environment Programme (UNEP) has already started to enhance coordination between environmental secretariats and treaties (Wolfrum and Matz 2003). Building on its initiatives, various options are available, including providing a common housing to secretariats and increasing the frequency of secretariat meetings (Hicks 1999), holding simultaneous COPs or holding them at a permanent location (von Moltke 2005), harmonizing reporting requirements or the timing of reporting, and streamlining guidance to financial mechanisms. The latter is particularly relevant to the Montreal Protocol–Kyoto Protocol interactions, as the conflict stems from two different financial mechanisms—the Montreal Protocol's Multilateral Fund and the Global Environment Facility—with diverging financial incentives (Oberthür 2001). All these proposals face legal and practical barriers. A legal barrier may be that the treaty in question does not provide for the desired change in institutional infrastructure or procedure (Oberthür 2002). A practical barrier might be the impossibility of organizing joint COPs, or the lack of financial or human resources. Another important practical barrier is the difference in mandates of treaty secretariats, in particular the varying degrees of independence from their member states.

Yet another proposal is to cluster environmental treaties (Oberthür 2002). Von Moltke (2005, 177–178) describes clustering as "[i]nstitutional and organisational arrangements short of a merger that will increase the efficiency and effectiveness of existing agreements without requiring elaborate changes in legal or administrative arrangements" (see also Young 1996). Clustering could entail the grouping of MEAs by issue area (e.g., an atmosphere or biodiversity cluster), by region (e.g., a European or Southeast Asia cluster), by function (e.g., review of implementation or reporting), by human activity (e.g., transport or industrial production), or by environmental policy instrument (e.g., trade restrictions) (Oberthür 2002; Biermann 2005). However, creating an "atmosphere cluster" that includes the climate- and ozone-related treaties would probably encounter opposition from developing countries arguing that this approach would downplay the development aspects of those treaties. More generally, an atmosphere cluster might draw attention away from other interactions, like those with biodiversity treaties or with the law of the sea. Finally, clustering in itself cannot resolve problems of interplay per se; it merely addresses them on a higher level.

A proposal that goes further than clustering agreements is to create a World Environment Organization (WEO) (see Biermann and Bauer 2005 and references therein). A WEO could improve coordination among MEAs, facilitate their implementation at the national level, and provide incentives for financial and technology transfer to developing countries (Biermann 2005). Furthermore, it could serve as a counterweight to the WTO (Charnovitz 2005). However, creating a WEO could provoke resistance from existing environmental regimes, including the climate regime, and the parties responsible for financial support might be less willing to transfer control over the funding mechanisms (von Moltke 2005). How a possible WEO could deal in practice with interactions involving the climate regime is a pertinent question, but one that lies beyond the scope of this chapter.

Enhanced Coordination and Cooperation with Nonenvironmental Regimes

Proposals to enhance institutional coordination and cooperation between the WTO and the UNFCCC face significant barriers (van Asselt, Gupta, and Biermann 2005). The first is the conflict of ideology and interests between the two regimes: trade liberalization and cheap production processes (WTO) versus environmental protection and sustainable production processes (UNFCCC/Kyoto Protocol).[4] Second, the WTO has a strong institutional framework that has developed over time. A third point that complicates addressing trade and climate interactions concerns the critical differences in memberships to both agreements—notably, the

United States is a member of the WTO but has not ratified the Kyoto Protocol. Finally, those who engage in the negotiations of the two different issues are usually not the same individuals: generally it is representatives of trade ministries that attend WTO discussions and negotiations, whereas representatives from environment ministries attend UNFCCC negotiations. Nevertheless, a first option would be for parties to the UNFCCC and WTO to conclude a non-legally binding memorandum of understanding that could address outstanding contentious issues, such as the legality under the WTO of unilateral trade measures taken by parties to the Kyoto Protocol. Parties to the WTO and the UNFCCC could also establish a consultative mechanism (Stokke 2004) to discuss the competitiveness effects of climate policies, or they could establish a joint WTO/UNFCCC working group (Assunção and Zhang 2002). Politically, decisions of the WTO require the consensus of its members, including the United States. Pursuing this path is hence likely to require sufficiently safeguarding the interests of the latter (van Asselt and Biermann 2007).

Implications of Political Approaches to Interplay Management

Ongoing or proposed coordination and cooperation activities can be categorized in several ways:

Ad hoc and structural   At times, coordination or cooperation consists of a one-off political effort in response to current affairs or a COP decision of another treaty. An example is the organization of joint meetings on biodiversity and climate change interactions. Other forms of coordination and cooperation, such as the JLG, are more structural. The most structural proposal is the creation of a WEO that would deal with interactions among and between environmental regimes.

Legal basis   Treaties occasionally spell out the purpose of coordination and cooperation efforts (as with the Kyoto Protocol's mandate to cooperate with the IMO concerning bunker fuels). Other provisions, however, are more open-ended regarding the outcomes, such as the general provisions on cooperation with "relevant" international bodies in the climate agreements.

Involvement of treaty bodies   Coordination and cooperation may involve different treaty bodies, including decision-making bodies such as the COPs, and administrative bodies such as the secretariats. Because of the intergovernmental nature of decision-making bodies, activities from these bodies arguably have a higher potential impact on the interaction.[5]

It might appear that coordination and cooperation efforts that are structural, have a clear legal mandate, and involve decision-making treaty bodies are likely to be more effective as a means of interplay management. However, this need not be the case. While some structure is necessary to ensure continuity of coordination and cooperation activities, the creation of a permanent body that would merely discuss interactions rather than conceiving of ways of managing them is in itself insufficient. The existence of a clear legal mandate is also not always enough for dealing with interactions, as is clear in the case of bunker fuels (Oberthür 2006). Finally, with respect to treaty bodies, activities that involve secretariats often result in more practical recommendations to address interactions than do the decisions produced by intergovernmental bodies.

Although these various activities and proposals do much to address the need to enhance synergies between treaties, one important barrier remains: realizing the initiatives will be difficult, or even impossible, if the political will to cooperate or to coordinate is limited or nonexistent. This barrier has been particularly evident in climate and trade interactions, where, on the one hand, the CTE discussions have not led to substantive outcomes on the WTO's relation to the climate regime, and on the other hand, the actors in the climate regime have largely avoided the issue. Indeed, concerns over loss of national sovereignty may induce states to resist interinstitutional cooperation (Wolfrum and Matz 2003). More specifically, if the interests of states are not served by jointly or cooperatively addressing a case of interactions, they are likely to try to stall progress in cooperation or coordination. As Yamin and Depledge note (2004, 527), the SBSTA "has been at pains to underscore the advisory nature of the [JLG], safeguarding the authority of Parties . . . to take decisions on inter-convention cooperation." Although there is thus potential for dealing with interactions through coordination and cooperation, the extent to which this potential is fulfilled will depend on the willingness of states to engage in these activities.[6]

Concluding Thoughts

The proliferation of international agreements poses an enormous challenge, as different international norms may have a bearing on any given situation. This is particularly the case for climate change, since both the causes and impacts of climate change have implications for many sectors of society and the environment. Interactions between the climate regime and other treaty-based regimes may be conflictive, synergetic, or neutral. To enhance the effectiveness of the regimes involved, it is vital for interplay management to aim at avoiding or reducing conflicts, while promoting synergies to the greatest extent possible.

Taking the fragmented structure of global climate governance as a starting point, this chapter has shown how different means of interplay management could complement each other. Both legal and political approaches to mitigate conflicts and enhance synergies have their limits. For legal approaches these are that, first, the restrictive definition of conflict often used by legal scholars fails to cover all the divergences and inconsistencies between treaties with negative effects, such as those between MEAs. Second, conflicts can be created by decisions made by treaty bodies (e.g., COPs), which are not covered by the international law of conflicts. Third, although different norms may apply in a particular situation, they do not necessarily point in diverging directions. However, while sufficient potential remains for exploiting synergies between the climate treaties and other agreements, international law has focused on conflict avoidance and resolution. Political efforts to enhance interinstitutional coordination and cooperation are also limited, in that parties to one of the interacting regimes may not be willing to respond to the interactions because of sovereignty concerns. Furthermore, some coordination and cooperation efforts do not structurally address the interactions involved. Finally, such efforts do not seem to have been particularly successful in interactions between "stronger" and "weaker" regimes—here we may note the case of the WTO and the UNFCCC.

The distinction made in this chapter between legal and political approaches is in practice not as straightforward as described here. Attempts to address interactions through legal techniques will also have political ramifications; conversely, coordination and cooperation efforts may have legal implications as well. Nevertheless, the broad distinction applies for different actors in the international arena, with legal approaches being more relevant for judicial bodies and political approaches more relevant for states and treaty bodies.

In conclusion, neither legal nor political approaches are a panacea for interplay management. However, the example of interplay management in global climate governance shows that there is potential for the one approach to address the lacunae in the other. Where international law does not address synergies between environmental treaties, stronger political coordination and cooperation between them could. Where political efforts may not be sufficient to deal with the tension between the trade and climate regimes, a groundbreaking ruling by a dispute settlement body based on forward-looking legal techniques could do so, although that would still most likely take place within the WTO context. While this complementary relationship may not be so clear-cut in practice, this chapter has shown the value of investigating how legal techniques and political means can work together in reaping synergies and addressing conflicts among multilateral regimes in global environmental governance.

Acknowledgments

This chapter was prepared in the context of the Adaptation and Mitigation Strategies: Supporting European Climate Policy (ADAM) project, funded by the European Commission (CONTRACT 018476 (GOCE)). The author wishes to thank Frank Biermann, Joyeeta Gupta, Nele Matz-Lück, Sebastian Oberthür, Olav Schram Stokke, and Fariborz Zelli for thoughtful comments on earlier drafts.

Notes

1. Attention to synergy in international legal literature is arguably evident in studies of the role of international law in resolving conflicts and promoting coherence. However, the lens through which most international lawyers look is that of conflict resolution.

2. Articles 7.2(l) and 8.2(e) of the UNFCCC; Articles 8.1, 22.2(i), and 23.2(d) of the UNCCD; Articles 5, 23.4(h), and 24.1(d) of the CBD. See also Articles 13.4(i) and 14.2 of the Kyoto Protocol.

3. A similar case is the coordination sought with the International Civil Aviation Organization (ICAO) on emissions from aviation. The ICAO has not yet recommended specific policies to address these emissions.

4. This conflict is partially mitigated by the WTO's strengthening of its sustainable development component over time, through rulings under its dispute settlement mechanism and the climate agreements' explicit statements on compatibility with the multilateral trading system. Yet fundamental differences remain, as Charnovitz (2003, 143) argues: "The climate regime is driven by the need to correct market failure. Therefore, governments want maximum flexibility at the national level in using economic instruments to influence individual behavior. By contrast, the trade regime is not a response to market failure; it is a response to government failure, that is, the distortions of policy fomented by mercantilism and protectionism."

5. Another classification of coordination and cooperation efforts could be along the line of the type of interaction. Zelli (in this volume) provides such a classification for conflicting interactions.

6. In practice, responsibility for the implementation of MEAs often falls to specific national focal points (Velasquez and Piest 2003). As these are not always the same for the different conventions, a corresponding need for coordination and collaboration exists at the national level. Nevertheless, a role remains for interinstitutional coordination and cooperation among treaty bodies. These bodies can help to enhance synergies through implementation support, awareness raising, and capacity building.

References

Assunção, Lucas, and Zhong Xiang Zhang. 2002. *Domestic Climate Policies and the WTO*. United Nations Conference on Trade and Development Discussion Paper No. 164. Geneva: UNCTAD.

Biermann, Frank. 2005. The Rationale for a World Environment Organization. In *A World Environment Organization: Solution or Threat for Effective International Environmental Governance?*, ed. Frank Biermann and Steffen Bauer, 117–144. Aldershot, UK: Ashgate.

Biermann, Frank, and Steffen Bauer, eds. 2005. *A World Environment Organization: Solution or Threat for Effective International Environmental Governance?* Aldershot, UK: Ashgate.

Borgen, Christopher J. 2005. Resolving Treaty Conflicts. *George Washington International Law Review* 37 (3): 573–648.

Brown Weiss, Edith. 1993. International Environmental Law: Contemporary Issues and the Emergence of a New Order. *Georgetown Law Journal* 81: 675–710.

Brunnée, Jutta. 2002. COPing with Consent: Law Making under Multilateral Environmental Agreements. *Leiden Journal of International Law* 15 (1): 1–52.

CBD. 2000. *Decision V/4, Progress Report on the Implementation of the Programme of Work for Forest Biological Diversity*. Convention on Biological Diversity. UN Doc. UNEP/CBD/COP/5/23 of 22 June 2000.

CBD. 2004. *Decision VII/15, Biodiversity and Climate Change*. Convention on Biological Diversity. UN Doc. UNEP/CBD/COP/7/21 of 13 April 2004.

CBD. 2008. *Decision IX/16, Biodiversity and Climate Change*. Convention on Biological Diversity. UN Doc. UNEP/CBD/COP/9/29 of 30 May 2008.

Chambers, W. Bradnee, ed. 2001. *Inter-linkages: The Kyoto Protocol and the International Trade and Investment Regimes*. Tokyo: United Nations University Press.

Chambers, W. Bradnee. 2008. *Interlinkages and the Effectiveness of Multilateral Environmental Agreements*. Tokyo: United Nations University Press.

Charnovitz, Steve. 2003. Trade and Climate: Potential Conflicts and Synergies. In *Beyond Kyoto: Advancing the International Effort against Climate Change*, ed. Elliott Diringer, 141–170. Washington, D.C.: Pew Center for Global Climate Change.

Charnovitz, Steve. 2005. Toward a World Environment Organization: Reflections upon a Vital Debate. In *A World Environment Organization: Solution or Threat for Effective International Environmental Governance?* ed. Frank Biermann and Steffen Bauer, 87–116. Aldershot, UK: Ashgate.

Doelle, Meinhard. 2004. Linking the Kyoto Protocol and Other Multilateral Environmental Agreements: From Fragmentation to Integration? *Journal of Environmental Law and Practice* 14:75–104.

French, Duncan. 2006. Treaty Interpretation and the Incorporation of Extraneous Legal Rules. *International and Comparative Law Quarterly* 55 (2): 281–314.

Gehring, Thomas, and Sebastian Oberthür. 2006. Comparative Empirical Analysis and Ideal Types of Institutional Interaction. In *Institutional Interaction in Global Environmental Governance: Synergy and Conflict among International and EU Policies*, ed. Sebastian Oberthür and Thomas Gehring, 307–371. Cambridge, Mass.: MIT Press.

Hicks, Bethany Lukitsch. 1999. Treaty Congestion in International Environmental Law: The Need for Greater International Coordination, Comment. *University of Richmond Law Review* 32 (4): 1643–1674.

ILC. 2006. *Fragmentation of International Law: Difficulties Arising from the Diversification and Expansion of International Law.* Report of the Study Group of the International Law Commission. ILC Doc. A/CN.4/L.682 of 13 April 2006. Geneva: International Law Commission.

IPCC. 2002. *Climate Change and Biodiversity.* Geneva: Intergovernmental Panel on Climate Change.

Jacquemont, Frédéric, and Alejandro Caparrós. 2002. The Convention on Biological Diversity and the Climate Change Convention 10 Years after Rio: Towards a Synergy of the Two Regimes? *Review of European Community & International Environmental Law* 11 (2): 139–180.

Jenks, Wilfred. 1953. The Conflict of Law-Making Treaties. *British Yearbook of International Law* 30:401–453.

Kornicker Uhlmann, Eva M. 1998. State Community Interests, *Jus Cogens* and Protection of the Global Environment: Developing Criteria for Peremptory Norms. *Georgetown International Environmental Law Review* 11 (1): 101–135.

Linnér, Björn-Ola. 2006. Authority through Synergism: The Roles of Climate Change Linkages. *European Environment* 16 (5): 278–289.

McCabe, Daniel G. 2007. Resolving Conflicts between Multilateral Environmental Agreements: The Case of the Montreal and Kyoto Protocols. *Fordham Environmental Law Review* 18:433–466.

McLachlan, Campbell. 2005. The Principle of Systemic Integration and Article 31(3)(c) of the Vienna Convention. *International and Comparative Law Quarterly* 54:279–319.

Oberthür, Sebastian. 2001. Linkages between the Montreal and Kyoto Protocols: Enhancing Synergies between Protecting the Ozone Layer and the Global Climate. *International Environmental Agreements: Politics, Law and Economics* 1 (3): 357–377.

Oberthür, Sebastian. 2002. Clustering of Multilateral Environmental Agreements: Potential and Limitations. *International Environmental Agreements: Politics, Law and Economics* 2 (4): 317–340.

Oberthür, Sebastian. 2003. Institutional Interaction to Address Greenhouse Gas Emissions from International Transport: ICAO, IMO and the Kyoto Protocol. *Climate Policy* 3 (3): 191–205.

Oberthür, Sebastian. 2006. The Climate Change Regime: Interactions with ICAO, IMO, and the EU Burden-Sharing Agreement. In *Institutional Interaction in Global Environmental Governance: Synergy and Conflict among International and EU Policies*, ed. Sebastian Oberthür and Thomas Gehring, 53–77. Cambridge, Mass.: MIT Press.

Oberthür, Sebastian. 2009. Interplay Management: Enhancing Environmental Policy Integration among International Institutions. *International Environmental Agreements: Politics, Law and Economics* 9 (4): 371–391.

Oberthür, Sebastian, and Thomas Gehring. 2004. Reforming International Environmental Governance: An Institutionalist Critique of the Proposal for a World Environment Organization. *International Environmental Agreements: Politics, Law and Economics* 4 (4): 349–381.

Paulus, Andreas L. 2005. *Jus Cogens* in a Time of Hegemony and Fragmentation. *Nordic Journal of International Law* 74 (3–4): 297–334.

Pauwelyn, Joost. 2003. *Conflict of Norms in Public International Law. How WTO Law Relates to Other Rules of International Law*. Cambridge: Cambridge University Press.

Pontecorvo, Concetta Maria. 1999. Interdependence between Global Environmental Regimes: The Kyoto Protocol on Climate Change and Forest Protection. *Zeitschrift für ausländisches öffentliches Recht und Völkerrecht* 59 (3): 709–749.

Ramsar. 2002. *Resolution VIII.3, Climate Change and Wetlands: Impacts, Adaptation, and Mitigation. Eighth Conference of the Parties, 18–26 November 2002*. http://www.ramsar.org/pdf/res/key_res_viii_03_e.pdf (accessed 13 April 2010).

SCBD. 2003. *Interlinkages Between Biological Diversity and Climate Change: Advice on the Integration of Biodiversity Considerations into the Implementation of the United Nations Framework Convention on Climate Change and Its Kyoto Protocol*. Montreal: Secretariat of the Convention on Biological Diversity.

Scott, Karen N. 2005. The Day after Tomorrow: Ocean CO_2 Sequestration and the Future of Climate Change. *Georgetown International Environmental Law Review* 18 (1): 57–108.

Stokke, Olav Schram. 2001. *The Interplay of International Regimes: Putting Effectiveness Theory to Work*. FNI Report No. 14. Lysaker, Norway: Fridtjof Nansen Institute.

Stokke, Olav Schram. 2004. Trade Measures and Climate Compliance: Institutional Interplay between WTO and the Marrakesh Accords. *International Environmental Agreements: Politics, Law and Economics* 4 (4): 339–357.

UNCCD. 1999. *Review of Activities for the Promotion and Strengthening of Relationships with Other Relevant Conventions and Relevant International Organizations, Institutions and Agencies: Collaboration and Synergies among Rio Conventions for the Implementation of the United Nations Convention to Combat Desertification*. Note by the Secretariat. United Nations Convention to Combat Desertification. UN Doc. ICCD/COP(3)/9 of 28 September 1999.

UNCCD. 2005. *Review of Activities for the Promotion and Strengthening of Relationships with Other Relevant Conventions and Relevant International Organizations, Institutions and Agencies, in Accordance with Article 8 and Article 22, Paragraph 2 (i) of the Convention*. Note by the Secretariat. United Nations Convention to Combat Desertification. UN Doc. ICCD/COP(7)/5 of 5 August 2005.

UNEP/WTO. 2009. *Trade and Climate Change: A Report by the United Nations Environment Programme and the World Trade Organization*. Geneva: United Nations Environment Programme and the World Trade Organization.

UNFCCC. 1999. *Report of the Subsidiary Body for Scientific and Technological Advice on Its Tenth Session Bonn, 31 May–11 June 1999*. United Nations Framework Convention on Climate Change. UN Doc. FCCC/SBSTA/1999/6 of 23 August 1999.

UNFCCC. 2001. *Report of the Subsidiary Body for Scientific and Technological Advice on Its Fourteenth Session, Bonn, 24–27 July 2001*. United Nations Framework Convention on Climate Change. UN Doc. FCCC/SBSTA/2001/2 of 18 September 2001.

UNFCCC. 2003a. *Decision 13/CP.8, Cooperation with Other Conventions*. United Nations Framework Convention on Climate Change. UN Doc. FCCC/CP/2002/7/Add.1 of 28 March 2003.

UNFCCC. 2003b. *Cooperation with Relevant International Organizations: World Trade Organization*. Note by the Secretariat. United Nations Framework Convention on Climate Change. UN Doc. FCCC/SBSTA/2003/INF.7 of 14 May 2003.

UNFCCC. 2004. *Options for Enhanced Cooperation among the Three Rio Conventions*. Note by the Secretariat. United Nations Framework Convention on Climate Change. UN Doc. FCCC/SBSTA/2004/INF.19 of 2 November 2004 Annex.

van Asselt, Harro, and Frank Biermann. 2007. European Emissions Trading and the International Competitiveness of Energy-Intensive Industries: A Legal and

Political Evaluation of Possible Supporting Measures. *Energy Policy* 35 (1): 497–506.

van Asselt, Harro, Joyeeta Gupta, and Frank Biermann. 2005. Advancing the Climate Agenda: Exploiting Material and Institutional Linkages to Develop a Menu of Policy Options. *Review of European Community & International Environmental Law* 14 (3): 255–264.

Velasquez, Jerry, and Uli Piest. 2003. Case Studies on Inter-linkages and Environmental Governance in 14 Asia and Pacific Countries. *Global Environmental Change* 13 (1): 61–68.

Vierdag, E. W. 1988. The Time of the "Conclusion" of a Multilateral Treaty: Article 30 of the Vienna Convention on the Law of Treaties and Related Provisions. *British Yearbook of International Law* 59:75–111.

Voigt, Christina. 2009. *Sustainable Development as a Principle of International Law: Resolving Conflicts between Climate Measures and WTO Law*. Leiden: Brill.

von Moltke, Konrad. 2005. Clustering International Environmental Agreements as an Alternative to a World Environment Organization. In *A World Environment Organization: Solution or Threat for Effective International Environmental Governance?*, ed. Frank Biermann and Steffen Bauer, 175–204. Aldershot, UK: Ashgate.

Vranes, Erich. 2006. The Definition of "Norm Conflict" in International Law and Legal Theory. *European Journal of International Law* 17 (2): 395–418.

Werksman, Jacob. 1999. *Formal Linkages and Multilateral Environmental Agreements*. http://www.geic.or.jp/interlinkages/docs/jake.PDF (accessed 13 April 2010).

Werksman, Jacob, Kevin A. Baumert, and Navroz K. Dubash. 2003. Will International Investment Rules Obstruct Climate Protection Policies? *International Environmental Agreements: Politics, Law and Economics* 3 (1): 59–86.

Wolfrum, Rüdiger, and Nele Matz. 2003. *Conflicts in International Environmental Law*. Berlin: Springer-Verlag.

Yamin, Farhana, and Joanna Depledge. 2004. *The International Climate Change Regime: A Guide to Rules, Institutions and Procedures*. Cambridge: Cambridge University Press.

Young, Oran R. 1996. Institutional Linkages in International Society: Polar Perspectives. *Global Governance* 2 (1): 1–24.

4

Savings Clauses and the "Chilling Effect"

Regime Interplay as Constraints on International Governance

Mark Axelrod

The situations that environmental treaties address are necessarily linked to other policy fields, such as trade and human rights. Recent research suggests that environmental treaties are weakened by multilateral trade rules that address related issues (Conca 2000; Eckersley 2004; Stilwell and Tuerk 1999; see also Gehring in this volume). As these studies argue, the "chilling effect" prevents nations from establishing robust environmental treaties out of concern for potential conflicts with international trade rules. Unfortunately, accounts of this relationship have been limited to examples in which environmental cooperation does seem to have been chilled. To determine whether environmental agreements are particularly susceptible to these constraints, environmental treaties should be compared with nonenvironmental treaties negotiated under similar conditions. It is equally important to explore the conditions under which new agreements take the opposite approach, overriding existing international law.

This chapter explores the chilling effect, showing that it does have an impact on international environmental negotiations. Although environmental agreements demonstrate concern for existing rules at a rate similar to agreements in other policy fields, they are more likely than others to consider existing international law in other policy fields. In accordance with the chilling effect hypothesis, existing international law (in other policy fields) therefore is an important factor limiting the scope of international environmental agreements. This effect points to the need for analysts and activists to better understand the nature of institutional interplay and the conditions under which regimes influence each other.

As discussed in this chapter, established techniques of interplay management in international law tend to be biased toward preserving the status quo and against institutional change. Although new institutions continue to emerge, negotiators have long employed legal means to limit the scope of new agreements and their effects on existing regimes. Using an original data set, I find support for the claim that this practice has not only helped avoid regime conflicts but has also led to weakened environmental regimes in particular. This status quo bias of international law may contribute to the relatively stable division of labor between different international institutions, once established (see Stokke and Oberthür in this volume).

The next section reviews existing research on institutional interaction, focusing on the possibility that these interactions affect negotiated outcomes. It explores various types of hierarchies among international regimes and further discusses the chilling effect hypothesis. The subsequent sections explain a series of empirical tests used to assess that claim and offer results from this analysis. The concluding section discusses the implications of these findings.

Institutional Interaction and the Chilling Effect

Institutional Linkages
Rather than looking at international institutions as completely separate entities, recent scholarship examines interactions between international regimes. Raustiala and Victor (2004), for example, examine "regime complexes" rather than individual agreements because they recognize that negotiations take place in the shadow of existing law.

Of course, interaction does not occur only between formal institutions; it also results from the broader relationship between different policy fields in international politics. For instance, the notion of sustainable development inherently touches on trade, agriculture, environmental protection, and human rights, among other concerns. In a world of overlapping issues, the traditionally separate legal approaches to these concerns cannot help but overlap as well.

The study of institutional interactions is still in its infancy. However, this new body of research has begun to explore the effects of multiple institutions on behavioral outcomes, noting that the existence of more than one regime may complicate prospects for enforcement. Young (2002), for instance, suggests that "horizontal interplay" between institutions has resulted in both conflicting and symbiotic results. Helfer (2004) describes how parties attempt to circumvent undesirable rules by moving to a different negotiating forum.

Oberthür and Gehring (2006a) explain that interactions can take place at any stage of the process, from negotiation to implementation, and may be positive or negative in nature. Rules from one regime may enhance the efforts made in another institution or they may conflict, as will be explored further in the following section. By providing the important insight that interactions should be analyzed on an individual basis, with one institution serving as the "source" and the other as "target" of the source's influence, these authors advance the empirical study of institutional overlap and provide a means for comparison.

This chapter draws on those studies, looking at potential target regimes to see which ones are constrained by existing source institutions.

Hierarchy among International Institutions

Conventional wisdom counsels us to expect many conflicting rules in international law as the number of treaties continues to increase (Kingsbury 1999). Within countries, centralized decision making facilitates the establishment of a hierarchy of rules. In the international context, however, even if negotiations take place in completely separate issue areas (e.g., human rights and trade), the resulting agreements may contain specific rules that substantively overlap. If the rules covering a particular type of action in separate international regimes are inconsistent, countries may not be able to comply with both commitments simultaneously. For instance, a country cannot simultaneously prevent environmentally damaging imports and keep its borders open to all foreign goods. In contrast to formal domestic political institutions, the lack of centralized legal-political institutions for choosing, implementing, and adjudicating among rules at the international level should result in their overlap (Pauwelyn 2003). This lack of linkage should encourage states to pursue the best possible outcome each time without considering the results of previous negotiations in which their preferences were not realized (Young 2002). In addition, countries send different representatives to negotiate in each subject area. Their different stances should lead to a lack of coherence, even within one country's positions, on different negotiations (Davis 2004).

Despite the absence of a central international legal system, recent years have witnessed a drastic increase in the number of global regimes covering a variety of topics. As D'Amato (1983, 8) notes, increasing the complexity of the law, rather than filling voids, tends to create space for uncertainty. The same would appear to be true at the international level. As the international legal system becomes more and more complex, the need for interplay management increases. To some extent, we should expect the various subject matter regimes to operate independently of each other. However, to the extent that different subjects overlap, states necessarily encounter situations requiring a choice. As Trachtman (2002, 89) notes, "while there is room for creative ambiguity . . . at certain junctures one organization's norms will have to trump another's."[1]

Such concerns about conflicting obligations may be addressed through various management techniques. Legally speaking, "secondary rules" (Hart 1961), those defining the relationship between existing laws, should guide the analysis of treaty interaction. As I argue below, hierarchical relationships are important in efforts to enhance legal certainty. Uncertainty increases the degree of risk one faces in carrying out any action (D'Amato 1983, 5). In an economic sense, this risk raises the expected costs and makes a transaction less likely (Coase 1988; Williamson 1985). Lack of clarity about the hierarchy among laws compromises the legal system. Law cannot guide behavior unless people are clear on what to expect from a legal system. Without knowing which law applies, they have no chance of acting appropriately, or of bargaining in the shadow of these rules (Mnookin and Kornhauser 1979). Such situations invite noncompliance (Gehring and Oberthür 2006, 335–339).[2]

At the second, or systemic, level of international law, therefore, we would expect to see some mechanism that coordinates treaties to determine which one is applicable in which situation. Secondary rules accomplish this coordination by establishing a hierarchy among international provisions.

Nonhierarchical relationships lead to legal uncertainty and its associated problems. Hierarchy establishes a means for conflict resolution and legal certainty. Therefore, we might expect negotiators to consciously introduce some form of order between institutions. As the next section shows, default rules in international law indicate the supremacy of the most recent agreement. The following sections describe conflicting possibilities for legal hierarchy.

The Vienna Convention and Legal Change

The idea of a central convention for understanding conflicts and making them part of a coherent legal system is not new. The best-known attempt is the Vienna Convention on the Law of Treaties (VCLT).[3] The VCLT is a treaty of treaties, intended to bring all international legal rules under one guiding body that would codify customary rules for common treaty interpretation. The convention includes regulations for where and when treaties apply, how they enter into force, and how they may be amended. The rules in general serve a coordinating function.

The VCLT provides a set of rules with which to interpret and enforce treaties. Article 30 lays out the rules designed to manage interplay among conflicting international laws. All states are expected to follow the same set of rules to understand which treaty takes precedence when applicable conventions conflict. Paragraph 2 of Article 30 allows treaties to state explicitly that they are subject to, or "not to be considered incompatible with, an earlier or later treaty," in which case "the provisions of that other treaty prevail." Next, the article provides that, without an explicit statement and if all parties are members of both regimes, "the earlier treaty applies only to the extent that its provisions are compatible with those of the later treaty" (Article 30, para. 3). That is, barring language to the contrary, new treaties should be interpreted as replacing old provisions if their rules conflict. The rationale is that parties would not bother to negotiate a new treaty if they wanted the old rules to remain in place, so any contradiction must represent a change in the law. Finally, if one state is party to both agreements and another state is party to only one, "the treaty to which both States are parties governs their mutual rights and obligations" (Article 30, para. 4(b)).

The Vienna Convention, therefore, codifies some default rules of hierarchy in international law. Although such rules are not applicable in all situations, the convention codifies the rule of *lex posterior*, meaning that more recent treaties should prevail when a conflict arises, so we might expect that later negotiations trump previous results. This strictly legal orientation simply replicates the power relationships evident in institutional design.

In the realist view of international relations, as power alignments change, newly powerful parties can easily introduce rules that override earlier agreements. Krasner claims that distributional consequences lead to power-based bargaining (Krasner 1991). Accordingly, renegotiation reflects a change in relative power and may occur whenever power shifts. As such, the more powerful states are able to guide negotiations no matter what rules are already in place. If that were the case, we should expect the most recent rules to represent current power dynamics and to overrule any previous enactments. Consistent adherence to the *lex posterior* rule, therefore, would provide legal support for the realist view that more recent negotiations can easily overrule past agreements (Krasner 1991).

Status Quo Bias

In contrast, Oberthür and Gehring (2006a, 36–38) posit that commitment to existing rules sometimes constrains negotiators. International regimes are, in fact, often characterized by persistence (Keohane 1984, 100–103). That is, rules do not change easily, and new configurations frequently reflect existing rules (North 1990, 92–104). Under such circumstances, at least some parties are happy with the rule as set forth by institution 1. Any efforts to renegotiate that rule during the framing of institution 2 would face an uphill battle, since powerful interests prefer maintenance of the status quo. If institutions emerge consecutively, a first-mover advantage limits the "room for maneuver within negotiations of the later institution by strengthening the actors preferring the earlier institution's objectives" (Gehring and Oberthür 2006, 338).

This act of preserving benefits that derive from existing rules is an explicit indication that parties wish to protect past gains achieved from international cooperation. Rather than merely accepting the Vienna Convention's default, parties to international law have taken pains to protect their previous winnings across issue-areas. As Pierson (2000, 2004) notes, existing institutions constrain the possible configuration of later rules. Institutional path dependence does not merely happen as a result of existing institutions but requires positive action by groups who wish to block change from taking place. Influential parties are able to consolidate power by introducing institutions that benefit them (Moe 1990; Pierson 2000). These arrangements, therefore, protect their position in later negotiations on other issues. States, and the beneficiary groups within them, often work hard to retain institutional benefits, even in the face of changing power relationships.

Kahneman and Tversky (1979) shed further light on such institutional entrenchment: their "prospect theory" holds that taking something away from someone who has been given a particular benefit is harder than denying them that pleasure in the first place. Put simply, we place a higher value on the things we have than on those we aspire to obtain. Therefore, a loss hurts an individual (or country) more than a comparable gain helps that same person (or country).

This desire to protect the status quo runs contrary to Krasner's suggestion that powerful countries can easily overturn existing institutions. Despite changing power dynamics, countries are often able to prevent legal change, leading to relatively stagnant regime complexes. Realist theory expects to see countries relying on the VCLT's *lex posterior* rule, with newly powerful actors overturning institutions they accepted when they had less power to influence negotiations. Historical institutionalists, on the other hand, should anticipate efforts to entrench existing law. Not surprisingly, neither theory appears to be correct in all situations, and scholars have therefore begun to ask *under what conditions* we should expect deference to existing international law. The remainder of this chapter examines why negotiators defer to existing law in some circumstances but overturn it in other situations.

The Chilling Effect Hypothesis

Stilwell and Tuerk (1999) provide one possible answer to this question, suggesting that multilateral environmental agreements (MEAs) are more likely than others to defer across policy fields. They note the potential for a "chilling effect" of existing international trade institutions (specifically the World Trade Organization, WTO) on new environmental treaties because of the value that actors place on earlier trade regimes. This line of argument expects environmental agreements in particular to be weakened in the face of a desire to maintain existing international law (Conca 2000). Eckersley (2004, 27) notes that environmental agreements are particularly threatened because they tend to use trade measures as enforcement devices. In light of the WTO's well-established dispute settlement mechanism, countries are concerned about any potential legal conflict that could lead to the overturning of trade rules (Eckersley 2004, 36).

In terms of Oberthür and Gehring's (2006b, 32–33) mechanism of "interaction through commitment," the chilling effect hypothesis suggests that trade regimes (the "source" of influence) change the behavior of important actors on trade issues, thus leading to altered preferences or behavior regarding the "target" institutions, which they try to influence accordingly. Actors value the existing institution because of the gains that come in exchange for their commitment. "Hence, once sincere cooperators have entered into an obligation within one institution, they become interested in avoiding incompatible decisions in other forums, because otherwise they might not be able to comply with their commitments" (Oberthür and Gehring 2006b, 37).

However, Eckersley's explanation is limited by its failure to consider why the WTO developed these stronger rules for dispute settlement in the first place. If countries are actually more concerned with environmental cooperation, they should establish similarly robust institutions in that area. The existing asymmetry indicates a deeper concern for strong trade institutions at the international level and a much weaker desire to regulate the global environment more generally. In addition to governmental concerns about protecting existing law, trade agreements also create enforceable private rights, which should lead to domestic political pressure on negotiators to avoid any restrictions on gains resulting from the prior bargain. I therefore hypothesize that, even before the WTO Dispute Settlement Understanding came into force in 1995, environmental agreements were more likely to show deference toward existing agreements in other policy fields. The combination of frequent inclusion of trade provisions and a generally lower-priority position in politics makes environmental agreements vulnerable to chilling from other issue regimes.

Chilling Effect Hypothesis: Environmental institutions are more likely than those in other policy fields to defer to existing rules in other policy fields.

While existing research on the chilling effect provides valuable evidence about the impact of WTO rules, these studies do not offer any comparison with situations in which this impact was *not* experienced. As Gehring and Oberthür (2006, 356) note, it is important to study instances of interaction as well as noninteraction, and to expand the research to other policy fields beyond the environment. This chapter follows these suggestions by exploring a random sample of treaties from environmental and other policy fields.

Modeling the Chilling Effect Hypothesis

Savings Clauses
This section compares situations in which chilling does and does not take place. By examining factors present when these different outcomes occur, I seek to derive a better understanding of why negotiators pay attention to existing law in some contexts but not in others.

One tactic for interplay management and protection of existing rules is the introduction of a "savings clause," which parties sometimes use to state explicitly that the new treaty does not preempt old rules. Since, without additional guidance, the Vienna Convention leads us to assume that the later treaty will prevail, savings clauses allow negotiators to protect their previous rights and responsibilities and apply the new rules only insofar as they do not conflict.

When the parties want to preserve the gains achieved from a previous negotiation, "they may specify that some or all of the provisions of the [current] treaty shall not prevail" (United Nations 2003, 87). Some of these savings clauses require deference to all previous agreements. Others may merely subordinate the current accord to some subset of treaties in the same or another policy field; or they may preserve only those treaties that enshrine broader rights to individuals (ibid., 88). For instance, the

Constitution of the International Labour Organization (1919) subordinates itself to existing law only if the preexisting provision "ensures more favorable conditions to the workers concerned."

The wish to preserve institutional benefits need not lead to savings clauses. Instead, some parties may oppose new rules entirely, or they may only consent to join a weaker form of the new institution.[4] The introduction of savings clauses is a very direct way for states, and the beneficiary groups within them, to retain their preferred institutions, even in the face of changing power relationships. This chapter, therefore, endeavors to explain the use of savings clauses in multilateral treaties, assessing the chilling effect hypothesis by comparing the use of savings clauses in a random sample of environmental treaties with similar outcomes in a more general sample.

The Samples

I randomly sampled two sets of treaties and coded each observation on the basis of its relationship to existing international law.[5] The first sample represents a broad range of policy fields (including the environment) and is drawn from the 4,631 multilateral agreements contained in the United Nations Treaty Series (UNTS). The UNTS publishes all treaties in force that have been registered by member countries (Koremenos 2005).[6]

I focused only on multilateral treaties (i.e., those open to participation by more than two country parties). While selecting on values of an explanatory variable (i.e., number of participants) should not bias results (King, Keohane, and Verba 1994), this truncation may make it less valid to generalize from these findings to bilateral negotiations. However, as bilateral treaties account for more than 90 percent of the total (Koremenos 2005), their inclusion in a uniform random sample would reduce variation on this independent variable.[7] After eliminating bilateral agreements, I further reduced the sample size by removing treaties with unavailable text or with less than three potential member countries.[8] Neither of these restrictions should bias the results because they simply exclude irrelevant accords in which negotiation between sovereign states is not present or testable. Including 10 percent of UNTS multilateral agreements leaves 201 observations in the general sample.

A second random sample, drawn from Ron Mitchell's (2003a; 2003b) International Environmental Agreements database (IEA database), contains only environmental treaties. Mitchell defines agreements as environmental "if they seek, as a primary purpose, to manage or prevent human impacts on natural resources" (see http://iea.uoregon.edu/page

.php?query=static&file=definitions.htm). As of 2008, this accessible resource contains a list of environmental treaties, their dates of negotiation and entry into force, and most of the treaty texts. I analyzed 101 of 557 multilateral environmental agreements (MEAs) (just under 20 percent of the available treaties) from the IEA database.[9] With these 101 treaties, I employed the same rules for dropping observations as for the UNTS data. In addition, to maintain comparability, I eliminated any treaties that, as of early 2008, were not yet in force. As a result, 67 treaties remain in the environmental sample. None of these 67 MEA observations is included in the UNTS sample. There is no overlap between the two random selections.

Three shortcomings of the data should be noted before continuing. First, because many less-developed countries are slower to report to the United Nations (Kohona 2002, 402), the UNTS (but not IEA database) data may underrepresent their treaties, raising concerns about comparability between the samples. However, I also conducted the same analyses after dropping any treaties that are not reported to UNTS, and both samples showed almost the same results as they do here. Therefore, the samples appear to be sufficiently comparable.

Second, the material may underrepresent legal deference because there are various ways of diluting agreements, not all of which require language that directly addresses existing treaties. Finally, my reliance on existing treaties in force means that the study cannot account for negotiations that failed completely on these grounds (Dimitrov et al. 2007).[10] Nonetheless, on both of these accounts, there is no reason to believe that this type of dilution should be limited to specific types of treaties.

Dependent Variable—Use of a Savings Clause

The data set contains 201 randomly selected UNTS multilateral agreements and 67 randomly selected MEAs. Although a number of observations have already been omitted for the aforementioned reasons, others had to be left out of the analyses owing to missing information on key independent variables. As a result, the sample sizes cited below are smaller than 201 for the general sample and 67 for the environmental sample.

I coded each treaty's relationship to other international law/treaties according to the following rules:

1 = no mention, or overriding, of past agreements (legal default).

2 = use existing international law to interpret certain provisions, or reiterate commitment to previously agreed international law (e.g., "States

situated between the sea and a State having no sea-coast shall . . . in conformity with existing international convention accord" [Convention on the High Seas 1958]).

3 = defer to past treaties *if* they are in the same spirit ("In no case shall the adoption of any Convention or Recommendation by the Conference, or the ratification of any Convention by any Member, be deemed to affect any law, award, custom or agreement which ensures more favorable conditions to the workers concerned than those provided for in the Convention or Recommendation" [International Labour Organization Constitution 1919]).

4 = defer to particular past treaties in the same policy field (e.g., "Nothing in this Convention shall be interpreted as in any way limiting or detracting from the obligations assumed by any State under the Protocol for the Prohibition of the Use in War of Asphyxiating, Poisonous or Other Gases, and of Bacteriological Methods of Warfare" [Chemical Weapons Convention 1992].)

5 = defer to particular past treaties in a different policy field[11] (e.g., "The provisions of the preceding articles shall be without prejudice to: 1. the right to mail documents direct to interested parties who are abroad; . . . In each of the above cases the right in question shall be deemed to exist only if it is recognized in Conventions between the States concerned" [Convention Relating to Civil Procedure 1954]).

6 = defer to all past treaties (e.g., "Nothing in this Convention shall be construed as altering the rights or obligations of any Party under any other convention or international agreement" [International Convention On Oil Pollution Preparedness, Response And Cooperation 1990]).

In order to represent the overall degree of deference in a given negotiation, each treaty is coded at the highest category of deference achieved in its text.[12]

Table 4.1 shows the distribution of this variable in the UNTS (general) and IEA database (environmental) samples, and figure 4.1 depicts it graphically.

The first thing to note from this summary is that more than 75 percent of multilateral agreements in both samples rely on some aspect of existing law, at least for interpretation (types 2–6). That level speaks to the importance of institutional interplay. Negotiators are not merely focusing on the policy issue they address: they are also conscious of the legal environment within which they operate.

Table 4.1
Descriptive statistics: Observations in each category for each sample

Type of deference	General sample (%)	Environmental sample (%)
1. No mention, or overriding, of existing international law	24.10	20.97
2. Maintain existing international law	35.54	35.48
3. Defer to existing international law if it has the same goals	3.01	3.23
4. Defer within the same policy field	20.48	14.52
5. Defer across policy fields	3.61	4.84
6. Defer to all existing international law	13.25	20.97

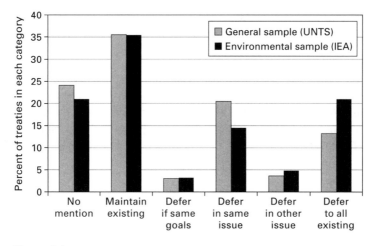

Figure 4.1
Comparing deference in the general and environmental samples

Second, it should be apparent from the data that the debate over institutional change remains alive. As discussed earlier, neither the VCLT default nor savings clauses are always in effect. More than one-third of the agreements in each sample contain some form of deference to existing international law (types 4–6). That proportion raises the question as to why deference appears in some situations and not others. The remainder of this chapter focuses on that question.

As table 4.1 indicates, savings clauses are only slightly more common in the environmental sample. However, most of that difference, as the chilling effect hypothesis anticipates, is among *external* savings clauses, in which treaties include deference to existing agreements of *other* policy fields (types 5 and 6). The following section employs multivariate regression to determine whether these relationships are statistically significant after controlling for other factors.

Explanatory and Control Variables

Various factors should be able to explain path dependence in international law, as measured by the inclusion of savings clauses in multilateral treaties. This section considers a few potential explanations and the data that have been collected to assess them.

Environmental Chilling Effect   As explained above, the chilling effect hypothesis suggests that environmental agreements are more prone to the inclusion of savings clauses than are other types of treaties. I code treaties as dealing with the environment and resources in two different ways, depending on the sample from which they originate. If they come from the environmental agreements database (Mitchell 2003b), I automatically consider them to be environmental in nature. That database includes observations as "environmental" if

they seek, as a primary purpose, to manage or prevent human impacts on natural resources; plant and animal species (including in agriculture); the atmosphere; oceans; rivers; lakes; terrestrial habitats; and other elements of the natural world that provide ecosystem services (internal reference omitted). Primary purpose was operationalized by searching for terms corresponding to this conception in agreement titles, preambles, or articles specifically designating agreement goals. (Mitchell 2003b)[13]

Second, I code agreements from the UNTS list as environmental if the UN subject coding includes any of the following terms: "Pollution," "Resource(s)," "Natural," or the name of a particular resource. Table 4.2 presents summary statistics for observations that have complete data available.

Control Variables   To properly test the power of the environment variable, one must control for other characteristics that are likely to affect deference in international law. By introducing these controls, I can be sure that the environmental policy field does not simply track some other obvious predictor of savings clauses.[14] Two control variables are in focus here: the number of parties and the number of previous commitments.

Table 4.2
Summary statistics for the explanatory variable: environment or resource treaties

Sample	Number of environmental treaties in the sample	Number of nonenvironmental treaties in the sample	Percentage of the sample constituted by environmental treaties
Full sample	74	154	32
Environmental sample (IEA database)	62	0	100
General sample (UNTS)	12	154	7

First, the involvement of more countries should mean a greater possibility of affecting a group that fears change. Treaties that involve more participants should also be more likely to contain savings clauses because of the complexity of negotiations, as well as the greater opportunity for any country to raise concerns about existing law. If bargaining constraints originate in domestic politics, additional participants should make negotiations more difficult (Koremenos 2005). Thus, the more countries that are involved, the more likely savings clauses should be. Similarly, a veto points model (Tsebelis 2002) would expect that more parties should make cooperation more difficult.[15]

Each regression includes the number of parties. Table 4.3 shows summary statistics for this variable in each sample, as well as the natural log of that value. The regression models use only the natural log of the number of parties because that function allows me to test whether the impact of additional parties makes a greater difference at the lower end.[16] I expect the changing number to make more difference at lower levels. That is, the shift from three to four parties should complicate bargaining much more than the addition of a 101st participant: there is less likelihood that any two out of four parties will take the same position, whereas if 100 parties are involved, it seems quite plausible that some subset of the larger group will take a similar position and possibly form a negotiating bloc.

In operational terms, by "number of parties" I mean those that have signed each treaty. I rely on signatories rather than ratifiers because the signatories are those who had to agree in order to adopt the resulting text. Ratification is an up-or-down vote on the existing text and should be distinct from negotiation results. Signatures are included in the official version of each agreement published in the UNTS.[17] For environmental agreements outside the UNTS I have relied on official information about signatures from the treaty secretariat, and have occasionally consulted the IEA database itself.

The second control variable concerns participants' existing commitments at the time of negotiation. Because legal deference focuses on past agreements, we should expect more savings clauses when there are more agreements that countries may want to protect. We should not expect to see savings clauses unless those provisions can refer to some preexisting agreements. The Correlates of War project includes an International Governmental Organizations Data Set (Pevehouse, Nordstrom, and Warnke 2004), which codes each country's memberships in each of approximately 500 treaties in any given year.

I used these data to construct a measure of existing commitments among the parties to a subsequent negotiation. This variable identifies the average number of existing commitments for parties to a given negotiation in a given year. It can be written as the following equation:

Table 4.3
Summary statistics for the control variables

Variable (sample)	Observations	Minimum[a]	Maximum	Mean
Number of parties				
(Full sample)	226	2	160	17.24
(Environmental sample—IEA database)	62	2	160	13.69
(General sample—UNTS)	164	2	133	18.59
Natural log of the number of parties				
(Full sample)	226	0.69	5.08	2.29
(Environmental sample—IEA database)	62	0.69	5.08	2.14
(General sample—UNTS)	164	0.69	4.89	2.35
Existing commitments of the average participant				
(Full sample)	228	0	102.8	56.4
(Environmental sample—IEA database)	62	0	102.8	56.6
(General sample—UNTS)	166	2.3	89	56.3

a. See notes 18 and 19.

$$\textit{Average commitments} = \frac{\displaystyle\sum_{i=1}^{p} [\text{memberships}_{it}]}{p}$$

where:

p = number of parties to the current treaty

i = the set of countries that are party to this treaty

t = the year of negotiation

memberships$_{it}$ = country i's existing IO memberships in year t

Figure 4.2
Average commitments equation

Table 4.4
Expected relationship of explanatory/control variables to savings clauses

Environment or natural resources treaty	Savings clauses more likely than in other policy fields (+)
Number of parties (logged)	Savings clauses more likely as the number of parties increases (+)
Existing commitments of the average participant	Savings clauses more likely as the number of existing commitments increases (+)

I expect a positive correlation between the average number of existing commitments and the likelihood of including a savings clause. This variable should also pick up the impact of an increase in number of treaties over time, since countries are more likely to have more commitments over time, as treaties become more pervasive.

Table 4.3 includes summary statistics for both control variables. There is a great deal of variation on these measures, indicating that a regression model will show whether they affect the negotiation process. The number of signatories to a treaty ranges from 2 to 133 in the general sample[18] and from 2 to 160 in the environmental sample.[19] The average number of existing treaty commitments for participants ranges from 2.3 to 89 for treaties in the general sample and from 0 to 102.8 in the environmental sample.

Table 4.4 summarizes the expected relationship between control or explanatory variables and the prevalence of savings clauses.

I tested the chilling effect hypothesis by using statistical analysis to see whether deference to existing law outside of the policy field is more prevalent in environmental treaties. Because the dependent variable is categorical and sequential but not intervallic (the categories represent rising levels of deference, but they are not evenly spaced), linear regression techniques cannot provide accurate results (Long and Freese 2006). I used ordered probit models to demonstrate what factors correlate with a rising value on the six-point dependent variable scale. Then, to differentiate between deference to the status quo more generally and a chilling effect on environmental issues, I compared the factors that correlate with all savings clauses (categories 4–6 on the deference scale) to those present in the subset of treaties containing savings clauses for *other* policy fields (categories 5 and 6 on the deference scale). The latter test is most relevant for this chapter because the literature on the chilling effect suggests that environmental negotiations are influenced by nonenvironmental treaties. All analyses were conducted using STATA statistical software (Long and Freese 2006).

Results

This section outlines and reports two different and mutually supportive analytical approaches to evaluating the model's validity. One examines all observations, while the other pinpoints differences between the patterns that emerge in the general and the environmental samples.

Full Sample

One way to determine the difference between environmental and other agreements is to pool all data and then see whether an agreement's classification as "environmental" also correlates with its likelihood of containing a savings clause.

Table 4.5 shows results from the pooled data set while controlling for the other variables mentioned above. The positive coefficient for the environment variable provides further evidence that environmental agreements are indeed more likely to contain savings clauses than other types of treaties. However, the environment coefficient was not statistically significant when I tested the ordered dependent variable (model 1) or the dichotomous variable for all savings clauses (model 2). Environmental agreements do not achieve higher outcomes overall on the deference scale, nor are they more likely—on the whole—to contain a savings clause (any value above 3). On the other hand, as the chilling effect hypothesis suggests, environmental agreements are significantly more likely to contain savings clauses that protect institutions in *other* policy fields, as evidenced by the statistically significant coefficient for the environment in model 3.

Table 4.5
Results for the full (pooled) sample

Variable	(1) All 6 categories (full model)	(2) Any savings clause (full model)	(3) External savings (full model)
Environment or resources treaty	0.173 (0.15)	0.114 (0.19)	0.395* (0.21)
Parties' existing commitments	0.011** (0.00)	0.007 (0.01)	0.015** (0.01)
No. of parties (logged)	0.385*** (0.08)	0.378*** (0.09)	0.283*** (0.10)
_cut1	0.788 (0.36)		
_cut2	1.813 (0.37)		
_cut3	1.900 (0.37)		
_cut4	2.507 (0.38)		
_cut5	2.673 (0.38)		
Constant		−1.629 (0.45)	−2.586 (0.54)
No. of observations	226	226	226
χ^2	27.183	16.936	13.645
Pseudo-R^2	0.0389	0.0564	0.0620

Notes: Standard errors in parentheses. "Cut points" indicate the likelihood of an outcome higher on the dependent variable scale when all independent variables are held to zero. The constant indicates the likely result for a dichotomous dependent variable under those conditions. These values are reported for replication/verification purposes. χ^2 is a measure of the model's overall goodness of fit. Lower values indicate greater accuracy of the model. Pseudo-R^2 is a measure of how much variation in the dependent variable can be explained by the variables included in the model. It is adjusted to account for the addition of more independent variables. Pseudo-R^2 ranges from 0 to 1, with higher values suggesting that the model is a more complete explanation. Standard errors indicate the difference between actual observations and the predicted regression line. Statistical significance is determined by the ratio of each coefficient to its standard error. If that result (z-statistic) is greater than 1.64, then we can say there is a less than 10 percent likelihood that the relationship between explanatory and dependent variables happened by chance. A z-statistic greater than 1.96 indicates a less than 5 percent likelihood of a chance relationship, and 2.57 indicates a less than 1 percent likelihood.
*Statistically significant at the 90% level; **statistically significant at the 95% level; ***statistically significant at the 99% level.

The control variables also influence the use of savings clauses, which demonstrates the importance of including them in these statistical models. The number of existing commitments for participants also appears to play a role in pushing negotiators to protect institutions outside the policy field, although these memberships (surprisingly) do not make all savings clauses more likely (compare models 2 and 3). Finally, the significance of the logged number-of-parties variable indicates that a more complex negotiating environment, as measured by the number of signatories, makes savings clauses of all types (including those that address other policy fields) more likely.[20]

I also employed Clarify software (King, Tomz, and Wittenberg 2000; Tomz, Wittenberg, and King 2001) to demonstrate substantive effects of the environmental policy field in the regressions discussed above. This program allows the user to predict the likelihood that some outcome (here, savings clauses) will change when one explanatory variable (here, whether or not it is an environmental issue) changes values and all others are held at their mean value. I used Clarify to determine the difference in the likelihood of a savings clause (or a savings clause for other policy fields) when shifting between environmental and other issue areas. When testing the dependent variable for all savings clauses (table 4.5, model 2), and holding all other variables at their mean, a shift from nonenvironmental to environmental agreements yielded a very small (approximately 4 percent) rise in the likelihood of a savings clause. Once again, it appears that negotiators are not significantly more likely to use savings clauses in environmental treaties.

The same test with the "external savings clause" dependent variable yielded a much more noticeable increase (more than 11 percent) in the likelihood of environmental agreements deferring to other policy fields. That is, environmental agreements are only 4 percent more likely than others to contain a savings clause, but they are 11 percent more likely to contain a clause that protects agreements *across* policy fields.

Figure 4.3 shows the difference in the likelihood of savings clauses between environmental and other agreements. These tests support the hypothesis that environmental negotiations are more likely to be chilled by existing law in other policy fields.

Differences between Samples
To check the robustness of my findings, I also analyzed the environmental (IEA database) and general (UNTS) samples separately. This arrangement allowed me to see whether negotiators face the same kinds of

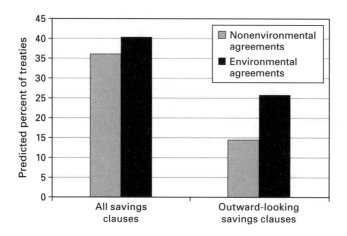

Figure 4.3
Legal deference: comparison between environmental and other agreements

constraints in environmental negotiations as they do in other policy fields. A comparison of columns 6 and 7 in table 4.6 shows that treaties in the IEA database sample are significantly more likely to contain an external savings clause when the participants have a large number of existing commitments. That is, in line with the chilling effect hypothesis, environmental negotiators demonstrate more concern for the protection of earlier agreements across policy fields. The general (UNTS) sample does not exhibit such a relationship, indicating that nonenvironmental negotiators do not feel as constrained by their countries' previous commitments. Since the number of commitments has risen over time, this result also provides support for Eckersley's claim that the environmental chilling effect parallels the strengthening of the GATT/WTO Dispute Settlement process (Eckersley 2004), whereas a similar relationship is not evident among treaties more generally. Unfortunately, there are not enough post-1995 observations to determine whether new WTO rules act as a threshold event after which environmental agreements are further chilled. Figure 4.4 shows the strong effect of this variable in the IEA database sample and its negligible impact in the general sample.

In contrast, concerns about negotiating complexity seem most relevant for deference *outside* the environmental realm. The greater significance of the logged number-of-parties variable in the UNTS sample shows that environmental negotiators are less likely than others to employ a savings clause in reaction to a complex negotiating environment. That is not to say that they ignore this complexity but that they are not as consistently

Table 4.6
Results for environmental (IEA database) and general (UNTS) samples

Variable	(4) Any savings clause (IEA database)	(5) Any savings clause (UNTS)	(6) External savings (IEA database)	(7) External savings (UNTS)
Parties' existing commitments	0.012 (0.01)	0.005 (0.01)	**0.027**** **(0.01)**	0.008 (0.01)
No. of parties (logged)	0.271 (0.19)	0.407*** (0.11)	**0.206** **(0.20)**	**0.276**** **(0.12)**
Constant	−1.495 (0.69)	−1.603 (0.57)	−2.679 (0.84)	−2.120 (0.68)
No. of observations	62	164	62	164
χ^2	3.772	14.085	7.479	5.099
Pseudo R^2	0.0451	0.0651	0.1056	0.0348

Note: Standard errors in parentheses (see note to table 4.5 for an explanation). *Statistically significant at the 90% level; **statistically significant at the 95% level; ***statistically significant at the 99% level.

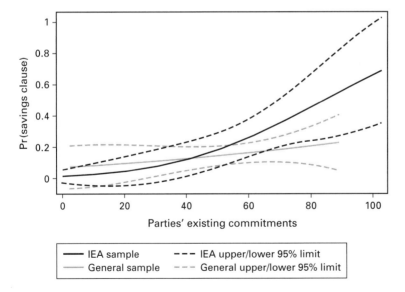

Figure 4.4
Predicted probability of savings clauses based on parties' existing commitments

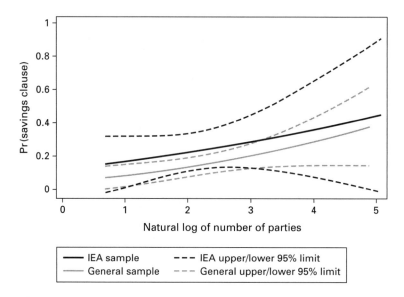

Figure 4.5
Predicted probability of savings clauses based on natural log of the number of parties

driven to adapt by means of savings clauses. Perhaps this lack of correlation occurs because environmental negotiators are already more likely to show concern for existing agreements. As figure 4.5 shows, the number of parties has a similar substantive effect on both samples, but the error is much greater among environmental treaties.

Conclusion

The data sets in this chapter provide substantial insights into international treaty negotiations and the importance of interplay management in them. Perhaps the most important finding is that more than 75 percent of multilateral agreements at least acknowledge the importance of some existing international law. Negotiators have systematically and for a long time engaged in interplay management to avoid disruptive regime conflicts. Given such an interconnected environment, it would be erroneous to think of each treaty negotiation as a completely independent event. The notion of regime complexes is surely a more accurate way of looking at international negotiations (Raustiala and Victor 2004). Moreover, the interactions between those complexes should receive further attention as well.

Contrary to the legal default provided by the Vienna Convention, more than one-third of all multilateral treaties explicitly defer to existing international law. Rather than each negotiation serving as an opportunity for newly empowered countries to overturn provisions with which they have been dissatisfied (Krasner 1991), international law and "legal" interplay management (see also van Asselt in this volume) frequently retain a bias toward the status quo through the use of savings clauses. Far from being epiphenomenal (Strange 1983), international law is difficult to change, and this feature may be one of the root causes for the relative stability of a division of labor between international institutions once established.

But in what kinds of agreements do negotiators resort to this type of interplay management? Environmental negotiations appear to operate in a slightly different fashion than other international treaty conferences. Environmental treaties are no more likely than others to contain some form of a savings clause but environmental negotiators are significantly more likely to take account of existing international agreements outside their own policy field. Existing international law is highly valued and will be defended by its beneficiaries against new rules that could weaken existing provisions. Environmental advocates should be aware of these effects and search for solutions that allow for the continued development of international environmental law while addressing very real concerns about existing treaties.

Acknowledgments

I owe many thanks to Sebastian Oberthür and Olav Schram Stokke for their wide-ranging thoughts and suggestions on earlier drafts. Previous versions of this chapter were presented in seminars at Michigan State University and the Centre for Policy Research, New Delhi, India, as well as during a panel at the 2007 Annual Meeting of the International Studies Association. I benefited greatly from the comments of participants in each of those settings, in addition to thoughtful suggestions from Doug Bushey, Seth Jolly, Emily Meierding, and Steven Wilkinson. Ron Mitchell provided feedback on a related project, as well as access to his comprehensive database of international environmental agreements.

Notes

1. There is little evidence for this proliferation of legal conflicts, although two notable cases come to mind. First, the EU and Chile simultaneously initiated

disputes about swordfish fisheries in the WTO and Law of the Sea tribunals, respectively (WT/DS193/3 [6 April 2001]). Also, decisions by NAFTA and WTO tribunals in 2007 provided conflicting solutions for the U.S.–Canada softwood lumber dispute (WT/DS277/20/Add.1 [9 March 2007]).

2. In the swordfish case (see note 1), the lack of a clear hierarchy between institutions resulted in the reduced influence of each available legal institution.

3. 1969. Vienna Convention on the Law of Treaties. *8 I.L.M. 679.* See also the discussion of relevant provisions of the VCLT by van Asselt in this volume.

4. These subsequent negotiations may include treaty amendments, protocols, or entirely new agreements. For analytical reasons, the empirical tests discussed below include only the latter two categories.

5. Random samples were obtained by placing each full set of treaties in chronological order and conducting a random-number draw to identify treaties for analysis.

6. As discussed below, UNTS includes treaties from all policy fields. I have coded the policy field for each agreement in the sample. Coding rules for the environment category are discussed below. A full set of field codings is available in Axelrod 2008.

7. Additionally, although bilateral treaties represent 90 percent of all treaties, they do not account for 90 percent of all international cooperation. Rather, a multilateral treaty with eight parties should actually count as a much greater coordination event than a bilateral accord. As such, a true random sample should weight each treaty on the basis of the number of participants.

8. UNTS multilateral agreements include treaties, such as loan agreements, negotiated between one country and international organizations (e.g., the World Bank). Because these international organizations do not respond directly to domestic political interests, I cannot consider them to be governments for the sake of testing this theory.

9. The smaller population necessitated analysis of more than 10 percent.

10. The importance of including "nonregimes" to avoid selection bias is developed by Dimitrov et al. (2007).

11. For purposes of this distinction, I refer to broad policy fields such as the environment or human rights. For example, if an agreement on biological diversity defers to a treaty on transboundary pollution, it is coded in category 4. However, if that same agreement deferred to existing international trade law, it would be coded in category 5.

12. As I performed all coding by myself, there is no guarantee of universally reliable data. However, my coding rationale for each provision is available for replication and critique at www.fw.msu.edu/~axelrod3.

13. For the particular search terms, see http://iea.uoregon.edu/overview/definitions.htm#environmental.

14. Statistically speaking, a control variable allows the analyst to examine the impact of an important explanatory variable (here, the environment) while all

other aspects of the issue remain constant. It allows the researcher to compare across a large number of cases while still following John Stuart Mill's method of difference, which requires that all variables except one remain at the same value in order to isolate the impact of the one factor that varies across cases (Bennett 2004, 31–32).

15. In essence, all treaties analyzed here involve consensus decision making, as signatures would not reach the treaty unless each country is satisfied (though not necessarily pleased) with the outcome. In that sense, every participant has a veto to the extent that its participation is valued by the other parties. However, unlike the process in domestic politics, powerful actors can decide to exclude some weaker parties if their demands are not acceptable to the rest of the group.

16. The natural log function tracks the inverse of the exponential function for the constant e (approximately 2.71828). The function demonstrates the exponent to which that constant must be raised in order to reach x (Larson et al. 2005, 322–323). Use of this function allows the analyst to test whether marginal change in the variable x (here, parties) has a greater impact on the dependent variable (here, the likelihood of a savings clause) at lower values than it does after reaching a high level (Griffiths, Hill, and Judge 1993, 258–260, 345–347).

17. This measure encounters some confusion in determining whether to count regional integration organizations or their member states in treaties to which both are signatories. I have counted the regional organization when it is the only participant among the group, and the individual member states otherwise.

18. One treaty in the data set is a multilateral scientific research agreement between the European Economic Community and Norway. However, because the EEC member states delegated authority to the European Commission in this instance, they are not counted individually (see note 17). As a result, this multilateral treaty appears to have only two signatories.

19. The United States and Costa Rica are the two original parties to the Convention for the establishment of the Inter-American Tropical Tuna Commission (1949). However, Article V (para. 3) allows for the inclusion of other countries "whose nationals participate in the fisheries" covered by the treaty.

20. However, I have shown elsewhere that the complexity of the negotiating environment is significant only when the average participant can be considered to have declined in relative power since World War II (Axelrod 2008).

References

Treaties Cited

Convention on the High Seas. 1958. 450 U.N.T.S. 11 (No. 6465). Agreed at Geneva, 29 April 1958 (entered into force 30 September 1962).

Convention on the Prohibition of the Development, Production, Stockpiling, and Use of Chemical Weapons and on Their Destruction. 1992 (Chemical Weapons Convention). 1974 U.N.T.S. 45 (No. 33757), 32 I.L.M. 800. Agreed at Paris, 3 September 1992 (entered into force 29 April 1997).

Convention Relating to Civil Procedure. 1954. 286 U.N.T.S. 265 (No. 4173). Agreed at The Hague, 1 March 1954 (entered into force 12 April 1957).

International Convention on Oil Pollution Preparedness, Response and Cooperation. 1990. 1891 U.N.T.S. 51 (No. 32194), 30 I.L.M. 733 (1991). Agreed at London, 30 November 1990 (entered into force 13 May 1995).

International Labour Organization (ILO), Constitution of the International Labour Organization (ILO). 1919. Agreed at Versailles, 1 April 1919 (entered into force 28 June 1919). http://www.ilo.org/public/english/about/iloconst.htm.

Vienna Convention on the Law of Treaties. 1969. 1155 U.N.T.S. 331 (No. 18232), 8 I.L.M. 679. Agreed at Vienna, 23 May 1969 (entered into force 27 January 1980).

Other Sources

Axelrod, Mark. 2008. Saving Institutional Benefits: Path Dependence in International Law. PhD diss., Duke University, Durham, N.C. http://dukespace.lib .duke.edu/dspace/handle/10161/628 (accessed 19 April 2010).

Bennett, Andrew. 2004. Case Study Methods: Design, Use, and Comparative Advantages. In *Models, Numbers, and Cases: Methods for Studying International Relations*, ed. Detlef F. Sprinz and Yael Wolinsky-Nahmias, 19–55. Ann Arbor: University of Michigan Press.

Coase, Ronald H. 1988. *The Firm, the Market and the Law*. Chicago: University of Chicago Press.

Conca, Ken. 2000. The WTO and the Undermining of Global Environmental Governance. *Review of International Political Economy* 7 (3): 484–494.

D'Amato, Anthony. 1983. Legal Uncertainty. *California Law Review* 71 (1): 1–55.

Davis, Christina L. 2004. International Institutions and Issue Linkage: Building Support for Agricultural Trade Liberalization. *American Political Science Review* 98 (1): 153–169.

Dimitrov, Radoslav S., Detlef F. Sprinz, Gerald M. DiGiusto, and Alexander Kelle. 2007. International Nonregimes: A Research Agenda. *International Studies Review* 9 (2): 230–258.

Eckersley, Robyn. 2004. The Big Chill: The WTO and Multilateral Environmental Agreements. *Global Environmental Politics* 4 (2): 24–50.

Gehring, Thomas, and Sebastian Oberthür. 2006. Comparative Empirical Analysis and Ideal Types of Institutional Interaction. In *Institutional Interaction in Global Environmental Governance: Synergy and Conflict among International and EU Policies*, ed. Sebastian Oberthür and Thomas Gehring, 307–371. Cambridge, Mass.: MIT Press.

Griffiths, William E., R. Carter Hill, and George G. Judge. 1993. *Learning and Practicing Econometrics*. New York: Wiley.

Hart, Herbert L. A. 1961. *The Concept of Law*. Oxford: Clarendon Press.

Helfer, Laurence R. 2004. Regime Shifting: The TRIPs Agreement and New Dynamics of International Intellectual Property Lawmaking. *Yale Journal of International Law* 29:1–83.

Kahneman, Daniel, and Amos Tversky. 1979. Prospect Theory: An Analysis of Decision under Risk. *Econometrica* 47 (2): 263–292.

Keohane, Robert O. 1984. *After Hegemony: Cooperation and Discord in the World Political Economy*. Princeton, N.J.: Princeton University Press.

King, Gary, Robert O. Keohane, and Sidney Verba. 1994. *Designing Social Inquiry: Scientific Inference in Qualitative Research*. Princeton, N.J.: Princeton University Press.

King, Gary, Michael Tomz, and Jason Wittenberg. 2000. Making the Most of Statistical Analyses: Improving Interpretation and Presentation. *American Journal of Political Science* 44 (2): 347–361.

Kingsbury, Benedict. 1999. Foreword: Is the Proliferation of International Courts and Tribunals a Systemic Problem? Symposium on Proliferation of International Tribunals: Piecing Together the Puzzle. *New York University Journal of International Law & Politics* 31 (4): 679–696.

Kohona, Palitha T. B. 2002. The United Nations Treaty Collection on the Internet: Developments and Challenges. *International Journal of Legal Information* 30:397–425.

Koremenos, Barbara. 2005. Contracting around International Uncertainty. *American Political Science Review* 99 (4): 549–565.

Krasner, Stephen D. 1991. Global Communications and National Power: Life on the Pareto Frontier. *World Politics* 43 (3): 336–366.

Larson, Ron, Robert P. Hostetler, and Bruce H. Edwards. 2005. *Calculus of a Single Variable*. Boston: Houghton Mifflin.

Long, J. Scott, and Jeremy Freese. 2006. *Regression Models for Categorical Dependent Variables Using Stata*. College Station, Tex.: StataCorp.

Mitchell, Ronald B. 2003a. International Environmental Agreements Database. http://www.uoregon.edu/~rmitchel/IEA/ (accessed 15 January 2008).

Mitchell, Ronald B. 2003b. International Environmental Agreements: A Survey of Their Features, Formation, and Effects. *Annual Review of Environment and Resources* 28:429–461.

Mnookin, Robert H., and Lewis Kornhauser. 1979. Bargaining in the Shadow of the Law: The Case of Divorce. *Yale Law Journal* 88:950–997.

Moe, Terry. 1990. Political Institutions: The Neglected Side of the Story. *Journal of Law Economics and Organization* 6:213–254.

North, Douglass Cecil. 1990. *Institutions, Institutional Change, and Economic Performance: Political Economy of Institutions and Decisions*. Cambridge: Cambridge University Press.

Oberthür, Sebastian, and Thomas Gehring. 2006a. Conceptual Foundations of Institutional Interaction. In *Institutional Interaction in Global Environmental*

Governance: Synergy and Conflict among International and EU Policies, ed. Sebastian Oberthür and Thomas Gehring, 19–51. Cambridge, Mass.: MIT Press.

Oberthür, Sebastian, and Thomas Gehring, eds. 2006b. *Institutional Interaction in Global Environmental Governance: Synergy and Conflict among International and EU Policies*. Cambridge, Mass.: MIT Press.

Pauwelyn, Joost. 2003. *Conflict of Norms in Public International Law: How WTO Law Relates to Other Rules of International Law*. Cambridge: Cambridge University Press.

Pevehouse, Jon C., Timothy Nordstrom, and Kevin Warnke. 2004. The COW-2 International Organizations Dataset Version 2.0. *Conflict Management and Peace Science* 21 (2): 101–119.

Pierson, Paul. 2000. Increasing Returns, Path Dependence, and the Study of Politics. *American Political Science Review* 94 (2): 251–267.

Pierson, Paul. 2004. *Politics in Time: History, Institutions, and Social Analysis*. Princeton, N.J.: Princeton University Press.

Raustiala, Kal, and David G. Victor. 2004. The Regime Complex for Plant Genetic Resources. *International Organization* 58 (2): 277–310.

Stilwell, Matthew, and Elisabeth Tuerk. 1999. *Trade Measures and Multilateral Environmental Agreements: Resolving Uncertainty and Removing the WTO Chill Factor*. Geneva: World Wide Fund for Nature/Center for International Environmental Law.

Strange, Susan. 1983. *Cave! hic dragones*: A Critique of Regime Analysis. In *International Regimes*, ed. Stephen D. Krasner, 337–354. Ithaca, N.Y.: Cornell University Press.

Tomz, Michael, Jason Wittenberg, and Gary King. 2001. CLARIFY: Software for Interpreting and Presenting Statistical Results. Version 2.0. http://gking. harvard.edu/stats.shtml (accessed 19 April 2010).

Trachtman, Joel P. 2002. Symposium: The Boundaries of the WTO: Institutional Linkage: "Trade and . . . ." *American Journal of International Law* 96:77–93.

Tsebelis, George. 2002. *Veto Players: How Political Institutions Work*. Princeton, N.J.: Princeton University Press.

United Nations. 2003. *Final Clauses of Multilateral Treaties: Handbook*. http:// untreaty.un.org/English/FinalClauses/english.pdf (accessed 19 April 2010).

Williamson, Oliver E. 1985. *The Economic Institutions of Capitalism: Firms, Markets, Relational Contracting*. New York: Free Press.

Young, Oran R. 2002. *The Institutional Dimensions of Environmental Change: Fit, Interplay, and Scale*. Cambridge, Mass.: MIT Press.

5

Managing Policy Contradictions between the Montreal and Kyoto Protocols

The Case of Fluorinated Greenhouse Gases

Sebastian Oberthür, Claire Dupont, and Yasuko Matsumoto

The international regimes for the protection of the ozone layer and for combating climate change have been at the forefront of global environmental governance since the mid-1980s. The ozone regime is based on the 1985 Vienna Convention for the Protection of the Ozone Layer and its 1987 Montreal Protocol on Substances that Deplete the Ozone Layer. The Montreal Protocol determines the phase-out of the production and consumption of several groups of ozone-depleting substances, most prominently chlorofluorocarbons (CFCs). For more than a decade, it was paradigmatic for global environmental governance, and it has been heralded as one of the most effective international environmental agreements (e.g., Parson 1993, 2003; Benedick 1998; Wettestad 2002; Andersen and Sarma 2002). The climate regime is based on the 1992 UN Framework Convention on Climate Change (UNFCCC) and its Kyoto Protocol of 1997, which, for the first time in history, introduced restrictions on greenhouse gas (GHG) emissions. While not yet as successful as the ozone regime, it contains several important innovations, most prominently three market-based mechanisms (including international emissions trading) (Oberthür and Ott 1999; Yamin and Depledge 2004). Climate change has replaced ozone depletion as the number one global environmental issue, even superseding most nonenvironmental issues on the international political agenda.

Both regimes are interlinked and have influenced each other in various ways. Since they are global in scope and regulate closely related issue areas, it is not surprising that the younger climate regime has in many respects been modeled on the older, successful ozone regime. Both regimes follow the framework-convention-plus-protocol approach and incorporate a strong differentiation between industrialized and developing countries (see, e.g., Thoms 2003). Furthermore, several specific features of the Montreal Protocol, including its compliance system, have informed the design of the climate regime. Moreover, the Montreal Protocol makes an important contribution to climate protection, because CFCs and other ozone-depleting substances phased out under the protocol are also powerful GHGs (Oberthür 2001, 2006; IPCC/TEAP 2005; Velders et al. 2007).

Perhaps more surprisingly, partially halogenated fluorocarbons—powerful GHGs manufactured primarily as substitutes for the major ozone-depleting substances (IPCC/TEAP 2005; Velders et al. 2007)—have given rise to two policy contradictions between the regimes. First, the Montreal Protocol has undermined efforts to mitigate climate change by directly and indirectly promoting the use of hydrochlorofluorocarbons (HCFCs) and hydrofluorocarbons (HFCs) as substitutes for ozone-depleting substances (Oberthür 2001). Second, the implementation of certain projects under the Kyoto Protocol's Clean Development Mechanism (CDM) implies an incentive to increase the production of the ozone-depleting substance HCFC-22, thus potentially undermining the Montreal Protocol (Schneider, Graichen, and Matz 2005; Wara 2008).

This chapter analyzes the management of these policy contradictions in four steps, with particular emphasis on the case of problematic projects under the Kyoto Protocol's CDM. The next section provides further background on the two underlying interactions between the ozone and climate regimes with respect to HCFCs and HFCs. Subsequently we explore in some detail the related interplay management as it has evolved and intensified since the late 1980s, then assess the options available in the climate regime to mitigate and remove the policy contradiction with the Montreal Protocol regarding CDM projects. In the concluding section we assess the effectiveness of interplay management so far and its future prospects, and also discuss the pros and cons of the fragmentation of governance of both issue areas.

Background: Underlying Interactions

We can distinguish two underlying disruptive interactions between the regimes for the protection of the ozone layer and the global climate regarding fluorinated GHGs. These interactions run in different directions: one of them undermines the implementation of the Montreal Protocol, while the other runs counter to the objectives of the UNFCCC and the Kyoto Protocol. They constitute "behavioral interaction" (Oberthür and Gehring 2006, 39–41) because each protocol provides incentives for actors during implementation that are contrary to the objectives of the other regime.

First, the Montreal Protocol undermines efforts to mitigate climate change by promoting the use of fluorinated GHGs. The phase-out of CFCs and other fully halogenated ozone-depleting substances agreed to under the Montreal Protocol also contributes significantly to protecting the climate, but agreement on this phase-out was contingent on the availability of appropriate substitutes (for use in, e.g., refrigeration, air conditioning, and as a foam-blowing agent), the most important being HCFCs and HFCs (Anderson 2001). Consequently, parties to the Montreal Protocol allowed the continued use of the ozone-depleting HCFCs in industrialized countries until 2020/2030 and in developing countries until 2040. Developing countries were even allowed unrestricted growth of production and consumption until 2015 (see table 5.2). Because HFCs have no ozone-depleting properties, they were not controlled under the Montreal Protocol at all and have been considered particularly suitable substitutes. Emissions of HFCs not only arise from their use as substitutes but also occur inadvertently as a significant by-product during the production of the most important HCFC, HCFC-22. Both HCFCs and HFCs are potent GHGs (Oberthür 2001).

Second, the CDM of the Kyoto Protocol potentially undermines efforts to protect the ozone layer. In accordance with Article 12 of the Kyoto Protocol, the CDM allows industrialized countries to invest in climate change mitigation projects in developing countries. Credits gained for GHG emission reductions achieved in CDM projects can be used by industrialized countries for compliance with their emission reduction targets under the Kyoto Protocol. In addition, the CDM aims at promoting sustainable development in developing countries that host projects. In principle, projects for the destruction of HFC-23 during the production of HCFC-22 are eligible under the CDM. However, such CDM projects can provide a considerable "perverse incentive" to continue and increase the production of HCFC-22 beyond normal market demand, thereby detrimentally affecting the ozone layer and the implementation of the Montreal Protocol. This interaction and its management are the major focus of this chapter.

The aforementioned perverse incentive stems from the enormous financial gains to be reaped from HFC-23 abatement projects under the CDM (Schneider, Graichen, and Matz 2005; McCulloch 2004; Wara 2008; UNFCCC 2005a). HFC-23 possesses a particularly high global

Table 5.1
Economics of HFC-23 destruction under the CDM

	Scenarios		
Assumptions	Low impact	Reference	High impact
HFC-23/HCFC-22 ratio (%)	1.5	2.2	3.0
HFC-23 abatement costs (USD/CO_2e)	1.0	0.6	0.2
Market price for CERs (USD/CER)	5	10	15
Market price for HCFC-22 (USD/kg)	2.4	1.7	1.1
CER market price/abatement cost ratio	5	16.7	75
Net financial gain/HCFC-22 market price ratio	0.33	2.45	5.1

Source: Adapted from Schneider, Graichen, and Matz 2005

warming potential: each ton of HFC-23 contributes as much to global climate change as 11,700 tons of CO_2.[1] The gains from related CDM projects depend on the ratio of HFC-23 inadvertently produced per ton of HCFC-22 production, the cost of HFC-23 abatement, and the market price of the emission credits known as Certified Emission Reductions (CERs). Table 5.1 gives an overview of various scenarios on the basis of plausible ranges of these factors. Even in the best case ("low impact"), the financial gains from HFC-23 abatement projects under the CDM would exceed the costs by a factor of five. In a "high-impact" scenario, the gains-cost ratio could even increase to around 75. In the lowest case, HFC abatement projects would constitute a significant subsidy to HCFC-22 production, equaling roughly a third of HCFC-22 market prices. Already in a moderate "reference" scenario, the profits exceed the HCFC-22 market price. In reality, CER prices on the European spot market and for CER futures have regularly exceeded the USD 15 assumed in the high-impact scenario since 2005 and have never dropped to the level of the reference scenario. Thus, the gains from HFC-23 abatement projects under the CDM have by far exceeded the costs.[2]

The impact of HFC-23 destruction projects under the CDM is considerable also in terms of the absolute number of emission credits. Under the Montreal Protocol, HCFC production in industrialized countries has been restricted, but it has been allowed to grow in developing countries. In 2004, approximately thirty HCFC-22 production plants existed in developing countries, with a combined output of about 210,000 tons and a combined annual production capacity of about 340,000 tons (UNFCCC 2005a; McCulloch 2004). Furthermore, the worldwide production of HCFC-22 was set to increase from 491,000 tons in 2000 to 707,000 tons by 2015 (IPCC/TEAP 2005, 395–396; TEAP 2007, 25–37). Even without any artificially inflated production, CDM projects for the destruction of HFC-23 could thus generate emission credits of up to 160 million tons annually during the Kyoto Protocol's first commitment period, 2008–2012 (see also Schneider, Graichen, and Matz 2005, 44; Cames et al. 2007, 38–41). The amount of 160 million tons exceeds Belgium's 2005 emissions by roughly 15 million tons. The resulting five-year total of 800 million tons compares to a total of around 2.7 billion CERs that are to be issued during the first commitment period. At prices of 15 to 20 euros per ton, they would have a value of around 12 to 16 billion euros (approximately USD 16 to 21 billion at the exchange rate of 1.33).[3]

HFC-23 abatement projects under the CDM may not only seriously undermine the Montreal Protocol, they also entail several other problematic effects for the climate regime and the CDM itself. First, HFC-23 abatement projects under the CDM could result in a net increase in global GHG emissions. CDM projects reduce the costs of compliance for industrialized countries with emission targets, but they do not contribute to a reduction in global GHG emissions. One CDM emission credit transferred to an industrialized country to meet its emissions commitment would relieve that country of reducing one ton of GHG emissions domestically (Oberthür and Ott 1999, 169). Although CDM emission reductions are required to be additional to what would have occurred without the CDM project activity, a significant portion of CERs have been shown to exist only on paper. With respect to HFC-23 projects, the danger is further reinforced, both because HCFC-22 production may be shifted from industrialized countries (where HFC-23 abatement has become the standard) to developing countries in order to gain emission credits and because HCFC-22 production may be increased for the sole purpose of earning CERs from HFC-23 abatement. Industrialized countries may thus offset domestic emissions with emission credits that exist only on paper (Schneider, Graichen, and Matz 2005; Schneider 2007; Wara 2008; Wara and Victor 2008).

Furthermore, HFC-23 abatement projects score particularly poorly on secondary benefits. HFC-23 abatement through "thermal oxidation" (burning) does not produce any further environmental or social benefits.

It does not provide additional advantageous spillover effects, induce structural change in the energy sector, or help diffuse technology to developing countries (Schneider 2007). Relevant projects also reinforce the unequal distribution of CDM projects by focusing on a few large developing countries, such as India and China, which together account for over 80 percent of HCFC-22 production in the developing world (UNFCCC 2005a). Finally, these projects distort market competition by providing a competitive edge to the relevant chemical industry in developing countries (Schneider, Graichen, and Matz 2005; TEAP 2007; Wara 2007).

More stringent controls on HCFC production and consumption (defined as production minus exports plus imports) under the Montreal Protocol could only partially resolve the issue. While the CDM's economic clout may impede attempts to strengthen these restrictions, production of HCFC-22 for feedstock—especially in the production of polytetrafluoroethylene (Teflon)—is not controlled under the Montreal Protocol because it results in comparatively minor emissions (Schneider, Graichen, and Matz 2005). The share of total HCFC production used for feedstock was projected to increase from about one-third in 2003 to about 40 percent by 2015 (McCulloch and Lindley 2007, 1563; IPCC/TEAP 2005, 396). Even with stringent controls under the Montreal Protocol, the CDM could thus create a considerable incentive to increase HCFC production for feedstock purposes—a major concern for efforts to protect the ozone layer.

Intensifying Interplay Management

Early Interplay Management: Building the Foundations (1989–1999)

The tensions between efforts to protect the ozone layer and combat climate change were acknowledged early, but the first decade of interaction saw little targeted political effort to address them. The emergence of the UNFCCC and its Kyoto Protocol as the foundation of the global regime on climate change, on the one side, and the maturation of the Montreal Protocol on the other, set the stage for the policy contradictions and their political management. The interplay management that occurred proceeded unilaterally in each of the institutions, without explicit coordination.

Although parties to the Montreal Protocol have long been aware of the climate-damaging potential of fluorinated substitutes, they began to focus on developing controls for HCFCs only in the 1990s. After scientific advice had indicated in May 1989 that the global warming potential of HCFCs and HFCs should be "taken into account when their suitability as substitutes is being considered" (UNEP 1989, para. 19), parties in 1990 requested the Scientific Assessment Panel of the Montreal Protocol to include an evaluation of the global warming potentials of these gases in its work (Decision II/13).[4] Parties then agreed to restrictions on HCFC consumption in 1992, strengthened them in 1995, and added controls on production in 1999. Accordingly, industrialized countries had to freeze their HCFC production in 2004 and phase out 99.5 percent of HCFC consumption in stages until 2020, with a "service tail" of 0.5 percent allowed until 2030. Developing countries had to freeze HCFC consumption and production in 2016 and to phase out consumption by 2040. No intermediate reductions were determined between the freeze in 2016 and phase-out in 2040 (see table 5.2).

Throughout this process, the impacts of these gases on climate change played a limited role. The global warming potential of HCFCs remained clearly subordinate to considerations related to the protection of the ozone layer (Benedick 1998; Oberthür 2000; Parson 2003). In particular, industry had received assurances of continued HCFC availability when it agreed to phase out CFCs. Consequently, parties to the Montreal Protocol supported HCFCs and HFCs against more climate-friendly alternatives in 1992 by requesting that both the "direct and indirect global-warming effects" of alternatives be taken into account (Decision IV/13), since HCFCs and HFCs were believed to generate indirect climate change benefits from energy-efficiency gains.

On the side of the climate regime, two features shaped the relationship with the Montreal Protocol. In order to delimit clearly the regulatory authority of the two regimes, the UNFCCC determined, first, that it would not cover GHGs already controlled by the Montreal Protocol. As a result, HFCs fall under the climate regime, while authority for regulating HCFCs rests solely with the Montreal Protocol. Second, the Kyoto Protocol includes HFCs in the "basket" of six controlled gases and groups of gases (CO_2, CH_4, N_2O, HFCs, perfluorocarbons, and sulfur hexafluoride) covered, in aggregate, by industrialized countries' emission targets for 2008–2012. As a result, HFCs are generally controlled under the Kyoto Protocol, but their production and use are not subject to any specific restrictions. With HFCs having so far contributed less than 5 percent to total emissions, industrialized countries can thus further increase the use of these gases as long as growth in emissions is offset by reductions in the emissions of other GHGs (Oberthür and Ott 1999, 124–126).

The Use of Fluorinated GHGs: Focus on Scientific Cooperation (1998–2005)

The disruptive effect of the Montreal Protocol's promotion of HCFCs and HFCs on the climate regime triggered scientific and technical cooperation between both regimes, in two phases. This cooperation improved the consensual knowledge base about the options for limiting the emissions of fluorinated GHGs. While it did not lead to consequential political decision making in either regime—let alone by the regimes jointly—the resulting scientific reports made a valuable contribution to the political discussions on strengthening HCFC controls under the Montreal Protocol and the treatment of HFC-23 destruction projects under the CDM.

Both regimes initiated scientific cooperation in 1998. The parties to the Montreal Protocol and the parties to the UNFCCC then each called for a joint workshop of their respective scientific advisory bodies—the Intergovernmental Panel on Climate Change (IPCC) and the Technology and Economic Assessment Panel (TEAP) of the Montreal Protocol—to assess available and potential means of limiting HFC and perfluorocarbons emissions. Held in May 1999, the workshop resulted in a report on options for the limitation of these emissions (IPCC/TEAP 1999). Written submissions from parties provided further input into the political debates under the UNFCCC, while TEAP provided an additional report on the matter to the parties to the Montreal Protocol (TEAP 1999; see also Oberthür 2001, 368–369).

The subsequent political debates remained largely inconclusive. Parties to the climate regime could have, for example, directly restricted emissions of fluorinated GHGs, and parties to the Montreal Protocol could have given clear priority to existing non-GHG alternatives. Coordination between the regimes could have made it more difficult for the laggards to play both regimes against each other and would have provided the opportunity to prioritize available climate- and ozone-friendly alternatives to fluorinated GHGs (Velders et al. 2007; Matsumoto 2008). However, both parties to the Montreal Protocol and parties to the UNFCCC took up the issue again separately during their annual conferences in 1999. While political discussions under the Montreal Protocol failed to result in any decision at all, parties to the climate regime merely agreed to invite individual parties to assess the information presented, and mandated the Subsidiary Body for Scientific and Technological Advice (SBSTA) to consider the issue further (Decision 17/CP.5; Oberthür 2001, 369).[5]

The ensuing process in the climate regime led to a second joint IPCC/TEAP report in 2005 which served as a fig leaf for taking the issue off the agenda. With several parties (among them the United States, Japan, and China) opposing further decisions, the climate regime emphasized providing further "policy-neutral, user-friendly information." Following discussions with the respective advisory bodies, both the parties to the UNFCCC (Decision 12/CP.8) and the parties to the Montreal Protocol (Decision XIV/10) requested the IPCC and TEAP in 2002 to prepare an integrated report by early 2005. The joint IPCC/TEAP special report, titled *Safeguarding the Ozone Layer and the Global Climate System: Issues Related to Hydrofluorocarbons and Perfluorocarbons* (IPCC/TEAP 2005), provided a face-saving opportunity for proponents of action like the EU to rest their case in view of insurmountable political opposition. On the basis of the joint report, the SBSTA heralded a last round of discussions in May 2005 "with a view to finalizing the consideration of this agenda item" by mid-2006 (UNFCCC 2005b, 16). A year later this aim had been achieved, with SBSTA simply encouraging parties to ensure good interministerial communication and the secretariats of the two regimes to continue their cooperation (UNFCCC 2006, 20). The IPCC/TEAP special report did, however, contribute to discussions on strengthening HCFC controls under the Montreal Protocol and provided useful information with respect to HFC-23 destruction projects under the CDM (see next subsections).

Kyoto Protocol: HFC-23 Destruction Projects under the CDM (2003–2010)

Beyond HFC emissions, relevant political discussions under the climate regime have focused on the treatment of HFC-23 destruction projects under the CDM. Interplay management of the issue has been primarily pursued unilaterally within the institutional framework of the Kyoto Protocol. As a result, HFC-23 destruction projects have been approved in "existing" HCFC-22 production plants, while discussions on the treatment of projects in "new" plants have stalled (as of 2010).

The CDM is an innovative market-based mechanism with a unique governance structure. CDM projects need to be based on approved methodologies for the calculation of baselines and the monitoring of emissions and emission reductions. Proposed methodologies require approval by the CDM Executive Board, composed of ten elected members, who supervise and govern the CDM. Once the board, assisted by a "Methodology Panel," approves a methodology, project implementation can proceed and certainty about the calculation of resulting credits exists. The approved methodology serves as the basis for so-called Designated

Operational Entities to oversee and independently validate the projects and the certification of emission reductions (Oberthür and Ott 1999, 168–171; Wilkins 2002; Yamin and Depledge 2004, chap. 6.6; Streck 2007).

HFC-23 destruction projects were among the first projects initiated under the CDM, but soon proved controversial. The CDM Executive Board first approved the methodology for HFC-23 abatement projects in July 2003, but decided to put it on hold and to review it in September 2004, in the face of serious concerns about possible negative effects. The board then agreed on a two-track approach in December 2004. It first decided to modify the approved methodology by limiting it to "existing production sites," which were defined as having at least three years of operating history by the end of the year 2004. Second, it decided to seek guidance from the conference of the parties on the treatment of "new" plants.[6]

The ensuing discussions among parties produced a specification of the approach toward "existing" plants but has remained inconclusive with respect to "new" facilities (as of early 2010). In December 2004, parties mandated SBSTA to develop, in collaboration with the CDM Executive Board, a recommendation for the treatment of "new" production sites (Decision 12/CP.10). The next annual conference in 2005 specified the meaning of "new HCFC-22 facilities" as those without an operating history of at least three years between 2000 and 2004. In addition, increased production of HCFC-22 in "existing" plants above the maximum historical annual production level during any of the last three years of operation between the beginning of 2000 and the end of 2004 would be considered "new" and thus not covered by the approved methodology for existing facilities. Finally, the conference encouraged industrialized countries and multilateral financial institutions to provide funding for HFC-23 destruction projects in new facilities separately from the CDM (Decision 8/CMP.1). No agreement has since been reached on the treatment of new facilities under the CDM. While China, as one of the major potential beneficiaries, pushed for making projects in "new" plants eligible, European and Latin American delegations resisted on the grounds of environmental and competitiveness concerns (see also Gehring and Plocher 2009). Consequently, HFC-23 destruction projects concerning "new" production facilities have remained ineligible under the CDM.

The limitation of eligibility to "existing" plants has effectively halved the estimated potential of HFC-23 destruction projects under the CDM. In all, nineteen relevant projects had been registered under the CDM as of May 2010 (eleven in China, five in India, and one each in the Republic of Korea, Mexico, and Argentina). These projects are expected to generate more than 70 million CERs per year during the first commitment period. Including emission credits from the prompt-start phase of the CDM prior to 2008, a total of around 450 million tons could be generated from these projects by the end of 2012, which would be more than 15 percent of all CERs anticipated to be generated (see data available at http://cdmpipeline.org/cdm-projects-type.htm and http://cdm.unfccc.int/index.html).

The limitation of eligibility to existing plants reduces the negative impacts. Given the growing demand for HCFCs in developing countries especially, current projects do not create a significant direct incentive to expand production beyond demand. However, they generate considerable subsidies that could distort international competition and constitute a significant incentive to continue production. Windfall profits could also be used to cross-subsidize an expansion of HCFC-22 production in order to acquire additional market shares from the chemical industry in industrialized countries. Since any such expansion of production would probably occur without ensuring HFC-23 abatement (also in the hope of becoming eligible under the CDM later on), which is the norm in industrialized countries, it could paradoxically lead to an overall increase in HFC-23 emissions.

Montreal Protocol: Strengthening HCFC Controls (2007)
Parties to the Montreal Protocol eventually responded to the policy contradiction with the Kyoto Protocol by strengthening HCFC controls in 2007. Discussions on HFC-23 destruction projects under the CDM and broader climate change concerns contributed to the agreement, which promises significant benefits for both the ozone layer and the global climate.

Parties to the Montreal Protocol remained extremely reluctant to address the policy contradictions with the Kyoto Protocol regarding fluorinated gases at the beginning of the twenty-first century. In 2001, EU suggestions to launch discussions to strengthen HCFC controls received a cold reception, especially by many developing countries, which cited the risk of "creating chaos among governments and industry" (UNEP 2001, 8). In 2002, agreement to join the climate regime in initiating a special IPCC/TEAP report (see above) was secured only after opponents had received assurances that the parties to the Montreal Protocol were to consider the special report only "in so far as it relates to actions to address ozone depletion" (Decision XIV/10)—in other words, they would not attempt to restrict HFCs.

Accordingly, parties focused their attention on HCFCs in the wake of the 2005 IPCC/TEAP Special Report. Progress was driven more by the changed political context (with the rising salience of climate change in international relations and the emerging HFC-23 issue) than the hardly revolutionary content of this report. Hence, parties to the Montreal Protocol first requested TEAP to identify the ozone regime implications of the report more clearly (UNEP 2005, para. 97). On the basis of TEAP's supplementary report (TEAP 2005), parties agreed to convene an experts' workshop to elaborate a list of practical measures in late 2005 (Decision XVII/19). At their meeting in 2006, they mandated TEAP to provide a further assessment of the measures identified at this workshop in 2007. Signifying the increasing prominence of the issue, parties requested TEAP to give "full consideration" to the influence of the CDM on HCFC-22 production (para. 2 of Decision XVIII/12). The news that the recovery of the ozone layer could be delayed to between 2060 and 2075—ten to twenty-five years later than previously thought—further contributed to a sense of urgency. Higher production of HCFC-22 than anticipated was among the factors responsible for the delay (WMO 2007).

The requested TEAP report, presented in August 2007, paved the way for an adjustment of HCFC controls under the Montreal Protocol. TEAP reported that an "accelerated HCFC phase-out had been demonstrated to be technically and economically feasible" (UNEP 2007, para. 72) and emphasized that the adverse impacts of HFC-23 abatement projects under the CDM on the ozone layer were a major rationale for tighter controls. The panel further pointed out that, under the current phase-out timetable, total emissions of ozone-depleting substances could reach an estimated 900 million tons of CO_2 equivalent per year from 2025 to 2040—thus highlighting the significant climate gains of an accelerated HCFC phase-out (TEAP 2007).

In addition to the TEAP inputs, several other factors facilitated the 2007 agreement on strengthened HCFC controls under the Montreal Protocol. A progressive stance taken by the United States, which cited the climate benefits of an accelerated phase-out as a major motivation, advanced the negotiations. Furthermore, agreement on providing financial assistance for the phase-out in developing countries was crucial for sealing the deal (Depledge 2007). The stalled negotiations on HFC-23 destruction projects under the CDM had a twofold positive effect. First, the diminished prospect of receiving credits under the CDM reduced the

Table 5.2
HCFC phase-out schedule under the Montreal Protocol

Industrialized countries		Developing countries	
Pre-2007	Post-2007	Pre-2007	Post-2007
Consumption:	Consumption:	Consumption:	Consumption:
1996: freeze	1996: freeze	2016: freeze	2013: freeze
2004: −35%	2004: −35%	2040: −100%	2015: −10%
2010: −65%	2010: −75%		2020: −35%
2015: −90%	2015: −90%		2025: −67.5%
2020: −99.5%	2020: −99.5%		2030: −97.5%
2030: −100%	2030: −100%		2040: −100%
Production:	Production:	Production:	Production:
2004: freeze	2004: freeze from 2010: as consumption	2016: freeze	As consumption
Baseline (consumption): 1989 HCFC consumption + 2.8% of 1989 CFC consumption.		**Baseline (consumption):** 2015	**Baseline:** Average of 2009 and 2010 consumption and production, respectively.
Baseline (production): Average of: (1) 1989 HCFC production + 2.8% 1989 CFC production; and (2) 1989 HCFC consumption + 2.8% of 1989 CFC consumption.		**Baseline (production):** Average of 2015 HCFC consumption and production.	

Sources: UNEP 2006; UNEP 2007, Decision XIX/6 and Annex III

temptation for countries with "new" HCFC-22 production plants to block progress under the Montreal Protocol so as to secure a future source of income. Second, progress under the Montreal Protocol reduced the policy contradiction with the Kyoto Protocol and thus had the potential to advance negotiations under the climate regime.

Table 5.2 provides an overview of HCFC controls before and after the 2007 adjustment. The most significant change with respect to industrialized countries was the alignment of controls of production with those of consumption. Developed countries thus relinquished the prospect of net exports to developing countries—not much of a sacrifice, given the growing production capacity in China and India in particular (whose competitiveness was further enhanced as a result of CDM HFC-23 destruction projects). More important, the overall phase-out in developing countries was effectively brought forward by ten years, to 2030, with significant intermediate control steps in 2013, 2015, 2020, and 2025. In addition, the baseline of controls was changed from 2015 to the average of 2009 and 2010. Remaining production and consumption allowances after 2020 for industrialized countries and after 2030 for developing countries apply to servicing existing equipment. The need for this "service tail" is to be reviewed in 2015 and 2025, respectively. Owing to the special "adjustment procedure" applicable to strengthening existing control measures under the Montreal Protocol, the 2007 agreement entered into force automatically, without any need for ratifications, in May 2008.

The accelerated phase-out of HCFC consumption and production promises moderate positive effects for the ozone layer and the global climate. Assuming full compliance, the accelerated phase-out could speed up the recovery of the ozone layer by a few years (WMO 2007; TEAP 2007, 106–108). As regards the climate benefits, the HCFC emissions avoided would amount to about 15,000 million tons of CO_2 equivalent until 2040, which is equivalent to about three times the current annual GHG emissions of the EU (own calculations based on TEAP 2007, esp. 7–9). The net climate effect is significantly reduced, however, because several of the most promising substitutes are also powerful GHGs—the most important being the HFCs controlled under the Kyoto Protocol (Velders et al. 2007, 2009; Norman, DeCanio, and Fan 2008). Nothing in the agreement reached under the Montreal Protocol restricts the use of these substitutes. However, a second positive effect is that reduced HCFC production in developing countries automatically leads to reduced HFC-23 emissions. Consequently, the potential for gaining CDM credits and thus the perverse incentive to continue or increase the production of HCFC-22 was effectively limited—without disappearing altogether.

Epilogue: Discussions on HFC Controls (since 2008)

HFC emissions came onto the agenda of the Montreal Protocol and, to a lesser extent, the UNFCCC in 2008 and 2009. After parties to the Montreal Protocol had agreed to hold a dialogue in 2008, Mauritius and the Federated States of Micronesia, as well as Canada, Mexico, and the United States, tabled concrete proposals in 2009 to regulate and phase down the production and consumption of HFCs by 85–90 percent within twenty to twenty-five years under the Montreal Protocol. Their proposals also covered a ban on HFC-23 emissions from HCFC-22 production plants not covered by the Kyoto Protocol's CDM, with funding for developing countries provided through the Montreal Protocol's Multilateral Fund. While authority for regulating HFCs legally rests with the climate regime, the Montreal Protocol's experience with the relevant industrial area and its existing institutional infrastructure, including the Multilateral Fund, speak in favor of making it the major forum for HFC controls. In the 2009 discussions under the UNFCCC on a post-2012 climate agreement, the EU thus tabled a proposal calling for the delegation of authority to regulate and phase down HFCs to the Montreal Protocol, which aimed to ease concerns about the competency of the ozone regime to address non-ozone-depleting substances (Depledge 2009).

Given the longstanding opposition of major stakeholders to specifically targeting HFCs under either regime, and in particular under the Montreal Protocol (see above), how can we explain the momentum toward regulating HFCs in the context of the Montreal Protocol at the end of the 2000s? Besides the more environmentally minded administration of U.S. president Obama, two interacting and interconnected factors can be identified. First, the chemical industries in developed countries had come to support, and push for, HFC controls because of the imminent expiry of their patents on HFC production processes and their advances in research on alternatives (which could again receive patent protection). The proposed HFC controls were thus in line with the traditionally strong industrial interests in the framework of the Montreal Protocol, raising concerns about the overall environmental integrity of the proposals (environmental impact of substitutes, continued production of HFCs) and their compatibility with the polluter-pays principle. Second, forecasts for future HFC production and consumption were revised upward, thus making clear the considerable need for HFC controls.[7] The "indirect" effects of HFC use on energy efficiency, previously highlighted to protect these gases from regulation (see above), now received less attention (Velders et al. 2009; Depledge 2009).

As of early 2010, no agreement on HFC controls had been achieved under either the Montreal Protocol or the UNFCCC. Legal complications due to the allocation of regulatory authority for HFC controls to the climate regime have hindered progress under the Montreal Protocol. However, developing countries have opposed the proposals under both regimes (including proposals under the UNFCCC addressing the legal issues) also because of substantive concerns regarding costs and the availability of substitutes (Depledge 2009). The proposals tabled under the Montreal Protocol in 2009 were reintroduced to the debate in spring 2010.

HFC-23 Destruction Projects under the CDM: Further Options

Among the various options that have been put forward in the climate regime as well as in the literature (see, e.g., summary in TEAP 2007, 55–57), we assess in this section the merits of three principal options that aim to counter the perverse incentive created by HFC-23 destruction projects under the CDM: (1) excluding these projects from the CDM, (2) reducing the amount of emission credits issued for such projects, and (3) taxing emission credits from such projects, either nationally or internationally.[8]

These options could in principle be applied to both "new" and "existing" HCFC-22 production facilities, but proposals to date have focused on the treatment of "new" facilities because changing the rules for "existing" facilities is unrealistic. Such a rule change would require the agreement of the beneficiaries of the current arrangements, which is highly unlikely, and could infringe on the property rights of those who have invested in existing CDM projects. Under the current rules, approved CDM projects gain crediting for ten years, or for seven years with the possibility of two renewals. Most HFC-23 destruction projects (with the exception of those in India) have chosen the second option (TEAP 2007, 53) and are thus up for renewal between 2012 and 2014. In the absence of other political guidance by the conference of the parties (which would again require the agreement of the beneficiaries of approved projects), there is little scope for denying them renewal. The possible resolution of the issue in the context of a broader climate agreement post-2012 remains hypothetical at the time of writing. While the options discussed are in principle also applicable to "existing" facilities, the discussion therefore is de facto primarily relevant for the question of how to treat "new facilities" for the benefit of the environment.

Excluding HFC-23 Destruction from the CDM

Excluding HFC-23 destruction projects from the CDM would remove the perverse incentive to increase HCFC-22 production inherent in such projects. Since CDM projects do not reduce global GHG emissions, the additionality of HFC-23 destruction projects is in doubt, and, as these projects hardly produce secondary benefits (see above), the overall environmental and climate balance of an exclusion may even be positive. As of 2010, the political stalemate in the related discussions under the Kyoto Protocol has rendered "new" HCFC-22 production facilities de facto ineligible under the CDM.

The related emissions could be addressed through means other than the CDM. If the costs of HFC-23 destruction, including the costs of installing and running the necessary equipment, were covered from other sources, this could lead to real reductions in global emissions. Several parties to the Kyoto Protocol—including Argentina, the EU, Mexico, Nicaragua, Panama, Switzerland, and the United States—have supported such an approach (UNFCCC 2005c). In Decision 8/CMP.1 (2005), the parties to the Kyoto Protocol encouraged industrialized countries and multilateral financial institutions to provide funding separately from the CDM (see above). The Global Environment Facility, which operates the financial mechanism of the climate regime, is an obvious candidate for providing multilateral funding (Schneider, Graichen, and Matz 2005). Recent proposals under the Montreal Protocol suggest its Multilateral Fund as a source of financing.

However, implementing this alternative approach faces several challenges in the current regulatory environment. Firstly, industrialized countries have shown reluctance to provide the additional funding required (Wartmann, Hofman, and de Jager 2006), so that no such funding has yet been forthcoming. Second, the prospect of HFC-23 destruction projects under the CDM has dissuaded plant operators and developing countries from accepting alternative sources of funding. Even with this prospect declining, plant operators and developing countries might require incentives beyond the coverage of incremental costs to engage in related projects. The rise of climate change on the international agenda may give reason for heightened expectations in this respect.

Restricting the Amount of Emission Credits from HFC-23 Projects

The effectiveness of restricting the issuance of emission credits from HFC-23 projects will depend on the specifics of the discount. If the discount is set too high, the incentive to engage in these projects may disappear; if it is set too low, the perverse incentive emanating from such projects may persist. The difficulty of determining a discount rate is aggravated by the uncertainty of future prices on the carbon market. Table 5.1 indicates that the discount would have to exceed 90 percent in order to reduce the perverse incentive significantly. Such a discount could also ensure that HFC-23 destruction projects would contribute to global GHG emission reductions, because a large part of the emission reductions achieved would not be offset in industrialized countries (Schneider 2007, 62).

The definition of ambitious technology benchmarks may be the most appropriate way of implementing this option. Other proposals include a flat-rate discount rate of, for example, 95 percent and the flexible adaptation of the amount of emission credits issued so as to generate an agreed fixed monetary income (TEAP 2007, 56). However, these proposals would appear to require major deviations from the current regulatory framework of the CDM. In contrast, Schneider's proposal (2007, 62) of defining ambitious technology benchmarks for HFC-23 destruction projects to calculate emission reductions could achieve a similar result, while being compatible with the existing regulatory framework.[9]

Irrespective of the specific approach, reaching agreement on this option may prove elusive. On the one hand, several parties have suggested a level that would cover only the costs of installing and operating an incinerator for the destruction of HFC-23 or a small addition to this level (see UNFCCC 2005c). On the other hand, China has resisted such restrictions and has itself introduced a moderate national levy of 65 percent on the revenues from emission credits from HFC-23 destruction projects (Schneider 2007, 48; see also below). The task of reconciling differing positions is aggravated by fluctuations on the carbon market: Since 2005, prices for CERs on the European market have varied roughly between 10 and 30 euros (http://www.ecx.eu/ECX-Monthly-Report).

Taxing Emission Credits

The major difference between taxing emission credits and discounting emission reductions is that taxing generates revenues for the tax authorities, whereas discounting creates a benefit for climate protection. In both schemes, the perverse incentive for plant operators is addressed by reducing the gains to the operator. To make the taxing scheme also contribute to climate protection, the tax revenues could be allocated to activities that create further climate benefits, whether with respect to mitigation or adaptation (TEAP 2007, 56–57).

As noted above, China has introduced a levy of 65 percent on the revenue generated by emission credits from HFC-23 destruction projects. The revenue gained is to support domestic climate-change-related activities in China (Schneider 2007, 48; TEAP 2007, 59). However, this national scheme, although covering the lion's share of HCFC-22 production in developing countries, is at best an imperfect response to the underlying problem. In line with the above analysis, the tax level is insufficient to counter the perverse incentive. In addition, national tax schemes shift the perverse incentive from the plant operator to the government—a situation that might lead a government to encourage production of HCFC-22 (Wartmann, Hofman, and de Jager 2006).

Devising a more appropriate internationally coordinated taxation scheme faces major political hurdles. As in the case of restrictions on the issuance of emission credits, parties are likely to have varying views on the level of such a tax that would need to be agreed upon internationally (see above). Agreement would also be required on who would collect the tax, and for what purposes the income generated should be spent. National tax schemes may simply shift the perverse incentive from the plant operator to the government. They would also require agreement on the use of the tax revenues in order to exclude uses that defeat the purpose of the tax. Such agreement would also be needed in the case of an international scheme run by an international institution. In one variant, emission credits would be allocated to an international institution such as the Global Environment Facility, which could then reimburse plant operators, either at a fixed rate or with a predetermined share of the emission credits (UNFCCC 2005c).[10] As in the case of a discount, achieving agreement on such complicated matters may well prove elusive.

Concluding Assessment

The international ozone and climate regimes have a history of problematic interaction with respect to fluorinated GHGs. On the one hand, the Montreal Protocol has explicitly and implicitly promoted the use of fluorinated GHGs (HCFCs and HFCs) as substitutes for ozone-depleting substances. This has created space for increased production and consumption of these gases, and hampered efforts to limit and reduce their emissions—as well as enhancing the viability of projects under the Kyoto Protocol's CDM for the destruction of HFC-23 in HCFC-22 production plants. These CDM projects, on the other hand, have the potential to inflate HCFC-22 production artificially, thus harming efforts to protect the ozone layer.

Both regimes have primarily managed these policy contradictions unilaterally. Cooperation between the regimes has addressed scientific and technical assessments and the exchange of information, which have provided an important but not an essential input to decision making. Parties to the Montreal Protocol have long been aware at the declaratory level that fluorinated GHGs are negatively implicated under the climate regime. However, concrete regulatory activity to deal with the issue intensified only after 2005. HCFC controls under the Montreal Protocol were strengthened in 2007, also to address the perverse incentive created by HFC-23 destruction projects under the CDM. Proposals for regulating HFCs under the Montreal Protocol have been discussed since 2009. Parties to the Kyoto Protocol, on their side, have so far excluded HCFC-22 production facilities established after 2002 from the CDM. Significantly, interplay management in both regimes has been considerably motivated by consideration of the objectives of the other regime, but justified by reference to their own objectives. In this respect, the HFC controls proposed under the Montreal Protocol would, if adopted, constitute an innovation.

The unilateral interplay management has so far delivered mixed environmental results. On the side of the climate regime, existing CDM projects for HFC-23 destruction have provided a significant subsidy for the production of an ozone-depleting substance (HCFC-22), and could continue to do so until 2026–2028, but parties to the Kyoto Protocol have significantly limited the damage by not extending the subsidy to new production facilities. On the other side, the Montreal Protocol's strengthened HCFC controls make a meaningful, if modest, contribution to both the protection of the ozone layer and the global climate, with the exact net effect on climate change depending on individual actors' choice of substitutes for HCFCs. Proposed HFC controls under discussion at the time of writing could contribute significantly to combating climate change and enhancing policy consistency between both regimes.

Several factors provide reason to expect that further negative effects can be prevented. The issue of CDM projects for HFC-23 destruction in "new" production plants has been moved to the political level, so a change of the status quo will require consensus by all parties to the Kyoto Protocol. Since extending eligibility to new facilities would not only endanger the protection of the ozone layer but could also have considerable negative climate-related effects, interested parties to the Kyoto Protocol have sound reasons to resist related demands. Furthermore, the strengthening of HCFC controls under the Montreal Protocol limits the potential of HFC-23 destruction projects in new facilities, thereby reducing the overall importance of the issue.

Two particularly promising options for further dealing with HFC-23 emissions of HCFC-22 production plants would have synergistic effects for the protection of both the ozone layer and the global climate. First, a strict benchmarking resulting in a large discounting of achieved emission reductions could help address concerns about the additionality of projects and their potentially negative consequences. However, political agreement on an environmentally beneficial technology benchmark or discount rate may be difficult to achieve, judging from the current stalemate in the climate regime. Second, and perhaps more important, ongoing negotiations on HFC controls under the Montreal Protocol and on a global post-2012 agreement on climate change may provide sufficient financial and political incentives to developing countries with new HCFC production facilities to implement HFC-23 destruction.

The story of HFC-23 destruction projects under the CDM illustrates the potential for unintended effects and unanticipated institutional interaction that can result from the introduction of policy innovations in general and the establishment of market mechanisms and the accompanying privatization of global governance in particular. When the CDM was established, negotiators were guided by the principal rationale of this instrument: to unleash the power of the market in order to identify the best way of mitigating GHG emissions. They did not take into account the side effects of employing the power of the market and directly involving private actors: First, market participants aim at maximizing economic benefits (rather than reducing emissions) and will exploit opportunities for reaping excessive profits from investments in emission reductions, even in the face of negative externalities on other issue-areas. Second, the direct involvement and central role of private actors in the CDM further restricts the potential for changing the status quo and strengthening the existing regulatory framework. Politically, private investors, who demand a stable policy framework, acquire leverage in the policy process because the effectiveness of the CDM hinges on their acceptance and investment. Legally, their direct involvement gives them the option, and a strong motivation, to pursue their interests and newly acquired "rights" by legal means, including by bringing cases to national courts (Gehring and Plocher 2009). The privatization of global governance thus brings its own path dependency, with corrective action becoming more difficult, once the benefits have been privately appropriated.

Would institutional aggregation under an overarching framework deliver better results? That seems questionable. Integration of the ozone and climate regimes might overburden the climate agenda and distract the climate regime from its central task: steering the transition of national and international energy systems. Further, it might lead to a dominance of climate change considerations, with lack of attention to the protection of the ozone layer and the implicated fluorinated gases. Arguably, progress on fluorinated GHGs has been facilitated by their having a separate regulatory "home." It is difficult to imagine how the 2007 agreement on strengthening HCFC controls under the Montreal Protocol could have come about in an integrated regime. In this case, the politics of climate change (without the progressive decision-making rules of the Montreal Protocol) might easily have poisoned the negotiations and blocked clear U.S. support (by the administration of President George W. Bush, which otherwise largely dismissed international climate regulation).

However, delimitation of regulatory authority of overlapping institutions is not necessarily enough. Both the international ozone and climate regimes are legally clearly delimited because the UNFCCC and the Kyoto Protocol exclude from their scope gases controlled by the Montreal Protocol. However, this delimitation of regulatory authority has not prevented the aforementioned problematic interactions because it did not "fit" the underlying functional interlinkages between both regimes (on the concept of "fit," see Young 2002; Galaz et al. 2008). It defines the regulatory boundaries and thus tells the members of each regime to keep their hands off what is under the authority of another regime (negative coordination). This has facilitated the attempts of interested parties in fending off moves to establish controls to minimize use and emission of fluorinated GHGs.

While a more integrated approach might facilitate the development of mutually supportive policies in both regimes that prioritize climate- and ozone-friendly alternatives to fluorinated GHG, a slight readjustment of the division of labor and regulatory authority may be an even more promising route for further progress: delegating decision-making authority on phasing down, or out, HFCs to the Montreal Protocol.

Acknowledgments

Support from the following projects is gratefully acknowledged: (1) Interdisciplinary Study on Policy Interlinkages between Global Warming and Ozone Depletion Issues (Japan, FY2008 Grant-in-Aid for Scientific Research, Basic Research (B): 20310025); (2) Environmental Policy Integration and Multi-Level Governance (EPIGOV), which was funded under the European Community's 6th Research Framework Programme (contract no. 028661). We would also like to thank Ms. Mari Nishiki, Mr. Hiroaki Sakamoto, and Ms. Melanie Jung for their valuable assistance.

Notes

1. The 2007 assessment of the Intergovernmental Panel on Climate Change (IPCC) suggests that HFC-23 may actually have a global warming potential of 14,800 over a 100-year period (IPCC 2007). However, the global warming potential of 11,700 has been fixed as a basis of calculations under the Kyoto Protocol for the first commitment period 2008–2012.

2. See monthly price reports of European Climate Exchange, available at http://www.ecx.eu/ECX-Monthly-Report.

3. See http://cdm.unfccc.int/index.html for latest data on the CDM, including registered projects and expected issuance of CERs (accessed 3 May 2010). For historical and current CER prices on the European market, see monthly price reports of European Climate Exchange available at http://www.ecx.eu/ECX-Monthly-Report (accessed 3 May 2010).

4. All decisions of the Meeting of the Parties to the Montreal Protocol referred to in the following are available at http://ozone.unep.org/Meeting_Documents/mop/index.shtml.

5. All decisions of the Conference of the Parties to the UNFCCC (COP) and the Conference of the Parties serving as the Meeting of the Parties to the Kyoto Protocol (COP/MOP) referred to in the following can be accessed via http://unfccc.int/documentation/decisions/items/3597.php.

6. Gehring and Plocher 2009 and reports of the 10th, 15th, and 17th meetings of the CDM Executive Board, available at http://cdm.unfccc.int/EB/index.html (accessed May 2010).

7. These upward revisions were in line with projections made earlier by environmental nongovernmental organizations and others. They were also supported by scientists of major chemical companies in developed countries (see Velders et al. 2009).

8. Members of the climate regime identified the crediting of emission reductions for project activities that substitute the production or consumption of HCFC-22 under the CDM as an option in 2006 (e.g., TEAP 2007, 56; UNFCCC 2005c). However, this option would have faced severe legal problems, since the climate regime does not cover GHGs controlled by the Montreal Protocol. Consequently, this option has not been pursued further, and it is not included in the analysis here.

9. A further proposal concerns restricting CDM eligibility to HCFC production for feedstock uses (TEAP 2007, 57). While this would exclude HCFC production for immediate use and thus address concerns regarding increased HCFC emissions, it would not deal with the perverse incentive to increase HCFC production for feedstock uses in order to gain cheap emission credits.

10. If the surplus emission credits collected internationally were to be canceled, as some have suggested (*Earth Negotiations Bulletin* 12, no. 313, 2006; available at http://www.iisd.ca/vol12/), this solution would be equivalent to the option of restricting the issuance of emission credits discussed before.

References

Andersen, Stephen O., and K. Madhava Sarma. 2002. *Protecting the Ozone Layer: The United Nations History*. London: Earthscan.

Anderson, Jason. 2001. Keeping Cool without Warming the Planet: Cutting HFCs, PFCs, and SF_6 in Europe. Climate Network Europe. http://www.bdix .net/sdnbd_org/world_env_day/2001/sdnpweb/sdi/issues/climate_change/articles/ keeping%20cool%20without%20warming%20the%20planet-eu.htm (accessed 7 May 2010).

Benedick, Richard Elliot. 1998. *Ozone Diplomacy: New Directions in Safeguarding the Planet*, 2nd ed. Cambridge, Mass.: Harvard University Press.

Cames, Martin, Neils Anger, Christoph Böringer, Ralph O. Harthon, and Lambert Schneider. 2007. *Long-Term Prospects of CDM and JI*. Dessau: Umweltbundesamt.

Depledge, Joanna. 2007. Adjustments: A Double Hit for Ozone and Climate. *Environmental Policy and Law* 37 (6): 448–452.

Depledge, Joanna. 2009. Montreal Protocol/MOP-21: The "Climate MOP." *Environmental Policy and Law* 39 (6): 274–277.

Galaz, Victor, Per Olsson, Thomas Hahn, Carl Folke, and Uno Svedin. 2008. The Problem of Fit among Biophysical Systems, Environmental and Resource Regimes, and Broader Governance Systems: Insights and Emerging Challenges. In *Institutions and Environmental Change: Principal Findings, Applications, and Research Frontiers*, ed. Oran R. Young, Leslie A. King, and Heike Schroeder, 147–186. Cambridge, Mass.: MIT Press.

Gehring, Thomas, and Isabel Plocher. 2009. Making an Administrative Trustee Agent Accountable: Reason-Based Decision-Making within the Kyoto Protocol's Clean Development Mechanism. *International Studies Quarterly* 53 (3): 669–693.

IPCC. 2007. *Climate Change 2007: Synthesis Report*. Contribution of Working Groups *I, II and III to the Fourth Assessment Report of the Intergovernmental Panel on Climate Change*. Geneva: Intergovernmental Panel on Climate Change.

IPCC/TEAP. 1999. *Report of the Joint IPCC/TEAP Expert Meeting on Options for the Limitation of Emissions of HFCs and PFCs*. Petten: World Meteorological Association/United Nations Environment Programme.

IPCC/TEAP. 2005. *Safeguarding the Ozone Layer and the Global Climate System: Issues Related to Hydrofluorocarbons and Perfluorocarbons. Intergovernmental Panel on Climate Change/Technology and Economic Assessment Panel Special Report*. Cambridge: Cambridge University Press.

Matsumoto, Yasuko. 2008. Chikyukankyou Regime kan no Seisaku-mujun to Inga Mechanism: HFC-23 Hakai CDM Jigyou no Jirei [Addressing Policy Inconsistencies between the Climate and Ozone Regimes: The Clean Development Mechanism and the Destruction of HFC-23]. [Review of Environmental Economics and Policy Studies] *Kankyou Keizai, Seisaku Kenkyuu* 1 (1): 54–64.

McCulloch, Archie. 2004. Incineration of HFC-23 Waste Streams for Abatement of Emissions from HCFC-22 Production: A Review of Scientific, Technical and Economic Aspects. Internal background paper prepared for the UNFCCC. http://cdm.unfccc.int/methodologies/Background_240305.pdf (accessed 7 May 2010).

McCulloch, Archie, and A. A. Lindley. 2007. Global Emissions of HFC-23 Estimated to Year 2015. *Atmospheric Environment* 41 (7): 1560–1566.

Norman, Catherine S., Stephen J. DeCanio, and Lin Fan. 2008. The Montreal Protocol at 20: Ongoing Opportunities for Integration with Climate Protection. *Global Environmental Change* 18 (2): 330–340.

Oberthür, Sebastian. 2000. Ozone Layer Protection at the Turn of the Century: The Eleventh Meeting of the Parties to the Montreal Protocol. *Environmental Policy and Law* 30:34–41.

Oberthür, Sebastian. 2001. Linkages between the Montreal and Kyoto Protocols: Enhancing Synergies between Protecting the Ozone Layer and the Global Climate. *International Environmental Agreements: Politics, Law and Economics* 1 (3): 357–377.

Oberthür, Sebastian. 2006. The Climate Change Regime: Interactions with ICAO, IMO, and the EU Burden-Sharing Agreement. In *Institutional Interaction in Global Environmental Governance: Synergy and Conflict among International and EU Policies*, ed. Sebastian Oberthür and Thomas Gehring, 53–78. Cambridge, Mass.: MIT Press.

Oberthür, Sebastian, and Thomas Gehring. 2006. Conceptual Foundations of Institutional Interaction. In *Institutional Interaction in Global Environmental Governance: Synergy and Conflict among International and EU Policies*, ed. Sebastian Oberthür and Thomas Gehring, 19–51. Cambridge, Mass.: MIT Press.

Oberthür, Sebastian, and Hermann E. Ott. 1999. *The Kyoto Protocol: International Climate Policy for the 21st Century*. Berlin: Springer-Verlag.

Parson, Edward A. 1993. Protecting the Ozone Layer. In *Institutions for the Earth: Sources of Effective International Environmental Protection*, ed. Peter M. Haas, Robert O. Keohane, and Marc A. Levy, 27–73. Cambridge: Cambridge University Press.

Parson, Edward A. 2003. *Protecting the Ozone Layer: Science and Strategy*. Oxford: Oxford University Press.

Schneider, Lambert. 2007. *Is the CDM Fulfilling Its Environmental and Sustainable Development Objectives? An Evaluation of the CDM and Options for Improvement. Report Prepared for WWF*. Berlin: Öko-Institut e.V. http://www.oeko.de/publications/dok/616.php (accessed 7 May 2010).

Schneider, Lambert, Jakob Graichen, and Nele Matz. 2005. Implications of the CDM on Other Conventions: The Case of HFC-23 Destruction. *Environmental Law Network International Review* 1:41–52.

Streck, Charlotte. 2007. The Governance of the Clean Development Mechanism: The Case for Strength and Stability. *Environmental Liability* 15 (2): 91–100.

TEAP. 1999. *The Implications to the Montreal Protocol of the Inclusion of HFCs and PFCs in the Kyoto Protocol.* October 1999. Nairobi: United Nations Environment Programme, Technology and Economic Assessment Panel.

TEAP. 2005. *Supplement to the IPCC/TEAP Report.* Nairobi: United Nations Environment Programme, Technology and Assessment Panel.

TEAP. 2007. *Response to Decision XVIII/12. Report of the Task Force on HCFC Issues (with particular focus on the impact of the Clean Development Mechanism) and Emission Reduction Benefits Arising from Earlier HCFC Phase-Out and Other Practical Measures.* Nairobi: United Nations Environment Programme, Technology and Assessment Panel.

Thoms, Laura. 2003. A Comparative Analysis of International Regimes on Ozone and Climate Change with Implications for Regime Design. *Columbia Journal of Transnational Law* 41 (3): 795–859.

UNEP. 1989. *Report of the First Meeting of the Parties to the Montreal Protocol on Substances That Deplete the Ozone Layer (Helsinki, 2–5 May 1989).* United Nations Environment Programme. Doc. UNEP/OzL.Pro.1/5.

UNEP. 2001. *Report of the Thirteenth Meeting of the Parties to the Montreal Protocol on Substances That Deplete the Ozone Layer (Colombo, 16–19 October 2001),* United Nations Environment Programme. Doc. UNEP/OzL.Pro.13/10

UNEP. 2005. *Report of the Twenty-fifth Meeting of the Open-ended Working Group of the Parties to the Montreal Protocol (Montreal, 27–30 June 2005).* United Nations Environment Programme. Doc. UNEP/OzL.Pro.WG.1/25/9.

UNEP. 2006. *Handbook for the Montreal Protocol on Substances That Deplete the Ozone Layer,* 7th ed. Nairobi: Ozone Secretariat, United Nations Environment Programme. http://ozone.unep.org/Publications/MP_Handbook/index .shtml (accessed 7 May 2010).

UNEP. 2007. *Report of the Nineteenth Meeting of the Parties to the Montreal Protocol on Substances That Deplete the Ozone Layer (Montreal, 17–21 September 2007).* United Nations Environment Programme. Doc. UNEP/OzL. Pro.19/7.

UNFCCC. 2005a. *Issues Arising from the Implementation of Potential Project Activities under the Clean Development Mechanism: The Case of Incineration of HFC-23 Waste Streams from HCFC-22 Production.* Technical Paper. United Nations Framework Convention on Climate Change. Doc. FCCC/TP/2005/1.

UNFCCC. 2005b. *Report of the Subsidiary Body for Scientific and Technological Advice on Its Twenty-second Session (Bonn, 19–27 May 2005).* United Nations Framework Convention on Climate Change. Doc. FCCC/SBSTA/2005/4.

UNFCCC. 2005c. *Implications of the Establishment of New Hydrochlorofluorocarbon-22 (HCFC-22) Facilities Seeking to Obtain Certified Emissions Reductions for the Destruction of Hydrofluorocarbon-23 (HFC-23): Submissions from Parties.* United Nations Framework Convention on Climate Change. Doc. FCCC/ SBSTA/2005/MISC.10.

UNFCCC. 2006. *Report of the Subsidiary Body for Scientific and Technological Advice on Its Twenty-fourth Session, held at Bonn from 18 to 26 May 2006.*

United Nations Framework Convention on Climate Change. Doc. FCCC/SBSTA/2006/5.

Velders, Guus J. M., Stephen O. Andersen, John S. Daniel, David W. Fahey, and Mack McFarland. 2007. The Importance of the Montreal Protocol in Protecting Climate. *Proceedings of the National Academy of Sciences of the United States of America* 104 (12): 4814–4819.

Velders, Guus J. M., David W. Fahey, John S. Daniel, Mack McFarland, and Stephen O. Andersen. 2009. The Large Contribution of Projected HFC Emissions to Future Climate Forcing. *Proceedings of the National Academy of Sciences of the United States of America* 106 (27): 10949–10954.

Wara, Michael W. 2007. Is the Global Carbon Market Working? *Nature* 445:595–596.

Wara, Michael W. 2008. Measuring the Clean Development Mechanism's Performance and Potential. *UCLA Law Review 55* (6): 1759–1803.

Wara, Michael W., and David G. Victor. 2008. A Realistic Policy on International Carbon Offsets. Program on Energy and Sustainable Development Working Paper 74 (April). Stanford University, Palo Alto, Calif.

Wartmann, Sina, Yvonne Hofman, and David de Jager. 2006. *Instrumentations of HFC-23 Emission Reduction from the Production of HCFC-22: Assessment of Options for New Installations. Final Report.* Nürnberg: Ecofys.

Wettestad, Jørgen. 2002. The Vienna Convention and Montreal Protocol on Ozone-Layer Depletion. In *Environmental Regime Effectiveness: Confronting Theory with Evidence*, ed. Edward L. Miles, Arild Underdal, Steinar Andresen, Jørgen Wettestad, Jon Birger Skjærseth, and Elaine M. Carlin, 149–170. Cambridge: Cambridge University Press.

Wilkins, Hugh. 2002. What's New with CDM? *Review of European Community & International Environmental Law* 11 (2): 144–158.

WMO. 2007. *Scientific Assessment of Ozone Depletion: 2006.* Global Ozone Research and Monitoring Project, Report No. 50. Geneva: World Meteorological Association.

Yamin, Farhana, and Joanna Depledge. 2004. *The International Climate Change Regime: A Guide to Rules, Institutions and Procedures.* Cambridge: Cambridge University Press.

Young, Oran R. 2002. *The Institutional Dimensions of Environmental Change: Fit, Interplay, and Scale.* Cambridge, Mass.: MIT Press.

6

Interplay Management, Niche Selection, and Arctic Environmental Governance

Olav Schram Stokke

This chapter develops and applies a framework for analyzing strategic interplay management decisions on specialization and division of labor within larger institutional complexes. The framework identifies several institutional niches, or governance tasks, that an institution may focus on within the broader set of efforts to solve a particular environmental problem. Such strategic decisions are highly topical in Arctic environmental governance, which revolves around the relationship between global institutions like those based on the UN Convention on the Law of the Sea (UNCLOS) and several regional institutions concerning the Arctic in particular. The larger question of achieving cross-institutional interplay that can promote effectiveness is relevant in any region or issue area because efforts to solve specific problems usually involve more than one institution.

The next section links the notion of institutional niches to certain general tasks of governance: building knowledge, creating norms, enhancing capacity, and enforcing compliance. Findings from regime effectiveness research can help identify conditions for effective niche selection—that is, one generating interplay with other institutions that assists in mitigating or solving the problem at hand. Two questions guide this analysis. In the larger complex, which governance tasks are in particular need of strengthening? And does the focal institution have distinctive features that equip it to provide such strengthening? The next section elaborates on the niche approach by extracting, from four cases of Arctic environmental governance, some general lessons on institutional requirements for occupying each of the governance niches effectively. The concluding section summarizes the findings and draws some implications for interplay management in institutional complexes.

Niche Selection and Interplay: Aiming for Effectiveness

The human activities an international institution seeks to influence are often subject to rules or programs under several institutions operating at different levels of governance or focusing on different areas of activity, or aspects of the same activity. That macrofact, which Stokke and Oberthür in this volume term an "institutional complex," poses a micro-question for participants in each institution: How can they maximize its contribution to the overall system of governance with the aim of mitigating or solving a problem of environmental management?

Selection of Governance Niches

Institutional interplay means that one institution affects the contents, operations, or consequences of another; interplay management involves efforts to impede, trigger, or shape such impact.[1] Niche selection concerns a strategic aspect of interplay management: the governance tasks that those operating an international institution decide to focus on and where they challenge other institutions. In ecology, a "niche" denotes the position of a species or population in an ecosystem, notably that segment of a resource domain where it outcompetes other local populations. Used as a metaphor in organizational analysis, the niche concept highlights the relationship between institutional features and the ability to extract the resources necessary for organizational survival (Hannan and Freeman 1977; Aldrich 1999, 226).

In the environmental area, we may distinguish among four governance tasks, each defining a particular institutional niche. First, environmental governance requires knowledge about the severity of the problem and, preferably, of the effects of various options for dealing with it. A second governance task is elaboration of behavioral norms, whether soft-law instruments or binding rules. Third, multilateral institutions frequently seek to facilitate implementation of such norms in cases where some participants would otherwise be unable to heed them, for instance through funding or specific capacity-building programs. The fourth task, rule enforcement, is often a weak point in international environmental governance, since structures for behavioral monitoring, compliance review, and administration of sanction in cases of rule violation are often feeble or nonexistent.

Within an issue area, some institutions may attend to the full range of governance tasks, while others specialize in one or a few of them. For instance, regarding the management of cod in the Barents Sea, the

Norwegian-Russian Joint Fisheries Commission has carved out a broad niche aiming to engage in all four governance tasks, but it leans heavily on other institutions for two of them. In this particular complex, the International Council for the Exploration of the Sea (ICES) occupies a knowledge-building niche in the governance of these and other fisheries; and, as I show below, the North-East Atlantic Fisheries Commission (NEAFC) has become increasingly important in rule enforcement.

According to the principle of competitive exclusion, no two species can occupy the same niche for a long time: competition between species or populations will force the weaker party either to adapt by carving out another niche or to abandon the ecosystem. However, to assume that this competitive exclusion principle operates as powerfully in the realm of social institutions as in natural ecosystems would be ill-advised, for several reasons (Aldrich 1999, 301–306). As the fisheries example shows, cogovernance by several institutions can be mutually supportive: each institution may bring distinct capacities to bear on the overall problem-solving effort, enabling more forceful conduct of the governance task in question. Even when the institutions pull in different directions—as the World Trade Organization and some multilateral environmental regimes do on trade-related enforcement of environmental rules—tense coexistence is more common than one institution driving the other completely out of a governance niche (Gehring in this volume). Thus, each institution may opt for more than one niche, and each governance niche potentially leaves room for more than one institution.

In a dynamic institutional environment, consideration of whether an institution is better equipped than others to deal with one or more governance tasks should be an ongoing activity. The remainder of this section explores some findings from regime effectiveness research that can support the analysis of niche selection within institutional complexes.

International Regimes and Supportive Interplay

Key concepts in the study of regime effectiveness are useful when examining interplay management because, like effectiveness, institutional interplay involves a causal impact. In focus here are three general mechanisms that may help to explain institutional impact on problem solving and the conditions determining whether or not such impact is supportive. These mechanisms are cognition, obligation, and utility maximization.

An international institution is effective if it contributes significantly to solving the problem that gave rise to its creation, whether that relates to the state of the marine environment, the health of fish stocks, or some other challenge (Levy, Young, and Zürn 1995). To examine such institutional impact on problem solving, several large-scale transnational research projects over the past twenty years have devised intensive, loosely comparative case studies centering on certain causal mechanisms (Haas, Keohane, and Levy 1993; Stokke and Vidas 1996; Young 1999). Causal mechanisms are real-world processes that may, under certain conditions, connect *explanans* (the institution) and *explanandum* (behavior relevant to problem solving). The process that a causal mechanism spells out is simpler, more readily understandable, and closer to description than the causal connection that it supports. As Bunge (1997, 461) argues, mechanism hypotheses "burrow into the details of the composition or inner workings of the system they refer to." Identifying a causal mechanism is an inherent part of explanation and therefore necessary when examining institutional interplay.

Three general mechanisms capture most of the specific versions employed by regime effectiveness scholars (Stokke 2001a). One highlights cognition: regimes may affect behavior by influencing actor awareness about certain problems or the pros and cons of various mitigation options. A second general mechanism concerns obligation or normative pull: regimes may affect perceptions about what is right and proper conduct within an issue area by making certain norms more compelling. In the terminology that March and Olsen (1989, 21–26) elaborate, such compellingness concerns the "logic of appropriateness." A third general causal mechanism invokes their "logic of consequentiality" and pinpoints how regimes may affect behavior by altering the utility that actors assign to behavioral options within an issue area, for instance by providing incentives for rule adherence or adding costs to noncompliance.

This trichotomy of causal mechanisms is simple, but the cognitional and normative categories sensitize the analysis to causal processes frequently absent from studies of international relations, which tend to highlight incentives and material interest. Using the trichotomy to distinguish among types of interplay ensures the same substantive scope. Thus, cognitional interplay occurs whenever an institution influences how actors operating another institution define a problem, including their assessment of the risk it poses relative to other challenges and the options available for mitigating or solving the problem. Normative interplay denotes one institution reinforcing the compellingness of norms upheld by another. And finally, utilitarian interplay involves cases where rules or programs under one institution alter the costs or benefits of the activity dealt with by another institution. These distinctions are helpful when examining whether institutional niche selection is effective in the sense of triggering interplay with other institutions that supports problem solving within a larger complex.

Conditions for Effective Niche Selection

As seen by those operating an institution, institutional interplay can be disruptive, neutral, or supportive with respect to solving their problems. The regime literature in general has been criticized for giving an overly rosy picture of world affairs, with insufficient attention to turf struggles and conflicting interests (Strange 1982), but early studies of institutional interplay often highlighted disruption (Stokke 2001a). Typical points of departure were instances of normative discord, duplication of work, or institutional competition; hence the frequent appearance in the literature of negatively charged terms like "treaty congestion" and problems associated with increased "regime density" (Weiss 1993; Andresen 2001). Such negative framing may be due to a few high-visibility cases of inter-regime tension along the trade-environment border (see the review by Gehring in this volume). In contrast, an important finding in recent empirical studies of regime effectiveness is that cross-regime inefficiency and discord do not predominate in international environmental governance; instances of supportive or neutral interplay are also frequent (Stokke 2001b; Oberthür and Gehring 2006; Stokke and Hønneland 2007). One way to identify conditions for effective niche selection is to explore the factors capable of triggering, through one causal mechanism or another, supportive impact on each governance task, and then to examine whether the institution in question is especially well placed to influence those factors accordingly.

Knowledge Building Most international environmental institutions include, or link up to, a scientific body responsible for evaluating various kinds of data that inform risk and option assessment. Regime effectiveness research has indicated at least three factors that influence the problem-solving potential of such knowledge building: credibility, legitimacy, and saliency (Mitchell, Clark, and Cash 2006, 314–324). The first factor, credibility, highlights the cognitional mechanism and denotes a perception among decision makers that scientific input reflects the best available knowledge, in terms of expert consensus and certainty, concerning the problem in question (Haas 1989; Andresen et al. 2000). Knowledge building within or across international institutions may enhance credibility by diffusing research findings, thereby leveling the factual ground for assessment of risks and options. Legitimacy in this context refers to perceptions among users that scientific input reflects serious consideration of their concerns, values, and data provision (Mitchell, Clark, and Cash 2006, 320). Broad involvement in the process of developing input is one important way to support such a perception, which may prove decisive for generating normative commitment to the measures that scientists advise (Stokke and Vidas 1996). The third factor of interest here, saliency, concerns the extent to which scientific input is directly relevant to users by responding to urgent policy concerns or clarifying the costs and benefits of policy options available to them (Mitchell, Clark, and Cash 2006, 314–317; see also Underdal 1989, 264–265). Accordingly, opting for a knowledge-building niche is likely to prove effective if the institution is better equipped than others in the relevant institutional complex to enhance the credibility, the legitimacy, or the saliency of scientific input to decision making on an environmental problem.

Norm Building   Elaboration and adoption of behavioral norms under international institutions is typically a task for political regime bodies made up of representatives of member states. Three aspects of those norms deserve particular attention when examining their potential to advance problem solving: applicability, coverage, and substantive strength. The first of those factors, applicability, builds on Franck's (1990) extraction from the legal literature on international legitimacy certain "building blocks of due process": internal determinacy and external coherence with other norms acknowledged by the international community (Stokke and Vidas 1996). Determinacy enhances a norm's compellingness by communicating clearly what is expected of those addressed by the rule: a vague or nonbinding norm fails to direct behavior unequivocally and may indicate disagreement among those who created it, which may in turn be taken to justify nonadherence (Franck 1990). Coherence is evident when the UN Framework Convention on Climate Change (UNFCCC) reminds states that measures under that treaty "should not constitute a means of arbitrary or unjustifiable discrimination or a disguised restriction on international trade" (Article 3.5). This formulation is taken verbatim from the environmental provision of the General Agreement on Tariffs and Trade (GATT) and thus reinforces the applicability of liberal trade norms also where they might collide with environmental purposes (Stokke 2004). The second factor influencing an institution's potential to effectively occupy the norm-building niche is coverage, that is, whether it involves those states whose participation is the most important for solving the problem at hand (Barrett 2003, 356). Inadequate coverage is frequently a severe constraint in environmental governance, as illustrated by the nonparticipation of the United States in the climate Kyoto Protocol, or the many flag-of-convenience states that fail to join regional institutions for high-seas fisheries management. As Downs and associates (1996) point out, international institutions seeking to maximize coverage sometimes cede on the third aspect, thereby weakening the contribution that norm building can make to problem solving: substantive strength. If states seek to attract broader coverage by lowering the standard, the net effect on environmental problem solving will be uncertain (Barrett 2003, 356). Other things being equal, therefore, selecting a norm-building niche will tend to be effective if the institution is better equipped than others to raise the applicability, coverage, or substantive strength of normative commitments.

Capacity Building   A prominent feature of international environmental governance today is the acknowledgment that effective implementation may require the transfer of technology or other resources to states otherwise unable to comply with international commitments. As with knowledge building and norm building, the three effectiveness mechanisms help to identify certain factors that affect the problem-solving potential of such capacity building: models, commitment, and funds. The existence among regime members of models of implementation, including conducive technologies, that other states may learn from and adaptively apply is a basic requirement for occupying this particular governance niche. A second factor is normative commitment to provide such assistance, as found for instance under the Montreal Protocol on Ozone (Articles 5 and 10) and the UNFCCC (Article 4.1). Since the essence of capacity enhancement is resource transfer, a third factor is perhaps the most important requirement: willingness among some regime members to fund environmental projects in other states. To illustrate, a regional institution for Arctic military environmental cooperation raised the funds necessary to upgrade Russian treatment and storage facilities for liquid low-level radioactive waste in naval bases close to Norway (Stokke 1998). This project helped pave the way for Russia's joining the total ban on nuclear dumping under the London Convention 1996. In Barrett's (2003, 355) terms, the regional institution helped restructure

Russia's incentives to participate in and comply with the nuclear dumping ban, thus improving the effectiveness of the London Convention. Selecting a capacity-building niche is likely to prove effective, therefore, if the institution is better placed than others to provide model cases of how to go about solving the problem, to obtain commitments among leader states to contribute to practical problem solving beyond their own borders, or to raise the necessary funding for such projects.

Rule Enforcement   While capacity building supports problem solving by removing impediments to norm adherence, rule enforcement aims to deter noncompliance by adding costs—in practice, by raising the risk of exposure and sanctions. Key requirements for achieving such deterrence, and thus for occupying the rule-enforcement niche effectively, are capacities for verification, review, and punishment (Hovi, Stokke, and Ulfstein 2005, 2). Verification entails an assessment of the completeness and accuracy of compliance-related information and its conformity with pre-established standards for reporting. Such assessment is easier to achieve for institutions that have access to other sources of information besides the parties' own reports. The second factor is competence to review such factual information against a state's commitments and pass a compliance judgment. Under the climate regime, for instance, that judgment rests with the Enforcement Branch of the Compliance Committee and is based on reports by Expert Review Teams. Many other international institutions either leave such decisions to a conference of the parties or fail to provide for them at all. The third factor affecting the potential of an institution's rule-enforcement contribution is the readiness among participants to bear the political and other costs of administering punishment in cases of deliberate noncompliance, since otherwise some parties might well be tempted to cheat on their commitments. Accordingly, selecting a rule-enforcement niche is likely to be effective if an institution is better endowed than others to obtain verification of behavior based on independent sources of information, to prevent parties from blocking compliance review decisions, or to induce states to punish noncompliance.

An Interplay-Sensitive Framework for Effectiveness Analysis

This brief review of concepts and findings in regime effectiveness research provides a matrix of governance tasks and types of interplay that can support the analysis of strategic interplay management within institutional complexes. Table 6.1 summarizes conditions that favor fulfillment

Table 6.1
Effective niche selection: Conditions favoring supportive institutional interplay

Type of interplay	Governance niches			
	Knowledge building	*Norm building*	*Capacity building*	*Enforcement*
Cognitional	Credibility	Applicability	Model	Verification
Normative	Legitimacy	Coverage	Commitment	Review
Utilitarian	Saliency	Strength	Funds	Punishment

of four governance tasks, or niches, that an institution may seek to occupy either alone or jointly with other institutions. We see that an institution opting for a knowledge-building niche is effective if it can raise the credibility, legitimacy, or saliency of scientific input to decision making on the problem. Effective norm building requires applicability, coverage, and substantive strength. Occupying a capacity-building niche effectively means providing exemplary ways to solve the problem or to raise commitments or funds that enable broader use of such models. The final governance task, enforcement, requires means for verifying information, reviewing compliance, and punishing violation.

Niche Selection in Arctic Environmental Governance

The remainder of this chapter explores the niche approach to interplay management by applying this approach to four cases which together show Arctic institutions building knowledge, creating norms, enhancing capacity, or enforcing rules within institutional complexes for environmental governance. Throughout most of the postwar period, institutions for circumpolar or subregional governance across the East-West divide were few and far between. The main explanation for such institutional scarcity was the military rivalry between NATO and the Warsaw Pact, which was especially intense in the Arctic, since the ice cover can provide a shield for submarines carrying strategic nuclear missiles. Mikhail Gorbachev's 1987 "Murmansk initiative" sparked a hectic period for Arctic policymakers, with Western states welcoming the invitation to extend cooperation on Northern affairs (Stokke 1990). A window of opportunity emerged for achieving progress in numerous issue areas, including those in focus here: transboundary air pollution, marine contamination, hazardous waste treatment, and fisheries management.

Knowledge Building: Persistent Organic Pollutants

Arctic institutions have occupied a knowledge-building niche in the complex of institutions that govern activities generating harmful concentrations of hazardous chemicals in the High North. This niche selection has supported problem-solving activities by other institutions by raising the saliency, credibility, and legitimacy of scientific input to the process of negotiating two legally binding instruments.

Eight states govern territories within the Arctic Circle—Canada, Denmark, Finland, Iceland, Norway, Russia, Sweden, and the United States. In 1991 they created the Arctic Environmental Protection Strategy (AEPS), an intergovernmental vehicle with a set of permanent working groups engaging in various program activities. A few years later those working groups were incorporated into a new institution, the Arctic Council, which has now become the central high-level forum for dealing with a range of circumpolar matters (Stokke and Hønneland 2007). As a soft-law institution, the Arctic Council adopts nonbinding declarations at its biannual ministerial meetings. In-between those meetings, the Senior Arctic Officials of the eight member states oversee working group activities that rely on direct financial contributions from states willing to act as project leads and participants.

The pole-bound atmospheric and oceanic circulation systems and rivers draining into the Arctic waters transport a range of toxic substances that originate or volatilize further south, including such persistent organic pollutants (POPs) as organochlorine pesticides used in agriculture, industrial chemicals, and a range of combustion products. Low temperatures create an Arctic "cold trap," or sink, for some of these POPs, preventing further transport. The effects that POPs have on humans are more dramatic in the Arctic than at lower latitudes because these substances bioaccumulate in the fatty tissue and blood of mammals and seabirds that are important in the diet of Arctic indigenous residents. Today, the Inuit of Canada and Greenland have among the highest exposures to polychlorinated biphenyls (PCBs) on the planet, and fetuses and small children relying on breast milk are especially vulnerable (Dewailly and Furgal 2003). A similar situation applies to some of the Arctic megafauna. Some of the highest PCB levels ever measured in fat and blood are currently found in polar bears around Svalbard north of mainland Norway and the Russian archipelago of Franz Josef Land. Recent studies indicate negative impacts on immune systems and reproduction (Reiersen, Wilson, and Kimstach 2003, 76). Such effects are especially dramatic because several stocks of polar bear are already threatened by declining ice extension due to global warming and by increased hunting activities.

The role of the Arctic as a sink for hazardous compounds means that regional states and institutions cannot seriously address the POPs problem without engaging broader international regimes. Awareness of this limitation, and a general resistance among several Arctic states to the idea of developing the AEPS into a regulatory body (Stokke 1990), induced Canada to focus first on protocols under the UN Economic Commission for Europe Convention on Long-Range Transported Air Pollution (CLRTAP), which covers Europe and North America, and later on the UN Environmental Programme, when seeking global regulation of POPs in the 2001 Stockholm Convention (Selin 2000, 133). The Arctic Council and its predecessor contributed significantly to achieving such international instruments, which today commit states to eliminate, or in some cases restrict, the production, use, and trade of certain particularly harmful substances, primarily through cognitional interplay. Three distinctive features of the Arctic Council triggered supportive interplay with those other institutions: powerful membership, a collaborative research vehicle, and participatory inclusiveness.

The Arctic Council membership includes two political heavyweights in world affairs, which enhances the saliency of its knowledge input to regulatory decision making: the northern territories of the United States and Russia are major importers of pollution that originates elsewhere. Following adoption of the AEPS, delegates from the eight Arctic states expressed to the CLRTAP Executive Body their deep concerns about the Arctic health effects of POPs (Reiersen, Wilson, and Kimstach 2003, 61). This joint pressure added substantially to previous unilateral calls for action by the most concerned state, Canada, and contributed to the Executive Body's decision to strengthen the mandate of the new CLRTAP Task Force on POPs. In subsequent years as well, the articulation of an Arctic dimension of this issue has enhanced its overall saliency, since proven damage to human health and large mammals attracts greater public attention than does more "diffuse" information on toxic concentrations in air and water masses. At one point, the heavy emphasis on Arctic impacts induced those pressing for CLRTAP action to shift their focus and substantiate the benefits to be reaped further south as well, in order to secure broader support (Selin 2000, 133). The combination of powerful membership and the ability to demonstrate specific damage makes knowledge inputs from a regional institution more salient.

Another prominent feature of the Arctic Council is its Arctic Monitoring and Assessment Program (AMAP), a collaborative research instrument that has raised both the credibility and the legitimacy of scientific findings on the detrimental effects of POPs in the High North. The AMAP systematically examines the sources, pathways, and concentrations of regional pollution and their impacts on human health and Arctic flora and fauna. Such collaborative research and monitoring have emerged as the "specialization of the Arctic Council" (Stenlund 2002, 837) and are particularly consequential in connection with substances under consideration for stricter regulation. In fact, AMAP's attention to transport pathways and health impact on mammals and humans glove-fitted the CLRTAP criteria for chemical substances in particular need of regulation: transport range, persistency, toxicity, and bioaccumulation (Selin 2000, 142). This screening process coincided with the preparation of the first of two comprehensive AMAP Assessment Reports, and the fact that the co-chair of the CLRTAP Task Force also chaired AMAP ensured that Arctic findings were continuously fed into the process (Reiersen, Wilson, and Kimstach 2003, 68). Credible substantiation of threats to human health would have been far more difficult without the Arctic Council, since research and monitoring under CLRTAP rely on direct funding by interested states—and in the early 1990s, no such activities concerned POPs (Selin 2000, 126). The sixteen substances that were selected from an initial list of more than a hundred included those of greatest relevance to Arctic ecosystems, which indicates that AMAP inputs have been taken seriously.

Institutional interplay capable of triggering regulatory advances in broader regimes also resulted from the legitimacy gain deriving from a third distinctive feature of the Arctic Council, the unusually prominent place given to representatives of indigenous peoples. Six associations of indigenous organizations have status as Permanent Participants, which implies "active participation and full consultation." Inuit in North America and Greenland are particularly vulnerable to POP pollutants in marine mammals. The participation of Inuit representatives on the Arctic Council served to raise their awareness to and knowledge about international POP politics and thus their ability to exert influence. Through this Arctic institution, Inuit organizations have direct and regular access to high-level officials in the foreign ministries of Arctic states, biannually even to ministers. Such political access proved especially helpful when the locus of international POP regulation shifted from CLRTAP to the global Stockholm Convention (Fenge 2003). The Inuit participants gave priority to engaging U.S. support for an ambitious instrument, and the U.S. chairmanship of the Arctic Council during the run-up to the Stockholm Conference provided a platform for exerting Alaskan influence on relevant decision makers (Huntington and Sparck 2003, 221–222). Evidence of their success includes the Arctic Council's Barrow Declaration of 2000, in which ministers agreed to "strengthen efforts to finalize a comprehensive and verifiable convention at the last session of the Intergovernmental Negotiations Committee." According to the chair of the Stockholm Conference, representatives of indigenous and environmental organizations influenced the multilateral negotiations in a productive way and also ensured sustained publicity on the process (Buccini 2003, 250). The Arctic dimension of the POP problem was symbolized by a carving of an Inuit woman, which was placed on the chair's table, where it remained throughout the multilateral negotiations. The prominent role of indigenous organizations in the Arctic Council thus contributed first to the building of a common position among Arctic states on the desirability of a strong regulatory instrument and thereafter to maintaining pressure on negotiators to reach agreement.

Table 6.2 summarizes this brief case study of the management of interplay in the complex of international institutions that deal with POPs. The Arctic Council's decision to opt for a knowledge-building niche in this area appears effective, since certain features distinctive to this institution equip it well for raising the saliency, credibility, and legitimacy of scientific input to regulatory decision making. Some general institutional lessons from this case are worth examining in other empirical contexts: institutions that involve powerful states, that focus on issues of high policy saliency, that are capable of structuring collaborative

Table 6.2
Selecting a knowledge-building niche: The Arctic Council and persistent organic pollutants

Impact on conditions favoring knowledge building	Distinctive institutional feature
Raising saliency	Powerful membership
	Issue saliency: highlighting health damage
Raising credibility	Collaborative research: Arctic Monitoring and Assessment Program
Raising legitimacy	Victim prominence: involving indigenous peoples

research among member states, or that involve major victims of the problem in focus would appear especially well placed to occupy a knowledge-building niche in environmental governance.

Norm Building: Arctic Offshore Oil and Gas

In contrast to the case of POPs, half-hearted efforts within the Arctic Council to occupy a norm-building niche regarding offshore regional hydrocarbon development have not triggered significant supportive interplay with other institutions. Those efforts have been half-hearted because the Arctic Council norms in question are nonbinding and are not backed up by any reporting and review procedures. While this institution is capable of improving the coverage of relevant international norms, it is poorly equipped to raise their applicability or substantive strength.

Although earlier expectations of an Arctic "energy rush" have not materialized, the rapid warming currently under way in the region and the depletion of oil and gas in more southerly parts of Arctic states make an escalation of hydrocarbon operations likely (Offerdal 2007). Seismic activities and exploratory drilling are longstanding activities, and the first major Arctic offshore project, Northstar, to the north of Prudhoe Bay, Alaska, began oil production in 2001. Also, the Snøhvit gas field in the southern Barents Sea, off northern Norway, is now in production, while Russia's oil field Prirazlomnoye in the Pechora Sea is expected to reach this stage in a few years. Development of the Shtokman gas field in the Barents Sea, among the biggest in the world, is moving closer, although estimates of when production will start vary widely.

The main concern surrounding offshore oil and gas activities in the Arctic is the risk of a major accident involving large-scale oil spills. Regular operational discharges are unlikely to add significantly to the total load of hydrocarbons in Arctic waters, largely brought into the region from other areas through oceanic circulation. However, should an accident occur, climate and weather conditions, darkness, and long distances will hamper rescue and restoration. The probability of an accident is assumed to be higher than in temperate zones. Regional differences in industrial safety standards would indicate that particular attention should be paid to the Russian segment—which is also where most of the regional petroleum resources are likely to be found (Gautier et al. 2009). According to the Arctic Council's recent Arctic Oil and Gas Assessment, Canada, the United States, and Norway have mature systems for environmental regulation of the oil and gas sector, whereas Russia has been in a process of "constructing a new system of regulatory control" for the past decade and a half (AMAP 2008, x). Two experienced analysts conclude in a review of Russia's management of its Arctic hydrocarbon resources that "regulation systems on usage of the subsurface resources are lacking; opinions and interests of various groups of the population are rarely heard, and technical competencies for sustainable implementation of the projects are in short supply" (Andreyeva and Kryukov 2008, 284–285).

Accordingly, one distinctive feature of the Arctic Council, that it counts the Russian Federation among its members, can be seen as an asset for an institution opting for a norm-building niche in the governance of Arctic hydrocarbon activities. For more than a decade, Norway has tried in vain to persuade Russia to join the 1992 OSPAR Convention for the Protection of the Marine Environment of the North-East Atlantic, which commits parties to best available technology standards concerning drilling procedures and discharge levels (Stokke 2007). Russia is also among the few Arctic nonparties to the Espoo Convention, which obliges states to conduct environmental impact assessments prior to large-scale industrial projects with potential transboundary consequences. The Arctic Council therefore offers a potential vehicle for enhancing the coverage of normative commitments to best practices and environmental impact assessment.

Unfortunately, the applicability of the Arctic Offshore Oil and Gas Guidelines, recently revised and updated, is modest. Their coherence with broader international norms is considerable, as they derive from and invoke such existing and legally binding agreements as UNCLOS, various treaties drawn up under the International Maritime Organization, and regional instruments such as the OSPAR Convention. Such coherence adds somewhat to the normative compellingness of these guidelines and may also trigger supportive cognitional interplay by spelling out the implications of broader norms in the regional context. A study by Offerdal (2007), however, indicates very limited awareness of the Arctic Offshore Oil and Gas Guidelines within the relevant national bureaucracies. Moreover, their nonbinding nature implies low determinacy and constrains any normative or utilitarian interplay with other institutions. The Arctic Council is itself based in a soft-law instrument and lacks any mandate to adopt legally binding norms. On the other hand, experience with, for instance, the North Sea Conferences on marine pollution has shown that states may develop follow-up procedures also of nonbinding norms to enhance their clout (Skjærseth, Stokke, and Wettestad 2006). Following that example, the Arctic Council could carve its norm-building niche somewhat deeper, and enhance the determinacy of the Arctic Offshore Oil and Gas Guidelines by developing reporting and review procedures that would draw greater attention to the norms and their implementation by Arctic states.

Lack of mandate to adopt binding rules does not prevent an institution from providing a venue for states willing to negotiate and adopt a free-standing treaty, but a third institutional feature restricts the Arctic Council's potential to raise the substantive strength of regional hydrocarbon development norms: its membership is a mix of states with and without jurisdiction over the continental shelves of the Arctic. Under UNCLOS, coastal states enjoy exclusive management authority over resources found in the continental shelf, but they are strongly encouraged "to harmonize their policies in this connection at the appropriate regional level" (Article 2008). However, states with an Arctic shelf have few incentives to negotiate such constraint on their exercise of sovereignty within a venue framework that includes nonshelf states. Canada, Denmark, Norway, Russia, and the USA adopted in 2008 the Ilulissat Declaration, noting that by "virtue of their sovereignty, sovereign rights and jurisdiction in large areas of the Arctic Ocean the five coastal states are in a unique position to address these possibilities and challenges [and] ... see no need to develop a new comprehensive international legal regime to govern the Arctic Ocean." In Underdal's (2002) terms, negotiating stricter regulations on hydrocarbon activities within the Arctic Council would pose a malign problem because such rules would distribute the costs and benefits asymmetrically among the participating states. The loss of regulatory leeway, and perhaps of economic benefits if petroleum development is constrained, would afflict only the shelf states, whereas the political and environmental gains of more ambitious regulation would be shared by all.

Table 6.3 shows in capsule form this attempt by the Arctic Council to carve out a norm-building niche in offshore oil and gas activities. Failure to trigger major supportive interplay in this area reflects the lack of any distinctive features that could place this institution especially well for raising the applicability or substantive strength of international norms on hydrocarbon development, while Russia's participation is helpful for coverage. Among the general implications to be drawn from this case is that involvement of the major states whose behavior has given rise to the problem in question is an asset for an institution opting for a norm-building niche, as are a membership that includes states that are rather symmetrically affected by regulation and the possession of a

Table 6.3
Selecting (half-heartedly) a norm-building niche: The Arctic Council and offshore oil and gas activities

Impact on conditions favoring norm building	Distinctive institutional feature
Raising coverage	Membership including most relevant target states
Not raising applicability	Nonbinding norms Weak reporting and review procedures
Not raising strength	Asymmetrical interests: involving nonpetroleum states

formal mandate to adopt binding rules—or at least the ability to develop reporting and review procedures for following up on implementation activities.

Capacity Building: Management of Arctic Contaminants
While external flows of pollution into the Arctic are important, activities in the region also produce great amounts of toxic contaminants. Some of the largest and most heavily industrialized centers in Russia are found on the banks of rivers branching into the Arctic seas. Two-thirds of the atmospheric heavy metals found in the High Arctic originate from industrial activities in northwestern Russia, as does most of the sulfur found within the Polar Circle (AMAP 1997). The Arctic Council occupies a capacity-building niche in efforts to cope with such regional toxics. In this it has succeeded insofar as it provides models for better treatment of hazardous waste and raises commitments or funds enabling technology transfer.

The institutional feature of the Arctic Council most relevant to capacity enhancement is its Arctic Contaminants Action Program (ACAP), a collaborative structure for defining and implementing practical problem-solving projects, primarily in Russia. Such a program implies some political commitment among member states to contribute resources, but its main rationale is to stimulate broader use of state-of-the-art approaches to managing hazardous toxics. Several projects aim to eliminate PCBs in Russia (ACAP 2008). In addition to proposing legislative measures and outlining strategies for introducing substitutes for PCBs, the program has identified existing stockpiles and collected large amounts of this material for safer storage. Envisaging application of Western technology, this endeavor has now moved to demonstrations of how PCBs can be destroyed. A three-year plan developed in 2002 involved the destruction of nearly 10 percent of the PCBs believed to remain in Russia, but inability to identify, and receive permission for, an appropriate site for destruction facilities has constrained implementation (Stokke 2007; see also ACAP 2008). Obsolete pesticides are another area in which the Arctic Council has spurred international capacity-enhancement activities. Having identified priority regions where obsolete or prohibited pesticides threaten the Arctic environment, several projects have enabled inventorying of existing stocks as well as repackaging and safe storage of more than two thousand tons of pesticides, with destruction as the next step (ACAP 2009). Yet other projects target mercury, dioxins, and brominated flame retardants—thus far only by mapping releases, concentrations, and options for cleaner production options and by defining pilot projects (ACAP 2009).

A second distinctive feature that places the Arctic Council well to occupy a capacity-building niche is the role it plays in realizing a broader security objective held by Arctic states. Among the forces driving the creation of this institution was the determination to exploit a window of opportunity for enmeshing the Russian Federation and other Arctic states within a robust cooperative institution. This embeddedness in the global security structure generated willingness among Western states to raise a disproportionate share of the funds necessary for collaborative endeavors, including under ACAP, in the belief that practical action would reinforce cooperative ties in the region. Today, however, Western states are increasingly questioning the appropriateness of subsidizing capacity-building projects in Russia in view of the latter's very high, and rising, revenues from petroleum exports. This gradual change of mood among Western participants does not necessarily imply that the Arctic Council will abandon the capacity-building niche, only that the balance between Western and Russian funding sources for environmental projects is likely to change (ACAP 2008). In turn, this development puts to the test the effects of nearly two decades of problem-solving activities within Arctic and broader institutions on Russia's own willingness to give priority to combating regional discharges of hazardous contaminants.

Table 6.4 summarizes certain features of the Arctic Council that shape its ability to occupy a capacity-building niche with respect to the management of regional toxics. In focus are the collaborative vehicle that the council provides for transferring model solutions in the area and the project funds triggered by its role in furthering broader security objectives in the region. General lessons derivable from this case are that

Table 6.4
Selecting a capacity-building niche: The Arctic Council and destruction of persistent organic pollutants

Impact on conditions favoring capacity building	Distinctive institutional feature
Providing model	Technological asymmetry
Raising commitment	Structures for transfer: Arctic Contaminants Action Program
Raising funds	Fusion with broader concerns: security motivation

institutions seeking a capacity-building niche should have a membership with marked differences in the technological ability to solve the problem at hand, should include structures for organizing technology transfer, and, if funds are scarce in recipient states, should be able to link up to broader concerns that can motivate member states to fund projects beyond their own borders.

Rule Enforcement: Port-State Measures and Illegal Fishing
An international institution for managing regional high-seas stocks has effectively carved out an enforcement niche in the institutional complex for governing fisheries targeting the world's biggest cod stock, Northeast Arctic cod. Norway and Russia are the dominant actors in this complex, since the stock is found mostly in waters under their jurisdiction. During the past decade, however, steadily more landings from these fisheries have been occurring in EU states, a development that compounds the enforcement challenge. The supportive problem-solving role of a broader institution whose membership includes the major landing states, the NEAFC, derives from its ability to mobilize port-state jurisdiction in the verification of fisher reports and review of compliance, thereby enabling the flag state to expose and punish rule violation.

The major institution for managing Northeast Arctic cod is the Norwegian-Russian Joint Fisheries Commission, which meets annually to adopt and allocate total quotas and other binding regulations. Also, noncoastal states participate in the regime by accepting in separate bilateral or trilateral agreements the quotas and technical regulations that Norway and Russia establish. As Alcock elaborates in this volume, such regional institutions nest within the global fisheries regime codified primarily in the 1982 UNCLOS. An important aspect of that regime is the right of coastal states to establish exclusive economic zones (EEZs).

Within such 200-mile zones, coastal states enjoy "sovereign rights for the purpose of exploring and exploiting, conserving and managing" fish stocks and may enforce rules by "boarding, inspection, arrest and judicial proceedings" (Articles 56 and 73). A 1995 UN Fish Stocks Agreement specifies this global regime by committing parties to a precautionary approach to fisheries management, strengthening the duty to cooperate on management, and broadening the jurisdictional basis for enforcement activities beyond EEZs (Stokke 2001b). During the 1990s, coastal state use of trade-related measures to combat harvesting activities by nonmembers of the regime implied that trade regimes, including global rules under the GATT, became part of the relevant institutional complex (Stokke 2009). In addition, a broad set of international institutions within and outside the UN seek to constrain illegal, unreported, and unregulated (IUU) fishing (FAO 2002) and have facilitated the institutional changes in the NEAFC that have allowed it to occupy a rule-enforcement niche in the management of Northeast Arctic cod.

Large-scale quota overfishing, especially by Russian vessels, poses a severe management problem in this region (Stokke 2009). ICES (2007, 23) estimates total unreported catches of Northeast Arctic cod as high as 90 thousand tons in 2002 and rising to more than 160 thousand tons three years later; the latter figure represents roughly one-third of the entire legal catch. An important basis for these estimates is provided by satellite tracking data on fishing and transport-vessel movements to main ports, combined with assessments of vessel storage capacity that enforcement agencies derive from inspections and vessel registers (Directorate of Fisheries [Norway] 2009).[2] The consequences of such quota overfishing are grave for the stock's sustainability, the distribution of gains between fishers who play by the rules and those who cheat, and the readiness of fishers and managers to keep quotas and catches within scientific advice (Stokke 2009).

The Barents Sea coastal states are also parties to the NEAFC; they successfully recruited support among other regime members for carving out a port-state enforcement niche that reduced a loophole in the compliance system of the Joint Fisheries Commission. Large-scale quota overfishing had been possible as a result of the incorporation of Northwest Russia's fishing industry into the global market economy, following the radical reordering of Soviet society under Gorbachev in the late 1980s. Notably, the rapid rise in Russian landings in Western ports had undermined the fit between institutional reach and the activity under regulation, since domestic fisheries enforcement agencies were no longer able to verify fisher reports by cross-checking them with port delivery data. Accordingly, the leeway for rule violation increased considerably. Countermeasures under the Joint Fisheries Commission were without force when in the late 1990s Russian vessels shifted their landings from Norwegian to various EU ports. At-sea inspection had limited potential to correct the situation because Russia failed to share vessel quota information with Norway, and large parts of the EU deliveries involved at-sea transshipment to transport vessels, which made it easier to disguise the size of actual catches. The coastal state decision to use a broad institution, the NEAFC, for enforcement of rules concerning an EEZ stock thus responded to changes in the chain of production and distribution that made bilateral and national institutions ineffective.

Several features of the NEAFC equipped it well for narrowing this loophole in the system for enforcing Joint Fisheries Commission rules, but there were also initial limitations. First, the NEAFC membership includes most of the states that receive Northeast Arctic cod. States have jurisdiction over vessels voluntarily in their ports, and the Fish Stocks Agreement commits parties to use that competence "to promote the effectiveness of sub-regional, regional, and global conservation and management measures" (Article 23). Second, the NEAFC already had an extensive Scheme of Control and Enforcement in place for regional high-seas stocks, including a compulsory vessel monitoring system and provisions specifying port-state inspection and control commitments. A third feature constrained its potential to trigger supportive interplay with the Joint Fisheries Commission, however: that scheme applied only to "regulated resources" under the NEAFC—and Northeast Arctic cod is not among them, since it occurs mostly in waters under Norwegian or Russian jurisdiction.

After several years of pushing and shoving, Norway and Russia managed to remove the scope constraint in a new and stronger 2007 NEAFC Scheme of Control and Enforcement. The new scheme applies not only to high-seas stocks but to all "frozen catch of fisheries resources caught in the Convention Area," and the latter includes the regional EEZs as well. Among the conditions that favored such unorthodox broadening of an enforcement scheme beyond an institution's regulatory ambit was the keen attention within a wide range of international institutions, including the NEAFC, to the problem of IUU operations (Stokke 2009), which made it politically awkward for other NEAFC members to oppose the proposal on formalist grounds. Under the 2007 scheme, members may not allow a NEAFC vessel to land or transship frozen fish in its port unless the flag state of the vessel that caught the fish confirms that the vessel has sufficient quota, has reported the catch, and is authorized to fish in the area, and that satellite tracking information data correspond with vessel reports. This flag-state confirmation procedure is innovative and involves a recurrent external check on the flag state's implementation of authorization, data recording, and vessel monitoring commitments under global and NEAFC rules (Stokke 2009).

The latest estimate of Russian overfishing of Northeast Arctic cod indicates a significant decline, from 80 thousand tons in 2006 to around 15 thousand tons in 2008, following a steep rise in the number of vessel trips from the fishing grounds to domestic ports. Such changes presumably reflect also other developments, including the steady rise in purchasing power in Northwest Russia, but nevertheless indicate that port-state measures under the NEAFC are raising the effectiveness of the Norwegian–Russian Joint Fisheries Commission.

Table 6.5 summarizes the supportive institutional interplay that derives from the selection by parties to the NEAFC of a rule-enforcement niche in the management of Northeast Arctic cod. The distinctive features that equip this institution particularly well for this niche, which bilateral and national institutions no longer occupied effectively owing to Russian transshipment and foreign landings, are its broad membership and its Scheme of Control and Enforcement for high-seas stocks. In more general terms, the case demonstrates the significance of structures for verification, review, and punishment that span the spatial and actor ranges of the activity system regulated by an institution. Moreover, the ability to mobilize an existing structure for enforcement of high-seas rules in the management of Northeast Arctic cod also resulted from

Table 6.5
Selecting an enforcement niche: The North-East Atlantic Fisheries Commission and management of Northeast Arctic cod

Impact on conditions favoring enforcement	Distinctive institutional feature
Improving verification Permitting review	Fit with the activity system: involving port states
Raising willingness to punish	Fusion with broader concerns: saliency of IUU fishing

fusing this problem with a broader issue, the international combating of IUU fishing.

Conclusions

The framework developed in this chapter for analyzing interplay management in institutional complexes delineates four governance niches and helps to identify conditions for occupying them effectively—that is, in a way that supports overall problem solving. Applying the notion of institutional niches to four cases of Arctic environmental governance helps to identify distinctive features that can equip an institution particularly well for conducting the related tasks.

Knowledge building is a governance niche chosen by the Arctic Council in the complex of institutions for combating airborne POPs. The effectiveness of this niche selection is evident in the favorable impacts achieved on the saliency, credibility, and legitimacy of scientific input to the negotiation of two binding POP treaties. Effects on saliency derive from certain distinctive features of the Arctic Council: its membership, which includes two of the most powerful states in the world, and its substantive focus on issues capable of drawing public attention to the problem in question—here, the health situation among indigenous populations and the survival of media-amenable polar bears. Institutional features equipping this institution well for raising the credibility and legitimacy of scientific input are its structure for collaborative research among member states, notably a longstanding monitoring and assessment program, and the prominent representation it provides for groups especially vulnerable to the problem at hand.

Another governance niche is norm building, which the Arctic Council has made some attempt to fill regarding offshore hydrocarbon activities. Success here has been limited, mostly because the council is poorly equipped to raise the applicability and the substantive strength of international norms in this area, which are two conditions for effective occupation of this niche. Applicability requires a mandate to negotiate binding norms, which the Arctic Council lacks, or reporting and review structures to enhance follow-up. Agreement on substantively stronger norms is more likely if members are affected relatively symmetrically by the problem and by the regulation—and that is not the case for the Arctic Council. A high score on a third condition for effective norm building—coverage of all or most states that contribute to the problem—cannot compensate for low scores on applicability and strength.

Capacity building is a third governance niche and one that the Arctic Council occupies concerning regional management of hazardous contaminants, including PCBs and obsolete or prohibited pesticides. Significant variation among members in technology levels regarding the problem at hand is one institutional feature favoring occupation of this niche, since capacity enhancement requires model approaches that other states can learn from. Another relevant feature is normative commitment to stimulate such learning, which is not prominent in the case of the Arctic Council, despite its working group on Arctic contaminants. A third institutional feature favorable to capacity building stands out more clearly: the Arctic Council links up to broader concerns among member states that motivate them to fund projects beyond their own borders, in this case the security dimension of peaceful cooperation between Russia and the West.

The fourth governance niche in focus here is rule enforcement, which can be considered effective whenever an institution improves the basis for verifying the information states provide on problem behavior, for reviewing rule adherence, or for punishing noncompliance. In the institutional complex that cogoverns the harvesting of cod in the Barents Sea, the North-East Atlantic Fisheries Commission occupies this niche with steadily greater impact. That impact derives primarily from a membership which, unlike that of other institutions, covers most of the states now involved in the harvesting, landing, and port reception of this cod stock. Those seeking to use a second key feature of this institution, its elaborate compliance system, for managing a stock outside of its regulatory ambit succeeded because they were able to link the specific problem in question to a broader and more general one: the global combating of illegal, unreported, and unregulated fishing.

These brief case studies of Arctic environmental governance demonstrate the fruitfulness of examining strategic interplay management decisions that concern an institution's specialization and role within larger complexes of institutions as niche selection based on distinctive capacities to trigger cognitional, normative, or utilitarian processes conducive to problem solving. The case studies provide evidence that states are aware of such differences in institutional equipment for various governance tasks and actively seek to muster support for a corresponding niche selection. While success is hardly guaranteed, the cases examined here display the emergence of and changes in divisions of labor among institutions, reflecting their respective capacities to generate knowledge, norms, capacity, and enforcement structures in support of problem solving.

Acknowledgments

I would like to thank Thomas Gehring, Jon Hovi, Sebastian Oberthür, and Oran Young for very helpful comments on an earlier version of this chapter. Work was funded by the Research Council of Norway through the Geopolitics of the High North Program and by the Fridtjof Nansen Institute.

Notes

1. See the elaboration by Stokke and Oberthür in this volume.

2. Uncertainties regarding loading extent, species composition, and the mix of fillet and head-and-gutted products indicate that these figures should be treated with some caution; see Stokke (2009).

References

Aldrich, Howard. 1999. *Organizations Evolving*. London: Sage.

ACAP. 2008. ACAP Working Group, Minutes From a Meeting in Moscow, 4–5 March. Arctic Contaminants Action Program to Eliminate Pollution of the Arctic. http://www.arctic-council.org.

ACAP. 2009. ACAP Progress Report to Senior Arctic Officials, 12–13 November. Arctic Contaminants Action Program to Eliminate Pollution of the Arctic. http://www.arctic-council.org.

AMAP. 1997. Arctic Pollution Issues. Oslo: Arctic Monitoring and Assessment Program. http://www.amap.no

AMAP. 2008. *Arctic Oil and Gas 2007*. Oslo: Arctic Monitoring and Assessment Program.

Andresen, Steinar. 2001. Global Environmental Governance: UN Fragmentation and Co-ordination. In *Yearbook of International Co-operation on Environment and Development 2001/2002*, ed. Olav Schram Stokke and Oystein B. Thommessen, 19–26. London: Earthscan.

Andresen, Steinar, Tora Skodvin, Arild Underdal, and Jørgen Wettestad. 2000. *Science and Politics in International Environmental Regimes: Between Integrity and Involvement*. Manchester: Manchester University Press.

Andreyeva, Elena N., and Valery A. Kryukov. 2008. The Russian Model: Merging Profit and Sustainability. In *Arctic Oil and Gas: Sustainability at Risk?*, ed. Aslaug Mikkelsen and Oluf Langhelle, 240–287. London: Routledge.

Barrett, Scott. 2003. *Environment and Statecraft: The Strategy of Environmental Treaty-Making.* Oxford: Oxford University Press.

Brown Weiss, Edith. 1993. International Environmental Law: Contemporary Issues and the Emergence of a New World Order. *Georgetown Law Journal* 81 (3): 675–710.

Buccini, John Anthony. 2003. The Long and Winding Road to Stockholm: The View from the Chair. In *Northern Lights Against POPs: Combatting Toxic Threats in the Arctic*, ed. David L. Downie and Terry Fenge, 224–256. Montreal: McGill-Queen's University Press.

Bunge, Mario. 1997. Mechanism and Explanation. *Philosophy of the Social Sciences* 27:410–465.

Dewailly, Eric, and Christopher Furgal. 2003. POPs, the Environment, and Public Health. In *Northern Lights Against POPs: Combatting Toxic Threats in the Arctic*, ed. David L. Downie and Terry Fenge, 3–21. Montreal: McGill-Queen's University Press.

Directorate of Fisheries (Norway). 2009. *Status Report for 2008: Russian Catches of Northeast Arctic Cod and Haddock.* Bergen: Directorate of Fisheries. http://www.fiskeridir.no

Downs, George W., David M. Rocke, and Peter N. Barsoom. 1996. Is the Good News about Compliance Good News about Cooperation? *International Organization* 50 (3): 379–406.

FAO. 2002. *Implementation of the International Plan of Action to Prevent, Deter and Eliminate Illegal, Unreported and Unregulated Fishing. FAO Technical Guidelines for Responsible Fisheries.* Rome: UN Food and Agriculture Organization.

Fenge, Terry. 2003. POPs and Inuit: Influencing the Global Agenda. In *Northern Lights Against POPs: Combatting Toxic Threats in the Arctic*, ed. David L. Downie and Terry Fenge, 192–213. Montreal: McGill-Queen's University Press.

Franck, Thomas M. 1990. *The Power of Legitimacy among Nations.* New York: Oxford University Press.

Gautier, Donald L., Kenneth J. Bird, Ronald R. Charpentier, Arthur Grantz, David W. Houseknecht, Timothy R. Klett, Thomas E. Moore, et al. 2009. Assessment of Undiscovered Oil and Gas in the Arctic. *Science* 324:1175–1179.

Haas, Peter M. 1989. Do Regimes Matter? Epistemic Communities and Mediterranean Pollution Control. *International Organization* 43 (3): 377–405.

Haas, Peter M., Robert O. Keohane, and Marc A. Levy, eds. 1993. *Institutions for the Earth: Sources of Effective International Environmental Protection.* Cambridge, Mass.: MIT Press.

Hannan, Michael T., and John Freeman. 1977. The Population Ecology of Organizations. *American Journal of Sociology* 82 (5): 929–964.

Hovi, Jon, Olav Schram Stokke, and Geir Ulfstein. 2005. Introduction and Main Findings. In *Implementing the Climate Regime: International Compliance*, ed. Olav Schram Stokke, Jon Hovi, and Geir Ulfstein, 1–14. London: Earthscan.

Huntington, Henry P., and Michelle Sparck. 2003. POPs in Alaska: Engaging the USA. In *Northern Lights Against POPs: Combatting Toxic Threats in the Arctic*, ed. David L. Downie and Terry Fenge, 214–223. Montreal: McGill-Queen's University Press.

ICES. 2007. *ICES Advice 2007, Book 3*. Copenhagen: International Council for the Exploration of the Sea.

Levy, Marc A., Oran R. Young, and Michael Zürn. 1995. The Study of International Regimes. *European Journal of International Relations* 1 (3): 267–330.

March, James G., and Johan P. Olsen. 1989. *Rediscovering Institutions: The Organizational Basis of Politics*. New York: Free Press.

Mitchell, Ronald B., William C. Clark, and David W. Cash. 2006. Information and Influence. In *Global Environmental Assessments: Information and Influence*, ed. Ronald B. Mitchell, William C. Clark, David W. Cash, and Nancy M. Dickson, 307–338. Cambridge, Mass.: MIT Press.

Oberthür, Sebastian, and Thomas Gehring, eds. 2006. *Institutional Interaction in Global Environmental Governance: Synergy and Conflict among International and EU Policies*. Cambridge, Mass.: MIT Press.

Offerdal, Kristine. 2007. Oil, Gas and the Arctic Environment. In *International Cooperation and Arctic Governance*, ed. Olav Schram Stokke and Geir Hønneland, 138–163. London: Routledge.

Reiersen, Lars-Otto, Simon Wilson, and Vitaly Kimstach. 2003. Circumpolar Perspectives on Persistent Organic Pollutants: The Arctic Monitoring and Assessment Programme. In *Northern Lights Against POPs: Combatting Toxic Threats in the Arctic*, ed. David L. Downie and Terry Fenge, 60–86. Montreal: McGill-Queen's University Press.

Selin, Henrik. 2000. *Towards International Chemical Safety: Taking Action on Persistent Organic Pollutants (POPs)*. Linköping: Department of Water and Environmental Studies, Linköping University.

Skjærseth, Jon Birger, Olav Schram Stokke, and Jørgen Wettestad. 2006. Soft Law, Hard Law, and Effective Implementation of International Environmental Norms. *Global Environmental Politics* 6 (3): 104–120.

Stenlund, Peter. 2002. Lessons in Regional Cooperation from the Arctic. *Ocean and Coastal Management* 45:835–839.

Stokke, Olav Schram. 1990. The Northern Environment: Is Cooperation Coming? *Annals of the American Academy of Political and Social Science* 512:58–69.

Stokke, Olav Schram. 1998. Nuclear Dumping in Arctic Seas: Russian Implementation of the London Convention. In *The Implementation and Effectiveness of International Environmental Commitments: Theory and Practice*, ed. David G. Victor, Kal Raustiala, and Eugene B. Skolnikoff, 475–517. Cambridge, Mass.: MIT Press.

Stokke, Olav Schram. 2001a. *The Study of Regime Interplay: Putting Effectiveness Theory to Work*. FNI Report 4/01. Lysaker, Norway: Fridtjof Nansen Institute.

Stokke, Olav Schram, ed. 2001b. *Governing High Seas Fisheries: The Interplay of Global and Regional Regimes*. Oxford: Oxford University Press.

Stokke, Olav Schram. 2004. Trade Measures and Climate Compliance: Institutional Interplay between WTO and the Marrakesh Accords. *International Environmental Agreements: Politics, Law and Economics* 4 (4):339–357.

Stokke, Olav Schram. 2007. A Legal Regime for the Arctic? Interplay with the Law of the Sea Convention. *Marine Policy* 31:402–408.

Stokke, Olav Schram. 2009. Trade Measures and the Combat of IUU Fishing: Institutional Interplay and Effective Governance in the Northeast Atlantic. *Marine Policy* 33:339–349.

Stokke, Olav Schram, and Geir Hønneland, eds. 2007. *International Cooperation and Arctic Governance: Regime Effectiveness and Northern Region Building*. London: Routledge.

Stokke, Olav Schram, and Davor Vidas, eds. 1996. *Governing the Antarctic: The Effectiveness and Legitimacy of the Antarctic Treaty System*. Cambridge: Cambridge University Press.

Strange, Susan. 1982. *Cave! hic dragones*: A Critique of Regime Analysis. *International Organization* 36 (2): 479–497.

Underdal, Arild. 1989. The Politics of Science in International Resource Management: a Summary. In *International Resource Management: The Role of Science and Politics*, ed. Steinar Andresen and Willy Østreng, 253–268. London: Belhaven Press.

Underdal, Arild. 2002. One Question, Two Answers. In *Environmental Regime Effectiveness: Confronting Theory with Evidence*, ed. Edward L. Miles, Arild Underdal, Steinar Andresen, Jørgen Wettestad, Jon Birger Skjærseth and Elaine M. Carlin, 3–45. Cambridge, Mass.: MIT Press.

Young, Oran R., ed. 1999. *The Effectiveness of International Environmental Regimes: Causal Connections and Behavioral Mechanisms*. Cambridge, Mass.: MIT Press.

7

The Role of Expert Networks in Reducing Regime Conflict

Contrasting Cases in the Management of Plant Genetic Resources

Stefan Jungcurt

Introduction

A prominent example of institutional interplay is the disruption that has arisen among international institutions dealing with the conservation and use of genetic resources. Property rights to genetic resources are regulated by various international agreements that address the issue from different perspectives and with divergent objectives. Two main forces drive international regulation of property rights to genetic resources. On the one side, there is increasing awareness and scientific agreement that biodiversity is being lost at an accelerating rate and that urgent measures are needed to prevent such loss (MA 2005). On the other side, new biotechnologies greatly enhance the potential uses of biodiversity, leading to a sharp increase in the economic interest in genetic resources as inputs to biotechnological innovations in areas such as pharmaceuticals and plant breeding. As a result of these global drivers, the international discourse on property rights to genetic resources is increasingly marked by the interests of the suppliers of genetic resources (primarily indigenous and traditional farming communities in countries with high rates of biodiversity) and the users (pharmaceutical and plant-breeding industries in industrialized countries).

Suppliers are primarily interested in mechanisms that can ensure adequate compensation to the holders of genetic resources, and their participation in the benefit streams generated by the commercial use of their resources. Today, these interests are addressed by the Convention on Biological Diversity (CBD) and the Food and Agriculture Organization's (FAO's) International Treaty on Plant Genetic Resources for Food and Agriculture (ITPGR). By contrast, users push for the establishment of legally enforceable intellectual property rights (IPRs) on biotechnological innovations that can allow for the appropriation of their commercial value (Dutfield 1999). The most relevant international agreements on the user side are the WTO Agreement on Trade-related Aspects of Intellectual Property Rights (TRIPS) and the International Union on the Protection of New Varieties of Plants (UPOV).

Raustiala and Victor (2004) describe this group of interacting institutions as a "regime complex." Rather than being addressed by a single regime, property rights over genetic resources are dealt with in several institutional arrangements, which Raustiala and Victor refer to as "elemental regimes." This chapter describes the different types of institutional interplay that affect the relationships between these elemental regimes and efforts to establish mechanisms for interplay management. The following sections introduce the core elemental regimes of the institutional complex on plant genetic resources (UPOV, TRIPS, CBD, ITPGR) and develop a dyadic comparison of interplay among them. I show that relationships between supply-related agreements, on the one hand, and user-related ones on the other are generally synergistic. Interplay between the two sides has, however, generated strong disruptions that have negatively affected the implementation and effectiveness of the institutions involved. While efforts to consolidate CBD and TRIPS or to establish mechanisms for interplay management have been unsuccessful thus far, recent negotiations have substantially improved the prospects of solving the conflict between ITPGR and UPOV through the elaboration of an alternative approach to the management of the global pool of plant genetic resources for food and agriculture (PGRFA).

In the third part of this chapter, I explore why, under broadly similar conditions, these two instances of interplay have evolved in such different ways, leading to stalemate and disruption in one case and to successful interplay management in the other. The analysis shows that successful interplay management between ITPGR and UPOV is attributable largely to the influence of a network of scientific experts that has evolved into an epistemic community integrating the perspectives of both providers and users of PGRFA.

The Institutional Complex Concerning Plant Genetic Resources

International Union for the Protection of New Varieties of Plants
The first agreement to address the concerns of genetic resource users was the International Union for the Protection of New Varieties of Plants, adopted in 1968 and subsequently revised in 1972, 1978, and 1991. The objective of UPOV is to recognize, on an international basis, the IPRs of

plant breeders to their varieties. It provides a sui generis form of intellectual property protection,[1] specifically adapted for the process of plant breeding and aimed at providing incentives to plant breeders to develop new varieties of plants. Plant variety protection entitles breeders to appropriate the commercial benefits arising from their plant varieties for the duration of twenty years—twenty-five years in the cases of trees and vines (Article 19).[2]

There are two exceptions to the breeders' right: the breeders' exemption and the farmers' privilege (Article 15). The first refers to acts done for experimental purposes and for the purpose of breeding other varieties. The farmers' privilege allows farmers to save and replant seed on their own holdings without authorization from the breeder. The farmers' privilege was added during the 1978 revision of the UPOV Act and included a right that farmers may distribute the seed of protected varieties. The latter entitlement was removed during the 1991 revision. In both versions, implementation of the farmers' privilege is at the discretion of member countries.

The WTO Agreement on Trade-Related Aspects of Intellectual Property Rights

The general concerns of all industries making use of genetic resources, including plant breeding, pharmaceuticals, and other areas of biotechnology, are addressed under the Agreement on Trade-related Aspects of Intellectual Property Rights. TRIPS came into effect in 1994 as part of the global trade regime centered on the WTO, and must thus be implemented by all WTO members. The objective is to ensure the availability and harmonization of legislation for IPR protection in WTO member countries "in all fields of technology," including biotechnology (Article 27.3(b)).

The agreement embodies the WTO principles of *nondiscrimination* and *most-favored-nation treatment*. Nondiscrimination prohibits WTO members from regulating IPRs for foreign entities any differently than they would regulate the IPRs of domestic entities (Article 3). Most-favored-nation treatment requires member states to make available any IPR benefit to domestic and foreign actors alike (Article 4). Members may exclude from patentability plants and animals other than microorganisms and certain biological processes; however, with regard to plant varieties, they shall provide for protection "either by patents or by an effective *sui generis* system or any combination of the two" (Article 27.3(b)). Violations of TRIPS may be subject to the WTO's dispute settlement mechanism, potentially resulting in economic sanctions against the noncomplying party.

The definition and allocation of intellectual property follows a similar rationale under both UPOV and TRIPS. Technologies are, to large extent, information goods that are affected by problems of exclusion of non-authorized users and low degrees of rivalry in use. Once a piece of information has been disclosed, an unlimited number of actors can use it. The risk of unauthorized use and free riding substantially reduces the incentives for investments in research and development (Hess and Ostrom 2003). IPRs seek to counter this problem through the establishment of a legal mechanism that allows innovators to control the use of their inventions, and to implement sanctions against unauthorized uses. IPRs thus grant a temporary exclusive right for commercial use, to allow the IPR holder to recoup investments in research and development. Similarly, plant variety protection allows plant breeders to control the use and reproduction of their varieties by limiting the rights that a user acquires when buying seed or other propagative materials (Dutfield 1999; Helfer 2002).

The Convention on Biological Diversity

The Convention on Biological Diversity is the most comprehensive institutional framework to address the various concerns of biodiversity conservation and sustainable use on the international level. It came into force in 1993. In addition to the conservation of biodiversity and the sustainable use of its components, the CBD promotes the fair and equitable sharing of benefits arising out of the use of biodiversity and related traditional knowledge (Article 1). To this end, the CBD grants its member states *national sovereignty* over genetic resources on their territory and requires users to obtain the *prior informed consent* of the supplying party before accessing its genetic resources. The transfer shall take place on *mutually agreed terms* between the supplying party and the user, including arrangements to realize the suppliers' right to benefit sharing (Article 15).

These provisions establish a requirement to negotiate some form of a bilateral contract when genetic resources are transferred between countries. The providing country is the formal contracting partner for users who wish to access and use genetic resources. The intention is to create a market through which a part of the commercial benefits of genetic resource use is channeled to actors engaged in the conservation of biodiversity, thereby creating an incentive for continued investments in conservation. In 2002, parties to the CBD adopted the Bonn Guidelines on Access and Benefit Sharing, containing a set of voluntary principles and measures intended to assist parties in developing and implementing their national access and benefit-sharing (ABS) regimes (CBD 2002).

In response to a mandate by the World Summit on Sustainable Development in 2002 (UN 2002, para. 44(o)), the CBD initiated negotiations on an international ABS regime. Between 2001 and mid-2010 the CBD's Working Group on ABS met nine times to consider the design of a future regime. However, as of mid-2010, parties had yet to reach agreement on this future regime (IISD 2010).

The International Undertaking and the International Treaty on Plant Genetic Resources for Food and Agriculture

The FAO International Treaty on Plant Genetic Resources for Food and Agriculture addresses, among other issues, the concerns of suppliers of genetic resources that are important for agriculture and food security. It was negotiated under the auspices of the FAO Commission on Genetic Resources for Food and Agriculture and adopted by the FAO Conference in 2002. It is the successor agreement to the nonbinding International Undertaking on PGRFA, which had been in effect since 1983.

While the ITPGR has the same objectives as the CBD, it applies only to specific species of PGRFA and embodies a different approach to the definition of property rights over genetic resources. The treaty establishes a Multilateral System for ABS with regard to species of PGRFA (Article 10). Parties yield their sovereign right under the CBD to determine access to their genetic resources in exchange for facilitated access to materials supplied by other parties (Article 10.2). Annex I of the treaty identifies sixty-four crop and forage species covered by the Multilateral System. For other PGRFA species, the treaty supports the CBD's provisions regarding ABS, prior informed consent, and mutually agreed-upon terms as conditions for bilateral contracts for PGRFA transfers.

Access to materials within the Multilateral System is realized through a standard material transfer agreement, which spells out the rights and obligations of the suppliers and recipients of PGRFA (FAO 2006). Access is subject to the restriction that recipients may not claim intellectual property or other exclusive rights to PGRFA "in the form received" from the Multilateral System (Article 12.3(d)). The materials within the system thus have to remain in the public domain. A recipient claiming IPR protection over a product that incorporates material accessed from the Multilateral System must provide a fixed share of the commercial benefits to the financial mechanism of the Multilateral System (Article 13.2). The benefit-sharing mechanism of the Multilateral System seeks to provide incentives for the continued conservation of PGRFA by farmers in poor countries by channeling these contributions primarily to those farmers (Article 13.3).

Interplay in the Regime Complex

TRIPS, UPOV, CBD, and ITPGR can be differentiated according to their objectives and scope. With respect to objectives, the main difference lies in the focus on the protection of suppliers' rights, on the one hand (CBD and ITPGR), and on the protection of users' rights on the other (TRIPS and UPOV). With respect to scope, the CBD refers to all kinds of biological resources, whereas the ITPGR refers only to PGRFA. TRIPS expands the scope of patentable subject matter to all fields of technology, including those that make use of genetic resources, whereas UPOV addresses only the protection of new plant varieties. ITPGR and UPOV are much more narrowly focused on the specific problems associated with the conservation of PGRFA and the protection of farmers' rights and plant breeders' rights (table 7.1).

This section provides a cross-dyadic comparison of the types of interplay that have emerged among supply-related and use-related agreements (columns in table 7.1), as well as among those agreements that address all kinds of genetic resources and those that focus on genetic plant resources for food and agriculture (rows in table 7.1).

The analysis focuses on the degree of overlap and nesting between the different agreements and the extent to which their rules lead to synergies or disruptions in implementation. According to Oran Young's definition, overlapping agreements are created for different purposes but intersect "on a de facto basis producing substantial impacts on each other in the process," whereas an agreement is nested with another when its rules "fit into broader institutional frameworks that deal with the same general

Table 7.1
Scope and objectives in the institutional complex on PGRFA

Scope	Objective	
	Supplier rights	User rights
General	CBD	TRIPS
Specific to PGRFA	ITPGR	UPOV

issue-area, but are less detailed in terms of their application to the specific problem" (Young 1996, 2–3). Abbott and Snidal argue that nesting of international institutions is often incomplete, involving only a partial hierarchy between rules on particular issues. The resulting rule contradictions cannot be easily removed through top-down decision making and may require alternative ways of interplay management (Abbott and Snidal 2006, 4).

Synergy occurs if the implementation of one agreement effectively supports the implementation of another—for instance, by providing guidance on how general principles should be applied in specific cases, or by providing procedures that further joint implementation or resolve conflicts. Disruption occurs if conflicts in rules lead to actual conflicts in the behavior of actors who seek to implement different agreements—that is, if a conflict becomes *manifest* (see Zelli in this volume). Synergy and disruption thus refer to the outcome of institutional interaction rather than the relationship of rules alone. The nesting of rules as such does not necessarily lead to synergy in practice. Similarly, overlapping or contradicting rules do not always lead to effective disruptions.

The following analysis shows that the vertical relationships in table 7.1 are generally synergistic. The agreements with narrower scope (ITPGR and UPOV) determine how the rules of the agreements with broader scope (CBD and TRIPS) should be implemented in the specific area of PGRFA. The horizontal relationships, on the other hand, are more prone to disruptions and conflict. At the core of these disruptions are differing objectives and approaches to the allocation of property rights to genetic resources. Intellectual property rights and plant variety protection as provided for by TRIPS and UPOV make the whole commercial value of an innovation that is based on genetically encoded information appropriable to resource users. Access and benefit sharing under the CBD and ITPGR requires that at least some portion of that same benefit stream must be appropriable to suppliers of genetic resources. The simultaneous allocation of property rights to different actors involved in the supply and use of genetic resources leads to conflicts over the distribution of the benefits arising from their use.

Interplay between Agreements with Similar Objectives but Different Scope

CBD-ITPGR   Nesting is most evident in the interplay between the CBD and the ITPGR, where the nested nature is explicitly referred to in the objectives of the ITPGR. Article 1.1 states that the objectives of the treaty are pursued "in harmony" with the CBD; Article 1.2 adds that the treaty and the CBD will be closely linked. The treaty's Multilateral System is compatible with the CBD's principle of national sovereignty because states agree to create the system "in the exercise" of their sovereign rights (Article 10.2).

CBD parties have generally accepted the ITPGR's Multilateral System thus far. With regard to non-Annex I species, some provider countries have nevertheless expressed concern that the ITPGR's provisions for facilitated access to PGRFA under the Multilateral System may negatively affect their ability to negotiate bilateral agreements with PGRFA users. This is especially a problem for biodiversity-rich countries that are not members of ITPGR and that want to "sell" PGRFA products that are not part of the Multilateral System. Furthermore, some supplier countries fear that the principle of facilitated access may become a model for similar mechanisms for non-PGRFA products, which would, in their view, be detrimental to the negotiation of a regime on ABS (IISD 2005, 2006b).

TRIPS-UPOV   The nested relationship of TRIPS and UPOV is less obvious, mainly because the more specific agreement, UPOV, existed long before TRIPS was established. Therefore, UPOV does not contain direct references to TRIPS, nor does TRIPS explicitly state that UPOV is compatible with TRIPS principles. Nevertheless, UPOV obviously provides a readymade framework for states wanting to make use of the flexibility provided by TRIPS Article 27.3(b) and develop a sui generis system for the protection of plant varieties. In general, any legislation that follows UPOV rules should also be consistent with TRIPS, since UPOV embodies both the most important elements of TRIPS regarding the content of IPRs, as well as the general WTO principles of nondiscrimination and most-favored-nation treatment (Tsioumani 2005, 123). UPOV thus provides for the application of the general IPR principles laid out in TRIPS in the specific area of protection of new plant varieties.

This informally nested relationship does not rule out possible conflicts during implementation. The potential for conflict arises out of certain exceptions allowed under UPOV that may not be supported by TRIPS. For instance, countries may implement legislation under UPOV allowing breeders to use a protected variety for further breeding, based on the breeders' exemption. Similarly, a country adhering to UPOV '78 may allow farmers to reuse and distribute seeds harvested on their own land, based on the farmers' privilege. Such rights are usually limited under patent law, and as yet it is not clear to what extent such exceptions are permitted under TRIPS (Tsioumani 2005, 123). Despite these uncertainties, however, it can be expected that UPOV will most often support the implementation of TRIPS rather than hinder it.

In summary, while occasional conflicts may arise, institutional interaction between the supply-related and the use-related institutions will generally result in synergy rather than disruption. ITPGR and UPOV are complementary to CBD and TRIPS, respectively, because they determine how general principles should be implemented in the specific case of PGRFA (Jungcurt 2008; Andersen 2008; cf. Raustiala and Victor 2004).

Relationships between Agreements with Similar Scope but Different Objectives

CBD-TRIPS   The potential for disruptions is much more evident in the CBD-TRIPS relationship. The CBD gives states the right to control access to their genetic resources and to enforce the benefit-sharing obligations of the users of genetic resources. Effective implementation of these principles, however, requires both supplier and user countries to take legal action. Supplier countries must require users to comply with the requirements of benefit sharing, prior informed consent, and mutually agreed-upon terms, as a condition for access to genetic resources. User countries must inhibit imports of genetic resources that do not comply with these requirements (Rosendal 2006). So far, user countries have made scant efforts to this end.[3]

The TRIPS agreement is to some extent responsible for this lack of complementary action on the user side. TRIPS by itself does not accommodate claims of genetic resource suppliers, nor does it provide for the recognition of property rights that are based on collective systems of knowledge management and ownership, such as community or farmers' rights. These rights could, for instance, be safeguarded through a provision requiring the disclosure of origin of genetic resources in patent applications or proof of prior informed consent in accordance with supplier-country legislation on ABS (Correa 2003; de Carvalho 2005). However, TRIPS does not oblige countries to do so. The minimum standards for patent legislation spelled out in TRIPS are ill-suited for realizing the transfer of benefits to genetic resources suppliers in order to generate incentives for conservation as envisaged by the CBD (Rosendal 2006, 89).

To safeguard their rights under the CBD, supplier countries could design access laws requiring the disclosure of origin in applications for patents in the user country. This would lead to discrimination between users from countries that support the CBD objectives in their IPR laws and those that do not. Users from the latter countries would be obstructed from accessing genetic resources on grounds currently not supported by TRIPS. Such impediment would violate the WTO principles of non-discrimination and most-favored-nation treatment.

A second problem arises if supplier countries that are WTO members seek to incorporate CBD principles into their own IPR legislation. If they require the disclosure of origin and evidence of prior informed consent as conditions for granting IPR protection, such legislation would violate TRIPS Article 27.1, which states that the sole conditions for granting patents shall be that an innovation is new, involves an inventive step, and is capable of industrial application. Making the granting of a patent subject to compliance with benefit-sharing provisions would thus go beyond the conditions laid out in the TRIPS agreement and potentially constitute another form of illegal discrimination. In principle, user countries could bring such violations of the TRIPS agreement before the WTO dispute settlement mechanism. While in practice this has not yet occurred, the threat of economic sanctions may lead countries to give priority to TRIPS, even though it may be in their interest to fully implement the CBD (Rosendal 2006).

The main consequence of these tensions between CBD and TRIPS is an increase in legal uncertainty and transaction costs for both suppliers and users of genetic resources. Legal uncertainty has led to a rise in misappropriation claims, often referred to as biopiracy, in which suppliers accuse users of unauthorized access and use of genetic resources and traditional knowledge, or of not respecting the supplier's rights to benefit sharing. In 2005, an IUCN study of forty cases of misappropriation claims showed that the main problem in dealing with such cases was the absence of clear procedures and legal fora to address such disputes (IUCN 2005). Therefore, supplier organizations often turn to strategies such as public media campaigns to discredit the user for not complying with ABS standards. For users, the absence of clear legal procedures makes it impossible to achieve legal certainty with regard to potential misappropriation claims. Companies are unable to sign ABS agreements that effectively exclude further claims against them. Even worse, most claims are made against users that do make an effort to comply with benefit-sharing provisions: noncompliers go unpunished, since they are not obliged to disclose information that would enable misappropriation to be identified (IUCN 2005, 4).

Access legislation in many provider countries has raised the transaction costs associated with bioprospecting as well as research and conservation projects, mainly out of fear of misappropriation and to some extent unrealistic expectations about the benefits to be shared (Grajal 1999; Jinnah and Jungcurt 2009). Legal uncertainty and increased transaction costs caused by disruptions between CBD and TRIPS have thus reduced the overall benefits from research and development instead of achieving the desired change in their distribution.

Various initiatives have unsuccessfully undertaken to consolidate the two agreements. Most of these have aimed at amending the TRIPS agreement to allow for the recognition of the benefit-sharing rights of genetic resource providers in IPRs. Supplier countries have repeatedly suggested amending the TRIPS agreement to include an obligation in patent applications to disclose the origin of genetic resources and to provide evidence that these resources have been accessed in accordance with the CBD provisions for prior informed consent and mutually agreed terms.[4] Support for such proposals has increased since the adoption of the WTO's Doha Agenda in 2001, which specifically instructs the TRIPS Council "to examine the relationship between the TRIPS Agreement and the CBD" (WTO 2001, Article 19). Consideration of this matter has not yet gone beyond an initial exchange of views, during which it nevertheless became evident that key actors (among them Australia, Canada, the EU, Japan, Korea, New Zealand, Switzerland, and the United States) continue to oppose such an amendment, arguing that there is no substantial conflict between TRIPS and the CBD. Until the collapse of the Doha round of negotiations in 2008, this constellation had not changed (ICTSD 2006, 2008).

Under the CBD, negotiations on an international ABS regime have focused on the very same issues. Next to the general debate on the nature and scope of the new regime, much of the negotiating time has been devoted to discussing a certificate of origin, source, or legal provenance of genetic resources intended to become part of the required information to be submitted in patent applications (IISD 2005, 2006a, 2007).

In short, efforts toward consolidation have so far failed to improve legal certainty or reduce transaction costs in the exchange and use of genetic resources. Regarding the disruptive consequences arising out of the tension between CBD and TRIPS, the situation can well be described as stalemate.

ITPGR-UPOV   Similar problems of legal uncertainty and misappropriation claims might be expected between UPOV and the ITPGR. In some respects, the problem of legal uncertainty may be even greater for plant varieties than in other areas of biotechnology. A single plant variety contains genetic material from a large number of sources, typically acquired through gene banks. Since most of these materials were collected prior to the entry into force of the CBD and the ITPGR, no detailed information is available about the origin of most samples. Providers are unable to determine their claims, while it is impossible for users to comply with benefit-sharing requirements for all sources of genetic material (Cooper, Engles, and Frison 1994; Fowler 2000; Falcon and Fowler 2002).

The main potential for interaction arises out of the limitations that the ITPGR sets to the granting of breeders' rights and other forms of intellectual property. According to ITPGR Article 12.3, users cannot take out IPRs on materials "in the form received" from the Multilateral System. This means that the ITPGR limits the scope of protection to products derived from PGRFA resources, such that the original material has to remain publicly available through the Multilateral System. This provision is valid for patents and sui generis forms of IPRs alike, and thus also limits the scope of plant variety protection that can be granted under UPOV. In the latter case, the restriction is unlikely to lead to conflicts, as long as the UPOV requirements of novelty and distinctness are adhered to. These requirements ensure that protection can be granted only for varieties that are sufficiently different from any known variety, whether these are modern or traditional varieties.[5] It should therefore be possible to prevent cases of misappropriation through careful implementation of UPOV.

Users, however, have to negotiate with only one entity when accessing materials contained in the Multilateral System—the ITPGR Governing Body. The standard material transfer agreement specifies detailed rights and obligations of recipients of materials from the Multilateral System. Benefit-sharing obligations apply to any commercial product that incorporates materials from the Multilateral System and to which access for further research and breeding is restricted through plant variety protection or IPRs.

Furthermore, the standard material transfer agreement contains several easy-to-use forms of acceptance and procedures for arbitration, as well as procedures for dispute resolution and settlement for potential claims of misappropriation. These provisions substantially reduce uncertainty on the side of the recipients about potential claims to benefit sharing, and they minimize the transaction costs of using the system.

For PGRFA outside the Multilateral System, the ITPGR supports the relevant requirements under the CBD. As noted above, this can imply an obligation to disclose additional information in patent applications. Such disclosure requirements would be in conflict with UPOV Article 5, which states that distinctness, novelty, stability, and uniformity shall be the sole conditions for the granting of protection.[6] As with the relation between CBD and TRIPS, a high potential for disruptions thus exists. It remains to be seen whether the advantages of the Multilateral System will eventually convince member states to place all PGRFA materials under the Multilateral System, to avoid such disruptions.

The Multilateral System and the standard material transfer agreement provide for a process that decreases legal uncertainty and transaction costs for both suppliers and users of PGRFA. This leads to the expectation that misappropriation claims and other symptoms of disruption should be far less prominent for genetic materials governed by the ITPGR than those addressed only by the CBD. Two recent developments support this expectation. First, actors from both sides of the negotiating table, including representatives of the seed industry, hailed the conclusion of the ITPGR and of the standard material transfer agreement as a success (IISD 2006b; ISF 2005, 2007). Second, there has been a sharp increase in the conclusion of material transfer agreements since the standard agreement became available (FAO 2007). While the Multilateral System may not have completely removed the potential for disruption, it is at least proving to be a practical means to realize transfers of PGRFA that both users and suppliers of genetic resources accept.

However, the scope for interaction between ITPGR and UPOV extends beyond the mere realization of PGRFA transfers and benefit sharing. The ITPGR places much greater emphasis than UPOV on the protection of farmers' rights, including measures to promote the protection of traditional knowledge associated with PGRFA, benefit sharing by farmers, and farmers' participation in national-level decision making on matters related to the conservation and sustainable use of PGRFA (Article 9.2). These provisions are of fundamental importance for sustainable PGRFA conservation and use, as they provide support to those actors who bear the main responsibility for in situ conservation.

UPOV accommodates farmers' rights to some extent through the farmers' privilege. Even so, both UPOV and ITPGR leave the responsibility for implementing farmers' privilege and farmers' rights to the discretion of national governments. While this delegation avoids a formal

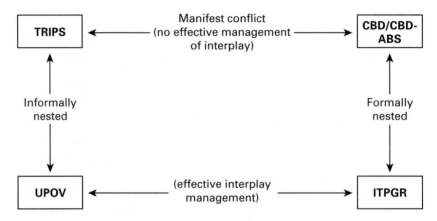

Figure 7.1
Institutional interplay in the regime complex on plant genetic resources

conflict between UPOV and ITPGR rules, it opens significant leeway for countries to decide whether and how strongly they will protect farmers' rights. In the absence of national legislation on farmers' rights in a UPOV member state, their influence will be very limited.

Overall Assessment
To summarize, the relationship between the two agreements addressing supply-related concerns and the relationship between those addressing use-related concerns are generally synergistic, whereas the relationships between supply- and use-related agreements are far more prone to conflict and disruption (figure 7.1). The potential for disruptions is, however, lower between the agreements with narrower scope (ITPGR and UPOV) than that between the two with wider scope (CBD and TRIPS). This difference can be attributed to successful interplay management during the negotiation of the ITPGR, resulting in a system that reduces legal uncertainty and transaction costs in regulating the conservation and use of PGRFA.

Explaining the Difference in Outcomes

The relationship between ITPGR and UPOV has developed very differently from that between CBD and TRIPS, even though the overlap and linkages giving rise to disruptions between them are similar. This section explores some factors that may have facilitated the development and adoption of provisions that reduced the scope for disruption in the course of the ITPGR negotiations. I begin with a brief account of how the respective mechanisms were negotiated under the ITPGR. I then turn to the analysis of some ways in which the ITPGR negotiations differed from the CBD and TRIPS negotiations, discussing to what extent these may have facilitated a consolidation of ITPGR and UPOV.

The empirical accounts in this section are based on a larger research project on institutional interplay in the regime complex related to PGRFA (Jungcurt 2008). Empirical evidence in this project is drawn from various sources, among them participatory observation in the negotiating processes, interviews with key participants in the negotiations, and analyses of meeting documentation, including submissions by countries and observers and independent reports of the negotiations.

The Influence of Experts

The main difference between the ITPGR and the CBD is their approach to realizing access to and sharing of benefits from the use of genetic resources and related provisions on property rights to genetic resources and their products. Under the CBD, discussions have centered on a contract-based approach providing for bilateral agreements between suppliers and users of genetic resources. The voluntary Bonn Guidelines on Access and Benefit Sharing are an attempt to specify the principles and respective rights and obligations of suppliers and users that should guide such contracts. While developing countries initially suggested a similar contract based approach in the ITPGR negotiations, many actors under the FAO did not feel that such an approach was adequate for the regulation of PGRFA. Instead, the negotiations led to the development of a Multilateral System for PGRFA conservation and exchange based on the principle of collaborative management of ex situ and in situ conservation by all parties.

The development of the Multilateral System was heavily influenced by representatives of the International Plant Genetic Resource Institute (now known as Bioversity International), speaking on behalf of the Consultative Group on International Agricultural Research (CGIAR). The CGIAR comprises sixteen public international agricultural research centers, most of which are situated in countries that are centers of origin of important crop species. Together the centers manage the largest collection of PGRFA materials in the public domain. Agreements between the FAO and the CGIAR centers designate the latter as "holders in trust" of these resources, with a mandate to conserve the resources and promote their use for the benefit of present and future generations (Bragdon 2004, 23). Equivalent agreements have been signed with the ITPGR Governing Body.

Representatives of the International Plant Genetic Resource Institute were involved in all stages of the ITPGR negotiations. Their involvement and influence on the negotiations resemble the work of "epistemic communities" described by Peter Haas and others (Haas 1989, 1992). Epistemic communities are "networks of experts with recognized expertise and competence in a particular domain and authoritative claim to policy-relevant knowledge within that domain or issue area" (Haas 1992, 3). The members of such networks share a common understanding of the nature of particular problems in their field of research and the need to address them through international cooperation, as well as an awareness of, and preference for, a set of technical solutions to these problems (Hasenclever, Mayer, and Rittberger 1997, 149).

The emergence of an epistemic community in the ITPGR negotiations was initiated by the participants representing the International Plant Genetic Resource Institute, who provided "timely and relevant technical information directly linked to the institute's domain of expertise" (Sauvé and Watts 2003, 308). In doing so, they were able to influence the perspectives and understandings of an increasing number of delegates and other participants, who developed a set of common understandings revolving around the core problems of international PGRFA conservation and use and who supported the Multilateral System as a preferred technical solution to these problems (ibid.).

Based on their experience in PGRFA management, representatives of the institute were the first to raise concerns that the transaction costs of bilateral contracts as provided for under the CBD and demanded by numerous developing countries would inhibit the exchange of PGRFA materials and thus prove detrimental to plant breeding. In particular, they pointed to the problem of determining the origin of materials that had been collected and stored in gene banks prior to the CBD's entry into force, and to the fact that plant breeding requires access to a vast variety of genetic materials, which would be impossible to monitor through bilateral contracts (see, e.g., Cooper, Engles, and Frison 1994; Fowler 2000; Falcon and Fowler 2002).

Representatives of the institute subsequently put forward proposals for the establishment of a Multilateral System, promoting it as a practicable alternative to a bilateral approach by actively seeking to persuade delegates and involving other actors in the discourse. This led to an expansion of the epistemic community to include other plant-breeding experts and a growing number of country delegates who shared the experts' concerns and supported the establishment of the Multilateral System. This growing support among country delegates eventually led to the adoption of the Multilateral System and the standard material transfer agreement as core elements of the ITPGR (IISD 2001, 2006b).

In contrast to the approach suggested by the CBD, the ITPGR treats PGRFA as an information resource rather than as commodities. Under the Multilateral System, the genetic information embodied in PGRFA must remain accessible to all of its members. Only the use rights to products developed on the basis of these resources can be privatized—subject to the condition that new genetic information must remain available for further research and development, or that the holder of such information must share the benefits of commercialization otherwise (Jungcurt 2008; Tsioumani 2005; IISD 2006b; Fowler 2004).

These rules create an interface between the property rights of PGRFA suppliers and the intellectual property rights of PGRFA users, which can realize ABS at low transaction costs. This interface significantly reduces the scope for disruptions in the joint implementation of ITPGR and UPOV or TRIPS and thus acts as an effective means of interplay management. The central aspects of this regulative structure—the Multilateral System and the standard material transfer agreement—were part of the consensual knowledge that was initially developed by the experts of the International Plant Genetic Resource Institute and later adopted by the broader epistemic community.

It should be noted that the experts involved in the epistemic community were not explicitly pursuing the objective of creating a mechanism for interplay management. Nevertheless, the ITPGR negotiation process provided an environment that was favorable to the development of an integrated approach that included both provider and user perspectives on PGRFA governance. Through the exchange of expert knowledge and experience, experts from both sides came to see the creation of an effective and manageable interface between the system for conservation and benefit sharing, on the one hand, and IPR legislation on the other, as an inherent technical problem of PGRFA governance and a common challenge to the realization of their interests.

Under the CBD and TRIPS such a common perspective between providers and users has not yet emerged. Part of the reason may be the absence of networks involving both negotiation processes under the CBD and TRIPS. In a straightforward extension of the epistemic communities approach, one might expect that such an interinstitutional network of experts would be required to initiate the development of consensual knowledge and integrated perspectives. The network under the ITPGR emerged spontaneously and then gradually evolved into a broader epistemic community involving both sides. This development was supported by several factors and characteristics of the process, which are explored in the following sections.

Scope, Issue Areas, and Functional Linkages

The similar scope of UPOV and ITPGR provided favorable conditions for the emergence of the epistemic community and its integrated perspective. Both ITPGR and UPOV are focused on PGRFA and their use as input to plant breeding, in contrast to the much broader scopes of the CBD and TRIPS. The definition of the scope also has an impact on the boundaries of the issue area and thus on the domestic institutions responsible for negotiations under the two agreements. Delegates to the ITPGR and UPOV negotiations have generally come from the agricultural ministries of their home countries. A common concern for agricultural production links the interests of plant breeders and PGRFA suppliers. In most countries, actor groups on both sides would turn to their agricultural ministries in order to have their interests represented at the international level. UPOV and ITPGR relate to a single domestic issue area, which favors a high degree of mutual understanding and coordination among actors in the different issue areas (Jungcurt 2008, 224).

The close relationship between issues addressed by ITPGR and UPOV and their association with the same domestic institutions made it easier for actors under the ITPGR to anticipate the views of plant breeders, whose interests in plant variety protection are addressed by UPOV. Furthermore, many delegates had precise knowledge of their countries' domestic situation with regard to plant variety protection and obligations under UPOV. The emergence of the expert network under the ITPGR was thus furthered because the negotiators had a much better understanding of the functional linkages between PGRFA conservation and the use of such resources in plant breeding than actors under the CBD. This situation arose because the two institutions concentrated on a specific set of genetic resources and because the interdependence between PGRFA supply and use has been far more pronounced in agriculture than in other sectors of genetic resource use, such as pharmaceuticals or bioengineering.

By contrast, the great majority of delegates negotiating under the CBD have come from environment ministries, whereas negotiators under TRIPS have tended to be from trade or commerce ministries or from their countries' bureaus for intellectual property. Only a few industrialized countries, such as the Netherlands and Switzerland, have sent representatives of their intellectual property institutions as part of their delegations to the CBD negotiations on ABS. The scientific and institutional distance between CBD and TRIPS is much wider. Many CBD delegates have only limited understanding of trade issues in general and TRIPS-related issues in particular. A study by Petit et al. (2001) found that, even though some mechanism for policy coordination existed between environment and trade ministries in most countries in their sample, links between officials dealing with environmental and trade-related aspects of the issue did not exist or did not work. "Trade ministry officials have been able to ignore any call for an exception to the TRIPS provisions of the WTO in the case of agricultural genetic resources" (Petit et al. 2001, 45).

Institutional Learning

A second factor that has favored the emergence of the expert network is the long institutional history of the relationship between ITPGR and its predecessor, the International Undertaking, and UPOV. Negotiations on UPOV were initiated as early as 1956, leading to the adoption of the first UPOV Act in 1968, and the first FAO technical conferences on genetic resources were held in 1961 and 1970, in parallel with efforts to create an international network of gene banks. In contrast, both CBD and TRIPs have been established much more recently. The CBD was adopted in 1992 during the Rio Conference, and TRIPS negotiations were concluded in 1993 as part of the Uruguay round of trade negotiations and the establishment of the WTO, which was also the first time that issues relating to IPRs were addressed in the context of trade liberalization.

Since their establishment, ITPGR and UPOV have interacted in various ways, which has allowed institutional learning on both sides. The first reaction to the 1968 UPOV Act, which had introduced private property rights over plant varieties, came in 1983 with the adoption of the International Undertaking. It declared that PGRFA are the "common heritage of mankind," referring to the treatment of genetic resources as belonging to the public domain and not owned or otherwise monopolized by a single group or interest (Brush 2005, 64). The "common heritage principle" was a reaction on the part of those who were concerned that removing PGRFA from the public domain would negatively affect the livelihoods of traditional farmers, including the possibility of farmers' conserving traditional plant varieties. The broader objective of this movement was to maintain free and unrestricted exchange of PGRFA as a basis for their continued conservation in farmers' fields (Berthaud 1997; Brush 2000).

Between 1989 and 1991, the FAO Conference responded to concerns about possible "incompatibilities" between the International Undertaking and UPOV by adopting a series of "Agreed Interpretations" of the former. The first Agreed Interpretation states that plant breeders' rights, as provided for under UPOV, are "not incompatible" with it—thereby accepting that access to some new varieties may be temporarily restricted (FAO 1989a). The second Agreed Interpretation endorses the concept of farmers' rights in order to provide farmers with financial and other assistance for the conservation and protection of plant genetic resources by participating in the benefits derived from the improved use of plant genetic resources (FAO 1989b). Finally, in 1991, the FAO Conference adopted a resolution explicitly stating that "the concept of mankind's heritage, as applied in the Undertaking, is subject to the sovereignty of the states over their genetic resources," and that "breeders' lines and farmers' breeding material should only be available at the discretion of their developers during the period of development." Furthermore, the resolution recognizes that "conditions of access to plant genetic resources need further clarification" (FAO 1991).

International cooperation on PGRFA conservation under the FAO resulted in a series of attempts to reconcile the interests of plant breeders with the concern for conservation and the interests of PGRFA providers. Prior to the emergence of the CBD and the WTO, actors under the FAO did not question the legitimacy of plant breeders' rights in general. Rather, they sought to complement the introduction of private property rights over plant varieties through the adoption of principles for the recognition of property rights on the supply side. When first adopted, farmers' rights "were largely a metaphor for the need to provide adequate resources and compensation to those farmers who bear the responsibility and cost of conservation activities" (Brush 2005, 88).

Originally, the concept of farmers' rights was thus in contrast to the idea of benefit sharing under the CBD. Actors under the CBD perceived the provisions on national sovereignty and benefit sharing as a mechanism allowing states to claim ownership to genetic resources and to enforce transfers of monetary and other benefits in bilateral access agreements. As a consequence, the discussion on property rights to genetic resources under the CBD became increasingly dominated by distributional concerns (Jungcurt 2008, 226). This emerging contention on the distribution of benefits from the use of genetic resources also had an impact on the understanding of farmers' rights under the ITPGR. In the context of benefit sharing under the CBD, farmers' rights became a "political slogan that was used by developing countries and NGOs to call for rules that realize benefit sharing" (Fowler 2004, 616).

The renegotiation of the ITPGR thus aimed primarily at balancing the objectives of conserving PGRFA and facilitating access to them, with the growing demand of supplier countries for benefit sharing under the CBD. While the "common heritage" principle proved unsuitable for the management of PGRFA, it nevertheless provided a shared idea of what the negotiations were designed to achieve. The principles of the Multilateral System allowed the ITPGR to return to the original objectives that had been articulated in the International Undertaking. The experts who promoted the Multilateral System were able to build on these past experiences. Moreover, they could appeal to the common objective of the International Undertaking to keep access to PGRFA unrestricted, in line with the common heritage principle.

Institutional Structure

The third factor that has supported the emergence of an expert network and its ability to influence negotiations is the institutional relationship between the FAO and the CGIAR. The CGIAR was created in 1971 by the World Bank, in collaboration with the FAO and other institutions. It led the first international expert discussion on PGRFA onservation and established a network of international public research centers and associated gene banks before the FAO became the official host for intergovernmental negotiations on genetic resources for food and agriculture in 1983. The CGIAR and its system of ex situ collections thus existed before any systematic international efforts were made regarding the conservation and sustainable utilization of genetic resources.

The substantive scientific knowledge and technical expertise accumulated by the CGIAR and its research centers allowed it to undertake a key role in those efforts. Furthermore, it became the main public provider of technical infrastructure for ex situ conservation of PGRFA. Notwithstanding the agreements designating the CGIAR as "holder in trust" of genetic resources for the countries of origin, the CGIAR's physical control over substantive PGRFA collections had a decisive impact on its role in the ITPGR negotiations. In contrast to other scientific advisory bodies, the CGIAR could offer advice as well as substantive resources toward the implementation of its preferred options. Since the attractiveness of the Multilateral System increases with the number of countries that make their resources available, it was important to convince countries that enough resources would be shared through the system from the beginning. If countries agreed to place the CGIAR's collections under the Multilateral System, a substantial amount of PGRFA would be available, regardless of other countries' participation or compliance. This provided a key incentive for parties to ratify the treaty, and assuaged fears of a "first-mover disadvantage" that might otherwise have delayed the treaty's entry into force.

The de facto control over its public PGRFA collections was, however, temporarily also a source of distrust that threatened to undermine the CGIAR's credibility as independent expert adviser. Sauvé and Watts (2003) describe three phases of influence of CGIAR experts on the negotiations. During the second phase, which marked the beginning of the CGIAR's active involvement, its proposals "were perceived by some delegations, rightly or wrongly, as favoring some players over others" (Sauvé and Watts 2003, 323). During this time, several supplier countries also accused the CGIAR of being a vehicle of biopiracy since it granted unrestricted access to "their" resources. This mistrust was eventually overcome, as CGIAR experts realized that their influence on political issues and those with distributional consequences was limited, and subsequently restricted their involvement to issues of a technical nature. This change in strategy served to restore the CGIAR's influence and eventually led to the expansion of the expert network into an influential epistemic community.

While the last two factors are arguably specific to the development of the ITPGR and UPOV, the first gives rise to an interesting question: might actors under the CBD and TRIPS take measures to facilitate the exchange of expert knowledge between the two sides and create a common community of negotiators who share a common perspective on the challenges of creating an international regime for ABS? Until 2008, negotiations under both CBD and TRIPS paid little attention to this need to create and exchange expert knowledge. The 2008 meeting of the CBD Conference of the Parties nevertheless decided to convene a series of expert meetings on legal and technical issues relating to access and benefit sharing. These meetings could provide the opportunity to initiate the creation of an integrative network of experts (IISD 2008).

Conclusions

The analysis of institutional interplay within the regime complex on plant genetic resources in the first part of this chapter has shown that the relationship between the two agreements that address supply-related concerns and the relationship between those that address use-related concerns are generally synergistic: each agreement with narrow scope provides substantive contributions to the implementation of the respective agreement with wider scope. By contrast, the relationships between supply- and use-related agreements are far more prone to conflict and disruption; however, the potential for disruptions between the agreements with narrow scope (ITPGR and UPOV) is less than that between the agreements with wider scope (CBD and TRIPS). This can be attributed to the establishment of mechanisms for interplay management during the ITPGR's negotiation, resulting in a system that reduces legal uncertainty and transaction costs in regulating the conservation and use of PGRFA. The provisions of the ITPGR are more detailed, and they define the boundary between resources in the public and in the private domains more clearly. Progress with respect to ITPGR and UPOV has been achieved largely through unilateral interplay management and without formal interinstitutional coordination, although some key actors were involved in both fora.

The second part of the chapter has shown that this success in interplay management is attributable largely to the influence of an expert network that evolved into a broader epistemic community. The influence of this network and its success in building an effective epistemic community were favored by a unique combination of factors that is difficult to emulate in efforts to establish mechanisms for interplay management in other processes. However, it may be possible to derive a few general lessons from this case with respect to improving the prospects for interplay management between the CBD and TRIPS. First, the focus on a specific area of plant genetic resource use—agriculture and plant breeding—facilitated mutual understanding and readiness to discuss alternative solutions. This was enhanced by the fact that both suppliers and users of PGRFA are usually part of the same domestic policy area and thus more likely to be in contact with each other and exchange views and opinions. By contrast, the broad scopes and distinct policy areas addressed by TRIPS and the CBD have so far prevented the emergence of such a common pool of knowledge and shared understandings of possible solutions.

Second, the case also shows that interplay management is a question of time and opportunities for institutional learning. The much longer history of UPOV and activities for PGRFA conservation under the FAO led to repeated adjustments in the institutional framework over time. As CBD and TRIPS evolve, similar opportunities for institutional learning and adjustments may arise, perhaps making it possible to resolve the relationship. However, even when an established division of labor between overlapping institutions is unsatisfactory, changing it may require specific windows of opportunity.

The third factor, the institutional structure that endowed the CGIAR with physical control over a large part of the resources at stake and the infrastructure needed for implementation, is probably most difficult to generalize. While various institutions have been set up with an explicit mandate to deliver expert advice for environmental negotiations, very few would be in a position to provide such means for implementation. Notwithstanding this particular role played by the CGIAR, the analysis here has confirmed the importance of expert knowledge for the development of shared understandings, the resolution of interinstitutional disruptions, and the establishment of mechanisms for interplay management.

Notes

1. The expression *sui generis* indicates an idea, an entity, or a reality that cannot be included in a wider concept. In intellectual property law, rights may be sui generis to owners of a small class of works, such as intellectual property rights in mask works, ship hull designs, databases, or plant species. Sui generis plant variety protection may thus deviate from the wider IPRs applicable in a country, such as patents, trademarks, or copyrights.

2. Unless indicated otherwise, reference is made to the 1991 version of the UPOV Convention. The UPOV acts are available online at http://www.upov.org/en/publications/conventions/index.html.

3. Belgium, Denmark, Germany, Norway, Sweden, and Switzerland have enacted patent laws that include requirements for the disclosure of origin; however, failure to comply does not affect the granting of a patent. Either the provisions are voluntary or noncompliance is subject to a fine (Chatham House 2006).

4. See, for example, WTO (2004), which refers to more than twenty-five communications that have been submitted on the subject to date.

5. While UPOV does not allow for the protection of traditional varieties because these do not meet the stability criterion, traditional varieties are regarded as "prior art" in the evaluation of applications for plant variety protection (Helfer 2002).

6. Article 6 in the earlier acts of UPOV.

References

Abbott, Kenneth W., and Duncan Snidal. 2006. *Nesting, Overlap and Parallelism: Governance Schemes for International Production Standards*. Princeton, N.J.: Princeton University Press.

Andersen, Regine. 2008. *Governing Agrobiodiversity: Plant Genetics and Developing Countries*. Aldershot, UK: Ashgate.

Berthaud, Julien. 1997. Strategies for Conservation of Genetic Resources in Relation with Their Utilization. *Euphytica* 96 (1): 1–12.

Bragdon, Susan, ed. 2004. *International Law of Relevance to Plant Genetic Resources: A Practical Review for Scientists and Other Professionals Working with Plant Genetic Resources*. Issues in Genetic Resources No. 10. Rome: International Plant Genetic Resources Institute.

Brush, Stephen B. 2000. The Issues of in situ Conservation of Crop Genetic Resources. In *Genes in the Field: On-Farm Conservation of Crop Diversity*, ed. Stephen B. Brush, 3–29. New York: Lewis.

Brush, Stephen B. 2005. Protecting Traditional Agricultural Knowledge. *Washington University Journal of Law & Policy* 17:59–110.

CBD. 2002. *Bonn Guidelines on Access to Genetic Resources and Fair and Equitable Sharing of the Benefits Arising out of their Utilization*. Montreal: Secretariat of the Convention on Biological Diversity.

Chatham House, ed. 2006. *Disclosure Requirements in Patent Applications: The State of the Art of National and Regional Measures. Report Produced for the European Commission under Its Sixth Framework Programme as Part of the Project, "Impacts of the IPR Rules on Sustainable Development" (IPDEV)*. London: Chatham House, Energy, Environment and Development Programme.

Cooper, David, Jan Engles, and Emile Frison. 1994. *A Multilateral System for Plant Genetic Resources: Imperatives, Achievements and Challenges*. Rome: International Plant Genetic Resources Institute.

Correa, Carlos. 2003. *Establishing a Disclosure of Origin Obligation in the TRIPS Agreement*. Geneva: Quaker United Nations Office.

de Carvalho, Nuno Pires. 2005. From the Shaman's Hut to the Patent Office: In Search of a TRIPS-Consistent Requirement to Disclose the Origin of Genetic Resources and Prior Informed Consent. *Washington University Journal of Law & Policy* 17:111–186.

Dutfield, Graham. 1999. Sharing the Benefits of Biodiversity: Access Regimes and Intellectual Property Rights. Science, Technology and Development, Discussion Paper No. 6. University of Oxford, Oxford, UK.

Falcon, Walter P., and Cary Fowler. 2002. Carving up the Commons: Emergence of a New International Regime for Germplasm Development and Transfer. *Food Policy* 27 (3): 197–222.

FAO. 1989a. *Agreed Interpretation of the International Undertaking. Twenty-fifth Session of the FAO Conference*. Rome: Food and Agriculture Organization of the United Nations.

FAO. 1989b. *Farmers' Rights. Twenty-fifth Session of the FAO Conference.* Rome: Food and Agriculture Organization of the United Nations.

FAO. 1991. *Resolution 3/91. Twenty-sixth Session of the FAO Conference.* Rome: Food and Agriculture Organization of the United Nations.

FAO. 2006. *Standard Material Transfer Agreement. First Session of the ITPGR Governing Body.* Madrid: Food and Agriculture Organization of the United Nations.

FAO. 2007. *Experience of the Centres of the Consultative Group on International Agricultural Research (CGIAR) with the Implementation of the Agreements with the Governing Body, with Particular Reference to the Standard Material Transfer Agreement. Second Session of the ITPGR Governing Body.* Rome: Food and Agriculture Organization of the United Nations.

Fowler, Cary. 2000. Establishing the Scope of a Multilateral System for Plant Genetic Resources for Food and Agriculture: Implications of Crop Exclusions. *Biopolicy Journal* 3 (2): 1–14.

Fowler, Cary. 2004. Accessing Genetic Resources: International Law Establishes Multilateral System. *Genetic Resources and Crop Evolution* 51 (6): 609–620.

Grajal, Alejandro. 1999. Biodiversity and the Nation State: Regulating Access to Genetic Resources Limits Biodiversity Research in Developing Countries. *Conservation Biology* 13 (1): 6–10.

Haas, Peter M. 1989. Do Regimes Matter? Epistemic Communities and Mediterranean Pollution Control. *International Organization* 43 (3): 377–403.

Haas, Peter M. 1992. Introduction: Epistemic Communities and International Policy Coordination. *International Organization* 46 (1): 1–35.

Hasenclever, Andreas, Peter Mayer, and Volker Rittberger. 1997. *Theories of International Regimes.* Cambridge: Cambridge University Press.

Helfer, Laurence R. 2002. *Intellectual Property Rights in Plant Varieties: An Overview with Options for National Governments.* FAO Legal Papers Online. Rome: Food and Agriculture Organization of the United Nations.

Hess, Charlotte, and Elinor Ostrom. 2003. Ideas, Artifacts and Facilities: Information as a Common-Pool Resource. *Law and Contemporary Problems* 66 (1–2): 111–145.

ICTSD. 2006. *Trade BioRes* 6 (19). Geneva: International Centre for Trade and Sustainable Development.

ICTSD. 2008. *Bridges Weekly Trade Digest* 12 (27). Geneva: International Centre for Trade and Sustainable Development.

IISD. 2001. Sixth Extraordinary Session of the Commission on Genetic Resources for Food and Agriculture: 24 June–2 July 2001. *Earth Negotiations Bulletin* 9 (191). Winnipeg: International Institute for Sustainable Development.

IISD. 2005. Summary of the Third Meeting of the Working Group on Access and Benefit-Sharing of the Convention on Biological Diversity: 14–18 February 2005. *Earth Negotiations Bulletin* 9 (311). Winnipeg: International Institute for Sustainable Development.

IISD. 2006a. Summary of the Fourth Meeting of the Working Group on Access and Benefit-Sharing of the Convention on Biological Diversity: 30 January–3 February 2006. *Earth Negotiations Bulletin* 9 (344). Winnipeg: International Institute for Sustainable Development.

IISD. 2006b. Summary of the First Session of the Governing Body of the International Treaty on Plant Genetic Resources for Food and Agriculture: 12–16 June 2006. *Earth Negotiations Bulletin* 9 (269). Winnipeg: International Institute for Sustainable Development.

IISD. 2007. Summary of the Fifth Meeting of the Working Group on Access and Benefit Sharing and the Fifth Meeting of the Working Group on Article 8(j) and related Provisions: 8–19 October 2007. *Earth Negotiations Bulletin* 9 (382). Winnipeg: International Institute for Sustainable Development.

IISD. 2008. Summary of the Ninth Conference of the Parties to the Convention on Biological Diversity: 19–30 May 2008. *Earth Negotiations Bulletin* 9 (452). Winnipeg: International Institute for Sustainable Development.

IISD. 2010. Summary of the Ninth Meeting of the Working Group on Access and Benefit-Sharing of the Convention on Biological Diversity: 22–28 March 2010. *Earth Negotiations Bulletin* 9 (503). Winnipeg: International Institute for Sustainable Development.

ISF. 2005. *Plant Genetic Resources for Food and Agriculture: Use and Conservation.* Santiago: International Seed Federation.

ISF. 2007. *Plant Genetic Resources for Food and Agriculture.* Santiago: International Seed Federation.

IUCN. 2005. *Analysis of Claims of Unauthorised Access and Misappropriation of Genetic Resources and Associated Traditional Knowledge: Research Report prepared for the Secretariat of the Convention on Biological Diversity.* Ottawa: World Conservation Union, IUCN-Canada.

Jinnah, Sikina, and Stefan Jungcurt. 2009. Could Access Requirements Stifle Your Research? *Science* 323 (5913): 464–465.

Jungcurt, Stefan. 2008. *Institutional Interplay in International Environmental Governance: Policy Interdependence and Strategic Interaction in the Regime Complex on Plant Genetic Resources for Food and Agriculture.* Aachen: Shaker.

MA. 2005. *Ecosystems & Human Well-being: Biodiversity Synthesis.* Millennium Ecosystem Assessment. Washington, D.C.: World Resources Institute.

Petit, Michel, Cary Fowler, Wanda Collins, Carlos Correa, and Carl-Gustaf Thornström. 2001. *Why Governments Can't Make Policy: The Case of Plant Genetic Resources in the International Arena.* Lima: International Potato Center.

Raustiala, Kal, and David G. Victor. 2004. The Regime Complex for Plant Genetic Resources. *International Organization* 58 (2): 277–309.

Rosendal, Kristin G. 2006. The Convention on Biological Diversity: Tension with the WTO TRIPS Agreement over Access to Genetic Resources and the Sharing of Benefits. In *Institutional Interaction in Global Environmental Governance: Synergy and Conflict among International and EU Policies,* ed. Sebastian Oberthür and Thomas Gehring, 79–102. Cambridge, Mass.: MIT Press.

Sauvé, Raphaël, and Jamie Watts. 2003. An Analysis of IPGRI's Influence on the International Treaty on Plant Genetic Resources for Food and Agriculture. *Agricultural Systems* 78 (2): 307–327.

Tsioumani, Elsa. 2005. International Treaty on Plant Genetic Resources for Food and Agriculture: Legal and Policy Questions from Adoption to Implementation. *Yearbook of International Environmental Law* 15:119–144.

UN. 2002. *Report of the World Summit on Sustainable Development, Johannesburg, South Africa, 26 August–4 September 2002.* New York: UN.

WTO. 2001. *Doha Ministerial Declaration.* Ministerial Conference, Fourth Session, Doha, 9–14 November 2001. Doha: World Trade Organization.

WTO. 2004. *The Relationship between the TRIPS Agreement and the Convention on Biological Diversity: Checklist of Issues.* Submission from Brazil, Cuba, Ecuador, India, Peru, Thailand and Venezuela. Geneva: World Trade Organization.

Young, Oran R. 1996. Institutional Linkages in International Society: Polar Perspectives. *Global Governance* 2 (1): 1–24.

8

Regime Conflicts and Their Management in Global Environmental Governance

Fariborz Zelli

Research on institutional interplay looks beyond the confines of a single institution, seeking to grasp its synergetic or disruptive interactions with other regimes or organizations. Despite the inherent centrality of institutional environments, however, most theoretical approaches stop short of considering the deeper structures in which these interactions are embedded. As Underdal (2006, 9) observes, the focus so far has been "primarily on interaction at the level of specific regimes and less on links to the kind of basic ordering principles or norms highlighted in realist and sociological analyses of institutions."

In this chapter, I address this research gap by introducing an analytical framework that includes "major determinants of human behavior and social outcomes" (Underdal 2006, 8) in the explanatory model. This framework deals with a particular type of institutional interplay—conflicts among international regimes—and aims to support the analysis of interplay management within institutional complexes. Over the past two decades, regime conflicts have become more frequent in global environmental governance, sometimes including not only environmental regimes but also regimes aimed at regulating other domains, such as international trade. These conflicts can have significant consequences for the functionality and effectiveness of the affected regimes. By bringing in such core determinants as knowledge and power structures, the framework permits a more in-depth analysis of those consequences. Specifically, it should help to elucidate whether one of these regimes prevails—and if so, why.

Building on international relations theories and pioneering studies on institutional interplay (Chambers 2001a; Oberthür and Gehring 2006a; Stokke 2001a), I successively introduce the various building blocks of the analytical framework. First I define the term "international regime conflict" in a broad manner, showing that conflict can emerge not only from legal incompatibility but also from related behavioral contradictions. This extensive understanding of regime conflicts provides a basis for including major determinants of social behavior.

I then introduce the framework's dependent variable: the prevalence of one of the involved regimes. For both pragmatic and substantive reasons, prevalence is framed in terms of a regime's output effectiveness, that is, the norms and rules it produces. A regime is considered to prevail if it generates stronger output on the contested issues than does the colliding regime. The development of third institutions may also be relevant if their output concerns these contested issues. This chapter thereby adumbrates one of the core topics of this volume, namely, the forces driving the emergence of institutional complexes.

The framework also attends to the second main research question of this volume, the role of interplay management. I establish the process of conflict management as the major intermediate process through which independent variables may affect the prevalence of a regime. I then introduce two independent variables central to international relations theories, power structure and knowledge structure. Power structure is presented as the constellation of power among countries, whereas knowledge structure is considered to be the basis of knowledge about the contested issues. For each of these determinants, I develop a configurational hypothesis and discuss obstructing or magnifying conditions. The concluding section summarizes the components and causal assumptions of this analytical framework. Throughout the chapter I illustrate the various components of this framework by referring to the conflict between the UN climate regime and the World Trade Organization (WTO).

Defining the Research Object: Conflicts among International Regimes

A *regime conflict* is here defined as a functional overlap among two or more international regimes that involves a significant contradiction of rules or rule-related behavior. This definition builds on three more generic terms: *international regimes*, *regime interactions*, and *conflict*. I follow Keohane's definition of international regimes as "institutions with explicit rules, agreed upon by governments, that pertain to particular sets of issues in international relations" (Keohane 1993, 28). How do such "institutions with explicit rules" interact? Oran Young (1996, 2–6) distinguishes several types of interaction, including "overlapping institutions," or regimes formed for different purposes and largely without reference to one another but intersecting "on a de facto basis, producing substantial impacts on each other in the process" (ibid., 6).

Young's understanding of overlapping regimes is a major building block of my definition of regime conflict, but "overlapping" does not necessarily mean "conflictive." Impacts flowing from a regime overlap may also prove to be synergetic. That is why I add the element of "contradiction" in both a legal sense (rules) and a behavioral sense (rule-related behavior). This twofold understanding of contradiction follows Dahrendorf's (1961, 201) broad definition of conflict as any kind of relation between elements that is characterized by "objective" (= latent) or "subjective" (= behavioral or manifest) contradictions.

The most straightforward indication of a conflict between regulatory systems is a contradiction between some of their rules. Such rule incompatibilities, or *latent conflicts,* may appear in the form of an obligation or a permissive rule under one regime and a prohibition of the same conduct under another regime (Vranes 2006, 398–401). A prominent example of such a latent conflict is the contradiction between Article 4 of the 1987 Montreal Protocol and the most-favored nation (MFN) principle of the General Agreement on Tariffs and Trade (GATT). Whereas the MFN principle obliges parties to give equal treatment to trading partners, the Montreal Protocol requires that parties discriminate among different groups of countries. The Montreal Protocol strictly bans the import and export of the controlled ozone-depleting substances from or to "any State not party to this Protocol" unless the non-party is "in full compliance" with the Protocol's phase-out and control measures (Article 4). Despite the latter qualification and the nearly universal membership in the Montreal Protocol, many observers hold that such import bans might be challenged under WTO law (see, e.g., Palmer, Chaytor, and Werksman 2006, 186; Neumann 2002, 266–267; Werksman 2001, 183). Likewise, the issue of full GATT/WTO compatibility of the Montreal Protocol's trade provisions has been the subject of several regime-internal debates and attempts at clarification (Chambers 2001b, 102–103).

My definition of regime conflicts exceeds a merely legal understanding of incompatibilities. With its inclusion of rule-related behavior, the definition also covers *manifest conflicts,* which can include any positional difference between actors who invoke existing rules of different regimes or seek to establish new regime rules. For instance, a manifest conflict arose when the Canadian Navy in 1995 arrested a Spanish-flag halibut fishing vessel on the high seas, just outside the Canadian 200-mile zone. Canada justified this action by reference to the rules of the Northwest Atlantic Fisheries Organization (NAFO), claiming that, at the time of the incident, NAFO's annual total allowable catch rates for halibut had already been taken. Spain, on the other hand, considered Canada's behavior as violating the UN Convention on the Law of the Sea, which grants extensive enforcement powers to coastal states for protection of marine resources only within their 200-mile zones (known as "exclusive economic zones") (see Bernauer and Ruloff 1999, 13–14, 36–38; Joyner 2001).

Given my broader sociological understanding of conflict as positional difference, not all manifest conflicts necessarily arise at the level of implementation. Various subtypes of manifest conflicts are possible, depending on *when* in a regime's life cycle they occur (e.g., during the norm-setting stage), *where* the actors conflict (e.g., within or outside regime organs), and *who* these actors are (e.g., parties, non-parties, or bureaucracies). For instance, whereas legal scholars with their focus on divergences and inconsistencies among existing rules may question whether the overlap between the UN climate regime and the WTO is conflictive, I conceive of it as a manifest conflict, owing to the longstanding positional differences among country coalitions on trade-restrictive measures under the climate regime.

The distinction between latent and manifest conflicts does not imply a static understanding, as conflicts are moving targets. They may change in character from latent to manifest or, in the best of cases, may even lose their disruptive implications altogether, thanks to successful conflict management.

The Concept of Regime Prevalence

Focusing on Output Effectiveness

Research on international regimes has adopted from the literature on policy analysis (Easton 1965, 351–352) the distinction between output (rules and decisions), outcome (behavioral effects), and impact (effects on the relevant subject matter) (Underdal 2002, 5–6; Wolf 1991, 104–107). Oberthür and Gehring (2006b) use these terms to pinpoint three levels of regime interaction.

Of those three levels, the output level is where we can expect immediate repercussions of contradictions among rules or rule-related behavior. As the next section shows in greater detail, important insights can be derived from a comparative assessment of the rules and decisions that regime members agree on in the further development of the regimes in question. Concentrating on the output level is helpful for identifying the immediate effects of regime conflicts. An assessment of various interactive processes within these regimes, such as agenda setting or norm building, may clarify to what extent concerns about a regime conflict affect these processes, for instance by hampering the generation of further output. The affected regimes are often the first or central place where actors discuss overlaps and various strategies for managing them. Output-related debates on contested issues are often traceable in the records of regime bodies such as working groups, panels, subsidiary bodies, or committees.

Unfortunately, an equally accurate and tractable causal analysis of changes on the outcome and impact levels would prove far more difficult. As Underdal (2006, 16) observes, the "number and range of potentially relevant variables increases the further 'out' we move along the causal chain, and most sharply as we go from studying effects on human behavior to examining consequences in terms of change in the biophysical environment itself." Avoiding these methodological impediments, the framework provided in this chapter is geared to the output level.

Indicating Regime Prevalence: Comparative Assessment of Output on Contested Issues

The analytical framework is based on an extended understanding of regime output. In traditional regime research, scholars have tended to equate output with regime formation and the respective processes (agenda setting, negotiation, and implementation). An extended or evolutionary understanding also takes into account the further growth or decline of a regime after its formation—the "regime development path" (Miles et al. 2002, 484).

Quantitative criteria for comparing the development of the involved regimes are (1) the amounts of subsequent output and (2) changes in membership. The first indicator includes additional agreements between states parties, which may be in the form of protocols, amendments, declarations, or decisions made at conferences of parties. The second yardstick highlights the support received for any such subsequent agreements and the regime as a whole. These two sets of figures may indicate the degree of acceptance of the regime as the (leading) regulative institution for a given issue area.

Alone, these two quantitative indicators (additional output and membership) are inadequate for characterizing and comparing the development of regimes. Additional decisions might be basically repetitions of existing ones, adding to the complexity rather than to the substance of a regime. For comprehensive assessment and cross-regime comparison of output effectiveness we need qualitative yardsticks as well. Based on Abbott et al. (2000), Underdal (2002, 5–6), and Wettestad (2001, 319–321), I propose three chief qualitative criteria:

Inclusiveness   The degree to which a regime has brought the targeted system of activities under its jurisdiction

Stringency   Indicators include:

• Degree of obligation (unconditional, with implicit conditions, contingent, hortatory, merely guidelines, or even explicit negation of legally binding treaty)

• Degree of precision (determinate rules, limited or broad issues of interpretation, or even too vague to determine when conduct complies)

Collaboration and delegation   The degree to which regime bodies and third parties have been granted authority, resources, and expertise; indicators include the type of dispute resolution, verification, and implementation mechanisms, decision rules, funding mechanisms, as well as available scientific expertise and bodies for the science–policy interface

Of course, it is important to exercise caution in interpreting any such quantitative or qualitative changes in regimes after the emergence of a regime conflict, for various other factors may account for the course of such overall regime developments. To render such causal analysis more tractable, I suggest focusing on the issues on which the regimes overlap, using the following approaches:

• Comparing the output produced by the colliding regimes on the contested issues

• Comparing the output produced by third institutions on the contested issues

A crucial step is hence the careful identification of the contested issues. In the conflict between the UN climate regime and the WTO, one major issue of controversy is trade-restrictive climate policies and measures (PAMs). Some parties, the most important being the EU, have tried to support and incentivize such measures by proposing stricter rules under the climate regime or by extending the scope of general exemptions under the trade regime. Or they already see a legal basis for such measures in existing rules such as Article 2 of the Kyoto Protocol, which lists the

PAMs that industrialized countries may take to meet their commitments. Although specifying that parties shall "minimize adverse effects . . . on international trade," Article 2 does not rule out approaches that might collide with WTO rules, including fiscal measures (e.g., subsidies granted to firms for research, development, or export of climate-friendly products; border adjustments through tariffs or taxes on energy-intensive imported goods) and regulatory measures (e.g., standards, technical regulations, and labeling reflecting minimum requirements for goods on the basis of their energy or greenhouse gas-intensity). Such measures might collide, for instance, with WTO provisions on subsidies, or with the GATT's national treatment principle, which prohibits discrimination of imported products compared to like domestic ones (see Cosbey and Tarasofsky 2007; Doelle 2004; McKibbin and Wilcoxen 2009).

Indications of a regime's claim to or leverage over such contested issues include willingness among major players to debate the respective subjects under a regime's umbrella and, ultimately, additional decisions and legal provisions. This focus on contested issues is especially pertinent to the inclusiveness criterion, asking to what extent a regime has managed to bring such issues under its jurisdiction, for instance by extending the list of substances for which trade restrictions apply. But the two other qualitative criteria may also be indicative: do subsequent decisions or provisions alter the degree of stringency and collaboration with regard to the contested issues, for instance by introducing binding targets or control measures and by strengthening the respective appraisal procedures?

Another look at the climate–trade case reveals that the climate regime's record on contested issues points to stagnation, if not downright deference. As for stringency, provisions on PAMs remain imprecise and nonbinding. Unlike in the ozone regime, where trade restrictions on ozone-depleting substances are included, parties to the climate regime have not adopted trade-restrictive measures concerning greenhouse gas–intensive products. Not even detailed agreement on good practices in this respect has been achieved. In terms of inclusiveness, the regime's compliance mechanism does not cover the trade effects of PAMs. Moreover, there has been no further elaboration of the dispute settlement procedure of the UN Framework Convention on Climate Change (UNFCCC), whereby "issues involving competing claims would be referred to WTO bodies" (Stokke 2004, 339). Since no extension of general exemptions under the world trade regime in favor of multilateral environmental agreements (MEAs) has taken place, the rights of WTO members to challenge trade-restrictive measures of such agreements remain intact (Eckersley 2004, 36). Likewise, the WTO's Committee on Trade and Environment (CTE) has so far been the only significant international arena where comprehensive conflict management approaches have been discussed.

Apart from an examination of the involved regimes, a second scope of analysis can address the broader institutional context of the regime conflict. Following Raustiala and Victor (2004) and their definition of "regime complexes," this wider context includes other institutions and agreements that also deal with the contested issues and the associated policy fields. These agreements can support one of the involved regimes if they apply a similar approach to the contested issues—that is, if they contain a similar understanding or solution.

In the case of trade-restrictive climate PAMs, developments outside both regimes hint at least indirectly at WTO prevalence. So far no multilateral system on respective measures—for instance, for coordinating product standards or adjustments at the border—has emerged. Multilateral climate or energy partnerships launched in the early 2000s, such as the Partnership on Clean Development and Climate or the Carbon Sequestration Leadership Forum, focus on market-based instruments while avoiding any trade-restrictive approach. These are voluntary initiatives aimed at the removal of trade barriers, especially with respect to climate-friendly technologies (see van Asselt 2007).

To summarize, we may determine the prevalence of a regime at the output level by answering two core questions:

• Which regime has been more successful in bringing the contested issues under its jurisdiction
    • by serving as the preferred arena for negotiations and decisions on these issues?
    • by producing more inclusive, stringent, and delegating provisions on these issues?
• Which regime's approach and jurisdiction in terms of the contested issues have been echoed or strengthened by third institutions (and their degrees of inclusiveness, stringency, and delegation)?

Conflict Management as an Intermediate Process

As one of the key processes for addressing contested issues, interplay or conflict management deserves special attention when we examine the

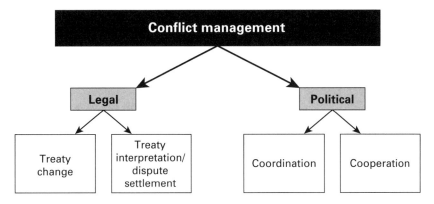

Figure 8.1
Approaches to managing international regime conflicts

consequences of a regime conflict. The term refers to any deliberate attempt to address, mitigate, or remove any incompatibility between the regimes in question. Such attempts to manage a regime conflict may occur within one or both of the regimes, or through cooperation between them. Third institutions may also be relevant as mediators or dispute settlers if they directly attend to the relations among the rivaling regimes and the contested issues. Conflict management responds to an already existing conflict and should not be confused with the conflict itself; it is an additional—not a necessary—element of the interaction between two regimes (Gehring and Oberthür 2006, 314; Stokke 2001a, 11; see also Stokke and Oberthür in this volume).

Figure 8.1 presents a brief overview of management approaches, building on existing taxonomies in international law (Neumann 2002, 317–512; Pauwelyn 2003, 237–439). These approaches may be differentiated according to whether they affect the wording or meaning of rules (legal approaches) or involve the active coordination or cooperation between regime bodies (political approaches) (see also van Asselt in this volume).

Legal approaches include negotiations among parties about treaty changes, for instance concerning the inclusion of priority clauses in favor of one or more regimes. The interpretation of treaty rules by state parties or dispute settlement bodies within the regime can provide another form of legal conflict management. Moreover, if appealed to, third parties such as regime-external dispute settlement agencies (e.g., the International Court of Justice) might provide interpretations of overlapping rules, by referring to superordinate regulatory systems (e.g., the Vienna Convention on the Law of Treaties).

As for political approaches, coordination refers mostly to ad hoc or temporary consultations between regime organs (especially secretariats or expert working groups), whereas cooperation implies continuous and intensive relations between regimes. Cooperation is often institutionalized by agreement or by establishing special agencies, such as the Liaison Group of the Convention on Biological Diversity, the UNFCCC, and the UN Convention to Combat Desertification (Neumann 2002, 92–108). Such agreements may address a range of different targets, such as the coherence of rules and national implementation, the common support of implementation, joint or coordinated scientific research and assessment, and information exchange (Yamin and Depledge 2004).

What role does conflict management play? In the analytical framework, conflict management is understood as an "intervening process [. . .] through which one variable exerts a causal effect on another variable" (Mahoney 2000, 531). Management approaches such as treaty change or interregime cooperation can influence the prevalence of a regime but do not genuinely cause such prevalence: the choice of one or more management approaches, as well as their course and outcomes, is itself rooted in the independent variables. As the remaining sections illustrate, analyzing the intermediate process of conflict management can help substantiate the causal significance of such independent variables for the prevalence of a regime.[1]

Important insights can be gained also when the management process does not lead to agreement. Whenever a policy response in favor of a certain regime is restricted or stalled, this points to deference on the part of that regime. In the CTE, various attempts to initiate processes for extending the scope of the general exemptions from the WTO's nondiscrimination principles to clearly cover trade-related measures under MEAs have failed to yield tangible results thus far. Moreover, since the mandate for the Doha round of trade negotiations was narrowed to binding rules under MEAs, the negotiations did not cover PAMs under the UN climate regime. In the absence of an extensive priority clause, some authors have argued that the shadow of WTO law and its strong dispute settlement system can provoke anticipatory conflicts or chilling effects in other regimes (Stilwell and Tuerk 1999; Eckersley 2004; see also Axelrod in this volume; Gehring in this volume). In such cases, negotiators of environmental regimes might prefer regime-internal autonomous adaptation and refrain from more ambitious policy responses (Gehring and Oberthür 2006, 314–316).

Determinants of Regime Prevalence: Power and Knowledge

This section employs two core independent variables from international relations theories for the study of regime conflicts: the power structure, and the knowledge structure in which the rivaling regimes are embedded. Bringing in these determinants in the following involves two crucial steps:

1. Framing the independent variable as an asymmetry (that is, which regime scores better in terms of this determinant?), then generating a "prime hypothesis" (Van Evera 1997, 11) that conveys the relationship between independent and dependent variables. In case of a conflict among international regimes, the one(s) with a higher score of factor A will prevail.

2. Moving from this prime hypothesis to a configurational one by attending to conditions, causal mechanisms, the role of conflict management, and rival explanations.

Power Structure

I derive the concept of power structure in regime conflicts in part from traditional power-based regime theories. They offer several structural determinants for the formation and robustness of regimes that can also help to explain regime prevalence. One of these theories is hegemonic stability theory, which "posits that regimes are neither created nor maintained unless there is hegemonic leadership in this issue-area" (Hasenclever, Mayer, and Rittberger 1997, 103). The hegemon may be benevolent (Snidal 1985), that is, willing to provide collective goods all by itself, or coercive (Gilpin 1981; 1987), using its power to impose its own will on others and forcing them to contribute as well. However, the claim that only states privileged by a hegemon are capable of generating international regimes has come under criticism. Snidal himself has shown that, through collective action, a group of states "may effectively substitute for hegemonic unilateral leadership" and succeed in achieving their common good (Hasenclever, Mayer, and Rittberger 1997, 101).

The broader concept of the most powerful coalition of countries—which may include the hegemon, but does not need to—is applicable to a wider array of cases of regime conflicts. Not every regime conflict takes place among regimes that include a (regional) hegemon. Moreover, the negotiations of major trade or environmental regimes have been dominated not by a single power but by blocs or coalitions of countries. In the case of the climate regime, for example, the EU, the Umbrella Group of non-EU developed countries, and the G-77 and China have formed such groups, with further subgroups such as the least-developed countries and small-island developing states.

The assessment of a coalition's power in a regime conflict may involve various dimensions. It clearly includes issue-specific power, that is, capabilities with respect to the subject matters of the involved regimes in general and the contested issues in particular. In addition, one could also consider classical yardsticks of power-based theories, such as the economic and military resources that may be used for threats or incentives as well as for concessions and side payments in other issue areas (Baldwin 2002, 180).

In the climate-trade case, power could be assessed in terms of capabilities or potentials in relation to climate change (using indicators such as the generation of greenhouse gas emissions and vulnerabilities to climate change impacts), general economic and trading capabilities (e.g., GDP and export figures), as well as military capabilities (e.g., military spending or troop strength). On all three counts, over an observation period from the establishment of the two regimes in the 1990s until the present, the various U.S.-led coalitions operating in these regimes can be considered the most powerful groups of countries. However, this dominance has been shrinking in recent years, especially for economic- and climate-related capabilities. In line with neorealist tenets, we could therefore expect other countries to have a growing incentive to balance against the United States and its allies. Another qualifying aspect is the relatively low degree of concurrence of these coalitions, a result of their heterogeneous membership and voting behavior. For instance, the Umbrella Group includes chief producers of fossil fuels, such as the United States, Australia, and Russia, but also Japan, which lacks significant domestic fossil fuel resources (Oberthür and Ott 1999, 17–21).

In addition to identifying the agents of power, it is also important to define more precisely the concept of power. Underdal (2002, 29–33) ascribes the poor performance of power-based propositions in regime research to rather inappropriate concepts that highlight the concentration of capabilities or overall structural power while neglecting the "distribution of power over the configuration of interests [in] the system of activities to be regulated" (ibid., 32). Unlike traditional understandings, the latter concept relates directly to the control over outcomes in collective problem solving and may hence prove more suitable for researching regime formation: "the probability that a particular solution will be adopted and successfully implemented is a function of *the extent to which it is perceived to serve the interests of powerful actors*" (ibid., 30; emphasis in original). In a regime conflict, such a "solution" might imply the prevalence of one regime over another concerning the contested issues. Accordingly, a prime hypothesis that forms the point of departure for the following configurations reads as follows: in case of a conflict among international regimes, the regime(s) supported by the more powerful coalition of countries will prevail.

To flesh out this assumption, I now turn to two major structural conditions for its validity: problem structure and decision structure. Like the independent variable, these structural conditions emerge from the literature on the formation and effectiveness of single regimes.

As Underdal (2002, 15–23, 30–31) points out, the structure of the problem constitutes an important condition for the influence of a powerful coalition in a regime. For a "benign problem" (one characterized by similar or slightly differing preferences among countries), it is relatively easy for the powerful group to generate support for a regime. But in case of a severe asymmetry of preferences ("malign problem"), the governments of less powerful countries will think twice: "concentration of power in the hands of *pushers* might generate fear among *laggards* and possibly also other prospective parties that *their* interests will not be accommodated within the regime" (ibid., 31).

According to Rittberger and Zürn (1990), the degree of problem malignancy (i.e., of asymmetry of preferences) depends on the object of contention. For instance, governments might differ about core values and goals, in which case they might be hardly willing to compromise despite the incentives that more powerful countries might offer. The chances for building or maintaining a regime that would contradict the core values of some members are hence very low. On the other hand, the prospects for regime formation and maintenance are better if governments disagree only on the means to achieve shared values and goals. Apart from values and means, Rittberger and Zürn distinguish two further types of conflict objects. These are absolutely assessed goods (where only one's own shares and gains in these goods matter; in short, How much do I get?) and relatively assessed goods (where relative shares and gains matter:

How much more than the others do I get?). Altogether, prospects for regime formation are best in conflicts about absolutely assessed goods, then decrease through conflicts about means and relatively assessed goods, to conflicts about values (ibid., 31–32).

Translating these insights from single-regime research to the study of regime conflicts, we could speak of benign and malign conflicts. A regime conflict brings together the problem structures underlying the separate regimes, thereby creating an overall problem structure on the contested issue. For instance, we could ask, do regimes collide on certain core values or goals? In such a case, it would be highly difficult for delegates of a powerful group of countries to achieve the prevalence of their favored regime. Or do regimes clash only concerning the means (fiscal instruments, binding targets, etc.) they prescribe in order to attain their objectives? (See Young 2002, 125–129; Rosendal 2001, 96–102.)

To illustrate, the climate and ozone regimes share the same general value, protection of the atmosphere, but differ with regard to the phase-out of certain dangerous greenhouse gases (Rosendal 2001, 99). Likewise, for the conflict between the climate and trade regimes, the objects of contention are the means (trade-related PAMs) considered appropriate for reaching the chief objective of the UN climate regime: "to prevent dangerous anthropogenic interference with the climate system" (UNFCCC Article 2).

Apart from the problem structure, a second condition affecting the influence of the powerful coalition is the decision structure, or the distribution of votes in the regimes' decision-making bodies (Underdal 2002, 31). If the size of their coalition in a "one country, one vote" procedure is too small, delegates of powerful countries might not be able to generate more inclusive and stringent output in favor of *their* regime. By the same token, this condition can affect the process of conflict management within or between the affected regimes. If representatives of powerful countries are not able to mobilize a sufficient majority during the management process, they may seek to influence the regime conflict through other channels, outside the affected regimes, in arenas where they can better exert their power.

In light of these qualifications, a modified and configurational hypothesis on the consequences of regime conflicts would read as follows:

In case of a conflict among international regimes, the regime(s) supported by the more powerful coalition of countries will prevail.

These countries will be successful in influencing the output generation on the contested issues
- if the conflict structure is benign;
- if the decision structure of the affected regimes does not disadvantage the powerful coalition.

Otherwise, the more powerful coalition will try to support the approach of its preferred regime to the contested issue through third institutions and agreements.

An in-depth examination of the causal mechanisms that power-based theories invoke can substantiate this hypothesis. Neorealists assume that countries try to maximize their interests through extended influence and relative gains, whereas interactions with other countries are characterized by a mutual lack of confidence and fear of cheating (Brooks 1997; Grieco 1988). Guided by these assumptions, we can explore whether the dominant coalition of states has indeed used its power to maximize its interests in the affected regimes—and whether lack of confidence has led them to seek solutions in alternative arenas—thereby leading to the observed consequences on the output level.

In the case of trade-related PAMs, the United States and its allies have indeed been "highly influential in establishing a market approach to managing climate change" (Boyd, Corbera, and Estrada 2008, 106). The Umbrella Group successfully rejected proposals tabled by the EU at Kyoto for a binding list and mandatory coordination of PAMs. Members of the group also ensured that the issue of taxing aviation or marine bunker fuels was delegated to other organizations (Oberthür 2006, 63; UNFCCC 2000, 17–29). On most occasions, the decision structure did not impede the interests of the United States and its allies on any of these contested issues. The consensus principle in both regimes equipped them with a de facto veto power against the EU proposals, and developing countries largely seconded the Umbrella Group's opposition to them.

Nevertheless, out of dissatisfaction with the overall course of the UN climate regime, in particular the differentiation of emission reduction responsibilities, the United States withdrew from the Kyoto Process in 2001. It colaunched new multilateral forums with better voice opportunities, including the Asia-Pacific Partnership and the Major Economies Process on Energy Security and Climate Change, where voluntary and WTO-consistent climate strategies have since been pursued (van Asselt 2007; McGee and Taplin 2009).[2]

The climate-trade example further illustrates how regime conflicts are moving targets. New developments may alter the interests of country coalitions and, given the shrinking power of the United States, also the drivers underlying the observed regime prevalence. Discussions on bunker fuels have continued to surface in the UN climate regime. Moreover, recent years have witnessed a shift of interests in U.S. domestic politics toward more trade-restrictive approaches. In June 2009, the House of Representatives adopted a legislative proposal that contains a provision that would oblige the president to impose tariffs or offsetting requirements on goods from countries that do not take comparable action to limit greenhouse gas emissions. At the Copenhagen climate summit in December 2009, some of the potentially affected importing countries such as China threatened to invoke the world trade regime's Dispute Settlement Body in such a case.

In examining the relevance of causal mechanisms, a focus on the intermediate process of conflict management can be particularly instructive. Have members of the more powerful coalition of countries successfully initiated or supported a certain type of conflict management? To what extent have such attempts favored the regime(s) backed by this powerful coalition? For instance, in terms of legal conflict management, such countries might have pushed for a treaty change, such as a priority clause favoring one or more regimes. Moreover, they might have appealed to a dispute settlement body (e.g., the International Court of Justice), arguing for the jurisdiction of a certain regime over a contested issue. Likewise, we could analyze whether the more powerful coalition has agitated for stronger interregime coordination or cooperation, for instance by calling directly on secretariats to take action, or by sponsoring a decision of the conference of the parties.

Such analysis could also try to show whether coalition members have successfully prevented or obstructed certain conflict management approaches favored by a competing group of countries. For instance, the continuous opposition by a U.S.-led coalition, along with most developing countries, stalled an initiative by the EU, Switzerland, and other countries for an "environmental window"—a priority clause for certain environmental regimes—in relevant WTO agreements (Sampson 2001, 74; Zelli 2006, 204–206). This opposition also led to the abovementioned restriction of the Doha mandate to existing and binding MEA rules, thereby excluding the issue of climate-related PAMs from the negotiations.

Knowledge Structure

Constructivists suggest an alternative organizing principle in international relations: they argue that actors, actions, and institutions are embedded in the profoundly normative structure of international society rather than in an international state of anarchy. The formation of regimes indicates that their underlying core norms have met the consent of a critical mass of key governments (Finnemore and Sikkink 1998, 897). However, applying this theoretical approach in empirical analysis proves rather difficult. Measuring the independent variable requires profound insight into the fundamental beliefs, values, and expectations that drive actors in their behavior. Moreover, the entire constructivist ontology and concept of causation are different from rationalist, unidirectional cause-and-effect approaches (Kratochwil and Ruggie 1986, 767).

In light of these challenges, "weak cognitivism" might offer a welcome refuge (Hasenclever, Mayer, and Rittberger 1997, 139–154). This camp of knowledge-based regime theories does not problematize the overall normative environment of regimes but focuses instead on the knowledge structure: the cognitive factors that shape actors' preferences and their understandings of available options. Weak cognitivism is even compatible with a rationalist ontology, by assuming that actors pursue and maximize their (knowledge-based) interests and preferences. According to this approach, the independent variable may be framed as the consensual basis of knowledge. The more negotiators agree on the nature of a problem and suitable solutions, and the firmer such common knowledge becomes due to better evidence and reasoning, the better the chances are for the formation and maintenance of a cooperative regime (Haas 1992, 29).

A focus on the contested issues can help tailor this theory to the subject of regime conflicts. In a regime conflict, the colliding regimes will obviously approach these issues differently. Either they conceive of them in a dissimilar manner (e.g., as harmful substances or as tradable commodities) or they devise different solutions for them. Weak cognitivism would indicate that such disparate approaches could result from different bases of knowledge. A prime hypothesis could read as follows: In case of a conflict among international regimes, the regime(s) whose approach to the contested issue is backed up by the stronger and more widespread basis of knowledge will prevail.

The relevance of the bases of knowledge might depend on several conditions, two of which I discuss here: the problem structure and the influence of knowledge brokers. The previous section introduced the concept of problem structure in terms of the malignancy of the regime conflict. I expect the relevance of the knowledge bases to decrease the more malign a conflict is: the more governments' preferences differ on the contested issue, the less susceptible will they be to new knowledge that supports positions other than their own. This assumption rests on research on institutional interplay. As Stokke (2001b, 22–23) observes, cognitive interaction across regimes is more likely in synergetic relations. Yet the more controversial a setting becomes, the harder it is to facilitate the prevalence, let alone the successful diffusion, of certain regime features or problem-solving policies.

A second condition for the relevance of a basis of knowledge in a regime conflict is the entrepreneurial leadership provided by "knowledge brokers." The list of potential knowledge brokers is quite extensive and includes members of regime secretariats, working groups, and subsidiary bodies, as well as private actors, transnational organizations, and informal networks (Underdal 2002, 35–36). Informal networks include epistemic communities, which have played a prominent role in the cognitivist regime literature. According to Haas (1992), the influence of epistemic communities depends on several conditions: the degree of uncertainty among policymakers on core aspects of the subject matter, the degree of consensus among scholars on these aspects, and the degree of institutionalization of scientific advice—that is, institutional openness to the advice.

To sum up these conditions, a configurational hypothesis on the relevance of the basis of knowledge would read as follows:

In case of a conflict among international regimes, the regime(s) whose approach to the contested issue is backed up by the stronger and more widespread basis of knowledge will prevail.

This stronger knowledge basis will have a high influence on the output generation on the contested issues
- if the conflict structure is benign;
- if the knowledge basis is shaped and supported by influential knowledge brokers such as epistemic communities.

Epistemic communities will be able to shape and support the knowledge basis on the contested issues
- if they feature a high degree of consensus on the contested issues;
- if the involved regimes feature a high degree of institutional openness to their advice.

Coming back to the climate-trade case, the role that the global climate regime assigns to the Intergovernmental Panel on Climate Change (IPCC) is one of the best examples of institutional openness. The panel's four assessment reports have induced social learning processes among policy-makers, thereby supporting and shaping the formation and evolution of the global climate regime (Siebenhüner 2006). Regarding the contested issue of trade-restrictive measures, the reports stress that the suitability of subsidies, subsidy removals, standards, regulations, energy taxes, and other instruments depends on a country's energy market, economic and political structures, and societal receptiveness. The Third and Fourth Assessment Reports refer explicitly to potential overlaps with WTO rules, discussing the controversial issues of border adjustments and product-related process and production methods. They suggest a multilateral agreement on trade-restrictive measures that would guarantee comparable actions across member countries, with a view to avoiding a direct collision with WTO rules (IPCC 2001, 430–437, 2007, 781–783). The IPCC's discussion of such measures has drawn criticism, including from the United States and Saudi Arabia, which would prefer a stronger focus on market-based mechanisms and less concentration on government activities such as border adjustments (IISD 2007, 8).

With respect to other knowledge brokers, various research institutes and think tanks providing expertise on trade-environment overlaps in general or trade-climate overlaps in particular have so far failed to establish an umbrella organization that can embody, identify, and regularly review consensual knowledge *among* them.[3] This state of affairs makes it difficult to identify alternative knowledge bases that might adhere to "a common vision about economic growth [and] trade liberalization" (Goldstein 1998, 146) and thereby compete with the IPCC's preference for a multilateral solution on trade-restrictive PAMs.

For epistemic communities to achieve a strong entrepreneurial role in a regime conflict, institutional openness must characterize all regimes involved. In the case of the global climate and trade regimes, however, such openness varies considerably across arenas. The WTO has no permanent "interface body" comparable to the climate regime's Subsidiary Body for Scientific and Technological Advice as a forum for regular interaction with major knowledge brokers. The possibilities for larger epistemic communities to interact with WTO representatives are confined to a few expert groups on specific topics, as well as conferences, seminars, and courses organized by the WTO Secretariat's Economic Research and Statistics Division. Otherwise, knowledge brokers must rely on the few channels of information exchange provided for NGOs, such as the annual WTO Public Forum. Ultimately, given its mandate, the External Relations Division has some influence on filtering which types of information enter the organization from the NGO community and which ones do not.

With respect to conflict management, the analysis may further examine the impact of the stronger knowledge basis on the process and the results of such management. Have knowledge brokers favored or opposed a certain form of conflict management, and have they been directly involved in it? While doing so, have they supported one regime's approach to the contested issues over others'? And have their recommendations been incorporated into the results of the management process? For instance, with regard to legal management approaches, we could examine whether epistemic communities or other knowledge brokers who advise governments or regime bodies have advocated a treaty amendment in favor of one regime. Epistemic communities may also inform the process of treaty interpretation and provide expertise or submit amicus curiae briefs to dispute settlement bodies (Neumann 2002, 619–622).

Regarding trade-restrictive PAMs, however, there has been no possibility for regular input by epistemic communities to the main venue for conflict management. The CTE does not provide for any direct contribution from outside experts or other non-state actors, not to mention any permanent observer status for them (Eckersley 2004, 34). Scientific experts can influence CTE discussions only ad hoc and indirectly, by briefing governmental representatives. In summary, unfavorable context conditions—the low institutional openness of the WTO in general and of the main conflict management venue in particular—might be one explanation for why the recommendations of the IPCC (presumably representing the strongest knowledge basis on the contested issues) were not pursued, and why no multilateral accord on trade-restrictive climate policies could be reached within or outside the involved regimes.

Rival Explanations

Considering the variety of theories on international regimes, several other factors are capable of shaping the generation of regime output on the contested issues. Presenting an exhaustive list of such further factors, let alone thoroughly deriving them from their respective theories, is beyond the scope of this chapter. Suffice it here to sketch some of them in the form of prime hypotheses, thus illustrating the scope of potential control factors to be examined when analyzing regime conflicts.

Strands of neoliberal institutionalism elaborate various output-related assumptions, including the assumption that the formation and design of a regime result from the collective action problem or strategic situation that the regime is trying to regulate.[4] Proponents of this situation-structural approach also establish secondary factors that may influence regime output, such as the number of actors in the issue area, the shadow of the future, or the salience of solutions (Hasenclever, Mayer, and Rittberger 1997, 44–59). These theories suggest that the regime regulating the more favorable strategic situation or scoring better on such secondary factors will prevail in a regime conflict.

With respect to constructivist factors other than knowledge structure, Müller (1994) and Risse (2000) apply the theory of communicative action to international relations research. They argue that wherever parties are open to persuasion and have high confidence in the authenticity of each other's statements, the strength and acceptance of arguments may significantly shape agreements. Accordingly, under such conditions, a regime based on the better argument would stand a greater chance of prevailing in a regime conflict.

Another strand of regime analysis focuses on the role of lead bureaucracies (secretariats) in the effectiveness of international institutions (Barnett and Finnemore 2004; Biermann and Siebenhüner 2009). This research agenda crosses the lines separating classic regime theories. On the one hand, in accordance with the tenets of sociological institutionalism, it conceives of international organizations as independent actors serving specific social purposes or values; on the other hand, secretariats might do so by following a rather rationalist logic of action, that is, with the intent of maximizing their interests by promoting their own autonomy and the effectiveness of the regime they serve. On the basis of this literature, it could be hypothesized that the prevalence of a regime is also a function of certain features of its secretariat, such as autonomy, coherence, and goal orientation (Biermann and Siebenhüner 2009).

Finally, liberal international relations theories scrutinize the emerging influence of business or civil society actors on regime output through various domestic and international channels (Putnam 1988; Wapner 1996). These theories might lead us to expect that the regime backed by more influential domestic and transnational actors will prevail.

Conclusions

The analytical framework advanced here relates the core themes of this book, institutional complexes and interplay management, to certain causal factors that loom large in the broader analysis of international regimes. Specifically, the framework draws attention to causal factors and processes that can explain which regimes prevail in conflictive institutional complexes and why, and it supports analysis of how interinstitutional conflicts influence the effectiveness of the regimes involved:

• Two independent variables adopted from regime theories: the power structure and the knowledge structure in which the competing regimes are embedded

• The dependent variable: regime prevalence, framed in terms of output strength within the colliding regimes as well as the wider regime complexes regarding the contested issues

• The intervening process of conflict management through which the independent variables may cause regime prevalence

• Cross-references and causal links between the different variables—in order to sustain the coherence of the proposed framework, instead of presenting a mere "toolbox" of loosely connected factors

Figure 8.2 summarizes the assumed causal relations among the three types of variables. According to this framework, analyzing the emergence and management of institutional complexes requires attention to power and knowledge structures that are partly independent of the international institutions in question.

The framework advanced in this chapter certainly does not provide a universal solution capable of dealing with the full range and depth of interaction effects, not least because of its focus on output effectiveness and its inherent cause-and-effect epistemology. It occupies a middle

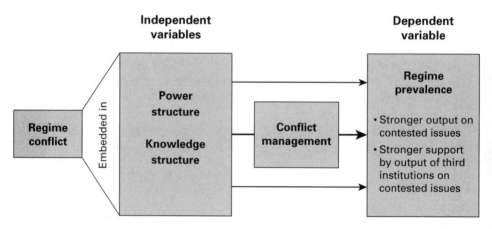

Figure 8.2
Overview of analytical framework

ground that attends to fundamental determinants while keeping research manageable.

The limited validity scope of the framework leaves theoretical ground for further research. Such research should relate not only to the explanation of regime prevalence but also to other aspects of regime conflicts, such as the causes of their emergence or the conditions for successful interplay management. These challenges should not deter but rather attract scholars, since the theoretical and empirical rewards are equally tempting. Insights from conflict analyses can help identify strategies to strengthen environmental regimes or to enhance synergies among free trade and global environmental protection. Explicit consideration of core determinants from social theories, as this chapter suggests, is an important prerequisite for developing such successful strategies.

Notes

1. This is not to say that the process analysis should focus solely on conflict management. Decisions on contested issues can also be made in other contexts and forums (including third institutions). Nevertheless, conflict management should be given specific attention, since of all output-related processes, it is most explicitly geared to addressing a regime conflict.

2. The process was continued by the new U.S. administration under President Obama as the Major Economies Forum on Energy and Climate.

3. These institutes include, to name a few, the Center for International Environmental Law, the International Centre for Trade and Sustainable Development, the International Institute for Sustainable Development, the International Development Research Centre, the South Centre, and the World Trade Institute.

4. To some extent, the preceding sections incorporate such interest-based assumptions by pinpointing the constellation of preferences and problem structure as major conditions for the impact of power and knowledge structures.

References

Abbott, Kenneth W., Robert O. Keohane, Andrew Moravcsik, Anne-Marie Slaughter, and Duncan Snidal. 2000. The Concept of Legalization. *International Organization* 54 (3): 401–419.

Baldwin, David A. 2002. Power and International Relations. In *Handbook of International Relations*, ed. Walter Carlsnaes, Thomas Risse, and Beth A. Simmons, 177–191. London: Sage.

Barnett, Michael N., and Martha Finnemore. 2004. *Rules for the World: International Organizations in Global Politics*. Ithaca, N.Y.: Cornell University Press.

Bernauer, Thomas, and Dieter Ruloff. 1999. *Handel und Umwelt: Zur Frage der Kompatibilität internationaler Regime*. Opladen: Westdeutscher Verlag.

Biermann, Frank, and Bernd Siebenhüner, eds. 2009. *Managers of Global Change: The Influence of International Environmental Bureaucracies*. Cambridge, Mass.: MIT Press.

Boyd, Emily, Esteve Corbera, and Manuel Estrada. 2008. UNFCCC Negotiations (pre-Kyoto to COP-9): What the Process Says about the Politics of CDM-Sinks. *International Environmental Agreements: Politics, Law and Economics* 8 (2): 95–112.

Brooks, Stephen G. 1997. Dueling Realisms. *International Organization* 51 (3): 445–477.

Chambers, W. Bradnee, ed. 2001a. *Inter-linkages: The Kyoto Protocol and the International Trade and Investment Regimes*. Tokyo: United Nations University Press.

Chambers, W. Bradnee. 2001b. International Trade Law and the Kyoto Protocol. Potential Incompatibilities. In *Inter-linkages: The Kyoto Protocol and the International Trade and Investment Regimes*, ed. W. Bradnee Chambers, 87–118. Tokyo: United Nations University Press.

Cosbey, Aaron, and Richard Tarasofsky. 2007. *Climate Change, Competitiveness and Trade: A Chatham House Report*. London: Royal Institute of International Affairs.

Dahrendorf, Ralf. 1961. *Gesellschaft und Freiheit: Zur soziologischen Analyse der Gegenwart*. Munich: Piper.

Doelle, Meinhard. 2004. Climate Change and the WTO: Opportunities to Motivate State Action on Climate Change through the World Trade Organization. *Review of European Community & International Environmental Law* 13 (1): 85–103.

Easton, David. 1965. *A Systems Analysis of Political Life*. New York: Wiley.

Eckersley, Robyn. 2004. The Big Chill: The WTO and Multilateral Environmental Agreements. *Global Environmental Politics* 4 (2): 24–40.

Finnemore, Martha, and Kathryn Sikkink. 1998. International Norm Dynamics and Political Change. *International Organization* 52 (4): 887–917.

Gehring, Thomas, and Sebastian Oberthür. 2006. Comparative Empirical Analysis and Ideal Types of Institutional Interaction. In *Institutional Interaction in Global Environmental Governance: Synergy and Conflict among International and EU Policies*, ed. Sebastian Oberthür and Thomas Gehring, 307–371. Cambridge, Mass.: MIT Press.

Gilpin, Robert. 1981. *War and Change in World Politics*. Cambridge: Cambridge University Press.

Gilpin, Robert. 1987. *The Political Economy of International Relations*. Princeton, N.J.: Princeton University Press.

Goldstein, Judith. 1998. International Institutions and Domestic Politics 1998: GATT, WTO, and the Liberalization of International Trade. In *The WTO as an*

International Organization, ed. Anne O. Krueger and Chonira Aturupane, 133–152. Chicago: University of Chicago Press.

Grieco, Joseph M. 1988. Anarchy and the Limits of Cooperation: A Realist Critique of the Newest Liberal Institutionalism. *International Organization* 42 (3): 485–507.

Haas, Peter M. 1992. Introduction: Epistemic Communities and International Policy Coordination. In *Knowledge, Power and International Policy Coordination*, ed. Peter M. Haas. Special Issue, *International Organization* 46 (1): 1–35.

Hasenclever, Andreas, Peter Mayer, and Volker Rittberger. 1997. *Theories of International Regimes*. Cambridge: Cambridge University Press.

IISD. 2007. Summary of the 27th Session of the Intergovernmental Panel on Climate Change, 12–17 November 2007. International Institute for Sustainable Development. *Earth Negotiations Bulletin* (Winnipeg) 12 (342).

IPCC. 2001. *Climate Change 2001: Mitigation*. Contribution of Working Group III to the Third Assessment Report of the Intergovernmental Panel on Climate Change. Geneva: IPCC.

IPCC. 2007. *Climate Change 2007: Mitigation of Climate Change*. Contribution of Working Group III to the Fourth Assessment Report of the Intergovernmental Panel on Climate Change. Geneva: IPCC.

Joyner, Christopher C. 2001. On the Borderline? Canadian Activism in the Grand Banks. In *Governing High Seas Fisheries: The Interplay of Global and Regional Regimes*, ed. Olav Schram Stokke, 207–234. Oxford: Oxford University Press.

Keohane, Robert O. 1993. The Analysis of International Regimes: Towards a European-American Research Programme. In *Regime Theory and International Relations*, ed. Volker Rittberger, 23–45. Oxford: Clarendon Press.

Kratochwil, Friedrich V., and John G. Ruggie. 1986. International Organization: A State of the Art on an Art of the State. *International Organization* 40 (4): 753–775.

Mahoney, James. 2000. Path Dependence in Historical Sociology. *Theory and Society* 29 (4): 507–548.

McGee, Jeffrey, and Ros Taplin. 2009. The Role of the Asia-Pacific Partnership in Discursive Contestation of the International Climate Regime. *International Environmental Agreements: Politics, Law and Economics* 9 (3): 213–238.

McKibbin, Warwick J., and Peter J. Wilcoxen. 2009. The Economic and Environmental Effects of Border Tax Adjustments for Climate Policy. *Brookings Trade Forum* 2008/2009:1–23.

Miles, Edward, Arild Underdal, Steinar Andresen, Jørgen Wettestad, Jon Birger Skjærseth, and Elaine M. Carlin, eds. 2002. *Environmental Regime Effectiveness: Confronting Theory with Evidence*. Cambridge, Mass.: MIT Press.

Müller, Harald. 1994. Internationale Beziehungen als kommunikatives Handeln: Zur Kritik der utilitaristischen Handlungstheorien. *Zeitschrift für Internationale Beziehungen* 1 (1): 15–44.

Neumann, Jan. 2002. *Die Koordination des WTO-Rechts mit anderen völker-rechtlichen Ordnungen: Konflikte des materiellen Rechts und Konkurrenzen der Streitbeilegung.* Berlin: Duncker & Humblot.

Oberthür, Sebastian, and Thomas Gehring, eds. 2006a. *Institutional Interaction in Global Environmental Governance: Synergy and Conflict among International and EU Policies.* Cambridge, Mass.: MIT Press.

Oberthür, Sebastian, and Thomas Gehring. 2006b. Conceptual Foundations and Institutional Interaction. In *Institutional Interaction in Global Environmental Governance: Synergy and Conflict among International and EU Policies,* ed. Sebastian Oberthür and Thomas Gehring, 19–52. Cambridge, Mass.: MIT Press.

Oberthür, Sebastian, and Hermann E. Ott. 1999. *The Kyoto Protocol: International Climate Policy for the 21st Century.* Berlin: Springer-Verlag.

Oberthür, Sebastian. 2006. The Climate Change Regime: Interactions with ICAO, IMO, and the EU Burden-Sharing Agreement. In *Institutional Interaction in Global Environmental Governance: Synergy and Conflict among International and EU Policies,* ed. Sebastian Oberthür and Thomas Gehring, 53–78. Cambridge, Mass.: MIT Press.

Palmer, Alice, Beatrice Chaytor, and Jacob Werksman. 2006. Interactions between the World Trade Organization and International Environmental Regimes. In *Institutional Interaction in Global Environmental Governance: Synergy and Conflict among International and EU Policies,* ed. Sebastian Oberthür and Thomas Gehring, 183–204. Cambridge, Mass.: MIT Press.

Pauwelyn, Joost. 2003. *Conflict of Norms in Public International Law: How WTO Law Relates to Other Rules of International Law.* Cambridge: Cambridge University Press.

Putnam, Robert D. 1988. Diplomacy and Domestic Politics: The Logic of Two-Level Games. *International Organization* 42 (3): 427–460.

Raustiala, Kal, and David G. Victor. 2004. The Regime Complex for Plant Genetic Resources. *International Organization* 58 (2): 277–309.

Risse, Thomas. 2000. "Let's Argue!" Communicative Action in World Politics. *International Organization* 54 (1): 1–39.

Rittberger, Volker, and Michael Zürn. 1990. Towards Regulated Anarchy in East–West Relations. In *International Regimes in East–West Politics,* ed. Volker Rittberger, 9–63. London: Pinter.

Rosendal, G. Kristin. 2001. Impacts of Overlapping International Regimes: The Case of Biodiversity. *Global Governance* 7 (1): 95–117.

Sampson, Gary P. 2001. WTO Rules and Climate Change: The Need for Policy Coherence. In *Inter-linkages: The Kyoto Protocol and the International Trade and Investment Regimes,* ed. W. Bradnee Chambers, 69–85. Tokyo: United Nations University Press.

Siebenhüner, Bernd. 2006. Social Learning in the Field of Climate Change. Draft paper. http://biogov.cpdr.ucl.ac.be/bioinstit/papers/SIEBENHUENER_paper.pdf (accessed 16 April 2010).

Snidal, Duncan. 1985. The Limits of Hegemonic Stability Theory. *International Organization* 39 (4): 579–614.

Stilwell, Matthew T., and Elisabeth Tuerk. 1999. Trade Measures and Multilateral Environmental Agreements: Resolving Uncertainty and Removing the WTO Chill Factor. WWF/Center for International Environmental Law International Discussion Paper No. TE 99-8.

Stokke, Olav Schram, ed. 2001a. *Governing High Seas Fisheries: The Interplay of Global and Regional Regimes.* Oxford: Oxford University Press.

Stokke, Olav Schram. 2001b. *The Interplay of International Regimes: Putting Effectiveness Theory to Work.* FNI Report No. 14/2001. Lysaker, Norway: Fridtjof Nansen Institute.

Stokke, Olav Schram. 2004. Trade Measures and Climate Compliance: Institutional Interplay between WTO and the Marrakesh Accords. *International Environmental Agreements: Politics, Law and Economics* 4 (4): 339–357.

Underdal, Arild. 2002. One Question, Two Answers. In *Environmental Regime Effectiveness: Confronting Theory with Evidence*, ed. Edward Miles, Arild Underdal, Steinar Andresen, Jørgen Wettestad, Jon Birger Skjærseth, and Elaine M. Carlin, 3–45. Cambridge, Mass.: MIT Press.

Underdal, Arild. 2006. Determining the Causal Significance of Institutions: Accomplishments and Challenges. Paper prepared for the IDGEC Synthesis Conference, Bali, Indonesia, 6–9 December 2006.

UNFCCC. 2000. *Tracing the Origins of the Kyoto Protocol: An Article-by-Article Textual History.* Technical paper prepared under contract by Joanna Depledge, August 1999/August 2000. United Nations Framework Convention on Climate Change. UNFCCC-Doc. FCCC/TP/2000/2. Bonn: UNFCCC.

van Asselt, Harro. 2007. From UN-ity to Diversity? The UNFCCC, the Asia-Pacific Partnership, and the Future of International Law on Climate Change. *Carbon and Climate Law Review* 1 (1): 17–28.

Van Evera, Stephen. 1997. *Guide to Methods for Students of Political Science.* Ithaca, N.Y.: Cornell University Press.

Vranes, Erich. 2006. The Definition of "Norm Conflict" in International Law and Legal Theory. *European Journal of International Law* 17 (2): 395–418.

Wapner, Paul. 1996. *Environmental Activism and World Civic Politics.* Albany, N.Y.: State University of New York Press.

Werksman, Jacob. 2001. Greenhouse-Gas Emissions Trading and the WTO. In *Inter-linkages: The Kyoto Protocol and the International Trade and Investment Regimes*, ed. W. Bradnee Chambers, 153–190. Tokyo: United Nations University Press.

Wettestad, Jørgen. 2001. Designing Effective Environmental Regimes: The Conditional Keys. *Global Governance* 7 (3): 317–341.

Wolf, Klaus Dieter. 1991. *Internationale Regime zur Verteilung globaler Ressourcen.* Baden-Baden: Nomos.

Yamin, Farhana, and Joanna Depledge. 2004. *The International Climate Change Regime: A Guide to Rules, Institutions and Procedures.* Cambridge: Cambridge University Press.

Young, Oran R. 1996. Institutional Linkages in International Society: Polar Perspectives. *Global Governance* 2 (1): 1–24.

Young, Oran R. 2002. *The Institutional Dimensions of Environmental Change: Fit, Interplay, and Scale.* Cambridge, Mass.: MIT Press.

Zelli, Fariborz. 2006. The World Trade Organization: Free Trade and Its Environmental Impacts. In *Handbook of Globalization and the Environment*, ed. Khi V. Thai, Dianne Rahm, and Jerrell D. Coggburn, 177–216. London: Taylor & Francis.

9

The Institutional Complex of Trade and Environment

Toward an Interlocking Governance Structure and a Division of Labor

Thomas Gehring

This chapter examines the dynamics of the institutional complex of trade and the environment. The relationship between the world trade system and the numerous multilateral environmental agreements (MEAs) with trade restrictions is difficult. These institutions do not operate in isolation from each other (Esty 1994; Charnovitz 1998; Brack 2002) but rather affect each other's effectiveness and even each other's normative development. Most observers argue, from the perspective of environmental policymaking, that the World Trade Organization (WTO) undermines the effectiveness of MEAs (Schoenbaum 2002; Shaw and Schwartz 2002) by "chilling" the negotiations of environmentally motivated trade-related obligations (Eckersley 2004). Some authors have voiced concern about the power of the WTO vis-à-vis MEAs, advocating the establishment of an equally powerful World Environment Organization (Whalley and Zissimos 2002). By contrast, authors arguing from a free trade perspective point to the limited relevance of WTO-related restrictions for environmental policymaking and emphasize that the world trade system has been responsive to environmental concerns in the past (Hudec 1996). However, institutional complexes that are characterized by multiple interactions among their component institutions tend to develop their own dynamics, which have so far largely escaped research on institutional interaction.

While the discussion in this chapter is founded on a theoretical understanding of institutional interaction that elucidates how institutions *can* influence each other, it draws attention to the nature and evolution of interlocking structures that evolve from continued interaction among competing international institutions of an institutional complex (Raustiala and Victor 2004). The chapter draws on the microconcept of causal mechanisms of institutional interaction that has been developed in greater detail elsewhere (see Oberthür and Gehring 2006a; Gehring and Oberthür 2009). Causal mechanisms reveal the pathways through which influence travels from a source institution to a target institution. In the next section this framework is expanded by the macroconcept of interlocking governance structures (Underdal and Young 2004). Such structures are characterized by a division of labor among the component institutions that reflects a specific configuration of these institutions within a given institutional complex.

Against this conceptual backdrop, the chapter explores the dynamics of the institutional complex of trade and environment. First it identifies the underlying problem. While the WTO sees trade restrictions as undesirable obstacles to trade, certain MEAs employ them as helpful governance instruments. The chapter then examines how the world trade system exerts influence on the normative development and the effectiveness of relevant MEAs. As has been widely recognized, the WTO changes the preferences of its member states on issues at stake in other institutions, thereby exerting a chilling effect on MEA negotiations. In addition, the WTO undermines the effectiveness of MEAs by creating incentives for free riding.

Subsequently, the chapter analyzes the influence of MEAs with trade restrictions on the world trade system. MEAs undermine the effectiveness of core WTO obligations by committing states to issue-specific trade restrictions that necessarily discriminate among countries. Even more, they encroach on the established jurisdiction of the WTO and push this institution toward redefining the scope and boundaries of its broadly formulated nondiscrimination provisions. Hence, and in contrast to the bulk of the literature on the subject, a careful analysis of interaction patterns demonstrates that influence is by no means unidirectional.

Finally, the chapter examines the emerging division of labor among the component institutions of this complex that evolves from mutually disruptive interaction among the WTO and relevant MEAs. The WTO has begun to elaborate general criteria for the acceptance of environmentally motivated trade restrictions, while MEAs acquire the role of defining the specific areas of application and the design of these restrictions. Instead of diminishing interaction, this arrangement perpetuates a specific form of interaction among the functionally specialized component institutions of the complex.

The chapter concludes that an interlocking governance structure of remarkable coherence is gradually evolving in the institutional complex of trade and environment. This structure accommodates the competing governance projects of the component institutions by limiting the freedom of operation of these institutions so as to minimize adverse interaction effects.

Conceptual Framework

Causal Mechanisms of Institutional Interaction

Institutional interaction always implies a causal relationship between the institutions involved, not mere coexistence. Causation means that one institution exerts influence on the existence, normative structure, or performance of another institution. In other words, it creates an observable effect in the realm of the target institution. Complex interaction situations like those in the trade-environment setting are accessible for causal analysis only if one decomposes them into suitable cases of interaction. A case includes the source institution from which influence originates and the target institution within which an observable effect occurs, as well as a clear direction of influence and a causal mechanism through which influence is transferred from the source to the target. Decomposition of complex interaction situations will be necessary if one institution exerts influence on another institution in different ways, if a situation involves more than two institutions, or if influence runs back and forth between the institutions in question.

Causal mechanisms can help elucidate *how* an institution succeeds in influencing another institution. They open the "black box" of the underlying cause-and-effect relationship (George and Bennett 2005, 135–145) and identify the particular pathways through which influence is transferred from the source institution to the target institution. Since institutions normally do not influence each other directly, causal mechanisms point to actors that adapt their perceptions, preferences, or behavior in the course of a case of institutional interaction (Hedström and Swedberg 1998).

Institutional interaction can take very different forms (see Gehring and Oberthür 2009 and this volume). Influence originating from one or more other institutions may affect either the decision process (and subsequently the norms and obligations) of a target institution or its effectiveness within its own domain. Two causal mechanisms of institutional interaction are particularly relevant for the trade-environment overlap.

Interaction through commitment affects the decision-making process of a target institution. It occurs when the commitments under the source institution induce member states to adjust their preferences with respect to issues dealt with under the target institution (Gehring and Oberthür

2006). For this type of interaction to occur, both the issue areas and the memberships of the institutions involved must overlap significantly. Without an overlap of issue areas, commitments under one institution will not be relevant for another institution. Without a significant overlap of memberships, actors committed under one institution will not participate in negotiations under the other institution.

If driven by the different objectives of the institutions involved, as in the trade-environment overlap, interaction through commitment is prone to conflict, typically creating disruptive effects on the target institution (Gehring and Oberthür 2009). Because of their diverging objectives, the institutions pull in different directions, and the source institution encroaches on the jurisdiction of the target institution. In interactions of this type, the institutions involved, as well as their constituencies, are in a "mixed motive" situation that resembles the game-theoretic constellation of the battle of the sexes (Stein 1982). On the one hand, they possess a general interest in some sort of separation of jurisdictions in order to avoid fruitless regulatory competition and reduced effectiveness of their respective institutions. On the other hand, they may have conflicting preferences as to the appropriate solution. While it is difficult to say how the balance will eventually be struck in a particular case (Gehring and Oberthür 2009), the earlier institution possesses a "first-mover advantage" (Mattli 2003). Commitments of the earlier institution limit the room for maneuvering by the later institution by strengthening actors that advocate the objectives of the earlier institution. Equilibrium in a coordination situation is generally fairly stable because neither side can expect to gain from resumption of conflict. Challenging an established distribution of jurisdictions by agreeing on incompatible commitments within one institution typically provokes open conflict among the institutions involved. The creation of such "strategic inconsistency" (Raustiala and Victor 2004, 301–302) is particularly relevant in promoting new regulatory objectives, such as environmental protection, in a field already governed by an existing institution.

Behavioral interaction influences the effectiveness of target institutions. It will occur if the source institution triggers behavior on the part of states and nonstate actors that is relevant for the implementation and effectiveness of the target institution (Oberthür and Gehring 2006b). Influence is channeled through the individual actions of relevant actors in response to the norms and obligations originating from the source institution. Relevant action includes the implementation of international obligations by the member states of an institution, as well as responding behavior by private actors, if it has a direct or indirect impact on the implementation of the target institution. Like interaction through commitment, behavioral interaction presupposes that the issue areas governed by the institutions involved, as well as the direct and indirect addressees of institutional obligations, are close enough to matter for each other.

Behavioral interaction driven by the different objectives of the institutions involved will usually constrain the effectiveness of both institutions (Gehring and Oberthür 2009). The existence of two contradictory sets of obligations provides norm addressees with additional freedom to choose between them (Raustiala and Victor 2004, 302–305). Each institution enlarges the room for national and subnational actors to interpret the obligations of the other institution to their liking, and thus to disregard these commitments at least partially, thereby jeopardizing the effective implementation of that institution's obligations. Hence, behavioral interaction driven by diverging objectives is expected to lead to the mutual disruption of the institutions involved, and creates demand for jurisdictional delimitation.

Institutional Complexes: Division of Labor and Interlocking Structures
The analysis of individual interaction cases does not reveal all properties of an institutional complex. In much the same way as an examination of individual trees and plants cannot grasp the emergent properties of a forest, the analysis of individual interaction cases cannot reveal such properties of an institutional complex that are not inherent in its components. It is one thing to examine how the WTO affects relevant MEAs, or vice versa, and quite another to explore how the overlapping area of environmentally motivated trade restrictions is jointly governed by these institutions. Since the properties of the forest emerge from the particular forms of coexistence of the trees and plants, including their mutual influence on each other's existence and development, we may expect that the interlocking governance structure relating to an institutional complex will be closely related to the particular forms of coexistence of its component institutions.

Over time, a particular division of labor may evolve among the component institutions of an institutional complex, if only because regulatory competition or duplication of work among two or more institutions established by a similar or identical group of actors is costly. The division of labor constitutes the ordering principle of an institutional complex and is enshrined in an institution of a higher order that emerges from interaction among, and mutual adaptation of, the component institutions (Sawyer 2001). It defines the specific functions to be fulfilled by these institutions within the broader system of divided labor; and it reflects generalized expectations as to how the component institutions ought to perform their particular tasks within their respective domains in order to avoid conflict and duplication of work. If respected within the regular operations of the component institutions, such an institutionalized division of labor will be automatically reproduced and stabilized. However, like any other social norm, it will change or break down if repeatedly ignored. Change of an established division of labor may occur unintentionally or deliberately through an act of strategic inconsistency in which interested actors design a component institution so as to challenge an established but undesired division of labor (Raustiala and Victor 2004, 301). Unlike the sector-specific institutions involved, a division of labor usually does not emerge directly from collective bargaining processes or from other forms of collective decision making because deliberately designed overarching institutions are difficult to create, especially in situations of interinstitutional competition. It constitutes a spontaneously emerging institution of a higher order.

An institutionalized division of labor among the component institutions of an institutional complex will create an interlocking governance structure (Underdal and Young 2004, 374–375). This structure is the aggregate result of the interaction of the institutions involved. On the one hand, it includes the component institutions with their issue area-specific substantive rules and decision-making apparatuses. On the other hand, it comprises an institutionalized division of labor that provides a systemic ordering principle and allocates specific functions to the component institutions. Accordingly, all substantive rights and obligations of an interlocking governance structure originate from the component institutions that perform the governance functions within this structure. However, these institutions operate in a configuration that is defined by the division of labor prevailing within the institutional complex.

The Trade and Environment Overlap: Same Issues, Different Objectives

The world looks quite different depending on whether it is viewed from a trade liberalization perspective or from an environmental protection perspective. The specific objectives of international institutions are of tremendous importance for intrainstitutional decision making. States establish and design institutions to help overcome particular cooperation problems and to change an undesired status quo in a given direction (Underdal 2002, 5–7; Gehring 1994, 433–449). Even if member states may struggle over specified obligations, institutional objectives are usually clearly identifiable and provide standards for the appraisal of proposals. Since their decision-making processes tend to ignore issues that are beyond their confines (Sebenius 1983), international institutions with different objectives can be expected to appraise a given set of policy measures differently, even if their memberships are identical (Gehring 2002). In practice, the representation of states through functional ministries corroborates this effect. While ministries of trade dominate within the WTO, ministries of the environment usually head the delegations to MEA negotiations.

The core objectives of the world trade system envisage liberalization of world trade. The General Agreement on Tariffs and Trade (GATT) of 1947 aimed at gradually removing tariffs and nontariff trade restrictions by its member states. Its core normative structure (Schoenbaum 1997, 271–280) is reflected in several general nondiscrimination provisions. According to the principle of equal treatment (GATT, Article III), states may not subject imported products to more restrictive regulation or taxation than comparable products that are domestically produced (Jackson 1999, 208–228). According to the "most-favored-nations" principle (GATT, Article I), member states shall extend to all other GATT/WTO member states any trade privilege they grant to any country, whether member state or not (Hoekman and Kostecki 1995, 26). In addition, quantitative restrictions on imports and exports are totally forbidden, apart from a few exceptions (GATT, Articles XI and XIII). During the past world trade rounds, GATT has been supplemented with several additional agreements, including the Agreement on Sanitary and Phytosanitary Measures (SPS), which is highly important for the trade-environment overlap. It applies particularly to foodstuffs, feed, and seeds, as well as living animals and plants. The SPS Agreement prohibits domestic product regulation unless based on a scientific risk assessment or on a product-specific international agreement or standard (Victor 2000).

The few core obligations of the world trade system have a significant impact on regulation in other issue areas. The principles of equal treatment and most-favored nations prohibit discrimination between like products by the importing country (Farber and Hudec 1996). Accordingly, member states cannot treat a good produced in a polluting plant, or originating from a country that is a pollution haven, differently from a qualitatively identical product from a clean plant, because that would amount to a discrimination of certain countries of origin. Member states are also precluded from submitting import products to their own process and production regulations (Hudec 1996). Under the SPS Agreement of 1994, they have even relinquished their power to independently define nondiscriminating product standards.

While the world trade system, against the backdrop of its core objectives, cannot be expected to consider any trade restriction as desirable, it does grant limited exceptions for well-justified environmentally motivated restrictions. Parties may apply measures "necessary to protect human, animal or plant life or health" (Article XX(b)) or "relating to the conservation of exhaustible natural resources" (Article XX(g)). However, these measures are subject to the requirement that they "are not applied in a manner which would constitute a means of arbitrary or unjustifiable discrimination between countries where the same conditions prevail, or a disguised restriction on international trade" (Article XX, chapeau). The scope of these exceptions is determined within GATT/WTO dispute settlement proceedings. To protect the world trade system from undesired regulations with protectionist effects, GATT/WTO dispute settlement panels for a long time interpreted these provisions very restrictively, repeatedly rejecting environmentally motivated trade restrictions that were in conflict with the GATT nondiscrimination obligations (Kingsbury 1995; Howse and Trebilcock 1997; Schoenbaum 2002, 701–702). In two widely recognized decisions, panels argued that, if contracting parties were permitted "to impose trade embargoes so as to force other countries to change their policies within their jurisdiction . . . , *the objectives of the General Agreement would be seriously impaired*" (GATT 1994, para. 5.38, emphasis added); moreover, "market access for goods could become subject to an increasing number of conflicting policy requirements for the same product *and this would rapidly lead to the end of the WTO multilateral trading system*" (WTO 1998a, para. 7.45, emphasis added).

In contrast, the objectives of the numerous MEAs relate to the protection of particular environmental goods or the resolution of specific environmental problems. While none of these institutions is intended to hamper international trade per se, an increasing number of them include issue-specific environmentally motivated trade measures (von Moltke 1997). A WTO (2007) compilation of MEAs with trade measures includes some twenty sector-specific institutions for international environmental governance, including some of the most important MEAs.

Environmentally motivated trade measures differ in form and purpose. Some MEAs aim expressly to restrict environmentally problematic parts of international trade, so that trade restrictions become part of their objective. For example, the purpose of the Convention on International Trade in Endangered Species of Wild Fauna and Flora (CITES) is to establish and maintain a system of restrictions on international trade in species of flora and fauna that are threatened with extinction (Sand 1997). This regime includes a ban of trade in certain species and a ban of trade in protected species with countries that do not comply with documentation requirements and other policy measures. Similarly, the Basel Convention prohibits trade in hazardous wastes between member states and nonmember states, as well as, upon a decision of the Conference of the Parties, between Organisation for Economic Co-operation and Development (OECD) countries and non-OECD countries (Kummer 1995). Other MEAs, among them the Montreal Protocol and the International Convention for the Conservation of Atlantic Tunas (ICCAT), put in place trade sanctions and limited boycotts against noncompliant member states or against nonmembers of the regime in order to enforce their obligations. Trade sanctions could be relevant to almost any standard-setting international institution aiming to increase compliance with costly obligations and to promote the performance of the institution (Howse and Trebilcock 1997, 192–208).

The issue areas governed by the WTO, on the one side, and by several MEAs on the other overlap with regard to environmentally motivated trade restrictions. Such measures appear highly problematic from the perspective of the world trade system, while they are conceived of as important, if not indispensable, devices for environmental protection from the perspective of MEAs.

WTO Influence on the Normative Development and Effectiveness of MEAs

Effects on the Normative Development of MEAs
The WTO exerts influence on the decision-making processes of MEAs, and subsequently also on their norms and rules. The WTO commits its virtually global membership of 153 members (as of early 2010) to the rules and norms of the world trade system. This commitment extends to the sincere implementation of these rules and norms, and to the nonacceptance of duties that violate WTO rules. It is enforceable through the courtlike WTO dispute settlement system. This commitment limits the

range of options available to WTO member states when negotiating environmentally motivated multilateral trade restrictions in MEAs, but it does not necessarily affect the preferences of all actors equally. While advocates of free trade may simply refer to their WTO obligations to undermine effective environmental policymaking, supporters of environmental protection might be prepared to ignore WTO commitments. The preferences of the middle group of actors intending to accommodate trade measures with the objectives of both the world trade system and relevant MEAs will be most visibly affected, and may modify the balance between the environmentalist camp and the free trade camp in favor of the latter. This result is known as the "chilling effect" (Eckersley 2004). However, it would be an oversimplification to attribute the absence of trade restrictions in several important MEAs, such as the Convention on Long-Range Transboundary Air Pollution (LRTAP), solely to WTO commitments. A group of actors may deliberately choose not to impose trade-related measures because such "hardening" of environmental obligations is unacceptable to the member states or because it is expected to trigger undesired side effects, such as more difficult decision making on substantive matters and even limited ratification of future agreements (see Abbott and Snidal 2000).

The rules and norms of several MEAs reflect the chilling effect (Brack 2002). For example, the UN Framework Convention on Climate Change stipulates that "the Parties should cooperate to promote a supportive and open international economic system. . . . Measures taken to combat climate change, including unilateral ones, should not constitute a means of arbitrary or unjustifiable discrimination or a disguised restriction on international trade" (Article 3.5). And the Kyoto Protocol states that parties "shall strive to implement policies and measures under this Article in such a way as to minimize . . . effects on international trade" (Article 2.3).

States frequently design trade-related enforcement mechanisms so as to minimize the detrimental effects on world trade. The Montreal Protocol on Substances that Deplete the Ozone Layer envisages restrictions of trade in certain goods with nonmember states (Werksman 1996), to provide incentives for states to join the protocol (Benedick 1995, 91–92) and to avoid the transfer of production facilities to nonmember states. To bring it somewhat in line with the WTO obligations and preclude undue discrimination of nonmember states, countries behaving like complying member states may apply for exemption from the restriction. ICCAT applies its trade restrictions equally prudently (see Palmer,

Chaytor, and Werksman 2006, 195–200). This intergovernmental organization, with more than forty contracting parties (among them Canada, China, the EC, Japan, and the United States), is responsible for the conservation of tunas and tunalike fish stocks in the Atlantic Ocean and adjacent seas, including the Mediterranean Sea. In response to the potential tensions with the WTO, ICCAT has developed a staged approach to the application of trade measures. With respect to its tuna and swordfish action plans, ICCAT first informs the flag state concerned of any illegal fishing carried out by its registered vessels. It then requests the cooperation of the flag state in bringing the activities of its vessels into compliance with ICCAT measures. Last, ICCAT warns the relevant flag state that nondiscriminatory, trade restrictive measures may be taken against it in the event of continued noncompliance.

The chilling effect has also significantly influenced the Cartagena Protocol. Negotiations on a "savings clause" intended to govern the relationship between the protocol and the WTO (Safrin 2002a) resulted in protocol provisions (in particular with respect to risk assessment, precaution, and socioeconomic considerations) that largely match and elaborate those of the SPS Agreement, so that both instruments *can* be interpreted in mutually supportive ways (Palmer, Chaytor, and Werksman 2006). The protocol obliges exporters of certain genetically modified organisms (e.g., genetically modified organisms, or GMOs, for use as seeds) to seek and receive an Advance Informed Agreement from the importing country before exporting—which in itself represents a significant restriction of free trade. However, the protocol also requires importing countries to base their decisions on a science-based risk assessment and to follow certain procedural steps. GMOs for direct use as food or feed or for processing, which account for about 90 percent of trade in GMOs (Eggers and Mackenzie 2000, 525, 530), are generally exempted from the Advance Informed Agreement procedure. GMO exporters (including Argentina, Canada, Chile, Uruguay, and the United States) that would probably have strongly opposed restrictions on free trade in GMOs even in the absence of relevant WTO rules most forcefully used the argument of WTO compatibility during the negotiations. Their position was strengthened because most other countries had an interest in avoiding incompatible regulations that could diminish the effectiveness of one or even both agreements (Oberthür and Gehring 2006c). Even the proponents of strong biosafety provisions, such as the EU and the Like-Minded Group of developing countries, significantly softened their stance because of their wish to avoid incompatible commitments. U.S.

nonmembership in the CBD further strengthened this interest by increasing the danger of challenges under the WTO dispute settlement procedures (Falkner 2000 and 2002).

However, the current tension between the WTO and MEAs would not have come about had the former been able to exert sufficient influence on the latter's norm-molding processes. The very existence of several MEAs with trade restrictions reflects a striking case of noninteraction and strategic inconsistency (Raustiala and Victor 2004, 301). MEAs have gradually assumed regulatory authority for areas of international relations that were already subject to regulation by another international institution. The GATT nondiscrimination commitments, in place since 1947, did not exert sufficient influence to prevent GATT/WTO member states from accepting numerous environmentally motivated multilateral trade restrictions (WTO 2007). If these states had been firmly resolved to honor their originally narrowly interpreted commitments under the world trade system, they could not have promoted, within other institutions, obligations that required them to limit severely the scope of the key nondiscrimination provisions. Hence, the earlier institution did not fully enjoy the expected first-mover advantage. Likewise, the SPS Agreement, adopted in 1994, did not preclude GATT/WTO member states from engaging in the negotiations of the Cartagena Protocol, which was adopted in 2000 (Oberthür and Gehring 2006c).

Consequences for the Effectiveness of MEAs
The WTO exerts influence on the effectiveness of MEAs especially by creating incentives for cost-effective but possibly environmentally detrimental production. The GATT nondiscrimination clauses largely rule out "process and production measures" (Farber and Hudec 1996; but see below). Accordingly, a WTO member state cannot normally make the import of a good conditional on the particular way in which it is produced or on the existence of, and compliance with, certain environmental protection regulations, *even if it requires domestic producers to fulfill these regulations*. In consequence, producers burdened with costs of environmental protection may have to compete even on the domestic market with external producers that do not incur similar costs. Thus the GATT nondiscrimination provisions create incentives for *not* sincerely honoring relevant international environmental obligations or for not becoming a member of relevant MEAs, to avoid adverse economic consequences.

This detrimental effect burdens the prospect of effective international environmental policymaking especially with respect to the protection of public goods and upstream or downstream situations. Many of the most important MEAs focus on the protection of global or regional public goods, such as the ozone layer, the global climate, or collectively exploited fish resources. International governance of such issues typically suffers because noncontributors to costly environmental protection measures cannot be excluded from the resulting benefits (Sandler 1997, 23–51). Accordingly, actors gain an interest in free riding. The GATT nondiscrimination obligations create an additional incentive for free riding because they ensure that goods produced cheaply within the jurisdiction of environmental free-riders may be freely exported to the markets of cooperating countries, whose own producers must bear the costs of environmental protection. A similar effect will occur if an environmental problem originates in one country but creates damage in another one, as with international rivers, where there are upstream and downstream riparian states. Such problems are notoriously difficult to solve because the costs and benefits are unevenly distributed. The GATT nondiscrimination duties have the effect of rewarding a noncooperative upstream country by ensuring that its industries can export their products freely to downstream countries that suffer from the resultant environmental degradation. And its producers enjoy a comparative advantage over the producers from downstream countries if the latter are burdened with costly environmental regulations (Esty and Geradin 1998, 7–21).

MEA Influence on the Effectiveness and the Normative Development of the WTO

Consequences for the Effectiveness of the WTO

The implementation of environmentally motivated trade restrictions originating from MEAs inevitably undermines the effectiveness of trade-liberalizing WTO obligations, especially the broadly formulated nondiscrimination clauses. Contrary to the rationale of the most-favored-nations clause, the principle of equal treatment, and the ban on import and export quotas, multilateral trade restrictions usually introduce some obligation to discriminate against goods according to their countries of origin. The Basel Convention, for instance, prohibits the export of certain wastes from OECD countries to non-OECD countries in order to protect the latter from environmentally dangerous substances. Whereas OECD countries may feed their waste-processing plants with imported wastes, non-OECD countries are deprived of this possibly remunerative business (Kummer 1995). While states may apply, without discrimination, the general restrictions to international trade in endangered species under CITES, this institution occasionally establishes quota systems for the protection of endangered species of flora and fauna and country-specific management plans that commit its member states to apply discriminating measures to imports from particular countries (Sand 1997). Discrimination is even more obvious if trade restrictions are employed to enforce MEA obligations. Commitments of the Montreal Protocol on Substances That Deplete the Ozone Layer to suspend trade in certain goods with identified noncompliant countries (Werksman 1996) oblige member states to discriminate openly against goods originating from one or more specified countries, irrespective of product quality. Collectively approved recommendations under CITES or ICCAT (Palmer, Chaytor, and Werksman 2006) to apply trade sanctions against noncompliant countries have a similar effect, because they urge member states to discriminate against products on the basis of country of origin.

MEAs are particularly successful in their struggle with the WTO when they succeed in committing their member states to issue-specific and clearly formulated trade restrictions. There is no evidence that the implementation of such commitments, even if formulated as formally unbinding recommendations, is seriously hampered by the norms and obligations of the world trade system (Brack 2002, 337). This may be attributed not least to the fact that clearly formulated issue-specific trade restrictions provide much less room for individual interpretation than the broadly formulated GATT nondiscrimination clauses, the opaque environmental exemptions under GATT Article XX, or the general rules of the SPS Agreement. States seeking to bring the diverging obligations into line will tend to follow the specific rather than the general rules.

As a result, the WTO partially loses its power to ensure that its member states can rely on the rights conferred on them in exchange for the acceptance of corollary obligations (GATT 1992, paras. 13–37). This effect is particularly important when the institutions in question differ not only in objectives but also in memberships. While states that have consented to an environmentally motivated trade restriction cannot reasonably claim that their rights under the world trade system have been unduly restricted, trade restrictions under MEAs may also infringe on the rights of certain WTO member states that have not consented to these measures or are not members of the relevant MEA.

Effects on the Normative Structure of the WTO

The commitment of numerous WTO member states to an increasing number of environmentally motivated multilateral trade restrictions gradually changes the normative structure of the world trade system. Trade-related MEA provisions almost inevitably lead to the tacit reinterpretation of the broadly defined GATT/WTO nondiscrimination clauses and the accompanying exemptions for environmental purposes. Unless they remain unintended or occasional violations of WTO provisions, they acquire an informal *lex specialis* function, introducing issue-specific and clearly defined exemptions to the more general WTO obligations. Applicable special provisions are widely used for the interpretation of general clauses (Wolfrum and Matz 2003, 155–158) and usually prevail, if only because they are less open to interpretation and offer clearer advice on disputed matters. For example, the ban on exports of certain wastes from OECD countries to non-OECD countries under the Basel Convention not only implicitly exempts OECD states from the GATT most-favored-nations obligation and from the ban on export quotas but tacitly implies that those restrictions fall under GATT's Article XX exceptions (see above). Otherwise, the ban could not have been acceptable to the WTO member states and it could not coexist with the nondiscrimination clauses within the WTO legal framework. Likewise, the Cartagena Biosafety Protocol governing international trade in GMOs spells out detailed rules on a particular subset of specific risks that are also subject to the more general rules of the WTO SPS Agreement. In doing so, the protocol tacitly broadens environmentally motivated exemptions from the general trade-enabling rules. For example, it includes environmental risks from GMOs, whereas the SPS Agreement merely deals with risks from pests and diseases (Qureshi 2000, 849). According to general international law, the legal interpretation of a treaty provision shall be made in light of other relevant agreements among the parties concerned (see Article 31 of the Vienna Convention on the Law of Treaties)—but the WTO and MEAs may have significantly different memberships.[1]

The tacit and stepwise redefinition of WTO obligations through the introduction of numerous environmentally motivated multilateral trade measures enjoys collective de facto approval by the WTO membership, because issue-specific restrictions strengthen the camp of those in favor of a tacit reinterpretation of WTO rules. Member states of a given MEA gain an interest in the accommodation of contradictory obligations through a tacit reinterpretation of world trade law because specific trade restrictions commit them to clear-cut duties that are less open to interpretation than the broadly defined provisions of the world trade system. The costs of this implicit consent are negligible for MEA member states because they have implicitly agreed to the tacit redefinition of relevant WTO rules by consenting to MEA-related trade measures. Owing to the broad membership of several MEAs with trade-restricting provisions, most WTO member states are committed at least to some environmentally motivated multilateral trade restrictions.

The tacit redefinition of WTO rules seems to have been generally accepted even by member states that are affected by an MEA-related trade restriction to which they have not agreed. Trade sanctions and other trade-related provisions will create particular difficulties if restrictions are imposed on members of GATT/WTO which are not also members of the respective standard-setting institution (GATT 1992, paras. 13–37), as this will mean depriving these WTO member states of some of their rights under the world trade system by an external decision made without their participation and consent. Such deprivation is highly dangerous for any contractual legal system, as it undermines the trust that member states have in the package of rights and obligations originally agreed on. While negative effects on third parties are contrary to Article 30 of the Vienna Convention on the Law of Treaties, environmentally motivated trade restrictions are unlikely to fall foul of the GATT requirements. A panel would have to argue that trade measures agreed on by the possibly almost global membership of a relevant MEA are not necessary to protect human, animal, or plant life or health according to the GATT exemptions (Sands 2003, 944–946). Although some countries reject this tacit encroachment on their free-trade rights, no state has so far responded to environmentally motivated multilateral trade measures by employing the WTO's dispute settlement mechanism to enforce those rights (Brack 2002, 334).

However, tacit agreement on the reinterpretation of WTO rules through issue-specific MEA provisions does not necessarily extend to enabling clauses. The United States, Argentina, and Canada, none of which is a party to the protocol, rejected the EU claim that the Cartagena Protocol might soften its obligations under the world trade system and provide an additional justification of its ban on GMO imports. The relevant WTO dispute settlement panel refused to consider the protocol when interpreting the obligations arising from the world trade system because the complainants were not parties to this instrument (WTO 2006, 328–336). However, this case did not address conflicting obligations, since the Cartagena Protocol does not *require* its member states to implement an outright ban of GMO imports and because the relevant treaties may be interpreted so as not to contradict each other (Howse and Meltzer 2002). Hence, these proceedings illustrate the potential conflict involved in the tacit reinterpretation of WTO commitments through environmentally motivated trade measures, but they do not indicate a reversal of the general tendency.

Assumption of regulatory authority over environmentally motivated trade restrictions by MEAs even threatens to encroach on the regulatory authority of the WTO to specify its own general rules and obligations. This is most clearly visible in the interaction between the Cartagena Protocol and the SPS Agreement. Against the backdrop of diverging objectives, the CBD began in 1995 to assume regulatory authority on trade in "living" GMOs. The commitment of the CBD parties to negotiate specific rules on trade in GMOs within this institution limited their range of available options. Negotiating these rules within the WTO would imply violation of their CBD commitments, although some WTO member states preferred this approach (Falkner 2000, 305). Proposals for regulating biotechnology under the WTO made by Canada, Japan, and the United States in the run-up to the WTO ministerial conference in Seattle were successfully rejected, in particular by developing countries, with explicit reference to the ongoing negotiations under the CBD (Palmer, Chaytor, and Werksman 2006). The camp of parties preferring free trade and WTO negotiations was significantly weakened by the decision to negotiate outside the WTO. As a result, the members of the WTO lost, at least for the moment, their ability to elaborate detailed rules for the subarea of trade in GMOs within this organization, although more specific rules may still emerge from legal interpretation under the WTO dispute settlement mechanism.

Toward a Recognized Division of Labor between MEAs and the WTO

The widespread occurrence of disruptive interaction in the trade-environment overlap creates a demand for the clear-cut allocation of competencies (Brack 2002, 340–342). Mutual disruption of the institutions involved is not advantageous for either side in this area, especially in light of the widely overlapping memberships of the WTO and relevant global MEAs. A group of actors cannot be interested in maintaining at the same time two or more institutions that thwart each other's governance projects. Careful reallocation of competencies, and the resulting separation of jurisdictions, promises to limit or even abolish the adverse effects of uncontrolled and undesired interaction. However, the proper form of this reallocation is not clearly visible from the analysis of the single interaction cases. While some actors may favor a retreat of MEAs from the disputed issue area in order to reinforce free trade, others will prefer the opposite.

In principle, governance of the trade-environment overlap could be assigned completely to one side (Brack 2002, 341–342). While this step might promise to minimize future interaction through commitment affecting the norm-molding process of the respective target institutions, it threatens to aggravate the disruptive effects of behavioral interaction. The originally bidirectional interaction with mutually disruptive effects would be replaced with an even stronger unidirectional interaction, if trade laws emerged irrespective of their negative implications for environmental policymaking, or environmentally motivated trade restrictions were designed irrespective of their disruptive effects on international trade.

The comparatively even distribution of power between the two major interests involved also militates against the clear-cut allocation of competencies to one side. Neither side dominates the trade-environment overlap entirely. The WTO has proved too weak to protect itself against environmentally motivated trade restrictions and it does not significantly complicate their implementation. MEAs, on their part, are subject to the chilling effect and cannot prevent the WTO from providing unintended incentives for noncompliant behavior that can undermine their effectiveness. This applies especially to areas that lack issue-specific environmentally motivated trade restrictions and are subject to international economic competition. Hence, states and nonstate actors predominantly interested in free trade preclude that governance of the overlap is entirely assigned to relevant MEAs, possibly through selective waivers (Schoenbaum 2002, 706). States and nonstate actors that prioritize environmental protection struggle against having this area completely assigned to the WTO. Likewise, it is inconceivable that the WTO will develop its own environmental policy to flank its market integration policy. As can be seen from the EU, such a development would dramatically strengthen the already powerful WTO and turn it into something like a socioeconomic world government—and that would most probably be unacceptable to the majority of its member states.

Instead of a clear allocation of regulatory competencies to one side, we observe the gradual emergence of a cogovernance scheme based on a functional division of labor among the institutions involved that assigns distinct governance functions to the WTO and to relevant MEAs. The WTO acquires the role of developing strategies for shaping and employing environmentally motivated trade restrictions so as to minimize their disruptive effects on free trade. In doing so, the WTO recognizes that there are important policies beyond free trade. It gives up its original claim to prioritize free trade over environmental protection, and even sacrifices its influence on the content of decisions on trade restrictions as instruments of international environmental policymaking, if certain general conditions are met (Charnovitz 2002). In contrast, MEAs acquire the role of defining the areas of environmental policymaking in which trade restrictions shall be employed, as well as the precise shape of these instruments. In exchange, they recognize that trade restrictions ought to be molded so as to minimize the disruptive effects on international trade.

The tacit emergence of this division of labor is most clearly visible in a remarkable change of GATT/WTO jurisprudence on trade-environment issues. While the dispute settlement mechanism has not yet dealt with the WTO compatibility of trade restrictions originating from MEAs, it has addressed the issue of environmentally motivated trade restrictions unilaterally imposed by member states. In the "shrimp/turtle case," the WTO Appellate Body rejected the previously well-established interpretation that GATT obligations rule out unilateral process-oriented requirements for import products (WTO 1998b, para. 121; see also above). It held that the world trade system aims to ensure that the interests of the importing state to enact meaningful environmental protection measures are weighed against the interests of the exporting states to accede to the import market (WTO 1998b, para. 156). It took stock of the practice that had actually evolved over time, and developed various criteria to which trade-restricting domestic measures must conform in order to be compatible with GATT rules. Of special relevance are the following four criteria (Hansen 1999, 1057): (1) the measures must aim to protect a legitimate object; (2) they must be reasonably closely related to achieving this task; (3) they must treat domestic and foreign producers as well as producers from different exporting countries equally; and (4) the regulating state must reasonably take into account the interests of adversely affected states during the preparation of its legislation. For this purpose, the regulating state must seriously attempt to reach a negotiated solution with these states. Some of these conditions will be almost automatically fulfilled if trade sanctions are not unilaterally imposed but emerge instead from an MEA. Arbitrary discrimination against single states and the abuse of (allegedly) environmentally motivated trade sanctions for protectionist purposes are unlikely to occur in multilateral frameworks (Howse and Regan 2000).

The emerging division of labor is also reflected in two other developments. First, the WTO has already formally accepted a similar scheme regarding product regulation. Two agreements concluded during the Uruguay round of trade negotiations, completed in 1994, refer explicitly to substantive product standards that are elaborated in competent international institutions outside the world trade system. Under the SPS Agreement, domestic product regulation is automatically acceptable, if it complies with established international standards like the *Codex Alimentarius*, a joint program of the World Health Organization (WHO) and the Food and Agriculture Organization (FAO) (Victor 2000). Second, many MEAs have reshaped their trade restrictions to minimize undesired negative effects. In particular, they pay attention to the situation of states that are, for whatever reason, not members of the respective MEA but do not violate its environmental policies. Measures that had been considered as being negatively affected by the chilling effect of the WTO (see Palmer, Chaytor, and Werksman 2006, 195–200) thus reflect the tacitly evolving division of labor and the mandatory search for measures that do not unduly restrict international trade and the rights of affected states.

The division of labor between the WTO and issue-specific MEAs with trade restrictions reinforces the importance of interaction through commitment, while tending to minimize the disruptive effects of behavioral interaction in the implementation stage. The emerging cogovernance scheme does not abolish institutional interaction in the trade-environment overlap. Instead, it diminishes the originally disruptive interaction effects on both sides. As a result, MEA-related norm molding is always influenced by the general WTO conditions for the acceptance of trade restrictions under the world trade system, while the specific content of the WTO commitments increasingly depends on decisions made outside the framework of this institution, as long as those decisions comply with the general WTO conditions. To put it more dramatically, the WTO now tacitly accepts that a considerable part of world trade law is made within the framework of MEAs. While this governance scheme applies only to the norm-shaping process on both sides, it allocates governance competencies more clearly to the institutions involved and diminishes the risk of contradictory obligations. If norm addressees are no longer forced to choose which of the two sets of obligations to violate, room for unilateral interpretation and maneuvering diminishes—and so does disruptive behavioral interaction resulting from normative ambiguity.

The Committee on Trade and Environment established within the WTO has gradually emerged as a forum for the management of the evolving cogovernance scheme. Although this forum does not have the power to decide on contentious cases, it scrutinizes environmentally motivated trade restrictions as to their WTO compatibility. Within the committee, members have discussed a range of trade and environment issues, including the application of the WTO rules to trade measures taken pursuant to MEAs, the application of WTO rules to measures based on process and production methods traditionally viewed as WTO-inconsistent, environmental labeling, especially with respect to GMOs, the relevance of the precautionary principle to risk assessments based on scientific evidence, particularly in the context of the SPS Agreement (Charnovitz 2002), and the environmental impact of certain subsidies, especially fisheries subsidies. While it may seem that environmentally motivated multilateral trade restrictions become subject to something like an informal licensing procedure under the WTO, this procedure forces both sides to reconsider the merits of each single measure and to examine whether the four conditions mentioned above are actually met.

Conclusions

In the institutional complex of trade and environment, an interlocking governance structure of remarkable coherence is gradually evolving that minimizes regulatory competition and interinstitutional conflict. It accommodates the competing governance projects of the component institutions by limiting the scope of the world trade system's free-trade obligations in light of legitimately enacted, environmentally motivated trade restrictions, and by simultaneously limiting the applicability of such trade restrictions to instances deemed acceptable within this scheme. This interlocking structure combines the issue area-specific rules and norms of the component institutions with normative expectations reflecting the appropriate way of accommodating their governance projects. The few existing overarching institutions, such as the Convention on the Law of Treaties and the International Court of Justice, play virtually no role in this interlocking structure.

The core of the interlocking governance structure involves a division of labor that assigns specific functions to the institutions involved and limits their regulatory freedom. The WTO acquires the role of defining requirements for the minimization of the trade-disruptive effects of environmentally motivated trade restrictions, while it has to recognize that environmental policies may overrule trade liberalization. For their part, MEAs acquire the role of defining the shape of environmental trade restrictions and the areas of their application, but have to accept the requirements for the minimization of trade-disruptive effects.

The emergence of a division of labor, and subsequently of an inter-locking structure, within the trade-environment overlap is based on numerous cases of interaction driven by two distinct causal mechanisms. Interaction through commitment is highly relevant, because commitments entered into under one institution modify the preferences of relevant actors on subjects negotiated within other institutions. It complicates negotiations and collective decision making and thus leads to disruption. Equally important is the behavioral interaction that occurs outside the institutional decision processes within the issue areas governed by the institutions involved. States and nonstate actors implementing, or otherwise responding to, the obligations originating from the source institution adapt their behavior in ways relevant for the implementation of the target institution. Obligations under one institution frequently require behavior that violates or undermines the implementation of the obligations of another institution, so that actors enjoy an enlarged margin for individual interpretation and maneuvering in deciding how to react to this trade-off.

In virtually all cases, interaction adversely affects the normative development and effectiveness of either MEAs or the WTO. The implicit assumption of the bulk of the literature that the world trade system hinders the normative development of MEAs is thus correct, but incomplete. The GATT/WTO had claimed regulatory authority over the entire trade-environment overlap. The broadly applicable GATT nondiscrimination obligations and the more recent market-liberalizing product regulation of the WTO serve to chill the negotiations on environmentally motivated multilateral trade restrictions. By restricting environmentally motivated import regulation and generating incentives for free riding and noncooperation, the WTO aggravates the cooperation problems and implementation difficulties of many MEAs. However, any MEA with trade restrictions also exerts disruptive influence on the world trade system. The regulatory approach of some MEAs is founded on restricting trade in certain goods, such as endangered species or hazardous wastes, under specified conditions, while other MEAs employ trade restrictions to ensure compliance. These institutions have gradually assumed authority in the trade-environment overlap, encroaching on the established

jurisdiction of GATT/WTO. The proliferation of environmentally motivated multilateral trade restrictions indicates remarkable strategic inconsistency and noninteraction. As a result, the WTO has gradually lost
control over the regulation of such trade restrictions. In addition, behavioral changes of states and nonstate actors in response to environmentally motivated trade restrictions inevitably undermine the implementation
and the effectiveness of WTO commitments.

Unlike the component institutions involved, the division of labor and
the resulting interlocking governance structure do not emerge directly
from collective bargaining processes or from other forms of collective
decision making. They lack the decision center that is present in virtually
all international institutions in environmental and socioeconomic affairs,
usually in the form of their conferences of the parties. The division
of labor emerges from the interaction effects produced by numerous
decentralized decisions made within either of the institutions involved,
or from action by the member states of either institution and by other
relevant (nonstate) actors (Raustiala and Victor 2004, 295–305). As a
spontaneous institution, it is produced and reproduced through the
occurrence of ever new interaction cases. The emerging interlocking
governance structure of the trade-environment overlap reflects the normative structures of the component institutions in the configuration
defined by the division of labor. It is therefore produced, reproduced,
and changed by activities occurring within the component institutions
that affect the normative structure of these institutions or the division of
labor among them.

This analysis of the institutional complex of trade and environment
demonstrates that the nature and dynamics of institutional complexes is
best examined by combining a microperspective with a macroperspec-
tive. While the exploration of causal mechanisms sheds light on the
causal influence present in specific interaction cases, the focus on the
division of labor among the component institutions elucidates the organizing principle of the complex that transforms a set of uncoordinated,
possibly mutually disruptive, issue-specific regulations into an integrated
interlocking governance structure.

Note

1. The *lex posterior* principle reflected in Article 30 of the Vienna Convention
on the Law of Treaties is less relevant in this regard. Since the new GATT 1994
and other WTO agreements are later than several important MEAs with trade
restrictions, such as the Montreal Protocol and CITES, they might formally

overrule trade provisions of these agreements. However, this fact does not seem to have had any practical consequences so far (Safrin 2002b, 624).

References

Abbott, Kenneth, and Duncan Snidal. 2000. Hard Law and Soft Law in International Governance. *International Organization* 54:421–456.

Benedick, Richard E. 1995. *Ozone Diplomacy: New Directions in Safeguarding the Planet*, 2nd ed. Cambridge, Mass.: Harvard University Press.

Brack, Duncan. 2002. Environmental Treaties and Trade: Multilateral Environmental Agreements and the Multilateral Trading System. In *Trade, Environment, and the Millennium*, 2nd ed., ed. Gary P. Sampson and W. Bradnee Chambers, 321–352. Tokyo: United Nations University Press.

Charnovitz, Steve. 1998. The World Trade Organization and the Environment. *Yearbook of International Environmental Law* 8:98–116.

Charnovitz, Steve. 2002. The Law of Environmental PPMs in the WTO: Debunking the Myth of Illegality. *Yale Journal of International Law* 27 (1): 59–110.

Eckersley, Robyn. 2004. The Big Chill: The WTO and Multilateral Environmental Agreements. *Global Environmental Politics* 4 (2): 24–50.

Eggers, Barbara, and Ruth Mackenzie. 2000. The Cartagena Protocol on Biosafety. *Journal of International Economic Law* 3 (3): 525–543.

Esty, Daniel C. 1994. *Greening the GATT: Trade, Environment and the Future*. Harlow: Longman.

Esty, Daniel C., and Damien Geradin. 1998. Environmental Protection and International Competitiveness. *Journal of World Trade* 32 (3): 5–46.

Falkner, Robert. 2000. Regulating Biotech Trade: The Cartagena Protocol on Biosafety. *International Affairs* 76 (2): 299–313.

Falkner, Robert. 2002. Negotiating the Biosafety Protocol. The International Process. In *The Cartagena Protocol on Biosafety: Reconciling Trade in Biotechnology with Environment and Development?*, ed. Christoph Bail, Robert Falkner, and Helen Marquard, 3–22. London: RIIA/Earthscan.

Farber, Daniel A., and Robert E. Hudec. 1996. GATT Legal Restraints on Domestic Environmental Regulations. In *Fair Trade and Harmonization. Prerequisites for Free Trade? Vol. 2, Legal Analysis*, ed. Jagdish Bhagwati and Robert E. Hudec, 59–94. Cambridge, Mass.: MIT Press.

GATT. 1995. *Report of the Chairman of the Group on Environmental Measures and International Trade presented to the Contracting Parties at Their Forty-ninth Session, General Agreement on Tariffs and Trade*. Vol. 40. General Agreement on Tariffs and Trade. 1992. "Trade and Environment." *Basic Instruments and Selected Documents*. Geneva: GATT.

GATT. 1994. Dispute Settlement Panel Report on United States Restrictions on Imports of Tuna. General Agreement on Tariffs and Trade. *International Legal Materials* 33:839–899.

Gehring, Thomas. 1994. *Dynamic International Regimes: Institutions for International Environmental Governance.* Frankfurt: Peter Lang.

Gehring, Thomas. 2002. *Die Europäische Union als komplexe internationale Organisation: Wie durch Kommunikation und Entscheidung soziale Ordnung entsteht.* Baden-Baden: Nomos.

Gehring, Thomas, and Sebastian Oberthür. 2006. Comparative Empirical Analysis and Ideal Types of Institutional Interaction. In *Institutional Interaction in Global Environmental Governance: Synergy and Conflict among International and EU Policies*, ed. Sebastian Oberthür and Thomas Gehring, 307–371. Cambridge, Mass.: MIT Press.

Gehring, Thomas, and Sebastian Oberthür. 2009. The Causal Mechanisms of Interaction between International Institutions. *European Journal of International Relations* 15:125–156.

George, Alexander, and Andrew Bennett. 2005. *Case Studies and Theory Development in the Social Sciences.* Cambridge, Mass.: MIT Press.

Hansen, Patricia I. 1999. Transparency, Standards of Review, and the Use of Trade Measures to Protect the Global Environment. *Virginia Journal of International Law* 39:1017–1068.

Hedström, Peter, and Richard Swedberg. 1998. Social Mechanisms: An Introductory Essay. In *Social Mechanisms: An Analytical Approach to Social Theory*, ed. Peter Hedström and Richard Swedberg, 1–31. Cambridge: Cambridge University Press.

Hoekman, Bernard M., and Michael M. Kostecki. 1995. *The Political Economy of the World Trading System: From GATT to WTO.* Oxford: Oxford University Press.

Howse, Robert, and Joshua Meltzer. 2002. The Significance of the Protocol for WTO Dispute Settlement. In *The Cartagena Protocol on Biosafety: Reconciling Trade in Biotechnology with Environment and Development?*, ed. Christoph Bail, Robert Falkner, and Helen Marquard, 482–496. London: RIIA/Earthscan.

Howse, Robert, and Donald Regan. 2000. The Product/Process Distinction: An Illusionary Basis for Disciplining "Unilateralism" in Trade Policy. *European Journal of International Law* 11 (2): 249–289.

Howse, Robert, and Michael J. Trebilcock. 1997. The Free Trade–Fair Trade Debate. Trade, Labour and the Environment. In *Economic Dimensions in International Law: Comparative and Empirical Perspectives*, ed. Jagdeep Bhandari and Alan O. Sykes, 186–234. Cambridge: Cambridge University Press.

Hudec, Robert E. 1996. GATT Legal Restraints on the Use of Trade Measures against Foreign Environmental Practices. In *Fair Trade and Harmonization: Prerequisites for Free Trade?* Vol. 2, *Legal Analysis*, ed. Jagdish Bhagwati and Robert E. Hudec, 95–174. Cambridge, Mass.: MIT Press.

Jackson, John H. 1999. *The World Trading System: Law and Policy of International Economic Relations*, 2nd ed. Cambridge, Mass.: MIT Press.

Kingsbury, Benedict. 1995. The Tuna–Dolphin Controversy, the World Trade Organization and the Liberal Project to Reconceptualize International Law. *Yearbook of International Environmental Law* 5:1–40.

Kummer, Katharina. 1995. *International Management of Hazardous Wastes: The Basel Convention and Related Legal Rules*. Oxford: Clarendon.

Mattli, Walter. 2003. Setting International Standards: Technological Rationality or Primacy of Power. *World Politics* 56 (1): 1–42.

Oberthür, Sebastian, and Thomas Gehring, eds. 2006a. *Institutional Interaction in International and EU Environmental Governance: Synergy and Conflict between Sectoral Legal Systems*. Cambridge, Mass.: MIT Press.

Oberthür, Sebastian, and Thomas Gehring. 2006b. Conceptual Foundations of Institutional Interaction. In *Institutional Interaction in International and EU Environmental Governance: Synergy and Conflict between Sectoral Legal Systems*, ed. Sebastian Oberthür and Thomas Gehring, 19–51. Cambridge, Mass.: MIT Press.

Oberthür, Sebastian, and Thomas Gehring. 2006c. Institutional Interaction in Global Environmental Governance. The Case of the Cartagena Protocol and the World Trade Organization. *Global Environmental Politics* 6 (2): 1–31.

Palmer, Alice, Beatrice Chaytor, and Jacob Werksman. 2006. Interaction between the World Trade Organization and International Environmental Regimes. In *Institutional Interaction in Global Environmental Governance: Synergy and Conflict among International and EU Policies*, ed. Sebastian Oberthür and Thomas Gehring, 181–204. Cambridge, Mass.: MIT Press.

Qureshi, Asif H. 2000. The Cartagena Protocol on Biosafety and the WTO: Co-existence or Incoherence? *International and Comparative Law Quarterly* 49 (4): 835–855.

Raustiala, Kal, and David G. Victor. 2004. The Regime Complex for Plant Genetic Resources. *International Organization* 58 (2): 277–309.

Safrin, Sabrina. 2002a. The Relationship with Other Agreements: Much Ado about a Savings Clause. In *The Cartagena Protocol on Biosafety: Reconciling Trade in Biotechnology with Environment and Development?*, ed. Christoph Bail, Robert Falkner, and Helen Marquard, 438–454. London: RIIA/Earthscan.

Safrin, Sabrina. 2002b. Treaties in Collision? The Biosafety Protocol and the World Trade Organization Agreements. *American Journal of International Law* 96 (3): 606–628.

Sand, Peter H. 1997. Whither CITES? The Evolution of a Treaty Regime in the Borderland of Trade and Environment. *European Journal of International Law* 8 (1): 29–58.

Sandler, Todd. 1997. *Global Challenges: An Approach to Environmental, Political, and Economic Problems*. Cambridge: Cambridge University Press.

Sands, Philippe. 2003. *Principles of International Environmental Law*, 2nd ed. Cambridge: Cambridge University Press.

Sawyer, R. Keith. 2001. Emergence in Sociology: Contemporary Philosophy of Mind and Some Implications for Social Theory. *American Journal of Sociology* 107 (3): 551–585.

Schoenbaum, Thomas J. 1997. International Trade and Protection of the Environment: The Continuing Search for Reconciliation. *American Journal of International Law* 91 (1): 268–313.

Schoenbaum, Thomas. 2002. International Trade and Environmental Protection. In *International Law and the Environment*, 2nd ed., ed. Patricia Birnie and Alan Boyle, 697–750. Oxford: Oxford University Press.

Sebenius, James K. 1983. Negotiation Arithmetics: Adding and Subtracting Issues and Parties. *International Organization* 37 (2): 281–316.

Shaw, Sabina, and Risa Schwartz. 2002. Trade and Environment in the WTO: State of Play. *Journal of World Trade* 36 (1): 129–154.

Stein, Arthur. 1982. Coordination and Collaboration: Regimes in an Anarchic World. *International Organization* 36 (2): 299–324.

Underdal, Arild. 2002. One Question, Two Answers. In *Environmental Regime Effectiveness. Confronting Theory with Evidence*, ed. Edward L. Miles, Arild Underdal, Steinar Andresen, Jørgen Wettestad, Jon Birger Skjærseth, and Elaine M. Carlin, 3–45. Cambridge, Mass.: MIT Press.

Underdal, Arild, and Oran R. Young. 2004. Research Strategies for the Future. In *Regime Consequences: Methodological Challenges and Research Strategies*, ed. Arild Underdal and Oran R. Young, 361–380. Dordrecht: Kluwer Academic.

Victor, David G. 2000. The Sanitary and Phytosanitary Agreement of the World Trade Organization: An Assessment after Five Years. *New York University Journal of International Law & Politics*. 32:865–937.

von Moltke, Konrad. 1997. Institutional Interactions: The Structure of Regimes for Trade and the Environment. In *Global Governance: Drawing Insights from the Environmental Experience*, ed. Oran R. Young, 247–272. Cambridge, Mass.: MIT Press.

Werksman, Jacob. 1996. Compliance and Transition: Russia's Non-Compliance Tests the Ozone Regime. *Zeitschrift für ausländisches öffentliches Recht und Völkerrecht* 96 (2): 750–773.

Whalley, John, and Ben Zissimos. 2002. Making Environmental Deals: The Economic Case for a World Environment Organization. In *Global Environmental Governance: Options and Opportunities*, ed. Daniel C. Esty and Maria Ivanova, 163–180. New Haven, Conn.: Yale School of Forestry and Environmental Studies.

Wolfrum, Rüdiger, and Nele Matz. 2003. *Conflicts in International Environmental Law*. Berlin: Springer.

WTO. 1998a. *United States Import Prohibition of Certain Shrimp and Shrimp Products*. Report of the Panel. Geneva: World Trade Organization. http://www.wto.org.

WTO. 1998b. *United States Import Prohibition of Certain Shrimp and Shrimp Products. Report of the Appellate Body.* Geneva: World Trade Organization. http://www.wto.org/english/tratop_e/dispu_e/58abr.pdf (accessed 18 May 2010).

WTO. 2006. *European Communities—Measures Affecting the Approval and Marketing of Biotech Products. Report of the Panel.* Geneva: World Trade Organization. http://www.wto.org/english/news_e/news06_e/291r_e.htm (accessed 18 May 2010).

WTO. 2007. *Matrix on Trade Measures Pursuant to Selected Multilateral Environmental Agreements.* WTO Committee on Trade and Environment. Doc. WT/CTE/W/160/Rev.4 of 14 March 2007. Geneva: World Trade Organization.

10

UNCLOS, Property Rights, and Effective Fisheries Management

The Dynamics of Vertical Interplay

Frank Alcock

Introduction

The Third United Nations Convention on the Law of the Sea (UNCLOS III) yielded one of the most profound institutional changes to global environmental governance during the twentieth century. It converted a vast swath of oceanic space from a global commons to a regime characterized by 200-mile exclusive economic zones (EEZs) that extend from the shores of every coastal state. Although UNCLOS III did not become binding international law until 1994, a wave of unilateral claims to extended jurisdiction that began in the mid-1970s and subsequent state practice rendered 200-mile EEZs customary international law by the time UNCLOS III was adopted in 1982. The establishment of EEZs transformed the prevailing property rights institutions among states: EEZs now account for more than 30 percent of oceanic territory and over 90 percent of its fisheries resources. The EEZs also triggered a cascade of changes to property rights institutions within states that has been more subtle and is still ongoing.

The performance of fisheries management since the emergence of EEZs is somewhat puzzling. Oceanic enclosure brought with it great expectations of increased industrial efficiency and enhanced sustainability (Eckert 1972; Royce 1987; Sydnes 2005). These expectations have not yet been realized. Three decades after EEZs were created, both the status of fish stocks and the efficiency of fishing fleets remain poor (Garcia and Newton 1997; FAO 2004). This puzzle is more easily understood if we examine the evolution of property rights institutions within coastal states. Oceanic enclosure could be seen as the maritime equivalent to Douglass North's account of the evolution of property rights in land-tenure systems, from first excluding outsiders from harvesting the resource to then limiting the intensity of exploitation by insiders (North

1981). However, coastal state fishing industries—the insiders—have been slow to limit the intensity of exploitation. Nevertheless, recent trends in fisheries management indicate that in the long run, North's observations may prove prescient.

This chapter explores the dynamics of vertical interplay in the institutional complex of international, national, and subnational property rights institutions in fisheries in the postwar era. It analyzes how institutional change at the global level that redistributed the division of competence between coastal states and others has led to adaptations of national and subnational fisheries arrangements.

The chapter is divided into three substantive sections. The next section surveys property rights institutions in fisheries with a view to clarifying how these institutions shape incentives and distributive outcomes. Subsequently, some concepts from the global environmental change literature on institutional interplay that are helpful for understanding the impact of UNCLOS III on property rights institutions in fisheries are introduced. This is followed by a concise historical assessment of evolving institutions, their most salient characteristics, and the prevailing paradigms that shaped them. It is divided into three periods: (1) the freedom of the seas era (1950s through mid-1970s), (2) the domestic expansion era (mid-1970s through 1980s), and (3) the fisheries governance reform era (1990s onward). For each period, relevant trends and developments are assessed at the international, national, and local levels of governance, as are the impacts of these trends on behavior and outcomes in fisheries sectors. In addition, each section offers reflections on these dynamics in the context of the concepts introduced in the preceding sections.

The chapter does not seek to capture all of the relevant interplay dynamics that affect fisheries institutions. Fisheries institutions have been the focus of a considerable amount of study on interplay, especially interplay between trade institutions and resource management institutions. The aim of this chapter is twofold: to explore the impacts of an institutional change at the international level (UNCLOS III) on national and local property rights institutions in fisheries, and to explore the impacts that evolving property rights institutions in national and local fisheries are having on international fisheries regimes (UNCLOS III and regional fisheries management organizations, RFMOs). Many international relations scholars are familiar with the significance of UNCLOS III as an instance of institutional change at the international level. Few, however, seem to fully appreciate the still ongoing evolution in property rights systems that has been triggered by this change.

Property Rights Institutions in Fisheries

This section discusses the impacts property rights institutions have on incentives and distribution in fisheries sectors. After a brief overview of some of the different forms of property rights found in fisheries, the discussion turns to incentives pertaining to "the race for the fish" and distributive outcomes pertaining to large-scale or industrial actors versus small-scale or artisanal actors. Monitoring and enforcement are addressed at the end.

Forms of Property Rights

Property rights arrangements are forms of institutions that delineate ownership, access, and usufruct rights in a given domain. In the marine environment, these rights are sometimes referred to as systems of marine tenure. Categories of property-rights systems in fisheries include (1) open-access rights, (2) state rights, (3) community rights, and (4) individual rights. Open-access rights are to a certain extent a lack of property rights, in that they refer to the inability to exclude or limit access to new actors. State rights are exclusive rights held by states; they can be used to regulate domestic actors as well as to exclude international ones. Specific forms of individual and community rights include limited-entry programs, individual fishing quotas (IFQs), community fishing quotas, and territorial use rights in fisheries (TURFs).

Limited-entry rules restrict access to a given fishery to a particular group or community of actors and are necessary preconditions for IFQs, community fishing quotas, and territorial use rights. IFQs are exclusive rights awarded to individual fishers or individual vessels, specifying a portion of a given fish species that can be harvested in a given year. They are often referred to as individual transferable quotas (ITQs) when rights can be transferred from one individual to another. Community fishing quotas involve the same basic concept as IFQs, but with the exclusive rights to harvest specific amounts of fish conferred on communities rather than individuals. Such communities are usually geographically defined but need not be ("communities" can include any distinct set of actors with common characteristics or goals). TURFs are exclusive rights to fish within a given area. They do not limit the amount of fish that can be caught but rather the time and place for fishing, and are often coupled with restrictions on harvesting methods. TURFs can be recognized for communities or individuals, or both. They have become a preferred method for regulating fishing activity in developing countries, where monitoring the landings of specific quantities of fish for large numbers of fishers is practically impossible (OECD 2006).

Many of the above property rights systems can be "nested" within others. For instance, EEZs are a form of exclusive state rights, but each of the other three forms can exist within EEZs. Individual rights arrangements can also exist within a broader framework of community rights, and community rights can also be incorporated into a broader framework of individual rights.

Incentives

Property rights arrangements affect fisheries behavior through their impact on incentives. Under open-access conditions, fisheries are especially sensitive to what has long been referred to as "the tragedy of the commons" (Hardin 1968). According to Hardin, the inability to exclude users of a common resource creates a situation in which each individual user receives the full benefit of his own resource consumption while bearing only a small fraction of the cost. Those inclined to conserve the resource witness the dissipation of benefits by others who exploit it. In the absence of institutional constraints, the rational choice for individual commons users is to exploit the resource before it is gone. In fisheries, this dynamic is sometimes referred to as "the race for the fish." When fish stocks can replenish themselves faster than a given set of fishers can harvest them, the race for the fish and the resulting tragedy of stock depletion do not apply. But when harvesting capacity exceeds a stock's replenishment rate, they do. Given the technological changes that have transformed the world's fishing fleets since the end of World War II and dramatically increased their fishing capacity, very few stocks today can maintain themselves without institutional constraints on fishing intensity.

Some attempts to avoid the tragedy by directly limiting the total harvest level can have perverse effects that actually accelerate the race for the fish. When technology and fishing capacity are left unconstrained, limiting the total amount of fish that can be caught or the season in which it can be caught generates incentives to invest in bigger and faster boats that allow actors to maximize their share of the quota or their share of the seasonal take. The race for the fish becomes intensified under such circumstances (Iudicello, Weber, and Wieland 1999).

IFQs have proved particularly effective in reducing the race for fish by changing behavioral incentives. The race for the fish is driven by the incentive of each individual fisher to maximize his or her share of the available fish by catching as many fish as possible as quickly as possible. Under an IFQ program, the share of each individual fisher is fixed in advance. Fishers are prohibited from landing more fish than they have been allocated, so catching fish before others do will do nothing to increase their share. Subject to adequate monitoring and enforcement mechanisms, the only way fishers can increase their share is by purchasing other fishers' quota in an ITQ program (if such exists). Since fishers can no longer affect the size of their slice of the pie, they focus instead on getting the most value out of the slice they have. The basic incentives under an IFQ program are to minimize the cost of catching a given share of fish and to maximize the price obtained for it. Where implemented, such programs have proved effective in eliminating the incentive to race for the fish, but they remain controversial, largely owing to concerns about the distributive impacts (Grafton, Squires, and Kirkley 1996; Iudicello, Weber, and Wieland 1999; Hannesson 2004).

In the absence of fixed individual quotas, the institutional design must focus on limiting the incentive to increase fishing intensities in order to capture larger portions of the stock, thereby limiting the race for the fish. To this end, new entrants, investments, and new technologies that would substantially impact fishing intensity can be restricted or constrained. Community fishing quotas and territorial use rights for relatively homogeneous communities of fishers with similar fishing gear, that are usually low impact or labor-intensive, are successful examples of non-IFQ arrangements (McCay and Acheson 1987; Pinkerton 1989; Ostrom 1990; Kurien 2003).

Distribution

Property rights arrangements are significant determinants of how the costs and benefits of fishing activity are distributed among actors operating in fisheries sectors. Prevailing property rights arrangements affect distribution across states and, perhaps more important, within them.

The fishing and seafood industry has historically consisted of fishers and merchants. A patron-client relationship known as the "truck system" defined many coastal fisheries for centuries. It was prevalent in the coastal fisheries of developed countries well into the twentieth century, and it continues to exist today in much of the developing world. The truck system characterizes an economic relationship in which merchants provide credit and supplies to individual fishers, who sell their fish back to the merchant on a credit-only basis. The merchant then markets the fish, often via export. The relationship has historically favored the merchants, who act as monopsonists. Fishers are often price-takers, dependent on a single merchant or dealer for the credit and supplies necessary for their annual operations (Apostle et al. 1998; Alcock 2003).

Glimpses into the longstanding political conflict between merchants and fishers can be gleaned through an examination of the history of domestic fisheries legislation in a number of countries. Much of this legislation concerns who can legally buy, sell, and export fish, along with the right to determine prices in the absence of competitive markets. Fisheries legislation also reflects battles over access to fisheries, the ownership of harvesting assets, and the introduction of new technologies. Merchants have long sought to bypass fishers and obtain direct access to fisheries by owning and controlling the harvesting assets, while fishers have long sought to block merchants from doing this. Whereas merchants have historically maintained the upper hand in most domestic struggles over prices and marketing arrangements, fishers have tended to fare better in terms of maintaining control over access to the fishery (Apostle et al. 1998; Alcock 2003).

The modern heirs to the merchant class in fisheries are industrial fishing operations. These are typically capital-intensive and are conducted by firms, while smaller-scale, artisanal fisheries are more labor-intensive and are conducted by fishers who own their own gear and fishing vessels. Artisanal and industrial fisheries each account for about half the world's fish catch, even though more than 90 percent of the world's fishers are artisanal fishers (FAO 2004).

Property rights arrangements have important distributive implications for each of these segments of the fishing industry through their effects on bargaining power over prices and access to fishing grounds. When harvesters receive exclusive quota rights, their bargaining power typically grows relative to that of downstream segments of the industry. Market gluts become less frequent as fishing seasons are often spread out more evenly during the year; harvesters begin to adjust their activity in response to market conditions; and quota owners bypass longstanding purchasing arrangements by shopping around for better deals. Where industrial or processing interests are precluded from owning quotas, IFQ programs will often redistribute fisheries rents in favor of harvesters. But if industrial fishing operations are awarded quota rights, or are allowed to purchase them, they often reassert control over fisheries access and the bargaining power associated with it. In the latter circumstance, "downstream" fishing interests often consolidate and capture rents from the fishery. Vertically integrated segments of the fishing industry tend to favor the introduction of ITQ programs more than smaller-scale interests do, but the ultimate distributive impact of a given program is largely a function of its programmatic details, such as the rules pertaining to program eligibility, initial quota allocation, and quota transfers (Alcock 2006).

Monitoring and Enforcement

Any primer on the issue of property rights in fisheries would be incomplete without brief reference to the issues of monitoring and enforcement. Sufficient levels of monitoring and enforcement are necessary conditions for the adequate performance of any property rights regime in fisheries. Poor monitoring and enforcement can undermine the incentives created by some forms of property rights, notably IFQs. Many of the world's fisheries are characterized by an industry structure (large numbers of actors and ports) that precludes the introduction of quota rights. Considerations as to what can be enforced often shape institutional changes, including changes to property rights arrangements.

In addition to affecting the performance of property rights regimes, monitoring and enforcement issues may themselves be affected by property rights regimes. New rule systems can affect incentives along with perceptions of legitimacy. IFQ programs in particular have been both applauded and criticized on this account. Advocates highlight how this form of property rights can strengthen the incentives for better stewardship, including investment and support for better monitoring and enforcement. Alternatively, when IFQ programs are introduced to a fishery where a number of actors resist them, a perceived lack of legitimacy can make monitoring and enforcement problematic (Copes 1996; Alcock 2003).

Interplay Concepts

Oberthür and Gehring in this volume provide a detailed overview of the conceptual development in the global environmental change literature on institutional interplay. They discuss the various approaches that have been used, before working through a series of classification schemes and conceptual typologies. The most relevant concepts for this chapter include Young's (1996) notion of embeddedness, nesting, and overlap; Stokke's (2001b) notion of ideational, normative, and utilitarian interaction; and Oberthür and Gehring's discussion of behavioral and cognitive interaction, as well as interaction through commitment. After briefly explaining the general approach taken in this chapter, in the remainder of this section I discuss how these concepts can help illuminate the dynamics of vertical interplay among property rights institutions in fisheries.

Jurisdictional Interaction

A common form of institutional interaction occurs when the jurisdictional boundaries of one institution subsume, overlap, encroach on, or in some way affect the jurisdictional boundaries of another institution. In Young's (1996) discussion, embeddedness, nesting, and overlap would all seem to involve some degree of jurisdictional interaction. "Nesting" in particular is a fairly common term in the institutional literature (Aggarwal 1983) and has previously been used with reference to vertical interplay dynamics in fisheries (Ostrom 1990). Drawing on Young (1996), Oberthür and Gehring (2006, 10) define nesting as "instances of interaction in which specific arrangements are folded into broader institutional frameworks that deal with the same issue area." They see nesting as a particular form of interaction in which the commitments under one institution affect the decision-making processes of another institution ("interaction through commitment").

Another form of interaction through commitment identified by these authors is jurisdictional delimitation, which is the redefinition of jurisdictional boundaries in response to regulatory conflicts that emerge in the presence of incompatible, overlapping commitments. This chapter uses the term "institutional displacement" to refer to a causal dynamic similar to what Oberthür and Gehring conceive of in their discussion of jurisdictional delimitation. It involves the delimitation of a given set of jurisdictional boundaries and associated institutional arrangements and their replacement with a different set of institutional arrangements associated with the expansion of a competing set of jurisdictional boundaries.

Utilitarian Interaction

Stokke's (2001b) typology of causal mechanisms associated with institutional interaction consists of ideational interplay, normative interplay, utilitarian interplay, and interplay management. He defines utilitarian interplay (2001b, 9) as "a case where rules or programmes that are undertaken within one regime alter the costs or benefits of behavioral options addressed by another regime." The concept relates to Oberthür and Gehring's discussion of behavioral interaction. Oberthür and Gehring (in this volume) suggest that "behavioral changes triggered by the source institution become relevant for the implementation of the target institution." They further refine the concept by specifying that the source institution must produce an output such as a set of prescriptions or proscriptions that cause relevant actors to change their behavior in response to the output. Ultimately, this behavioral effect exerts influence on the performance and effectiveness of the target institution. This chapter employs the term "utilitarian interaction" to denote behavioral changes that result from changes in incentives that are attributable to the arrangements in a given institution but that have implications for the effectiveness or performance of another institution.

Ideational Interaction

According to Stokke (2001b, 10), ideational interaction "involves processes of learning." He distinguishes between tributary institutions and recipient institutions to better elucidate the flow of ideas in a given mechanism. Tributary regimes provide "solutions of various sorts that are emulated or adapted for problem-solving purposes under the recipient regime." Oberthür and Gehring's (2006) notion of cognitive interaction appears consistent with Stokke's definition, if more specific in terms of causal pathways.

Interplay among Interaction Types

As previously noted, complex causal chains involving vertical interplay in fisheries sectors resulted from UNCLOS III. UNCLOS III dramatically curtailed the spatial dimensions of high-seas fisheries while expanding the jurisdictions of national fisheries institutions in the form of exclusive economic zones. EEZs created a space for national institutions that "displaced" a set of open-access rules operating at the international level. This was a clear instance of jurisdictional interaction among fisheries institutions at different scales of governance. Jurisdictional interaction triggered a cascade of utilitarian and ideational interaction across governance scales by changing incentives and promulgating ideas about fisheries policies and fisheries governance. Utilitarian and ideational interactions ultimately led to further jurisdictional interaction in the form of expanded or newly introduced RFMO mandates under the 1995 Fish Stocks Agreement, and additional jurisdictional modifications remain possible in the coming decades. Jurisdictional, utilitarian, and ideational interactions thus continue to influence one another.

Jurisdictional changes affect the incentives of coastal states, distant-water fishing nations, and distinct segments of the fishing industry. New ideas continue to emerge regarding how best to govern fisheries. Fishers, along with intergovernmental organizations, nongovernmental organizations, and epistemic communities, all learn from their experiences—and, in doing so, attempt to modify jurisdictional boundaries, in addition to the policies pursued within those boundaries. Institutions thus shape the behavior of actors, who in turn shape the evolution of institutions.

UNCLOS

This section examines the experience of UNCLOS, focusing on property rights arrangements at different governance scales with a view to elucidating the interplay concepts discussed above. This discussion is divided into three periods: the freedom of the seas era (1950s to mid-1970s), the domestic expansion era (mid-1970s through 1980s), and the fisheries governance reform era (1990s onward).

Freedom of the Seas Era (1950s to Mid-1970s)

In the immediate wake of World War II, the prevailing institutional framework at the international level can be characterized as a global commons. The world's fishing fleets were allowed to harvest as much fish as they could outside one another's territorial waters, which traditionally extended three miles from the coastline. Open-access conditions were underpinned by the freedom-of-the-seas paradigm. Various RFMOs also existed, but their efforts were focused largely on cooperative scientific research and the development of the sector (FAO 1999). Within RFMOs, it would seem that an industrial development paradigm held sway. RFMOs had neither the authority nor the desire to manage stocks by limiting access or constraining efforts during this period (Sydnes 2005).

At the national level, regulations and laws pertaining to fisheries varied considerably from one coastal state to another. In many developing countries there were no regulations at all; in such cases, "institutional void" is perhaps the most apt descriptor. The focus of much of the national legislation that did exist was on technology promotion and control, fisheries access, and price controls, and can best be characterized as measures to promote exports and privilege some segments of the fishing industry vis-à-vis others (Christy 1997; Apostle et al. 1998; Lear 1998; Alcock 2002).

A richer assortment of formal and informal rule systems existed at local governance levels within both the developed and the developing world. The focus of the vast majority of local fisheries institutions was on issues of controlling access to coastal fisheries and the use of particular technologies (McCay and Acheson 1987; Bailey 1997; Kurien 1998, 2003; Apostle et al. 1998; Ibarra, Reid, and Thorpe 2000b). Apparently no particular institutional paradigm was dominant at national and local levels of governance, although most state agencies with authority over fisheries policies seemed receptive to the idea of industrial development (Bailey, Cycon, and Morris 1986; Bailey 1988; Christy 1997; Lear 1998; Gelchu and Pauly 2007).

Perhaps the most salient behavioral drivers during this period were the rapid technological changes that affected the industry (Lear 1998). Fisheries technologies made quantum leaps in terms of their ability to locate, catch, process, freeze, transport, package, and distribute fish. In addition to expanding existing markets for fresh and salted seafood, these technological developments allowed for the creation of new ones, most notably frozen seafood retailing in American supermarkets. Global fisheries production grew rapidly.

The major beneficiaries of the prevailing institutional framework were the distant-water fishing nations (DWFNs), which had developed large fleets capable of exploiting unfettered access to global fish stocks. Challengers to this regime included various states with significant economic resources—including fisheries resources—near their coastlines or on the continental shelves that extended out from them. Several of these coastal states made unilateral claims to jurisdiction over the waters beyond their territorial seas and the living marine resources contained therein. Driven largely by concerns over energy resources, the United States was the first to advance this type of claim, in the form of the Truman Proclamation of 1945. Other coastal states concerned with fisheries resources soon followed suit, including Chile, Ecuador, Iceland, Mexico, Peru, and several African coastal states (Burke 1994; Juda 1996; Orrego Vicuña 2001). Many of these coastal states argued that monitoring and fisheries regulation could be improved by expanding coastal state jurisdiction.

Challenges to the freedom-of-the-seas paradigm resulted in the first United Nations Conference on the Law of the Sea in 1958 (UNCLOS I). A second conference (UNCLOS II) was held in 1960, but neither UNCLOS I nor II was able to resolve the jurisdictional disputes regarding fisheries. However, in the coming years, technological changes combined with considerations from outside the fisheries sector began to tip the balance of power in favor of a configuration of interests that supported expanded national jurisdictions. A coalition of coastal states supporting extended coastal jurisdictions ultimately prevailed during the UNCLOS III negotiations, which began in 1974. UNCLOS III was not codified until 1982, but many states unilaterally established EEZs during the 1970s, and most states had accepted the principle of 200-mile EEZs by the end of the decade (Burke 1994; Juda 1996; Orrego Vicuña 1999; 2001).

Vertical interplay among the prevailing fisheries institutions prior to the mid-1970s was modest, although the period did witness a gradual intensification of encroachments on the part of new actors and technologies that began to undermine and erode the efficacy of traditional institutional arrangements. Table 10.1 indicates the vertical dimensions of prevailing fisheries institutions and associated institutional paradigms during this period.

Domestic Expansion Era (Mid-1970s through 1980s)

Extended jurisdiction had immediate implications for the externalities associated with fishing activity and the distribution of fisheries rents at the international level. With respect to overfishing, EEZs internalized many externalities associated with the depletion of fish stocks that were largely contained within them. The new zones empowered coastal states to exclude other states from harvesting stocks within their respective EEZs, and granted them the authority to regulate fishing within their respective jurisdictions. Extended jurisdiction had less effect on internalizing externalities for straddling stocks and highly migratory species that moved across multiple EEZs, as the costs and benefits associated with harvesting activity for such stocks depended on the decisions made by more than one state. With respect to distribution, the EEZs implied a transfer of wealth from DWFNs or the "common heritage of mankind" to individual coastal states. The creation of EEZs is a clear example of jurisdictional delimitation or upward vertical displacement of an international institution by an emerging set of domestic institutions. It is also an instance of utilitarian interaction, as the incentives changed for coastal states and the actors operating within them.

Coastal states responded in various ways. Some countries saw the endowment as an opportunity to develop an industrialized, offshore fishing fleet to exploit the resources the DWFNs left behind. Several advanced industrialized countries, among them the United States, Canada, and New Zealand, did this independently (Shrank 1995; Hennessey and Healey 2000; Hersoug 2002). Many developing countries in Latin America and Southeast Asia did the same, with technical and

Table 10.1
Freedom of the seas era: 1950s to mid-1970s

Governance level	Fisheries management institutions	Institutional characteristics	Institutional paradigms
International	RFMOs; UNCLOS I and II.	Open access beyond territorial waters, but unilateral claims of expanded coastal jurisdictions begin to proliferate.	Oceans enclosure movement begins to contest freedom-of-the-seas paradigm; industrial development paradigm gains in strength.
Vertical interplay	Limited interplay. DWFN activity on continental shelves dampens the incentives for institutional reforms in waters under coastal state jurisdiction.		
National	Variation in domestic legislation, with voids in many developing countries.	Export promotion and elements of protection and privilege for different industry segments; technology, access to fisheries, and commodity prices are commonly subject to rules.	Various; tacit support for industrial development paradigm in most cases.
Vertical interplay	Limited but modestly intensifying interplay. Technological changes and associated DWFN fishing activity erode the effectiveness of traditional marine tenure arrangements at local governance levels.		
Local	Rich assortment of formal and informal rule systems.	Various, but exclusive community access and technology controls are common.	Various.

financial assistance from international development organizations or the DWFNs, or both (Bailey, Cycon, and Morris 1986; Christy 1997; Silvestre and Pauly 1997; Ibarra, Reid, and Thorpe 2000a). Still other developing countries in Africa and in Oceania allowed the DWFNs to maintain their access through leasing arrangements with coastal states (Queirolo, Johnston, and Zhang 1997; Gelchu and Pauly 2007). Most DWFNs responded to their displacement from EEZs by negotiating leasing arrangements or redirecting their fishing activity to the remaining high-seas fisheries.

At the national level, the mutual recognition of 200-mile EEZs triggered a wave of domestic fisheries legislation in many coastal states. In some cases the legislation implemented specific policies and strengthened organizations within existing regulatory frameworks, while in other cases it created new frameworks and organizations. The establishment of EEZs also stimulated a wave of capital investment in the fisheries sectors of those coastal states that were perceived as having more exploitable resources than their existing fishing capacity could harvest (Shrank 1995; Christy 1997; Silvestre and Pauly 1997; Hennessey and Healey 2000; Ibarra, Reid, and Thorpe 2000a, 2000b). The fisheries legislation enacted by several coastal states during the 1970s and 1980s reinforced the incentives for capital investment through subsidies, loans, and tax credits (Tvedten and Hersoug 1992; Shrank 1995; Hennessey and Healey 2000; Ibarra, Reid, and Thorpe 2000a, 2000b). Considerable variation is evident in the character of fisheries regulatory frameworks that coastal states established during this period. Many regulatory frameworks were (and continue to be) heavily influenced by a given country's sociopolitical history and its prevailing models for broader economic policies (Alcock 2006).

The creation of EEZs generated incentives that encouraged the adoption of the industrial development paradigm in some countries where that might not otherwise have happened. The industrial development paradigm emphasized fleet modernization, industrial upscaling, and export opportunities in American, European, and Japanese markets. The paradigm predates EEZs in its management logic for fisheries, but extended jurisdiction seems to have amplified its impact in some places. It emerged in the 1950s and 1960s, and was widely deployed by most DWFNs. Several developing countries did the same during this period, especially in Southeast Asia and Africa (Gelchu and Pauly 2007). For most coastal states, however, the reality of competing for access with the existing DWFNs dampened the prospects of developing an indigenous industrial capacity. Excluding the DWFNs from accessing the stocks contained within a coastal state's EEZs shielded coastal states from harvesting competition and created new opportunities for exploitation.

The agents responsible for spreading the industrial development paradigm were in many cases international organizations. The World Bank, along with regional development banks such as the Inter-American Development Bank (Christy 1997) and the Asian Development Bank (Bailey, Cycon, and Morris 1986), advocated and financed initiatives to industrialize the fisheries sectors of various developing countries. Also, the FAO's EEZ Programme was very active throughout the 1980s, shaping the policies of many developing countries. Although sensitive to the importance of managing fish stocks sustainably, the FAO largely promoted the industrial development paradigm during this period (Loftas 1981; Bailey, Cycon, and Morris 1986; Christy 1997; FAO 1999; Swan and Satia 1999; Sydnes 2005).

UNCLOS III thus led to a wave of policy changes at the domestic level that basically followed an industrial development paradigm. The causal dynamics involved a new jurisdictional delimitation at the international level that affected utilitarian calculations on the part of newly endowed coastal states, and international finance and fisheries development organizations facilitated the spread of ideas regarding how best to exploit these endowments.

Although UNCLOS III did not engage local levels of fisheries governance directly, several indirect impacts are discernible. For some local fishing communities, the banishment of foreign fishing fleets resulted in a brief respite from industrial fishing pressures. For most, however, the subsequent modernization and expansion of domestic fishing fleets soon allowed industrial fishing pressures to encroach on local fisheries institutions to an unprecedented degree. Encroachments were driven by the creation of domestic industrial fleets or the adoption of new technologies by some members of traditional fishing communities. Before UNCLOS III, many coastal and inshore fisheries within territorial waters, ranging from three to twelve miles from the coastline, had enjoyed a limited degree of protection from foreign industrial fleets. Although briefly benefiting from a 200-mile buffer from foreign fleets, many of these fisheries quickly became subject to more advanced technologies (trawlers) and industrial fishing pressures from domestic actors that had access not only to the EEZs but also to inshore fisheries within territorial waters.[1] Even in the absence of EEZs, many local communities would still have had a difficult time maintaining exclusive access to their traditional fishing grounds and protecting against encroachments from industrial harvesting assets, but the domestic institutional changes triggered by the EEZs probably accelerated these trends (McCay and Acheson 1987; Bailey 1997; Sunderlin and Gorospe 1997; Kurien 1998, 2003).

The relevant causal dynamics affecting local-level fisheries institutions included jurisdictional delimitation in the form of downward vertical displacement and utilitarian interaction. The industrial development policies pursued by many coastal states changed the behavior of some of the actors operating in coastal fisheries in two important ways. First, these policies introduced a new class of actors in the form of domestic industrial fishers that had not existed previously. Second, they provided incentives for existing small-scale or artisanal fishers to introduce or adopt new technologies that undermined the viability of traditional marine tenure arrangements. At one level of governance, coastal states changed their behavior in response to changing incentives in the wake of UNCLOS III. At another governance level, the policies enacted by coastal states (coastal state behavior) altered the incentives for actors operating in their respective fisheries sectors. These altered incentives led to behavioral changes on the part of these actors as well. Table 10.2 indicates the vertical dimensions of prevailing fisheries institutions and associated interplay from the mid-1970s through the 1980s.

Fisheries Governance Reform Era (1990s Onward)

As noted in the previous section, the creation of EEZs did well to internalize some of the fishing externalities associated with some fish stocks among states. However, this was not the case with straddling stocks, highly migratory species, and high-seas fisheries. For these latter groups of fisheries, UNCLOS III obliged states to cooperate but offered little in the way of frameworks for doing so. In fact, the displacement of DWFNs onto what remained of the high seas further undermined the efficacy of the freedom-of-the-seas principle. UNCLOS III provided a framework for protection of stocks within EEZs but increased the competition for stocks occurring outside them. Such competition was exacerbated by the fleets of newly industrialized coastal states that laid claim to straddling and migratory stocks that crossed into their respective jurisdictions (Burke 1994; Orrego Vicuña 1999; 2001).

Frustration with the impotence of RFMOs and the inability of UNCLOS to engender effective management of straddling stocks, highly migratory species, and other high-seas fisheries led to greater pressure for reforms. This pressure culminated in a collection of international

Table 10.2
Domestic expansion era: Mid-1970s through 1980s

Governance level	Fisheries management institutions	Institutional characteristics	Institutional paradigms
International	UNCLOS III; RFMOs with reduced jurisdictions.	200-mile EEZs; open access remains on high seas.	Curtailed freedom-of-the-seas paradigm; industrial development paradigm remains strong.
Vertical interplay	Jurisdictional interaction occurs when expanded EEZs curtail the spatial coverage of the high-seas regime. Utilitarian interaction occurs as coastal states react to changed incentives, and ideational interaction occurs as intergovernmental agencies promote industrial development paradigms within EEZs. Ideational interaction occurs as international organizations promote the industrial development paradigm to national governments.		
National	New wave of domestic fisheries legislation/regulatory frameworks appears.	Significant variation (including isolated IFQ programs); subsidies for capital investment are common.	Industrial development paradigm proliferates; emphasis is on capital investment, job creation, and exports.
Vertical interplay	Jurisdictional interaction occurs as national legislation overrides traditional institutional arrangements at local levels. Utilitarian interaction occurs as national policies create new actors or change the incentives of existing actors operating in local fisheries. Limited ideational interaction occurs where local actors embrace the industrial development paradigm.		
Local	Erosion of many local institutions occurs.	Local institutions can no longer constrain new actors and technologies.	National-level paradigms and policies overshadow and undermine local paradigms.

agreements that included the Agreement for the Implementation of the Provisions of the United Nations Convention of the Law of the Sea of 10 December 1982 relating to the Conservation and Management of Straddling Fish Stocks and Highly Migratory Fish Stocks (the 1995 Fish Stocks Agreement), and a nonbinding 1995 FAO Code of Conduct for Responsible Fisheries (the 1995 Code of Conduct). The 1995 Fish Stocks Agreement is notable for its attempt to further limit the freedom-of-the-seas principle by restricting access to high-seas fisheries to members of relevant RFMOs (new members with "real interests" in applicable fisheries are permitted, although the interpretation of this article remains contested). The responsibilities and mandates of RFMOs were also expanded in a manner that reemphasized the importance of responsible fisheries management (Stokke 2001a). The 1995 Code of Conduct further detailed the operationalization of "responsible" fisheries management.

These changes can be interpreted as instances of jurisdictional delimitation, in that they attempted to strengthen the authority of RFMOs in international waters and clarify obligations between open-access high-seas fisheries and coastal state jurisdictions. Although the changes have put greater pressure on several DWFNs to improve management practices within RFMOs, the RFMOs remain vulnerable to those DWFNs that have chosen not to sign and ratify the 1995 agreement or that operate through vessels flying under the flags of nonparties (Sydnes 2005; DeSombre 2006).

Within a decade or so after the establishment of EEZs, it became increasingly apparent to many coastal states that exclusive jurisdictional authority over fisheries resources could not guarantee effective fisheries management. By the end of the 1980s, after a brief period of rapid growth and prosperity within domestic fisheries sectors, many coastal states encountered depleted stocks and overcapitalized fishing fleets (Shrank 1995; Christy 1997; Hennessey and Healey 2000; Gelchu and Pauly 2007). To a certain extent, this outcome is attributable to the failure of the industrial development paradigm, with its dependence on problematic stock assessment models and its lack of caution in maintaining sustainable harvest levels. In addition, most coastal states failed to establish or reinforce marine tenure systems that could have reduced incentives to overcapitalize (Hannesson 2004).

Some coastal states had relatively successful experiences, however. Most notably, New Zealand and Iceland were the first countries to begin experimenting with individual fishing quotas (IFQs) (Eythorsson 2000; Hersoug 2002). IFQs remain controversial but, as noted earlier, they are widely acknowledged as reducing the incentives to overcapitalize and thus increasing the efficiency of fishing operations. Their primary drawback lies in the distributive impacts that accompany industry consolidation, vertical integration, and accompanying changes to bargaining power among different segments of the industry. If not carefully designed, IFQ programs may act to disenfranchise some industry segments and the communities that depend on them. As the 1990s progressed, several additional countries began to experiment with their own versions of IFQ programs, drawing on the lessons learned from the early movers. By the end of the 1990s, most developed countries with significant fisheries resources had at least considered them in some form, as had a handful of developing countries (Grafton, Squires, and Kirkley 1996; OECD 1997, 2006; Hannesson 2004).

The most salient interplay dynamics associated with the diffusion of IFQ programs can be characterized as instances of ideational interaction. The "sole-ownership theory" or privatization paradigm for fisheries management had been around since the 1950s (Gordon 1954; Scott 1955). Deployment of the paradigm was made possible by the creation of EEZs and the jurisdictional space they created for institutional experimentation. In the wake of UNCLOS III, advocates of the privatization paradigm began to champion the idea of exclusive, transferable rights in fisheries in the form of ITQ systems. Transgovernmental networks facilitated communication of the lessons learned through experimentation with ITQ systems in New Zealand and Iceland to fisheries officials in other countries (Slaughter 2004). More recently, however, various international organizations have acted as agents that have assisted in the proliferation of the privatization paradigm, including the World Bank (Sundar 2002), the OECD (2006), and the FAO (Shotton 2000). Learning from experiences with domestic fisheries institutions has shaped the prevailing paradigms in international organizations, which, in turn, help to spread these ideas to other countries. The institutional interplay is largely horizontal—coastal states learn from one another—but it is facilitated by international organizations that upload lessons from some coastal states and download them to others, consistent with previous conceptions of the role of international organizations in international policy diffusion (Weyland 2005). Accordingly, the governments of coastal states and international organizations might be considered as both tributaries and recipients of ideas pertaining to property rights institutions in fisheries.

At local levels, the 1990s witnessed growing resistance to the national fisheries policies of many coastal states. Local fishing communities often had to bear the economic and ecological costs of declining stocks and failing industries. The industrial development paradigm has been heavily criticized in many of these communities. Some have questioned the logic of the paradigm's privileging of the industrial segment of the industry, while others have focused their ire on the inability of state bureaucracies to manage fish stocks effectively (Shrank 1995; Kurien 1998; Ibarra, Reid, and Thorpe 2000a, 2000b).

Only a modest number of local communities have embraced the idea of IFQ programs, however. Most see such programs as further privileging large-scale industrial interests and as a mechanism for further depressing the economic viability and traditional values of local fishing communities. Of note, the sheer number of artisanal fishers and small-scale fishing communities has rendered IFQ programs infeasible in much of the developing world. Several local fishing communities, and the social scientists who have studied them, have advanced an alternative paradigm focusing on the idea of comanagement. Comanagement is a form of decentralization in which local fishing communities gain greater autonomy in managing the resources under their jurisdiction. Rather than looking toward the state or market for fisheries management solutions, the comanagement paradigm emphasizes the role of local communities (McCay and Acheson 1987; Pinkerton 1989). The virtues of comanagement stem from its perceived legitimacy by resource users and its ability to generate distributive outcomes that are often seen as fair. It also tends to privilege the concerns of small-scale, artisanal segments of the fishing industry over the large-scale, industrial segment. Its weakness lies in the lack of prescription of any particular property rights arrangements. Comanagement alone cannot guarantee outcomes that will be effective in structuring the appropriate incentives. Accordingly, IFQ programs and comanagement arrangements are not mutually exclusive (Berkes et al. 2001).

In contrast to the dynamics of transgovernmental politics characterizing the diffusion of the privatization paradigm, the decentralization paradigm has benefited from the dynamics of transnational politics involving a range of nongovernmental actors (Slaughter 2004). The decentralization paradigm is championed by an epistemic community that is in many ways distinct from that which embraces the privatization paradigm, although there are some overlaps (Haas 1992). Decentralization advocates include a larger proportion of social scientists from outside the economics discipline, and coalitions of stakeholders and NGOs that are at least as sensitive to equity considerations as they are to efficiency considerations (Alcock 2008). The dynamics of ideational interplay in the case of the decentralization paradigm can also be distinguished from those of the privatization paradigm, in that the vertical dimension of interplay largely involves the transfer of ideas and insights from local institutions to national-level institutions. Local-level institutions are the source of ideas, with national-level institutions and intergovernmental organizations as the recipients.

The period from 2000 to the present does not reflect a marked departure from the 1990s. However, some trends are worth mentioning. First, the proliferation of IFQ and comanagement programs seems to be accelerating, and there are indications of accommodation and coexistence in many instances. Second, some intergovernmental organizations that increasingly champion IFQs and the rights-based paradigm are becoming more and more receptive to governance insights arising from past failures to adequately consider and support artisanal and small-scale fishers (World Bank 2004; FAO 2005). Accordingly, the latest rounds of fisheries sector reforms and associated legislation in many countries seem more sensitive to local governance concerns and traditional fisheries institutions than in the 1980s and 1990s (Viswanathan et al. 2003; FAO 2005).

Future institutional arrangements in fisheries will likely continue to be shaped by both the privatization and decentralization paradigms. Perhaps the most intriguing interaction dynamic involves the potential for fisheries institutions at the domestic level to serve as tributaries of institutional ideas that become adopted by fisheries institutions at the international level. This could happen if RFMOs ever introduce IFQs, and it would serve as a striking example of vertical interplay that takes a specific form of marine tenure found at the domestic level and replicates it at the international level (Joseph 2005; Grafton et al. 2006; Trondsen, Matthiasson, and Young 2006; Alcock 2010). Even if this fails to happen, the freedom-of-the-seas paradigm has largely been repudiated by the 1995 Fish Stocks Agreement, although not all states have become parties to it. A few states continue to evoke the freedom-of-the-seas paradigm for reasons of self-interest, but it appears to have lost its perceived legitimacy as a viable institutional strategy for effective fisheries management outside of EEZs (Orbach 2002).

At the domestic level, coexistence among paradigms is likely within the EEZs of many coastal states, as is the potential for combining paradigms (embedding ITQ systems within comanagement institutions, or embedding community quotas or certain forms of territorial use rights within a broader IFQ/ITQ system). IFQ systems seem to have greatest resonance at national levels of governance and in OECD countries, but additional local communities and non-OECD countries may gravitate toward them. Privatization and decentralization schemes may incorporate some aspects of the old industrial development paradigm, but the failed policies of unbridled expansion in the absence of appropriate property rights arrangements and at the expense of local communities are unlikely to be rekindled en masse. Comanagement arrangements are likely to remain popular at local governance levels, and there are some indications that coastal states may be willing to accommodate traditional local institutions by nesting them within national fisheries legislation (Viswanathan et al. 2003; World Bank 2004; Alcock 2006).

Table 10.3 indicates the vertical dimensions of prevailing fisheries institutions and associated interplay from the 1990s to the present.

Conclusion

This chapter illuminates a fascinating set of vertical dynamics within the institutional complex of property rights regimes in marine fisheries. Extended jurisdiction associated with UNCLOS III has precipitated a cascade of utilitarian and ideational interactions across international, national, and local scales of human governance that may ultimately reverberate and lead to further jurisdictional changes at the international level. A set of exclusive national jurisdictions has displaced a global commons regime. While this institutional change at the international level has proven stable, the jurisdictional space thereby opened up at the national level has allowed experimentation with a diversity of new property rights arrangements, some of which have proved more effective than others. In many instances these new arrangements have undermined traditional fisheries institutions at local levels.

The initial wave of fisheries policies that accompanied institutional development in the wake of EEZs was shaped by the prevailing fisheries management paradigm at the time—industrial development. Under these circumstances, the behavior of actors operating in fisheries sectors was affected by incentives that changed in accordance with new institutional opportunities and ideas about how to exploit them. More often than not, the industrialization policies enacted in the absence of complementary property rights arrangements failed at local and national levels of governance alike. By changing jurisdictional boundaries, altering coastal state incentives, and contributing to the widespread adoption of an industrial development paradigm, UNCLOS III stimulated a top-down wave of action at lower levels of social organization.

Table 10.3
Fisheries governance reform era: 1990s onward

Governance level	Fisheries management institutions	Institutional characteristics	Institutional paradigms
International	UNCLOS III; 1995 Fish Stocks Agreement; 1995 FAO Code of Conduct.	200-mile EEZs; reinforced mandates and provisions within RFMOs and attempts to limit access to RFMO members.	Breakdown of freedom-of-the-seas paradigm for remaining international waters; recognition of need for better domestic governance and international cooperation.
Interplay	Jurisdictional interaction manifests in the Fish Stocks Agreement and expanded RFMO mandates. Ideational effects can be witnessed through institutional learning on the part of the FAO, World Bank, and OECD and their involvement in disseminating lessons learned about property rights regimes to coastal states. Ideational interaction also occurs as property rights ideas begin receiving consideration in RFMOs.		
National	Continued waves of domestic fisheries legislation and policy reforms.	Variation persists, but ITQ programs continue to proliferate.	Support for industrial development paradigm diminishes; privatization paradigm gains prominence; decentralization paradigm is endorsed to varying degrees.
Interplay	Jurisdictional interaction can be seen in the occasional nesting of local fisheries institutions within national legislation. Ideational interaction can be seen in the downward push of a privatization paradigm from national to local governance levels and the upward push of a decentralization paradigm from local to national governance levels.		
Local	Continued erosion of traditional institutions; some isolated cases of revival of traditional tenure systems and development of new comanagement regimes within national legislation.	Isolated cases of renewed local autonomy and discretion within regional and national regulatory frameworks are evident.	Some support for privatization paradigm appears; the decentralization paradigm is articulated as an alternative to the privatization paradigm.

During the 1990s, alternative fisheries management paradigms began to proliferate. Signifying the privatization paradigm, IFQs/ITQs are a property rights arrangement in the fisheries sector that has proved effective in removing incentives to "race for the fish" and in yielding significant efficiency gains where implemented. Distributive concerns on the part of small-scale, artisanal fishers and structural conditions (large numbers of artisanal fishers spread out over numerous port communities) have led to experimentation with other forms of communal property rights in the context of decentralization initiatives. Although the results of these latter institutional arrangements have been mixed, they have demonstrated the potential to be effective, sometimes more so than IFQs/ITQs.

As coastal state governments have shared experiences with one another, institutional learning has allowed the evolution and diffusion of these new forms of property rights in fisheries. A range of communicative mechanisms has facilitated direct communication between national governments, the uptake and dissemination of ideas by international organizations, and advocacy on the part of transnational networks of epistemic communities. All these mechanisms stand as important examples of ideational interactions that involve horizontal and vertical mechanisms of ideational transmission and diffusion.

With the international community moving toward granting RFMOs exclusive management authority over high-seas fisheries, and because of the merits of tradable quota arrangements as an RFMO management tool, an intriguing picture of the dynamics of the vertical institutional complex is unfolding. An initial change in property rights institutions at the international level has allowed institutional experimentation at the domestic level. Institutional learning has emerged, and the ultimate result may be a particular model of property rights that is adopted at the international level (within the framework of the unmodified extended jurisdiction). Taken together, these dynamics inform our understanding of how institutions, incentives, and ideas interact to produce the evolution of property rights regimes that we have been witnessing in the field of fisheries management.

Note

1. Not all coastal states were subject to this dynamic. Norway, for example, had existing legislation that banned trawlers from its inshore and coastal fisheries (Apostle et al. 1998).

References

Aggarwal, Vinod K. 1983. The Unraveling of the Multi-Fiber Arrangement, 1981: An Examination of International Regime Change. *International Organization* 37 (4): 617–646.

Alcock, Frank. 2002. Bargaining, Uncertainty and Property Rights in Fisheries. *World Politics* 54 (3): 437–461.

Alcock, Frank. 2003. Bargaining, Uncertainty and Property Rights in North Atlantic Fisheries. PhD diss., Duke University.

Alcock, Frank. 2006. Seafood Trade, Fisheries Management and Human Livelihoods. In *Proceedings of the Thirteenth Biennial Conference of the International Institute of Fisheries Economics & Trade*, 11–14 July 2006, Portsmouth, UK: *Rebuilding Fisheries in an Uncertain Environment*, ed. Ann L. Shriver. Corvallis, Ore.: International Institute of Fisheries Economics and Trade.

Alcock, Frank. 2008. Conflicts and Coalitions Within and Across the ENGO Community. *Global Environmental Politics* 8 (3): 66–91.

Alcock, Frank. 2010. Prospects for Use Rights in Tuna Regional Fisheries Management Organizations. In *Conservation and Management of Transnational Tuna Fisheries*, ed. Robin Allen, James A. Joseph, and Dale Squires, 251–268. Boston: Blackwell.

Apostle, Richard, Gene Barrett, Petter Holm, Svein Jentoft, Leigh Mazany, Bonnie McCay, and Knut Mikalsen. 1998. *Community, State and Market on the North Atlantic Rim: Challenges to Modernity in Fisheries*. Toronto: University of Toronto Press.

Bailey, Conner. 1988. The Political Economy of Marine Fisheries Development in Indonesia. *Indonesia* 46:25–38.

Bailey, Conner. 1997. Lessons from Indonesia's 1980 Trawler Ban. *Marine Policy* 21 (3): 225–235.

Bailey, Conner, Dean Cycon, and Michael Morris. 1986. Fisheries Development in the Third World: The Role of International Agencies. *World Development* 14 (10/11): 1269–1275.

Berkes, Fikret, Robin Mahon, Patrick McConney, Richard Pollnac, and Robert Pomeroy. 2001. *Managing Small-scale Fisheries*. Ottawa: International Development Research Centre.

Burke, William. 1994. *The New International Law of Fisheries: UNCLOS 1982 and Beyond*. Oxford: Clarendon Press.

Christy, Francis. 1997. *The Development and Management of Marine Fisheries in Latin America and the Caribbean*. Policy Research Paper. Washington, D.C.: Inter-American Development Bank.

Copes, Parzival. 1996. Adverse Impacts of Individual Quota Systems on Conservation and Fish Harvest Productivity. Institute of Fisheries Analysis Discussion Paper 96: 1. Simon Fraser University, Burnaby, British Columbia.

DeSombre, Elizabeth. 2006. *Flagging Standards: Globalization and Environmental, Safety and Labor Regulations at Sea*. Cambridge, Mass.: MIT Press.

Eckert, Ross. 1972. *The Enclosure of Ocean Resources*. Palo Alto, Calif.: Hoover Institute Press.

Eythorsson, Einar. 2000. A Decade of ITQ-Management in Icelandic Fisheries: Consolidation without Consensus. *Marine Policy* 24 (4): 483–492.

FAO. 1999. Trends and Issues Relating to Global Fisheries Governance. Paper prepared for the 23rd Session of the FAO Committee on Fisheries. Rome: Food and Agriculture Organization of the United Nations.

FAO. 2004. *State of World Fisheries and Agriculture*. Rome: Food and Agriculture Organization of the United Nations.

FAO. 2005. *Strategies for Increasing the Contribution of Small-Scale Fisheries to Poverty Alleviation and Food Security*. Rome: Food and Agriculture Organization of the United Nations.

Garcia, Serge, and Chris Newton. 1997. Current Situation, Trends, and Prospects in World Capture Fisheries. In *Global Trends: Fisheries Management*, ed. Ellen K. Pikitch, Daniel D. Huppert, and Michael Sissenwine, 3–27. Bethesda, Md.: American Fisheries Society.

Gelchu, Ahmed, and Daniel Pauly. 2007. Growth and Distribution of Port-Based Global Fishing Effort Within Countries' EEZs From 1970–1995. *Fisheries Centre Research Reports* 15 (4): 1–99.

Gordon, H. Scott. 1954. The Economic Theory of a Common Property Resource: The Fishery. *Journal of Political Economy* 62:124–142.

Grafton, R. Quentin, Dale Squires, and James E. Kirkley. 1996. Private Property Rights and Crises in World Fisheries: Turning the Tide? *Contemporary Economic Policy* 14 (4): 90–100.

Grafton, R. Quentin, Rognavaldur Hannesson, Bruce Shallard, Daryl Sykes, and Joe Terry. 2006. The Economics of Allocation in Regional Fisheries Management Organizations (RFMOs). Australian National University Economics and Environment Network Working Paper EEN0612. http://ideas.repec.org/p/anu/eenwps/0612.html (accessed 16 April 2010).

Haas, Peter M. 1992. Introduction: Epistemic Communities and International Policy Coordination. *International Organization* 46 (1): 1–35.

Hannesson, Rognavaldur. 2004. *The Privatization of the Oceans*. Cambridge, Mass.: MIT Press.

Hardin, Garrett. 1968. The Tragedy of the Commons. *Science* 162:1243–1248.

Hennessey, Tim, and Michael Healey. 2000. Ludwig's Ratchet and the Collapse of New England Groundfish Stocks. *Coastal Management* 28:187–213.

Hersoug, Bjørn. 2002. *Unfinished Business: New Zealand's Experience with Rights-based Fisheries Management*. Delft: Eburon.

Ibarra, Alonso, Chris Reid, and Andy Thorpe. 2000a. Neo-liberalism and Its Impact on Overfishing and Capitalization in the Marine Fisheries of Chile, Mexico and Peru. *Food Policy* 25:599–622.

Ibarra, Alonso, Chris Reid, and Andy Thorpe. 2000b. The Political Economy of Marine Fisheries Development in Peru, Chile and Mexico. *Journal of Latin American Studies* 32 (2): 503–527.

Iudicello, Suzanne, Michael Weber, and Robert Wieland. 1999. *Fish, Markets, and Fishermen*. Washington, D.C.: Island Press.

Joseph, James. 2005. Past Developments and Future Options for Managing Tuna Fishing Capacity, with Special Emphasis on Purse-seine Fleets. *FAO Fisheries Proceedings* 2:281–323.

Juda, Lawrence. 1996. *International Law and Ocean Use Management: The Evolution of Ocean Governance*. New York: Routledge.

Kurien, John. 1998. Small-scale Fisheries in the Context of Globalisation. Working Paper No. 289. Centre for Development Studies, Kerala, India.

Kurien, John. 2003. The Blessing of the Commons: Small-Scale Fisheries, Community Property Rights and Coastal Natural Assets. Working Paper No. 349. Political Economy Research Institute, University of Massachusetts, Amherst.

Lear, William. 1998. History of Fisheries in the Northwest Atlantic: The 500-Year Perspective. *Journal of Northwest Atlantic Fishery Science* 23:41–73.

Loftas, Tony. 1981. FAO's EEZ Programme: Assisting a New Era in Fisheries. *Marine Policy* 5:229–239.

McCay, Bonnie, and James Acheson, eds. 1987. *The Question of the Commons: The Culture and Ecology of Communal Resources*. Tucson: University of Arizona Press.

North, Douglass. 1981. *Structure and Change in Economic History*. New York: Norton.

Oberthür, Sebastian, and Thomas Gehring. 2006. Conceptual Foundations of Institutional Interaction. In *Institutional Interaction in Global Environmental Governance: Synergy and Conflict among International and EU Policies*, ed. Sebastian Oberthür and Thomas Gehring, 19–51. Cambridge, Mass.: MIT Press.

OECD. 1997. *Toward Sustainable Fisheries: Economic Aspects of the Management of Living Marine Resources*. Paris: Organisation for Economic Co-operation and Development.

OECD. 2006. *Using Market Mechanisms to Manage Fisheries: Smoothing the Path*. Paris: Organisation for Economic Co-operation and Development.

Orbach, Michael. 2002. Beyond the Freedom of the Seas. Fourth Annual Roger Revelle Commemorative Lecture, 13 November 2002, National Academy of Sciences Auditorium, Washington, D.C. http://www.southchinasea.org/docs/Orbach,%20Beyond%20Freedom%20of%20the%20Seas.pdf (accessed 16 April 2010).

Orrego Vicuña, Francisco. 1999. *The Changing International Law of High Seas Fisheries*. Cambridge: Cambridge University Press.

Orrego Vicuña, Francisco. 2001. The International Law of High Seas Fisheries: From Freedom of Fishing to Sustainable Use. In *Governing High Seas Fisheries:*

The Interplay of Global and Regional Regimes, ed. Olav Schram Stokke, 23–52. Oxford: Oxford University Press.

Ostrom, Elinor. 1990. *Governing the Commons: The Evolution of Institutions for Collective Action*. Cambridge: Cambridge University Press.

Pinkerton, Evelyn. 1989. *Co-operative Management of Local Fisheries: New Directions for Improved Management and Community Development*. Vancouver: University of British Columbia Press.

Queirolo, Lewis, Richard Johnston, and Zhengkun Zhang. 1997. The Nature and Evolution of Cooperative Fishing Arrangements in Extended Jurisdiction Zones. *Marine Policy* 21 (2): 255–266.

Royce, William. 1987. *Fishery Development*. Orlando, Fla.: Academic Press.

Scott, Anthony. 1955. The Fishery: Objectives of Sole Ownership. *Journal of Political Economy* 63:116–124.

Shotton, Robert, ed. 2000. *Use of Property Rights in Fisheries Management: Proceedings of the FishRights99 Conference*. Fremantle, Western Australia, 11–19 November 1999. Workshop Papers. FAO Fisheries Technical Paper No. 404/2.

Shrank, William. 1995. Extended Fisheries Jurisdiction: Origins of the Current Crisis in Atlantic Canada's Fisheries. *Marine Policy* 19:285–299.

Silvestre, Geronimo, and Daniel Pauly, eds. 1997. *Status and Management of Tropical Coastal Fisheries in Asian Countries*. Manila: Asian Development Bank & International Center for Living Aquatic Resources Management.

Slaughter, Anne Marie. 2004. *A New World Order*. Princeton, N.J.: Princeton University Press.

Stokke, Olav Schram, ed. 2001a. *Governing High Seas Fisheries: The Interplay of Global and Regional Regimes*. Oxford: Oxford University Press.

Stokke, Olav Schram. 2001b. *The Interplay of International Regimes: Putting Effectiveness Theory to Work*. FNI Report 14/2001. Lysaker, Norway: Fridtjof Nansen Institute.

Sundar, Aparna. 2002. Marine Fisheries. In *Marketing the Earth: The World Bank and Sustainable Development*, ed. Nancy Alexander, Pam Foster, Marcia Ishii-Eiteman, Ricardo Carrere, Aparna Sundar, Carol Welch, and Daphne Wysham. Friends of the Earth and Halifax Initiative. http://halifaxinitiative.org/content/marketing-earth-world-bank-and-sustainable-development-august-2002 (accessed 16 April 2010).

Sunderlin, William, and Maharlina Gorospe. 1997. Fishers' Organizations and Modes of Co-Management: The Case of San Miguel Bay, Philippines. *Human Organization* 56 (3): 333–343.

Swan, Judith, and Benedict Satia. 1999. *Contribution of the Committee on Fisheries to Global Fisheries Governance 1977–1997*. FAO Fisheries Circular No. 938. Rome: UN Food and Agriculture Organization.

Sydnes, Are. 2005. Regional Fisheries Organizations and International Fisheries Governance. In *A Sea Change: The Exclusive Economic Zone and Governance*

Institutions for Living Marine Resources, ed. Syma Ebbin, Alf Hakon Hoel, and Are Sydnes, 117–135. Dordrecht: Springer-Verlag.

Trondsen, Torbjorn, Thorolfur Matthiasson, and James Young. 2006. Towards a Market-oriented Management Model for Straddling Fish Stocks. *Marine Policy* 30:199–206.

Tvedten, Inge, and Bjørn Hersoug, eds. 1992. *Fishing for Development: Small-Scale Fisheries in Africa*. Uppsala: Scandinavian Institute for African Studies.

Viswanathan, K. Kuperan, Jesper R. Nielsen, Poul Degnbol, Mahfuzuddin Ahmed, Mafaniso Hara, and Nik Mustapha Raja Abdullah. 2003. *Fisheries Co-management Policy Brief: Findings from a Worldwide Study*. WorldFish Center Policy Brief 2. Penang, Malaysia: WorldFish Center.

Weyland, Kurt. 2005. Theories of Policy Diffusion: Lessons from Latin American Pension Reform. *World Politics* 57 (4): 262–295.

World Bank. 2004. *Saving Fish and Fishers: Toward Sustainable and Equitable Governance of the Global Fishing Sector*. World Bank Report No. 29090-GLB. Washington D.C.: Agriculture and Rural Development Department, World Bank.

Young, Oran R. 1996. Institutional Linkages in International Society: Polar Perspectives. *Global Governance* 2 (1): 1–24.

11

Interplay Management in the Climate, Energy, and Development Nexus

Sylvia I. Karlsson-Vinkhuyzen and Marcel T. J. Kok

The importance of integrating the three pillars of sustainable development—economic, social, and environmental—has been underscored in virtually every global policy process since the Brundtland Report was published in 1987. Even during the 1980s it was realized that environmental policies alone would not be able to ensure the attainment of environmental objectives (Lafferty and Hovden 2003). With the years has come growing recognition of the need for policies aimed specifically at the root causes of environmental problems and not merely at their symptoms. This requires the full involvement of all economic sectors in realizing environmental objectives. Equally weighty arguments can be made from the angle of economic development and social development: objectives in these domains are unsustainable unless they include the environmental dimension.

Interplay management (see Stokke and Oberthür in this volume) is concerned with realizing coherent governance for sustainable development, whether among different levels of policymaking (vertical interplay) or among different sectors of policymaking relevant to a specific topic (horizontal interplay). Interplay management is particularly challenging from the perspective of sustainable development as it requires realizing integration across scales, time, and sectors (UNEP 2007, 301–360), and within large institutional complexes that have often emerged without planned integration.

In this chapter we analyze *integration* (as defined below) in current global governance in the nexus of energy, development, and climate change and the associated institutional complex. In particular, we inquire how such integration can be achieved through improved interplay management. To answer that question, we specify functional interdependencies among the three policy domains, describe the essential elements of the related institutional complex, and identify possible means for interplay management. The urgent need for integration among these domains provides strong motivation for understanding more about their dynamics and interrelationships.

While the nexus of development, energy, and climate change has particular characteristics, the features of our object of study are not unique. An improved understanding of interplay management and the institutional complex in this area is therefore relevant to other domains as well. We are looking at a nexus of three very broad policy domains with multiple functional linkages in several directions, and in which the overall objectives of the main actors in each domain often diverge significantly. Furthermore, the type and number of global norms (including legally binding treaties and non-legally binding norms) differ significantly from one domain to another.

This chapter proceeds as follows. First we outline the analytical approach, then briefly sketch the functional linkages among the three policy domains. This is followed by an analysis of global governance and the associated institutions in each domain, focusing on the degree of legalization. Subsequently we analyze the directions of integration efforts at the climate-development, climate-energy, and energy-development domain interfaces, individually and for the entire nexus collectively. In the final section we draw some conclusions concerning the conditions for successful interplay management of an institutional complex in the broader context of sustainable development.

Analyzing Interplay Management

There are weighty arguments for interplay management to support integrating the three dimensions of sustainable development. To explore how such integration may be achieved, we suggest analyzing two aspects, the degree of legalization and the direction of integration.

Degree of Legalization

Interplay management to support integration may employ measures such as communication, policies and programs, organizational mergers or the adoption of common norms (often referred to as "institutions"), and organizational integration.[1] Legalization is a special form of institutionalization characterized by the adoption of (systems of) norms that have varying degrees of obligation, precision, and delegation associated with them (Abbott et al. 2000). Hard international institutions (also referred to as "hard law") usually come in the form of treaties; they score relatively high on these parameters (Abbott and Snidal 2000), while softer institutions ("soft law") score lower and may include codes of conduct, for example.

Legalization is an important avenue for interplay management, for two reasons. First, once in place, institutions are difficult to change. The very purpose of developing institutions is to stabilize behavior over time, so they are intentionally made difficult to change. This also means that, in the many situations in which institutions have been developed in individual sectors and support a narrow objective while ignoring concerns of other sectors or policy domains, alteration in support of interplay management is difficult.

A second and closely related reason for focusing on legalization is that integration takes a long time to accomplish, and maintaining consistency over time is essential. Information exchange or ad hoc policies to realize integration will not achieve much; neither will even the best-intended aspirations of single actors unless these influence the practices of key actors. If we want to explore the relative potential of interplay management in various policy domains that are functionally linked and therefore need to be integrated, we need to "measure" the density of institutions—including the density of norms in these different policy domains. If there is a high density of norms such that they hinder integration, they will have to be the target of change. If there are few or no formal norms in a domain, new ones will need to be created, or other instruments for interplay management might be required.

The degree of legalization and its related opportunities for interplay management is a question not only of the number of norms but also of the type of norms along the hard-soft continuum. Some analysts claim that softer norms are generally easier to establish and change (Reinicke and Witte 2000; Trubek, Cottrell, and Nance 2005) and facilitate cooperation (Chinkin 2000) and compromise over time (Abbott and Snidal 2000). Soft law is sometimes adopted as a first step toward subsequent hard law (Abbott and Snidal 2000; Shelton 2000). For these reasons, soft norms may be easier to change and develop. While there are diverging views on how much soft (and indeed hard) law can influence behavior when enforcement mechanisms are lacking, countries may follow such norms simply because they are considered legitimate (Karlsson-Vinkhuyzen and Vihma 2009).

By analyzing the degree of legalization of the various policy domains that need to be integrated, we can thus identify some of the opportunities for improving interplay management and making it effective over longer time-horizons.

The Direction of Integration

The direction of integration between policy domains is a second important analytical entry point in regard to interplay management. Interplay management aims at policy integration. Two of the definitions of integration in the *Oxford Dictionary* are "combine parts into a whole" and "bring into equal participation." These definitions indicate a two-way process between the components being integrated, with no special privilege given to either of them. However, in many cases the concept of policy integration implies a one-way direction reflecting specific policy priorities. With respect to environmental policy integration, for example, Lafferty and Hovden (2003) refer to the one-way integration of environmental concerns into other policy sectors. A more recent concept is mainstreaming, which suggests more clearly a unidirectional focus, putting one issue into the mainstream of one or many other policy domains and trying to accord it higher priority. In our analysis, we ask whether there are conditions that favor or hinder mainstreaming in one particular direction and enable a more multidirectional integration.

One such factor concerns which issue is privileged by being first. Persson (2004), for example, notes that adding a new issue such as the environment to existing policy agendas is likely to cause conflicts with existing interests (power relations, vested interests, public concerns). Given the generally high and increasing density of norms, the concept of being "first" may in many cases be questionable; as Gehring and Oberthür (2006, 2) note, "Whenever a new international treaty is adopted, it enters an institutional setting that is already densely populated." Even if whole new policy domains emerge (such as climate change), "new norms never enter a normative vacuum but instead emerge in a highly contested normative space where they must compete with other norms and perceptions of interest" (Finnemore and Sikkink 1998, 897).

There are further layers of complexity concerning integration between more than two policy domains. Achieving multidirectional integration, although this is repeatedly demanded in the political language on sustainable development, represents a considerable analytical and practical challenge, and successes are few. We approach this complexity by first analyzing governance in each domain. Only thereafter can we examine the potential of interplay management to achieve integration between two domains and in the whole nexus of the three domains. By focusing on conditions enabling and constraining one- or two-way integration in a nexus of three functionally linked policy domains and the associated institutional complex, we can identify the potential for improving interplay management and see which direction holds greatest potential.

Functional Interactions in the Energy, Climate, and Development Nexus

The basis for understanding the potential for interplay management among specific domains lies in their functional interactions. Functional interactions arise when "the substantive problems or activities that two or more institutions address are linked in bio-geophysical or socioeconomic terms" (Young 2002, 264). The very strong functional interactions among the issues of energy, climate, and development include both trade-offs and synergies that need to be considered in interplay management (see figure 11.1).

At the heart of several of these interactions is energy, which links up intimately with many aspects of development as well as with environmental, economic, and social sustainability. The world's energy systems are responsible for more than half the anthropogenic emissions of greenhouse gases (GHG) (WEHAB Working Group 2002). Development

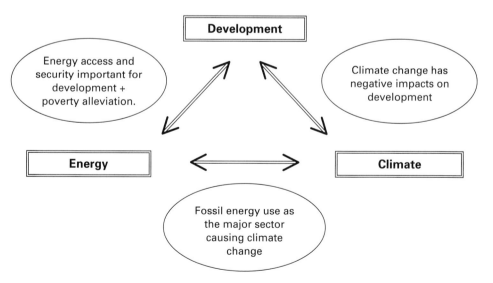

Figure 11.1
Functional linkages in the energy, development, and climate nexus

290 Sylvia I. Karlsson-Vinkhuyzen and Marcel T. J. Kok

without consideration of environmental impacts generates higher emissions of GHGs from energy, transport, agriculture, and deforestation. The impacts of climate change have negative consequences for social and economic development, especially for the poor (IPCC 2007). Climate change will seriously hamper development efforts, for example, through reduced economic growth due to climate change damage, threatened or underperforming investments, and lower food production because of maladaptation to climate variability and a changing climate (IPCC 2007; UNDP 2007). The Organisation of Economic Co-operation and Development (OECD) has shown that a significant part of the official flows of development assistance addresses activities that can be affected by climate risks (OECD 2005). The World Bank (2006) estimates the costs of climate change at 1–2 percent of its investment portfolio. Yet societies may achieve development objectives while also reducing their vulnerability by taking adaptation measures and moving toward a low-emissions economy. Research has also demonstrated the climate benefits of policies and measures taken by developing countries for non-climate-related reasons, such as economic growth, alleviation of poverty, energy and food security, health, and local environmental protection (Bradley and Baumert 2005; Halnaes and Garg 2006; OECD 2005).

Improving access to energy is an important condition for poverty reduction and realization of the Millennium Development Goals (Modi et al. 2005). For developing countries that lack fossil fuel reserves, ensuring energy supply is another component of the problem. Again, this impinges on the poorer population groups, because transport and food prices are affected most. Rural areas are especially vulnerable, as are small to medium-sized enterprises, which often cannot cope with the volatility of oil prices (ESMAP 2005). Rises in energy prices also result in macroeconomic losses that indirectly affect human well-being. The International Energy Agency (IEA) estimates that the poorest countries lose approximately 1.47 percent of their GDP with each USD 10 per barrel increase in the price of oil (IEA 2004). Some of the lowest-income countries suffer losses of up to 4 percent of their GDP (ESMAP 2005). Policies to reduce fossil fuel dependency may conflict with climate change mitigation, but they may also be synergetic.

The domains of energy, climate change, and development are closely knit in functional terms, and trade-offs between gains in the different domains lie side by side with considerable opportunities for win-win outcomes. Whereas Young (2002) observes that mutually supportive or benign functional interdependencies do not require further analysis and attention, we argue—as do Oberthür and Gehring (2006)—that both synergies and trade-offs should be subject to interplay management. Therefore, both the benign and the malign aspects of interdependencies are part of our analysis of the energy, development, and climate nexus.

Global Actors and Degrees of Legalization

The following subsections sketch the evolving global governance in the three domains, including the related institutional complexes, as the basis for analyzing challenges and opportunities for interplay management. Each subsection starts with an outline of the main organizational actors in the domain. Because specific actors usually have a closer association with one of the domains, this information is essential for identifying the existing and potential directions of integration in the nexus. We then analyze the degree of legalization in each domain, which is a prerequisite for exploring the best avenues for strengthening interplay management.

Global Development Governance

Major actors in global development governance consist of a broad range of intergovernmental organizations (IGOs), mostly belonging to the UN system and the Bretton Woods organizations. They include the International Labor Organization (ILO), the United Nations Development Programme (UNDP), the World Health Organization (WHO), the Food and Agriculture Organization of the United Nations (FAO), and the World Bank.[2] Although each of these IGOs focuses on different aspects and arenas of development intervention (workplaces, rural, urban, industrial, agricultural, and other issues), their common primary mandate is development. In addition, there are international nongovernmental organizations (NGOs) focusing on development. They are primarily active at the project level in developing countries, but also lobby in industrialized countries and in global arenas. While all these actors have development as their fundamental rationale for existence, other important actors, such as the World Trade Organization (WTO) and the International Monetary Fund (IMF), have development as part of their mandate and have sought to strengthen this dimension over time, although with debatable success. The same can be said of some multinational corporations that have taken on social and environmental development as part of their corporate social responsibility and have become engaged in their own development projects or in partnerships with other actors.

While variation across the domain is considerable, the existing degree of legalization is low. Some IGOs provide the forum for the development of binding multilateral treaties (such as the ILO and the WHO). The IGO hosting these treaties often provides considerable assistance to countries in support of compliance, for example through capacity building. Other IGOs, such as the UNDP, are not very active in developing norms, whether legally binding or voluntary, but concentrate instead on direct intervention programs and projects. Nevertheless, by steering financial flows and setting conditions, these institutions also have a strong direct impact on the policies of developing countries.

Furthermore, various UN-related intergovernmental processes have created a soft overarching framework of goals, directions, and priorities for development, with considerable potential to align actor objectives and guide interplay management. The UN General Assembly, the Economic and Social Council (ECOSOC), and the occasional World Summits have agreed on soft-law declarations and action programs. They form part of the international body of norms that influence international development actors both directly and indirectly. The most important of these are the Millennium Development Goals (MDGs) adopted at the Millennium Summit in 2000 (UN General Assembly 2000). Under this umbrella, the UN attempts to enhance the coherence of international support provided to developing countries through a set of more or less measurable goals aimed at reducing poverty and hunger as well as improving health and living conditions. The Johannesburg Plan of Implementation adopted at the World Summit on Sustainable Development (WSSD) in 2002 is also an overarching normative framework for international development (UN 2002), together with the outcome of the 2002 Monterrey Conference on development financing. An example of the impact of these norms is that actors like the UNDP and the World Bank have focused a substantial part of their activities on supporting the achievement of the MDGs.

The many large and small actors in global development governance imply a considerable risk of conflicting objectives, fragmentation, and overlapping activities. But it also gives an indication of the role that a coherent normative framework such as the MDGs or the concept of sustainable development could provide for interplay management if actors align their objectives accordingly. However, existing normative frameworks are of a very soft type. Compliance is voluntary and can be motivated only with arguments of their legitimacy—and such arguments may not carry equal weight with all actors.

Global Energy Governance

Energy has traditionally been addressed primarily by national governance because it is seen as a part of national security. While energy is often assumed to be an underlying driver for states' positions on conflict, peace, and development, it has remained on the sidelines of universal multilateral governance (Karlsson-Vinkhuyzen 2010). Within the UN system, no single strong IGO on general energy issues exists, but energy-related activities take place in many UN programs, agencies, and organizations, such as the World Bank, the UNDP, the United Nations Environment Program (UNEP), and the United Nations Industrial Development Organization (UNIDO). After many ad hoc efforts at coordinating the energy work in the UN system, UN-Energy with twenty member organizations was established in 2004 as an interagency coordination mechanism (UN-Energy 2006). Outside the UN system, oil-exporting countries have formed the Organization of Petroleum Exporting Countries (OPEC). Furthermore, bodies like the IEA, which is confined to OECD members, for example, provide expert information to national and international policymakers on energy issues. In 2009, the International Renewable Energy Agency (IRENA) was created with a similar aim, and the G-8 has also launched activities in support of cleaner energy. Many multinational corporations in the energy field tend to operate within a sphere of their own, rarely entering the corridors of the UN. In contrast, various renewable energy associations, together with a few energy-oriented international NGOs, do engage with UN processes when the opportunity arises.

There is very limited global-level legalization concerning the production and consumption of energy. One of the few examples of a multilateral legally binding instrument on energy is the 1994 Energy Charter Treaty, which, as of October 2009, had fifty signatory state parties, mostly EU member states, of which forty-six had ratified it.[3] It was negotiated outside the UN system and seeks to create an open international energy market and address energy security for consumers and suppliers alike (Westphal 2005).

This low degree of global-level legalization has created a vacuum that some actors have tried to fill with soft norms and processes, although with limited success. Within the UN, a few efforts to develop a more coherent normative framework for "energy for sustainable development" have been made, primarily in the Commission on Sustainable Development (CSD) and the WSSD. At the WSSD, an attempt to include quantifiable targets or timetables for the share of renewables in energy supply resulted in a compromise statement, that actions at all levels need to "[w]ith a sense of urgency, substantially increase the global share of renewable energy sources" (UN 2002, para. 20e). However, in a follow-up CSD meeting in 2007, the negotiations collapsed without an outcome, for the first time in CSD history (see below).

There is thus not much global energy governance into which the concerns of other policy domains could be incorporated. The many UN actors who provide support to developing countries in the energy field have some influence on the direction of energy investment in these countries. They may be susceptible to the influence of the emerging (admittedly very soft) norms in support of more sustainable energy options, but the more substantial influence is likely to come from global climate governance.

Global Climate Governance

The central international actor in global climate governance is the Secretariat of the United Nations Framework Convention on Climate Change (UNFCCC). Its role and size have increased with the development and growth of the regime. Furthermore, a large number of UN organizations engage in activities that support the ability of developing countries to implement the regime, such as through funding from the Global Environment Facility (GEF). Since its inception, the climate regime has been closely followed by a large number of organizations: national and international NGOs, international business associations, and companies.

Climate governance has moved from no legalization at all over imprecise hard law (UNFCCC) to more precise hard law (the Kyoto Protocol), although it is uncertain what legal status future agreements will have. Furthermore, the scope is wide and expanding. The UNFCCC, which entered into force in 1994, obliges all parties to work toward stabilizing atmospheric GHG concentrations at safe levels. With 194 parties (as of 2010), the convention is one of the most universal international environmental agreements. Under the Kyoto Protocol, industrialized countries have agreed to binding emissions limitations and reduction commitments in the period 2008–2012. The protocol allows industrialized countries to acquire, through three "flexible mechanisms" (Clean Development Mechanism, Joint Implementation, and emissions trading), emission credits from abroad that can be counted toward their own emission commitments. Adaptation to climate change has become the most important issue for many of the least-developed countries. While various funds are in place to support adaptation activities, there have been many calls for strengthening the legalization of the adaptation agenda.

Climate change has also moved to UN arenas beyond the UNFCCC and the Kyoto Protocol. The CSD addressed climate change in its 2006–2007 cycle. In 2007, the UN Security Council took up climate change as a common threat to the world's security, for the first time in its history (UN Security Council 2007), and the General Assembly addressed climate change in dedicated sessions in 2007 and 2009.[4] There are also less universal, soft arrangements on climate change outside the UN. For example, in 2005, the United States, Australia, China, India, Japan, and South Korea launched the Asia-Pacific Partnership for Clean Development and Climate (APP), focused on creating new investment opportunities, building local capacity, and removing barriers to the introduction of clean, more efficient technologies (APP 2006). In addition, the G-8 has become increasingly engaged since adopting the Gleneagles Plan of Action in 2005 (G-8 2005).

This brief overview of the rapidly evolving global climate governance illustrates that states remain the main actors for decision making. In addition, the regime relies heavily on the UNFCCC Secretariat, and several other IGOs fulfill key functions with regard to mitigation and adaptation in developing countries. The climate domain is characterized by a relatively high degree of legalization, which is, however, very patchy in geographic terms. While UNFCCC coverage is universal, it has been too imprecise to elicit substantial action in and of itself. Furthermore, the largest single emitter among the industrialized countries, the United States, has not ratified the Kyoto Protocol, which also does not address the emissions of the rapidly growing emerging economies.

Arenas for Integration

Given the strong functional linkages among the three policy domains of development, climate, and energy, the potential for synergies and the need to address possible trade-offs through integration are substantial. The domains also vary in the character of global governance. The climate regime is a very explicit regime with an elaborate and increasingly complex normative and institutional framework. The energy domain is more of a "nonregime," lacking both global norms and strong global legitimate actors. In contrast, the largest number of implementing international actors can be found in the development regime, each with its own governing structures and mandates but often willing (at least partly) to expand its agendas in response to new global norms and directions—especially if there is funding available. Each of the three policy domains is also closely associated with one of the dimensions of sustainable development: energy with the economic, climate with the environmental, and development with the social dimension.

Building on the preceding analysis, we now turn to a central question: How can stronger integration be achieved through improved interplay management? We approach this question by assessing, for pairs of policy domains, the current level of integration and the potential and need for further integration, in particular through further legalization. In the last subsection we look at the potential for interplay management in the whole nexus of the three policy domains.

Development and Climate Change

The mainstreaming of climate change into the development domain has emerged only slowly in recent years. According to various evaluations (see Klein et al. 2007; OECD 2005), development policies and projects have generally paid little or no attention to climate change and climate variability. International development organizations initially saw climate change as just another of many issues they would have to include in their daily operations. Increasing evidence of the importance of climate change for alleviating poverty and for development has begun to change this perception. In 2003, ten bilateral and multilateral donors published the report *Poverty and Climate Change: Reducing the Vulnerability of the Poor Through Adaptation* (African Development Bank et al. 2003) with a plea to address climate change because it is a precondition for meeting poverty reduction targets. The report suggests that the best way to address the impact of climate change on the poor is by integrating adaptation responses into development planning. Various international organizations, including the EU, OECD/DAC, and the World Bank, have since then published statements, green papers, and policy plans on mainstreaming climate change into development assistance (European Commission 2007; OECD 2006; World Bank 2006). However, even when climate change is mentioned in policies, specific operational guidance is generally lacking.

Pragmatically, implementation can be achieved by "climate proofing," that is, making new development resilient to a changing climate, by changing bilateral and multilateral norms, institutions, policies, financial flows, national and sectoral development planning, and community-based activities. To this end, donors are starting to screen their project portfolios. Denmark has developed a methodology for systematically going through its project portfolio with the aim of upscaling these experiences on a nationwide basis (Danida 2005). Special departments in development agencies have received responsibilities for climate change, particularly for adaptation, and they push for mainstreaming climate change in the development agenda.

The mainstreaming of development into climate governance is at least implicitly a prerequisite for the active participation of developing countries in the climate regime. On paper, the UNFCCC and the Kyoto Protocol already reflect development concerns. According to the UNFCCC, parties have a right to, and should, promote sustainable development (Article 3.4), and "responses to climate change should be coordinated with social and economic development in an integrated manner" (Preamble) to avoid negative impacts and deal with trade-offs. In practice, these provisions have failed to convince developing countries. Especially the Clean Development Mechanism (CDM), which emerged as part of the Kyoto Protocol to provide financial support for sustainable development projects in developing countries while reducing GHG emissions, has been widely criticized as lacking a development dividend.

The importance of development has become increasingly recognized in the climate policy domain. In 2002, industrialized countries, especially the EU, clashed with developing countries over the latter's desire to marry climate change with sustainable development (Davidson et al. 2003; Ott 2002). At the same time, research started to demonstrate possible synergies between development and climate policies. Overall, climate change research has increasingly adopted a sustainable development perspective. The Intergovernmental Panel on Climate Change (IPCC) moved from a perspective focused on mitigating climate change in its first report toward a sustainable development perspective in its fourth assessment report, including equity concerns and alternative development pathways (Najam et al. 2003). As a result, UNFCCC deliberations have come to put much more emphasis on linking development and climate. While development concerns are still not sufficiently recognized, such recognition might be a precondition for mainstreaming climate in the domain of development policy, as well as in other international frameworks and agreements (Kok and de Coninck 2007; Kok et al. 2008).

As a consequence of the differing degrees and types of legalization of the two policy domains, clear rules in the climate regime can have a direct and strong impact on, for example, financial transfers and mitigation or adaptation projects of relevance for development. On the development side, organizational cultures need to change; this will require changes in the structure of global development governance, the specific mandates of its major intergovernmental and state actors, and the guidelines for project planning and operation in organizations. Despite the dispersed and multi-organizational characteristics of development governance, the rise of climate change on the development agenda helps establish a broader normative framework that can enable organizational change. Consequently, it may be possible to change the organizational focus and culture of the many IGOs where the initiation of climate-related projects has so far been driven primarily by the availability of funds.

Interplay management at the global level might best focus on promoting the upscaling of best practices of integrating climate change into development aid. For example, integration of climate change risks in national poverty reduction and development plans could become a condition for access to funding (even if this is a politically sensitive issue). It will also be important for the development community that research and assessments undertaken by, for example, the FAO, the World Bank, and UNDP seek to demonstrate the relevance of climate change to their daily operations and identify options for adapting those operations. The UNDP's *Human Development Report 2007/2008* is a positive example in this respect.

Room for stronger integration exists between the climate domain and the implementation of development-related norms linked to adaptation. The International Strategy for Disaster Reduction (the Hyogo Framework for Action 2005–2015) can help countries integrate climate change risks into national and local disaster preparedness and risk reduction plans; various international human rights instruments can help address possible forced migration; the UN Convention for Combating Desertification can help with adaptation to drought, as can the Joint Liaison Group of the three Rio Conventions; and insurance mechanisms can assist in adapting to climate change as well. Further involvement of the insurance and financial sector and sectoral development agencies for food, water, and health would also be crucial.

In conclusion, interplay management of the climate and development domains requires mutual integration, and that poses different challenges for each domain. The development community seeks to include climate concerns in its daily operations, but operational guidance is still lacking and implementation is only just beginning. In the climate domain, development was initially considered only on paper, but this is gradually changing. The global climate regime is a regime with a very elaborate legally binding framework as well as many soft forms of legalization and activities by a multitude of actors. The resulting potential for significant positive or negative impacts on development makes it essential to internalize development concerns. Managing the interplay between the development and climate domains could focus on further collaboration in developing best practices and institutions that create conditions that can foster integration and help in dealing with trade-offs.

Energy and Climate Change

Global energy discussions, particularly on renewable energy, surfaced partly as a result of the rising prominence of climate change, also at Rio and the WSSD (Karlsson-Vinkhuyzen 2010). The mainstreaming of climate change mitigation issues into energy-related activities of IGOs in developing countries has gradually advanced, but faces the challenge of changing the overall focus and culture of the organizations that guide these activities. Energy activities in IGOs have tended to follow the dominant direction of the organization in question. Thus, the World Bank has primarily supported conventional energy production capacity (based on fossil fuels and large-scale hydro); the UNEP has supported efforts to reduce local, regional, and global pollution of fossil fuel use through renewable energy; the UNDP has concentrated on making energy available for the poor, while UNIDO has focused on the energy needs of the industrial sector. However, funding under the climate regime seems to enable an expansion of the energy activities of these organizations. The GEF provides the vast bulk of the funding for UNDP and UNEP energy-related projects. In the field of data and assessments, the traditional global actors that have produced basic energy data and scenarios for the energy sector, primarily the IEA, are now exploring alternative development paths to a low-carbon society (IEA 2006). The Global Energy Assessment (GEA), an initiative by a host of international partners, is working to develop energy scenarios that meet the requirements of mitigating climate change.[5]

Because of the strong functional linkages between the two domains, mainstreaming energy into global climate governance has occurred almost by default. The international climate change regime has thus had a heavy implicit focus on energy from its inception. But because countries with mandatory emissions reduction commitments enjoy discretion in how to achieve these reductions, the linkage between the international climate regime and national energy institutions has remained indirect. However, energy has been well integrated in international climate assessment activities, in particular by the IPCC, whose input is a recurrent agenda item within the UNFCCC. Energy-intensive sectors have been on the negotiation table of the post-2012 regime.

Functional linkages and societal priorities indicate that there is a greater need for mainstreaming climate considerations into the energy sector than vice versa. Such integration is feasible, however, only if it does not threaten the energy sector's objective of providing modern energy, because energy is central to the socioeconomic development of countries, the reduction of poverty, and providing livelihoods for societies. While the institutional and legalization vacuum for energy at the global level presents an opportunity to develop norms and organizations that would integrate concern for climate change from the start, building stronger energy governance at the global level faces considerable political sensitivities.

The virtual absence of a global energy regime provides few opportunities to integrate climate change into global energy governance through norm development. Still, international norms such as energy efficiency standards for products or preferential trade conditions for renewable energy technologies would be useful. There is a wider need to identify and adopt (inter)national policies with the highest potential to support the transition to a low-carbon society in countries at various stages of development. Particularly for countries without binding commitments and with limited resources for mitigation, there is room for global energy actors such as the IEA and the World Bank to do a much better job of integrating climate change as well as other energy concerns in their work to influence national energy policies.

The opportunities for interplay management between energy and climate domains lie primarily in strengthening the climate regime and thus indirectly setting the rules for the energy sector that support country-level policies to move toward a low-carbon society. If the future international climate change regime created a global market for carbon, with sufficiently long-term rules, that could provide incentives for private research and development and investments into low-carbon development in the energy sector. Political will is the crucial element to achieve this goal. A rich array of research exists, especially on the technical and economic side, to support such action (IPCC 2007).

Energy and Development

The dominant direction of mainstreaming between the energy and development domain has, in the early twenty-first century, been to bring energy into the global development domain.[6] While the MDGs failed to include energy access as a separate goal or even as a topic, the CSD pointed out that access to affordable energy services is a prerequisite to achieving the MDG of halving the proportion of people living in poverty by 2015 (CSD 2001, 22). Energy then emerged strongly in the Johannesburg Plan of Implementation sections on poverty eradication, despite the failure of efforts to include a target on the number of people that should receive access to energy (UN 2002). At the CSD-14/15 in 2006–2007, the importance of providing energy access to the poor was the one issue where consensus was relatively easy to reach. As part of this integration movement between energy and development, national ministries of development and the environment and IGOs have, after the WSSD, argued for including energy on the agenda of MDG implementation (see Kok et al. 2004). The fact that most UN agencies, programs, and organizations have development as one of their highest priorities provides an opportunity for mainstreaming energy issues in the development work of the UN system. However, without strong legalization and an appropriate institutional framework, this will be difficult to achieve.

Mainstreaming in the other direction—bringing development issues into the energy domain—has also occurred to some degree within and beyond the UN system. The new actors with an energy focus that have emerged in the UN early in the twenty-first century have a very close affinity to development needs (CSD 2001; United Nations 2002). These include the public–private partnerships created to support WSSD and CSD decisions. As of the end of 2007, the CSD-partnership database showed that 93 of the 332 registered partnerships reported they were concerned with energy for sustainable development.[7] In addition, the IEA has broadened its focus. In its *World Energy Outlook 2004*, the IEA analyzed a scenario in which the poverty-reduction target is assumed to be met by 2015, with electricity being provided to an additional half billion people (IEA 2004). Since then, IEA reports have systematically included the issue of energy for development, including both access and security of energy supply.

Research has further clarified the need for integration of these two policy domains. Most strikingly, research on the link between indoor air pollution from traditional cooking fuels and their health impacts has put this issue firmly on the international agenda. New data show that such pollution is the fourth largest risk factor contributing to mortality and disease worldwide (WHO 2007). In 2007, the WHO produced its first

302   Sylvia I. Karlsson-Vinkhuyzen and Marcel T. J. Kok

country-by-country estimates of the burden of disease due to indoor air pollution (WHO 2007).

It is difficult to say which of the two domains has primacy, as they are so closely linked in historical terms. Rapid development on a macroscale in industrialized countries was possible thanks to access to cheap energy. Opportunities for stronger interplay management through legalization in the future exist only along very soft fronts. For example, IGOs may take guidance from the CSD and WSSD decisions and the goals adopted by various "coalitions of the willing" in the form of networks and partnerships that seek to promote the use of renewable energy and improve energy efficiency. Despite this low degree of legalization, other forms of integration could be promoted—for example, improved collaboration among development actors themselves. However, the very weak structure for collaboration in the UN system in general, and on energy issues in particular, is a considerable obstacle. There are considerable political constraints linked to national security and sovereignty issues, as well as path dependence, which has severely hampered the support for such actions. Inter-institutional collaboration also faces the challenges of organizational competition and insistence on organizational independence. Closer collaboration among donors (bilateral and multilateral) and private finance actors would be one of the most important measures for channeling the necessary finances to provide access to modern energy in developing countries.

Opportunities for Aggregate Interplay Management
While integration among all three domains poses an even greater challenge, it also, because of the close functional linkages, provides a greater opportunity. If we focus on the root causes of problems rather than on symptoms, it makes most sense to look at energy as the central domain, as it drives both development and climate change. At the same time, multiple (perceived) trade-offs between particularly the development domain and both the energy and climate domains provide considerable challenges. Despite the norms, institutions, physical and economic infrastructure favoring a carbon-centered energy production system, and the political risks associated with trying to change this system, the functional need for interplay management makes it a route to be explored.

It seems as if the international community at least implicitly acknowledges the need to focus more explicitly on energy in global deliberations. "Energy for sustainable development" is a phrase that started to emerge in the 2000s in various soft declarations and decisions, epitomizing the move toward integration in this nexus (CSD 2001; UN ECOSOC 2000; WEHAB Working Group 2002). The legalization process of this aggregate agenda began in the context of the CSD and the WSSD in 2001 and was expected to continue during the "energy cycle" of CSD-14/15 in 2006 and 2007. In addition, the agenda item of energy for sustainable development has already provided opportunities for environment-focused IGOs to combine their climate- and environment-oriented agenda with a development agenda. Thus far, however, the dominant institutions and weighty political and economic interests mentioned above have hampered more far-reaching progress.

It is no coincidence that the CSD has become the predominant arena for deliberations concerning integration. Its explicit mandate is to ensure the integration of the three dimensions of sustainable development within the UN system. However, its ability to fulfill this objective is constantly put in question, and it is accused of prioritizing the environmental dimension of sustainable development at the expense of the others. The numerical dominance of environmental ministers who attend is taken as support of this criticism. Furthermore, the CSD's low standing in the UN hierarchy and its inability to influence the actions of states and the UN system allegedly render it ineffective. However, the CSD has earned a greater role on issues that do not have an organizational "home" within the UN system and have a low degree of legalization, such as water and energy.

CSD-14/15 on energy for sustainable development and climate change represented an unsuccessful test of the ability of the international community to support integration among all three policy domains.[8] While the sharing of experiences and priorities at CSD-14 indicated a high degree of consensus on the functional interplay among the three domains, negotiations at CSD-15 made conflicts visible, particularly conflicts between countries prioritizing climate-change mitigation or energy security and countries whose priority was to preserve the role of fossil fuels. For example, many developing countries made a forceful call for renewable energy at CSD-14 as a way to improve their development. Their position contrasted with that of some powerful developing countries that pursued their interest in the fossil fuel economy. Since the conflict could not be resolved, CSD-15 failed to adopt a decision document, and the process of soft legalization around energy for sustainable development came to a halt.

Other efforts at more aggregate interplay management around the energy domain have also had very limited success. The WEHAB (Water, Energy, Health, Agriculture and Biodiversity) report on energy (WEHAB

Working Group 2002) was initiated by the UN Secretary-General, written by an informal team of experts from different corners of the UN system, and released a few months prior to the WSSD. The report outlined the functional linkages between energy and the other four WEHAB themes, and identified challenges and frameworks for action, with examples of indicative targets, milestones, and actions. It provided another stepping stone for interplay management among agencies that in their approaches to energy emphasize different dimensions of sustainable development. However, governments failed to pick up the identified action frameworks, which thus did not become part of the formal outcome of the WSSD. The UN-Energy mechanism supports energy-centered aggregate integration through small steps, despite its limited mandate and lack of resources. A positive example is the framework for decision makers on sustainable bioenergy production, which it published as a timely contribution to the debate on biofuels and their impacts on environment and development (UN-Energy 2007).

The varying degrees of legalization among these domains shape the potential for aggregate interplay management. The resulting weak institutional complex is not able to balance the various domains. A domain with a high degree of legalization and organizational capacity can stand on its own, and can resist interaction with other weaker regimes. Thus, the climate change regime dominates global norm development on climate change to such a degree that taking up this issue in other fora—such as the CSD, where the potential for integration with energy and development is higher—becomes a very sensitive matter because of fears of a possible weakening of the climate regime. Similar concerns have been voiced even more strongly about efforts to create soft processes outside the UN that address climate change with a stronger focus on energy technology, such as the Asia-Pacific Partnership or the Major Economies Meetings organized by the United States in 2007–2009. The unequal presence of strong IGOs in the three domains, and in particular the weakness of the energy domain in this respect, is another obstacle to aggregate integration and an institutional complex that can support interplay management. As a result, the Johannesburg Renewable Energy Coalition of more than 80 countries that wanted to promote the use of renewable energy (created in 2002) found that not a single organization exists with the necessary competence across the entire field of energy for sustainable development, or the necessary legitimacy among all countries, to conduct a review on energy for sustainable development (JREC Secretariat 2007). Overall, the limited efforts to advance interplay management through norm development and enhanced interagency coordination have had little impact on the focus of investment by development financing organizations, which has remained on large-scale fossil fuel energy-supply projects rather than alternative energy sources or ensuring access for the poor (Spalding-Fecher, Winkler, and Mwakasonda 2005). Changing this situation will require much greater integration of both climate change and development concerns in the energy policies of countries, corporations, and IGOs.

What are the opportunities for strengthening aggregate integration? Advancing the energy domain would seem to require very soft legalization processes on energy for sustainable development outside the UN system in semiglobal coalitions of the willing, as assembled in IRENA, the G-8, the IEA, and various smaller partnerships. Otherwise, interplay management will have to progress primarily at the national level and in bilateral initiatives. Given the difficult political context of global energy governance, strengthening global climate governance where discussions on sectors have started may provide another starting point and opportunity. The slow pace of the post-2012 deliberations shows, however, the challenges involved in proceeding along this path.

Conclusions

While the prevailing unilateral interplay management in the nexus of climate, energy, and development has so far proved inadequate, the resultant institutional complex appears relatively stable. Lacking is a forum with the necessary clout to advance a more integrated, joint management of the interfaces between the three domains and related inter-institutional coordination, so decisions affecting the nexus have often been made in an uncoordinated manner within each of the domains. The strength of political interests favoring this status quo has tended to obstruct progress toward more integration and more similar levels of legalization in the different domains (which could support exchanges on a more equal footing). Although the international community has made attempts to capture some opportunities for synergies among domains, there is room for considerable improvement. Perceived and real trade-offs from old and persistent norms, institutions, and infrastructure pose challenges that so far have been difficult to overcome.

With respect to interplay management through legalization, an ambiguous picture emerges. On the one hand, truly aggregate integration and creating a balanced supportive institutional complex seem to require domains that are similarly strong in terms of legalization. On the other hand, lower levels of legalization in one or more of the domains may provide opportunities to build up and design norms with full consideration of other relevant domains at inception. The integration of climate and development concerns in the core energy domain is a nonstarter at the global level, because the regulatory institutions for this sector are found at the national, sometimes regional, levels. However, the normative vacuum for energy at the global level could also offer an opportunity to develop norms and institutions that integrate concern for climate change and development from the outset. Such legalization would most likely proceed along a very soft path, far from hard treaty frameworks, as governments have special concerns when it comes to strengthening global governance on energy. For the same reason, even soft legalization may advance only at a snail's pace. Still, there is space for old institutions to expand their agenda and for new institutions, such as IRENA, to chart new territory.

Whereas a balanced aggregate or multidirectional integration that assigns equal importance to each dimension of sustainable development may be the most appropriate, political realities frequently lead to a focus on unidirectional mainstreaming and may provide specific opportunities for advancing interplay management in more limited settings. The struggle to frame climate change as an environmental or development issue, and the struggle to get the energy domain to focus on poverty reduction (social development) and not merely on macroeconomic progress, exemplify the difficulties of achieving multidirectional integration. Furthermore, it is usually more feasible to initiate mainstreaming of other issues into policy fields that are closely related to daily operations and are prioritized by individuals and societies. An example is the mainstreaming of climate change and energy aspects into the development agenda, at least at the national and operational levels. Here, the low degree of legalization may also facilitate other forms of integration. Interplay could take place among the development actors themselves, but the very weak structure for collaboration in the UN system in general and on energy issues in particular makes this difficult.

Thus far, attempts to achieve aggregate integration at the global level have led to a complex struggle for supremacy among domains. Clear illustrations are the efforts to integrate in the CSD the traditional socioeconomic development agenda (now spearheaded by the MDGs), the environment and climate agenda, and the sustainable development agenda in the post-Rio process. While many actors commend the CSD's

mandate to be the forum for holistic analysis and institutional development among the three dimensions of sustainable development, there are
also complaints about the CSD's inability to achieve this. The commission has the potential for innovative interplay management in the nexus
we have analyzed, but it has not managed to utilize this potential.

The synergies and trade-offs within the nexus of energy, climate
change, and development, including the benefits of clean energy and the
possibilities energy offers for development, indicate the advantages of an
integrated approach. Some have argued that dealing with energy, climate
change, and development in an integrated manner complicates matters
to such an extent that policymaking becomes impossible. Similarly, some
have emphasized that mainstreaming climate change into the poverty
eradication agenda cannot work because poverty reduction has not yet
succeeded on its own. From this perspective, climate risks might be too
large to hide within another agenda. Others argue that climate change
might be the straw that breaks the camel's back, and that integrating
climate change into poverty reduction strategies is necessary in order to
reach the poor. Only by integrating macroscale development concerns of
large emitting emerging economies such as India and China may the
climate change regime itself be able to progress further.

Interplay management at the global level is not sufficient, but it is a
crucial element for supporting sustainable development. Global-level
action will have to be complemented by interplay management at other
levels of governance, and some matters of integration may best be solved
at the regional or national level. Nevertheless, global governance remains
important, particularly in the nexus analyzed here. What is required is
a governance structure within the UN that would allow coherent and
integrated policymaking on development, energy, and climate, along with
other related issues, at the global level, in support of interplay management at lower levels. This would require the slow buildup of an institutional complex that is more balanced among the energy, development,
and climate domains, in terms of the degree and level of legalization, and
in supporting integration rather than only mainstreaming in one direction. Such considerations need to be part of the UN reform discussions
that are currently under way.

Acknowledgments

We thank Bert Metz, Ton Manders, the editors, and three anonymous
reviewers for comments on earlier drafts of this chapter.

Notes

1. Finnemore and Sikkink (1998) suggest that "norms" refer to single standards of behavior while "institutions" refer to a collection of practices and rules. In the policy domains we analyze, however, it is difficult to identify very distinct individual norms. We still refer primarily to "norms" rather than "institutions" to highlight the distinction from organizations.

2. "Development" in the following is used to denote socioeconomic development focused on poverty reduction in developing countries.

3. See http://www.encharter.org/index.php?id=7.

4. For a summary of the proceedings, see http://www.un.org/climatechange/2007highlevel/summary.shtml and http://www.un.org/wcm/webdav/site/climate change/shared/Documents/Chair_summary_Finall_E.pdf.

5. See http://www.iiasa.ac.at/Research/ENE/GEA/index_gea.html.

6. Some international organizations with considerable programs supporting the energy sector in developing countries, such as the World Bank or UNIDO, are development-oriented organizations in a broader sense. Their efforts have focused on large energy infrastructure for national development priorities, which may support poverty eradication in the longer run.

7. See http://webapps01.un.org/dsd/partnerships/public/welcome.do.

8. This analysis is based on following the negotiations of CSD-14/15 on-site, and the analysis of associated statements and documents.

References

Abbott, Kenneth W., Robert O. Keohane, Andrew Moravcsik, Anne-Marie Slaughter, and Duncan Snidal. 2000. The Concept of Legalization. *International Organization* 54:401–419.

Abbott, Kenneth W., and Duncan Snidal. 2000. Hard and Soft Law in International Governance. *International Organization* 54:421–456.

African Development Bank, Asian Development Bank, Department for International Development United Kingdom, Directorate-General for Development European Commission, Federal Ministry for Economic Cooperation and Development Germany, Ministry of Foreign Affairs—Development Cooperation the Netherlands, Organization for Economic Cooperation and Development, United Nations Development Programme, United Nations Environment Programme, World Bank. 2003. *Poverty and Climate Change: Reducing the Vulnerability of the Poor Through Adaptation*. Washington, D.C.: UNDP, UNEP, World Bank, ADB, AfDB, GTZ, DFID, OECD, EC on behalf of the Poverty–Environment Partner. http://ec.europa.eu/development/icenter/repository/env_cc_varg_poverty_and_climate_change_en.pdf (accessed 18 May 2010).

APP. 2006. Charter for the Asia–Pacific Partnership on Clean Development and Climate. Inaugural Ministerial Meeting, Sydney, 11–12 January 2006.

Bradley, Rob, and Kevin A. Baumert, eds. 2005. *Growing in the Greenhouse: Protecting the Climate by Putting Development First.* Washington, D.C.: World Resources Institute.

Chinkin, Christine. 2000. Normative Development in the International Legal System. In *Commitment and Compliance: The Role of Non-Binding Norms in the International Legal System,* ed. Dinah Shelton, 21–42. Oxford: Oxford University Press.

CSD. 2001. *Report on the Ninth Session (5 May 2000 and 16–27 April 2001).* Economic and Social Council, Official Records, 2001, Suppl. No.9. Commission on Sustainable Development. Rep. E/CN.17/2001/19. New York: United Nations.

Danida. 2005. *Danish Climate Change and Development Action Programme: A Toolkit for Climate Proofing Danish Development Cooperation.* Copenhagen: Ministry of Foreign Affairs.

Davidson, Ogunlade, Kirsten Halsnæs, Saleemul Huq, Marcel Kok, Bert Metz, Youba Sokona, and Jan Verhagen. 2003. The Development and Climate Nexus: The Case of Sub-Saharan Africa. *Climate Policy* 3 (S1): S97–S113.

ESMAP. 2005. *ESMAP Annual Report 2005.* Washington, D.C.: International Bank for Reconstruction and Development, Energy Sector Management Assistance Program.

European Commission. 2007. *Adapting to Climate Change in Europe: Options for EU Action. Green Paper.* Brussels: European Commission.

Finnemore, Martha, and Kathryn Sikkink. 1998. International Norm Dynamics and Political Change. *International Organization* 52:887–917.

G-8. 2005. *Gleneagles Plan of Action: Climate Change, Clean Energy and Sustainable Development.* http://collections.europarchive.org/tna/20080205132101/www.fco.gov.uk/Files/kfile/PostG8_Gleneagles_CCChangePlanofAction.pdf (accessed 18 May 2010).

Gehring, Thomas, and Sebastian Oberthür. 2006. Introduction. In *Institutional Interaction in Global Environmental Governance: Synergy and Conflict among International and EU Policies,* ed. Sebastian Oberthür and Thomas Gehring, 1–18. Cambridge, Mass.: MIT Press.

Halnaes, Kirsten, and Amit Garg. 2006. *Sustainable Development, Energy and Climate: Exploring Synergies and Trade Offs. Methodological Issues and Case Studies from Brazil, China, India, South Africa, Bangladesh and Senegal.* Denmark: UNEP Risoe Centre.

IEA. 2004. *World Energy Outlook.* Paris: International Energy Agency.

IEA. 2006. *World Energy Outlook.* Paris: International Energy Agency.

IPCC. 2007. *Climate Change 2007: Synthesis Report. Contribution of Working Groups I, II and III to the Fourth Assessment Report of the Intergovernmental Panel on Climate Change.* Geneva: Intergovernmental Panel on Climate Change.

JREC Secretariat. 2007. *Towards an Effective Arrangement to Review Progress on Increasing the Global Market Share of Renewable Energy.* Draft discussion paper, Version 7. Prepared by an international team of experts with logistical support from the Secretariat, Johannesburg Renewable Energy Coalition.

Karlsson-Vinkhuyzen, Sylvia I. 2010. The United Nations and Global Energy Governance: Past Challenges, Future Choices. *Global Change, Peace & Security* 22 (2): 175–195.

Karlsson-Vinkhuyzen, Sylvia I., and Antto Vihma. 2009. Comparing the Legitimacy and Effectiveness of Global Hard and Soft Law. *Regulation & Governance* 3 (4): 400–420.

Klein, Richard, Siri E. H. Eriksen, Lars Otto Næss, Anne Hammill, Thomas M. Tanner, Carmenza Robledo, and Karen L. O'Brien. 2007. Portfolio Screening to Support the Mainstreaming of Adaptation to Climate Change into Development Assistance. *Climatic Change* 84 (1): 23–44.

Kok, Marcel T. J., Cees P. van Beers, Sascha N. M. van Rooijen, Max Wilton, and Steven J. Wonink. 2004. Energy for Development. Conference paper for the World Conference on Energy for Development held in Noordwijk, the Netherlands, 12–14 December 2004. Ministerie van Volkhuisvesting, Ruimtelijke Ordening en Milieu.

Kok, Marcel T. J., and Heleen C. de Coninck. 2007. Widening the Scope of Policies to Address Climate Change: Directions for Mainstreaming. *Environmental Science & Policy* 10 (7): 587–599.

Kok, Marcel T. J., Bert Metz, Jan Verhagen, and Sascha van Rooijen. 2008. Integrating Development and Climate Policies: National and International Benefits. *Climate Policy* 8:103–118.

Lafferty, William M., and Eivind Hovden. 2003. Environmental Policy Integration: Towards an Analytical Framework. *Environmental Politics* 12:1–22.

Modi, Vijay, Susan McDade, Dominique Lallement, and Jamal Saghir. 2005. *Energy Services for the Millennium Development Goals: Millennium Project.* New York: UNDP, UNEP, the World Bank, ESMAP. http://www.unmillenniumproject.org/documents/MP_Energy_Low_Res.pdf (accessed 18 May 2010).

Najam, Adil, Atiq A. Rahman, Saleemul Huq, and Youba Sokona. 2003. Integrating Sustainable Development into the Fourth Assessment Report of the Intergovernmental Panel on Climate Change. *Climate Policy* 3 (S1): S9–S17.

Oberthür, Sebastian, and Thomas Gehring, eds. 2006. *Institutional Interaction in Global Environmental Governance: Synergy and Conflict Among International and EU Policies.* Cambridge, Mass.: MIT Press.

OECD. 2005. *Bridge Over Troubled Waters: Linking Climate Change and Development.* Paris: Organisation for Economic Co-operation and Development.

OECD. 2006. *Declaration on Integrating Climate Change Adaptation into Development Co-operation, 4 April 2006.* Meeting of the OECD Development Assistance Committee and the Environment Policy Committee. Paris: Organisation for Economic Co-operation and Development.

Ott, Herman E. 2002. *Warning Signs from Delhi: Troubled Waters Ahead for Global Climate Policy.* Oxford: Oxford University Press.

Persson, Åsa. 2004. *Environmental Policy Integration: An Introduction.* PINTS— Policy Integration for Sustainability Background Paper. Stockholm: Stockholm Environment Institute.

Reinicke, Wolfgang H., and Jan Martin Witte. 2000. Interdependence, Globalization, and Sovereignty: The Role of Non-binding International Legal Accords. In *Commitment and Compliance: The Role of Non-Binding Norms in the International Legal System*, ed. Dinah Shelton, 75–100. Oxford: Oxford University Press.

Shelton, Dinah. 2000. Introduction: Law, Non-Law and the Problem of "Soft Law." In *Commitment and Compliance: The Role of Non-Binding Norms in the International Legal System*, ed. Dinah Shelton, 1–18. Oxford: Oxford University Press.

Spalding-Fecher, Randall, Harald Winkler, and Stanford Mwakasonda. 2005. Energy and the World Summit on Sustainable Development: What Next? *Energy Policy* 33:99–112.

Trubek, David M., Patrick Cottrell, and Mark Nance. 2005. "Soft Law," "Hard Law"and European Integration. In *Law and New Governance in the EU and the US*, ed. Grainne De Búrca and Joanne Scott, 65–94. Oxford: Hart.

UN. 2002. Plan of Implementation of the World Summit on Sustainable Development. In *Report of the World Summit on Sustainable Development. Johannesburg, South Africa, 26 August–4 September.* Rep. A/CONF.199/20. New York: United Nations.

UN-Energy. 2006. *Energy in the United Nations: An Overview of UN-Energy Activities.* http://esa.un.org/un-energy/pdf/un_energy_overview.pdf (accessed 30 April 2010).

UN-Energy. 2007. *Sustainable Bioenergy: A Framework for Decision Makers.* http://esa.un.org/un-energy/pdf/susdev.Biofuels.FAO.pdf (accessed 30 April 2010).

UNDP. 2007. *Fighting Climate Change: Human Solidarity in a Divided World. Human Development Report 2007/2008.* New York: United Nations Development Programme. http://hdr.undp.org/en/reports/global/hdr2007-2008/ (accessed 30 April 2010).

UNEP. 2007. *Global Environment Outlook 4. Environment for Development.* Nairobi: United Nations Environment Programme.

UN ECOSOC. 2000. *Report on the Second Session (14–25 August 2000). Economic and Social Council. Official Records.* Suppl. No. 12. Rep. E/C.14/2000/11. New York: United Nations, Committee on Energy and Natural Resources Development, United Nations Economic and Social Council.

UN General Assembly. 2000. *Resolution Adopted by the General Assembly: 55/2.* United Nations Millennium Declaration. Rep. A/RES/55/2. New York: United Nations.

UN Security Council. 2007. Security Council Holds First-ever Debate on Impact of Climate Change on Peace, Security, hearing over 50 Speakers. 5663rd Security Council Meeting, Tuesday, 17 April 2007, 10 a.m. New York: United Nations.

http://www.un.org/News/Press/docs/2007/sc9000.doc.htm   (accessed   2   July 2010).

WEHAB Working Group. 2002. *A Framework for Action on Energy*. New York: United Nations.

Westphal, Kirsten. 2005. The EU–Russian Relationship and the Energy Factor: A European View. In *A Focus on EU–Russian Relations: Towards a Close Partnership on Defined Road Maps?*, ed. Kirsten Westphal, 1–36. Berlin: Peter Lang.

World Bank. 2006. *Investment Framework for Clean Energy and Sustainable Development*. Washington, D.C.: World Bank.

WHO. 2007. *Indoor Air Pollution: National Burden of Disease Estimates*. Geneva: World Health Organization.

Young, Oran R. 2002. Institutional Interplay: The Environmental Consequences of Cross-Scale Interactions. In *The Drama of the Commons*, ed. Elinor Ostrom, Thomas Dietz, Nives Dolsak, Paul C. Stern, Susan Stonich, and Elke U. Weber, 263–291. Washington, D.C.: National Academy Press.

12

Conclusions

Decentralized Interplay Management in an Evolving Interinstitutional Order

Sebastian Oberthür and Olav Schram Stokke

This book has focused on two themes central to institutional interaction: interplay management and institutional complexes. The contributions to this volume have addressed one or both of these issues by exploring various fields of international environmental governance, frequently investigating changes over time. The authors have focused on specific institutional complexes, the interplay management of particular interinstitutional relationships, or relevant cross-cutting issues. In this concluding chapter, we pinpoint the main conceptual and empirical findings concerning the two core themes.

We present the main findings with respect to each of these themes. First, the contributions to this volume indicate that decentralized interplay management, short of joint or overarching approaches, dominates in global environmental governance—and probably beyond. Interinstitutional relationships seem to have evolved primarily on the basis of collective decisions made separately within one or more of the institutions involved, or through individual decisions by actors outside their formal decision-making processes. Much of this decentralized interplay management has contributed significantly to enhancing the effectiveness of global environmental governance, realizing synergy, or avoiding conflict among institutions. We identify three conditions for variation in such success: shared cross-institutional knowledge, problem malignancy, and political saliency.

Second, the volume indicates that, over time, institutional complexes tend to develop relatively stable internal divisions of labor among the elemental institutions. Rather than resulting from rational design, such divisions of labor emerge "spontaneously" from a political process that is framed by material interests in avoiding incompatible commitments and in preserving existing institutions, relatively weak normative frameworks, and evolving cognitional capacities. Once established, the divisions of labor are stabilized by the related mutual expectations of actors and reproduced through practice, but they remain susceptible to change where the underlying balance of power and interests alters significantly. As environmental concerns are relative newcomers in global governance, the rather lengthy processes required to modify the status quo within institutional complexes adds to the challenge of "greening" global governance in time to prevent irreversible damage.

Following these major findings, this final chapter highlights key priorities for future research on institutional interaction and institutional complexes. We conclude by summarizing the main findings and highlighting some policy-relevant conclusions that flow from them. In particular, the current prevalence of decentralized forms of interplay management and its success conditions identified (problem malignancy, political saliency, shared knowledge) raise doubts about the feasibility and suitability of proposals for restructuring and centralizing global environmental governance.

While we hope and believe that our findings constitute a significant contribution to an evolving scholarly debate, a note of caution seems in order regarding the generalizability or external validity of these findings. As explained in the introductory chapter, the volume is based on an inductive and exploratory approach. The contributions were not specifically designed to make up a representative empirical sample of the phenomena under study, although they do span a wide range of central areas in international environmental governance and were selected without any deliberate bias. As a consequence, the general insights that have been generated, and that are presented in this chapter, cannot claim to have general validity. However, we believe that they can stand as plausible conjectures, given the analyses on which they are based. For future research, they may represent useful working hypotheses waiting to be refuted, further refined, or corroborated.

Interplay Management

States, organizations, and individuals are often well aware that action under one institution can affect the evolution or consequences of actions under another, and therefore seek to influence those impacts. Actors pursue such interplay management by means that involve various degrees of coordination, ranging from general legal norms on the preeminence of rules to autonomous action by states or others aiming to strengthen one institution on a policy matter involving several institutions. The cases and policy areas examined in this volume indicate that decentralized interplay management, with modest or no overarching coordination across institutional boundaries, is a prominent feature of international environmental governance. Moreover, such interplay management often helps to ameliorate problems that many authors have associated with institutional interaction: fragmented and contested knowledge on overlapping issues (Alter and Meunier 2009), duplication of effort (Andresen 2001), and normative ambiguity due to conflicting commitments under separate institutions (Brown Weiss 1993; Drezner 2009). While such interplay management has produced considerable achievements in generating a common knowledge base regarding cross-institutional issues, achieving synergy, avoiding or mitigating normative conflict, and enhancing the environmental effectiveness of global governance, these successes are far from universal. Among the factors that the contributors to this volume indicate have influence on the success of interplay management efforts are the existence of cross-institutional knowledge, the political saliency of the interplay issue, and the problem malignancy in terms of compatibility of the interests underlying the policy objectives of each institution.

Pervasiveness of Decentralized Interplay Management

First of all, the contributions to this volume indicate that interplay management efforts in global environmental governance remain largely decentralized, with low levels of cross-institutional coordination. In the introductory chapter, we identified four levels of interplay management (see also Oberthür 2009): overarching institutional frameworks, such as the general rules of international law or the UN; joint management facilitated by designated structures for cross-institutional coordination; unilateral management based on collective decisions within one or more of the interacting institutions; and, at the lowest level, autonomous management efforts by states or other actors, such as civil society or business associations.

Practically all cases reported here of deliberate attempts to influence the nature and impacts of interplay concern either unilateral management within one institution or autonomous management by states or others. Van Asselt (chapter 3), for instance, notes the unilateral requests made by the Conference of the Parties (COP) of the Convention on Biological Diversity (CBD) that measures under the climate change regime be "consistent with and supportive of the conservation and sustainable use of biological diversity," as well as the Kyoto Protocol's provision that states should address greenhouse gas emissions from vessels through the International Maritime Organization. No less unilateral is the interplay management that Axelrod (chapter 4) reports, indicating that three-fourths of the multilateral treaties under study contain some type of savings clause invoking or deferring to existing agreements. Also, the interaction between the ozone and climate regimes has evolved predominantly through independent decision making within each of these institutions (Oberthür, Dupont, and Matsumoto in this volume). Stokke (chapter 6) focuses on how those operating an institution unilaterally define a niche within the overall governance system that corresponds to distinctive institutional capacities. Similarly, the new division of labor that Gehring (chapter 9) delineates, between multilateral environmental agreements (MEAs) and the World Trade Organization (WTO) regarding environmentally motivated trade restrictions, emerges not from extensive cross-regime communication but from decisions made within each institution and by individual states implementing their commitments under these institutions. Unilateral and autonomous interplay management efforts predominate in the areas studied in this volume—areas that cover important segments of global environmental governance.

In contrast, arrangements for overarching or joint interplay management are few and muted in the material reported here. One such structure is a set of fundamental principles of international law as codified in the 1969 Vienna Convention on the Law of Treaties, such as *pacta sunt servanda* (treaties are to be kept) and various general customary law rules of preeminence or treaty interpretation, the *lex posterior* (the most recent provision shall prevail) and the *lex specialis* (the most specific provision shall prevail) rules (Wolfrum and Matz 2003; see chapters by van Asselt and by Axelrod in this volume). While several contributions observe such processes in the policy areas under study (see in particular the chapters by van Asselt; Axelrod; Oberthür, Dupont, and Matsumoto; Jungcurt; Stokke; Alcock; and Gehring), those overarching rules are usually too general for settling specific cases of latent or manifest conflict. As we argue below, they tend to offer only a basis that may structure and thus facilitate more specific efforts at interplay management.

Coordination by overarching institutions appears difficult to realize even when interregime conflict is modest or absent. This is evident in the various attempts by agencies such as the United Nations Environment Programme (UNEP) to promote joint management to coordinate administrative and capacity-enhancement activities under international institutions to reap cost-efficiency gains in environmental governance. Relevant measures include common secretariat housing, back-to-back conferences of parties to treaties that involve largely the same state representatives, harmonizing reporting requirements, and streamlining the guidance to financial mechanisms (see discussion in von Moltke 2005; Chambers 2008). Such measures may be considered politically benign since the benefits to be gained are likely to be distributed relatively symmetrically among states (Underdal 2002). Van Asselt (chapter 3) lists such proposals, including those by a Joint Liaison Group set up to reap synergies across the three Rio Conventions on climate change, biological diversity, and desertification. However, as yet, most of these initiatives have failed to deliver their full potential. Van Asselt finds that practical results of the Joint Liaison Group have, beyond certain joint workshops and reports and mutual attendance at each other's meetings, been meager; he identifies a series of legal, practical, and political barriers that can help explain this outcome. Among those barriers are sticky procedures and practices within each institution, resistance within the issue-specific institutions to external coordination, and pervasive reluctance to involve others (including adjacent segments of national administrations and their associated stakeholders) in relevant decisions. In the case of UNEP, the failure of states to endow UNEP with strong institutional capacities for inducing interinstitutional coordination deserves mention (Ivanova 2007). Overall, our material does not provide strong cases where overarching institutions can be said to have played a central role in reaping cross-institutional efficiency gains.

The modest role that overarching structures have played in environmental governance so far and the paucity of actual attempts at joint management are somewhat at odds with the extensive debates among practitioners and scholars of the relative merits of various institutional means for streamlining and even hierarchically ordering relevant international regimes and agencies (for a recent review, see Biermann, Davies, and van der Grijp 2009). Actors within regimes continue to pay attention to coordination with other regimes and to identifying new options for improving practical linkages as well as the broader UN reform process, which should indicate that states still view this as a promising avenue (see also Chambers 2008). At the same time, the scarcity of actual cases of centralized interinstitutional coordination in global environmental governance indicates formidable counterforces to this mode of interplay management that are likely to continue to constrain its pervasiveness in the foreseeable future. That in turn directs attention to processes and conditions that allow states and other actors to achieve synergies, avoid normative conflicts, and enhance environmental governance also when cross-institutional hierarchy and coordination are modest or absent.

Interplay Management and Effective Environmental Governance

The contributors to this volume offer considerable evidence supporting the hypothesis that existing means of interplay management enhance the effectiveness of global environmental governance, and they identify several conditions that favor such impact. Given the methodological challenges involved in the causal substantiation of institutional effects (Underdal and Young 2004a), it is not surprising that most of the evidence concerns effects at the output level, in contrast to outcome- and impact-level effects, which require analysis of longer causal chains (Underdal 2008; see also Zelli in this volume).

Van Asselt (chapter 3) differentiates between legal and political approaches to interplay management, which may serve as a useful heuristic tool (see also Zelli in this volume). Legal approaches comprise the various means that international law provides for making, applying, or interpreting international norms, including conflict clauses and such judicial mechanisms as the WTO Dispute Settlement Body. Political approaches, in contrast, primarily involve political decision making or the activities of administrative bodies in international institutions and the means these provide for cooperation and coordination. As van Asselt argues, both political and legal means of management have important limitations and may therefore usefully complement each other. Admittedly, the distinction between legal and political approaches is hardly clear-cut, since political decision making is both constrained and enabled by international rules, while changes in international law often result from political decisions within or outside existing treaty regimes. However, one merit of this rough distinction is that it directs attention to different types of venues for interplay management, each of which may involve varying levels of coordination.

In the following, we explore the contribution of this volume to understanding the role of interplay management in effective environmental governance, in three steps. First, we examine how interplay management affects knowledge building on cross-institutional issues. Second, we argue that existing interplay management, despite the subordinate role of overarching cross-institutional interplay management, has contributed greatly to reaping interinstitutional synergy, mitigating conflict, and enhancing environmental governance, without realizing any principled priority for the environment in interinstitutional relationships. Third, we highlight the creation of shared knowledge across relevant institutions, the political saliency of interplay issues, and their problem malignancy as important conditions for successful interplay management.

Building Cross-Institutional Knowledge   Even with modest or insignificant levels of coordination, interplay management can help develop a shared understanding among states across different institutions about the consequences of institutional interplay and ways to improve it. Even when institutions spanning several issue areas are influential, their role is typically to encourage or inspire assessment work within the core institutions in each domain where subsequent action may or may not be taken. Otherwise, the contributors to this volume show that, even in the absence of such overarching institutional arrangements, efforts to influence how other institutions frame and define problems of shared relevance can succeed in counteracting the fragmentation of knowledge building that might otherwise undermine complementary action.

While attempts to build and diffuse cross-institutional knowledge may involve permanent or ad hoc bodies for linking relevant activities (overarching institutions), the evidence suggests that knowledge building itself relies mostly on the assessment bodies of each institution. Karlsson-Vinkhuyzen and Kok (chapter 11), for example, highlight the role of the UN Commission for Sustainable Development (CSD) in raising the saliency of affordable access to energy as a means for achieving the Millennium Development Goals and in diffusing this priority issue to various international venues and institutions in the energy and development domains, including the International Energy Agency (IEA). However, the specific framing, compilation, and analysis of relevant data at the energy-development interface have rested with the assessment bodies in the specialized institutions that possess considerable in-house expertise and other relevant resources. As one result, the IEA's high-profiled reports, such as the *World Energy Outlook*, now systematically attend to the development aspect of energy policies.

Other interplay management efforts at knowledge building reported in this volume demonstrate that success does not necessarily require involvement of overarching institutions. Oberthür, Dupont, and Matsumoto (chapter 5) show how assessment bodies under the climate and ozone regimes responded to calls from their respective decision-making bodies to develop a shared understanding of options for dealing with emissions of fluorinated greenhouse gases, which are major substitutes for ozone-depleting substances. The resultant joint scientific and technical assessments failed to lead to immediate action to reduce this policy inconsistency (mostly because of political resistance among leading states), but they were to prove important some years later, when the political saliency of the policy conflict had risen and pressure for taking action was mounting. Decentralized coordination of scientific activities and political saliency also figure prominently in Stokke's account (chapter 6) of how an Arctic Council monitoring program promoted regulatory strengthening under the UN Economic Commission for Europe (ECE) Convention on Long-Range Transboundary Air Pollution by documenting the serious health effects among Arctic indigenous residents from toxic agents bioaccumulating in marine mammals. That documentation raised the political saliency of the persistent organic pollutants issue (see also Stokke, Hønneland, and Schei 2010), because the Arctic finding dovetailed with the screening criteria in use by a special ECE task force identifying chemicals in particular need of regulation. Such mutual awareness of ongoing scientific or diplomatic activities in interacting institutions can suffice to generate cross-institutional knowledge about the interplay, in turn improving the basis for taking action.

Overall, the findings in this volume indicate that any fragmentation of knowledge building resulting from increasing institutional complexity may be counteracted by institutional inertia and determination among states to retain control of the knowledge-building process. Alter and Meunier (2009) have argued that institutional complexity yields fragmented knowledge building that compounds the problems of bounded rationality for state decision makers and makes them more reliant on various nongovernmental advisers or "knowledge brokers," such as civil society organizations or business actors. However, the findings reported in this book indicate that states are increasingly aware of the challenges of institutional interaction: they may create their own knowledge brokers by instructing assessment structures under existing international institutions to examine whether and how results from corresponding bodies under other international institutions might affect their scientific or technical inputs to political decision making.

Reaping Synergies, Mitigating Conflict, and Enhancing Environmental Governance   The chapters in this volume indicate that existing interplay management efforts have allowed states and other actors to realize some synergy in decision making and implementation, to avoid or mitigate normative conflicts among institutions that would undermine their compliance pull, and to enhance effective environmental governance. Whereas the major contribution of general rules of international law and the limited overarching institutional arrangements appears to consist in the overall framing of interinstitutional relations, more specific achievements emanate, within this framework, primarily from decentralized interplay management. It is obvious that the glass is still only half full, at best, as regards effective environmental governance: the results remain insufficient for maximizing environmental protection.

General rules of international law can best be understood as providing a broad framework, a basis and point of reference for concrete interplay management efforts. The few relevant rules are typically too vague or too easily counteracted for resolving issues of normative conflict or for reaping specific synergies among international institutions. As van Asselt argues in chapter 3, the ability of the aforementioned rules of *lex posterior* and *lex specialis* to reconcile norms or resolve questions of prevalence is limited by differences in treaty participation, as well as by such legal uncertainties as exactly when a given treaty provision came into existence, whether two treaties concern the same subject matter, and how to differentiate unequivocally the specificity of rules laid out in the various treaties. Moreover, such general rules are frequently overridden by specific treaty provisions, such as savings clauses that shield past agreements. Axelrod (chapter 4) notes that some 40 percent of the international agreements he examines explicitly defer to earlier treaties and thus cancel out any implication of the *lex posterior* rule. General norms of international law do frame interplay management, but the studies presented here do not indicate that such norms are powerful means for settling institutional conflict or enhancing the effectiveness of environmental governance.

Given the weakness of authority to coordinate international institutions in global environmental governance, the contributions to this volume point to the cognitional framing of policy choices across institutional borders as the main contribution of existing overarching institutional arrangements (beyond the general rules of international law discussed above). Overarching institutions have been active in seeking greater coherence among decisions and program activities undertaken by more specialized international institutions. Karlsson-Vinkhuyzen and Kok argue that various UN outputs create a soft, overarching framework that helps in setting priorities among development goals and in improving coherence and potential synergies among program activities within numerous bodies involved in development, energy, and climate issues.

When endowed with relevant resources, such institutions can also play a role in diffusing policy priorities across institutional boundaries, both horizontally and vertically. Furthermore, as Alcock shows in chapter 10, international organizations such as the UN Food and Agriculture Organization (FAO) and the World Bank have provided training programs and financial support to shape the effects of the UN Convention on the Law of the Sea on regional fisheries management regimes and national institutions in developing coastal states. Alcock also notes that this influence has involved a range of sometimes controversial policy priorities. Early on, the FAO and international financial institutions promoted an industrial development paradigm that favored the capital-intensive segment of the fisheries sector. Their more recent move to advocate the introduction of market-based governance instruments, such as individually tradable quotas, may have wide-ranging consequences for the evolution of fisheries management arrangements. These observations concur with more general findings that developing cross-institutional policy coherence involves processes of experimentation, emulation, and authoritative assessments of "best practices," which tend to shift over time (Scott and Davis 2007, 324–326), here facilitated by overarching institutions.

Nevertheless, specific progress toward enhancing synergy, mitigating conflict, and enhancing environmental governance appears to emanate predominantly from unilateral adaptation or even autonomous interplay management action by states and other actors. Groups of states that are similarly affected by a problem dealt with by several institutions can succeed in exploiting complementarity in institutional capacities to deal with it more effectively, even without overarching institutions. For instance, as Stokke argues in chapter 6, thanks to their participation in several relevant institutions, the Arctic states were able to marry the special capabilities of the Arctic Council to generate funds for monitoring sources, pathways, and health impacts of Arctic toxics to the greater ability of the broader ECE and UNEP conventions to get the relevant set of states to commit themselves, since these toxics largely originate outside the region. Also with respect to normative conflicts, contributors to this volume highlight notable successes achieved by decentralized, unilateral adaptation or even autonomous interplay management. Gehring argues that the sum of many independent decisions under MEAs and the WTO concerning trade-related environmental measures has produced a new governance structure marked by a division of labor rather than conflict. Underlying Gehring's argument is his assessment that MEAs have been able to make significant inroads into what was previously the unchallenged competence of the parties to the global trade regime. Furthermore, Jungcurt (chapter 7) demonstrates that states negotiating the FAO International Treaty on Plant Genetic Resources for Food and Agriculture (ITPGR) managed to find a solution that balances the interests of users and providers of plant genetic resources in food and agriculture, thus resolving a latent conflict with the International Union on the Protection of New Varieties of Plants (UPOV). Similarly, Oberthür, Dupont, and Matsumoto in chapter 5 argue that independent decision making within the climate and the ozone regimes has produced some positive results for both the ozone layer and the global climate, by limiting the eligibility of certain projects under the climate change regime's Clean Development Mechanism (CDM) and the production of ozone-depleting hydrochlorofluorocarbons. They also identify a significant potential for further progress through decision making in each of the regimes.

A note of caution seems in order, however, as regards the environmental effectiveness of these achievements. From an environmental perspective, the glass may be as much half full as half empty. The emerging balance between MEAs and the WTO concerning environmentally motivated trade restrictions may contain the interinstitutional conflict, but it hardly maximizes the level of environmental protection. While the tension between the ITPGR and UPOV may have been managed in a synergistic way, a positive resolution of the similar conflict between the WTO and the Convention on Biological Diversity (CBD) on broader issues of access to and use of plant genetic resources is still pending. And while the interplay management of the climate-ozone interactions has produced notable benefits for the environment, it has left an even greater potential for synergy to be exploited.

Reinforcing this note of caution, Axelrod finds that states are especially prone to insert savings clauses that uphold existing norms when negotiating environmental treaties. This pattern could reflect fear that MEA rules might otherwise be challenged under the WTO's compulsory and binding dispute settlement procedure, but it could also reflect, as Axelrod suggests, that free trade in general enjoys higher priority among leading states than environmental protection. Yet another possible explanation could be that the higher frequency of savings clauses in MEAs is due to their cross-cutting character, so that it would merely reflect the general desire of states to protect earlier agreements. The full understanding of Axelrod's empirical finding may thus require further investigation, which may also take into account that the inclusion of savings clauses does not necessarily mean outright subordination. (For the case of the Cartagena Protocol and the WTO, see Oberthür and Gehring 2006.) We return to the potential for further improvement of environmental governance below, in the section on institutional complexes.

Conditions of Success   Finally, the contributors to this volume point to certain key factors that may influence the success of interplay management. Given the inductive and exploratory approach of this collection, we cannot attempt to come up with an exhaustive or universally applicable list of factors conditioning success. However, the chapters point to at least three key factors that deserve particular attention as starting points for thinking about conditions for success: shared knowledge and understanding, problem malignancy, and political saliency.

The emergence of shared knowledge and understanding of interplay issues has supported successful interplay management in several of the cases examined here. Applying earlier work on epistemic communities (Haas 1992), Jungcurt finds that, during the negotiation of the ITPGR, a network of experts linked to the Consultative Group on International Agricultural Research and spanning the fields of several institutions proved instrumental in enabling a solution that avoids bilateral contracts—the controversial CBD approach to access and benefit sharing. Many consider that such contracts involve excessive transaction costs. According to Jungcurt, the network of experts paved the way for accommodating the interests of both suppliers and users of genetic resources, and thereby contributed to resolving the latent conflict with UPOV. Important conditions for this facilitating role of experts were the long history of mutual international accommodation in the area and the fact that most negotiators represented the same sector of government, namely, agriculture. Furthermore, Oberthür, Dupont, and Matsumoto (chapter 5), Stokke (chapter 6), and Alcock (chapter 10) highlight the role of shared knowledge and understanding across the boundaries of the individual institutions involved in problematic interaction for advances in interplay management. The building of cross-institutional knowledge, as indicated above, is frequently the result of interplay management and enhances the ability of states and others to reap synergies and to avoid or ameliorate conflict among institutions.

Problem malignancy is another key factor that appears to influence the success of efforts at interplay management. Here, "malignancy" refers to the (in)compatibility of the interests underlying the policy objectives pursued by the institutions in question (Underdal 2002; see Zelli in this volume). The relationship between the WTO and various MEAs is more malign than the Arctic cases examined in this volume (Stokke in this volume), since the latter generally involve institutions that pursue the same or compatible goals, but with different capacities. Yet, as Gehring notes in chapter 9, the WTO-MEA malignancy is softened by various WTO treaty provisions and dispute settlement decisions implying recognition of environmental protection and sustainable development as purposes that potentially justify restrictions on trade. Also, the relationship between the ITPGR and UPOV can be considered less malign than the interaction between the WTO and the CBD: the field of regulation of the ITPGR and UPOV was more limited in scope, which facilitated its insulation from the broader controversial field of access to and benefit sharing from genetic resources (Jungcurt in this volume). Finally, more progress on the interaction between the climate and ozone regimes became possible when the interests of major stakeholders of the ozone regime started shifting in the 2000s (Oberthür, Dupont, and Matsumoto in this volume). Problem malignancy complicates interplay management; it varies across issues, and may change over time.

As these examples demonstrate, problem malignancy may best be considered in the context of political saliency, which may outweigh and trump malignancy to some extent. Thus, Gehring argues that MEAs were able to make inroads into the WTO when environment rose as an international policy issue and proved strong enough to create strategic inconsistency with the WTO. Similarly, conditions for action in the ozone regime to support climate protection improved markedly when climate policy rose on the international agenda in the 2000s, and action within the climate regime got under way as the negative effects of its decisions on the ozone regime received more public attention (Oberthür, Dupont, and Matsumoto in this volume). In the management of Barents Sea fisheries, as Stokke shows, coastal state efforts to mobilize a broader institution for enforcing regulations applying in exclusive economic zones (EEZs) succeeded only when they managed to link this interplay management effort to the broader and highly salient issue of the global combat of illegal, unreported, and unregulated fishing.

These examples lend some support to the hypothesis, put forward by Karlsson-Vinkhuyzen and Kok in chapter 11, that the strength or degree of "legalization" influences the effect of interplay management on conflict resolution. They hypothesize, therefore, that cross-sectoral policy integration is more likely to succeed in arenas that feature strong institutions, as in most of the cases mentioned above. By contrast, in the weaker institutional framework of energy, states' concerns with their sovereignty over an area of strategic significance has so far both kept legalization at bay and hampered policy integration. The findings presented in this volume indicate that advances in such integration also depend on the extent of shared cross-institutional knowledge and the malignancy and political saliency of the issues in question.

Institutional Complexes: Structures Emerging from Complexity

Global environmental governance is characterized by the emergence of institutional complexes: sets of institutions that cogovern particular issue areas. Systematic examination of the structures, nature, and dynamics of such institutional complexes is still in an early stage. The contributions to this volume shed further light on the structures and division of labor within institutional complexes, their stability and change, and the underlying driving forces. They allow the conclusion that institutional interaction and its management have produced—and are reproducing—broader institutional complexes with a structuring division of labor, complexes that are relatively stable and difficult to change. In the following, we look into this finding by first examining the emergence of an interinstitutional division of labor and its underlying driving forces. We then investigate the relative stability of institutional complexes and identify factors that account for their stability and change.

Division of Labor among International Institutions

The contributions to this volume lend support to the hypothesis that, over time, relatively stable divisions of labor develop among the elemental institutions of a complex. Such division of labor does not arise accidentally but emerges from underlying mechanisms, including common and individual interests among the actors involved, established norms, and processes of learning. While the balancing of competing objectives within institutional complexes may rely more on power than on rules and thus hardly emerges from "rational" decision making, the resultant division of labor does provide for an order, an interlocking structure.

Several contributions to this volume find an emerging division of labor within the institutional complexes they study, one that serves to temper interinstitutional conflict and duplication while ideally creating meaningful complementarity among overlapping institutions. Stokke shows that Arctic states have been at pains to define niches for the new institution they set up, the Arctic Council, that would not intrude on the regulatory ambits of existing regimes on various environmental issues. They have worked to create a web of functionally differentiated and complementary institutions in which some attend to knowledge generation while others press for regulatory strengthening or generate funds for capacity building. With respect to environmentally motivated trade restrictions, Gehring finds that a division of labor has emerged between the international trade regime and MEAs: whereas the WTO defines the general criteria that states must heed when considering trade measures for environmental purposes, MEAs provide arenas for designing and adopting such measures. Finally, Jungcurt describes the emergence of a division of labor between two institutions within the broader complex of international governance of plant genetic resources. A system for access to and benefit sharing from specific plant genetic resources for food and agriculture elaborated under the ITPGR appears to have largely settled the latent conflict over property rights with the UPOV.

The contributors show that analyzing the evolution of institutional complexes and the emergence of an interinstitutional division of work requires the exploration of both causal chains and interaction clusters. As Gehring argues, the current balance between the world trade regime and MEAs regarding environmentally motivated trade restrictions is based on numerous connections between MEAs and global trade rules involving mutual influences in sequential interaction events. A similar pattern of multiple links and feedbacks marks the evolution of the regime complex on plant genetic resources (Jungcurt), the evolution of the governance complexes on Arctic resources and the environment (Stokke), and the coevolution of national and local fisheries management institutions with the UN Convention on the Law of the Sea (Alcock). Overall, institutions that cogovern a certain issue area of international relations may be expected to influence each other in multiple ways, with feedback effects evolving over time.

On the whole, the emerging divisions of labor identified in these contributions appear to enjoy relative stability and thus provide for interinstitutional order, a meta-institution distributing governance authority and tasks. That is not to say that such orders are not subject to challenge and change—an issue to which we return in the next subsection. However, the relative stability of these divisions of labor is remarkable in view of the paucity of strong instruments for joint or overarching interplay management substantiated above. It also puts into question the findings of those like Alter and Meunier (2009, 16), who have argued that "where preferences diverge, rule ambiguity will persist, allowing countries to select their preferred interpretation." The fact that institutional divisions of labor emerge even in such conflictual issue areas as the overlap of trade and the environment indicates important constraints on the selection of preferred interpretations by individual actors. The de facto collective acceptance of MEA authority to design and adopt specific environmental trade restrictions (and of WTO authority to determine general criteria in this respect) as part of an emerging interinstitutional division of labor constrains the choices available, and also constrains actors who have not explicitly approved this emerging division of labor and who prefer that trade-related measures remain within the exclusive domain of the WTO (or that MEAs receive complete authority in this area).

What are the mechanisms and driving forces behind the emergence of an interinstitutional division of labor and order? Contributors to this book provide evidence that order within institutional complexes emerges not from accidental interinstitutional relationships but from general forces and mechanisms that help to explain the resulting division of labor. Notably, interest maximization, normative frameworks, and processes of diffusion and learning frequently conspire to encourage some form of a division of labor and complementarity.

Thus, several contributions note how mechanisms rooted in individual or common interests, norms, and learning may support the emergence of interinstitutional order. Consider first the role of individual or parochial interest in Stokke's account of how the Arctic coastal states, which are well served by the current division of authority concerning offshore petroleum activities, have been both eager and able to fend off attempts to place related issues within the ambit of broader institutions involving noncoastal states as well. Vested interests in the status quo present impediments for those seeking change by pursuing "strategic inconsistency" (Raustiala and Victor 2004, 301). Under the circumstances, it may not be surprising that established institutions usually have a "first-mover advantage" over newcomers and therefore frequently prevail if there is competition. Karlsson-Vinkhuyzen and Kok consider the privilege of "being first" as one factor that determines whether integration of policy concerns is likely to proceed as one-sided mainstreaming or as multidirectional accommodation. Gehring argues that if a regulatory field is occupied by one regime, that will make it more difficult for other, newer regimes to make their concerns heard and reflected. Axelrod too finds evidence of a first-mover advantage in the inclination of states to safeguard existing rights and commitments when negotiating new treaties.

Nonparochial interests can also motivate states to pursue cross-institutional consistency and thereby reinforce the compliance pull of international rules. Gehring (chapter 9) highlights how a common interest among members of several institutions in avoiding incompatible commitments can in turn motivate these members to work toward and accept institutional adaptations in order to delimit regulatory authority in acceptable ways. Actors may differ in their preferences as to the accommodation of two or more institutions, but as members of these institutions they have an interest in avoiding inconsistencies that may jeopardize related cooperation gains. This shared interest in avoiding normative conflict may find a further, reinforcing rationale in the desire of actors to be seen as consistent and reliable partners (Keohane 1984). It may also derive from awareness of a normative mechanism, since internal consistency and external coherence with broader norms are important for the compliance pull of international rules and institutions (Franck 1990). Self-interest and normative obligation may thus together help to achieve complementarity even in constellations involving divergent objectives of the institutions involved, as in the relationship between the WTO and MEAs (see also Gehring and Oberthür 2006, 2009).

In international environmental governance, moreover, interests and obligation are often accompanied by a third mechanism that can advance cross-institutional compatibility: learning. Formulas that succeed in balancing competing concerns in a mutually acceptable way are frequently emulated within similar institutional constellations. Such learning is evident, for instance, in the rapid diffusion of the "cooperating state" concept under regional fisheries regimes, according to which nonmembers can avoid trade-related compliance measures by participating in the overall system for verification, review, and enforcement, which raises the WTO compatibility of such compliance measures (Stokke 2009). Alcock in chapter 10 similarly argues that intergovernmental organizations advocating the introduction of individual fishing quotas are increasingly accepting adaptations developed in some countries in order to avoid negative impacts on artisanal and small-scale fishers.

Because of the general relevance of these mechanisms deriving from interests, norms, and learning, we may expect them to operate also in other instances and thus be of broader significance. They may also help explain why the formation of additional institutions in a particular area of governance is rarely accompanied by the decay or clustering of pre-existing institutions.

Overall, the interinstitutional divisions of labor that emerge within institutional complexes are not primarily the outcome of legalized processes: instead, they tend to reflect political struggle among those operating the institutions. Interinstitutional division of labor results from sometimes conflictive political processes based on the distribution of power among institutional constituencies and the distribution of influence enshrined in the substantive norms and procedures of existing institutions. In this vein, Zelli's chapter elaborates on aspects of the power structure and the knowledge structure that may explain the prevalence of a regime in cases of interinstitutional conflict. Gehring argues that the emerging division of labor between MEAs and the global trade regime indicates a rough balance between these two sets of institutions. Reflecting the importance that governments attach to free world trade, the WTO's strong means for ensuring compliance with its norms and settling disputes are assets for states seeking to protect their rights under the international trade regime in this political struggle (Rosendal 2001; Stokke 2004; see also Axelrod in this volume). According to Gehring, however, the growing political saliency of environmental issues has allowed states that favor MEAs to gain ground and modify the balance over time.

In general, all contributions dealing with specific institutional complexes and their development over time seem to see the emergence of a division of labor as a result of politics based on interests, ideas, and knowledge, rather than as a straightforward application of established norms and procedures (see especially the chapters by Alcock, Gehring, Stokke, and Karlsson-Vinkhuyzen and Kok).

Any interinstitutional division of labor presents one possible balance between the institutions involved and, given the weakness of coordinated interplay management, results not from "rational design" but from politics. It follows that the existence of a division of labor does not necessarily imply mutual accommodation, equal weighting of concerns, or any rational distribution of competences. The roots of a division of labor in politics may also help us understand the insufficient effectiveness of interplay management from an environmental perspective, as discussed above. However, the existing divisions of labor may not merely be the result of "implementation politics" (Alter and Meunier 2009, 16; see also Raustiala and Victor 2004, 302–305) in which parties individually select which rules to follow (so that the most powerful states tend to determine the rules of the game). Rather, consecutive and interrelated collective decisions in the elemental institutions gradually establish—and then reproduce—a division of labor that individual actors will find costly to disregard.

The findings presented here do not allow firm conclusions about the advantages and disadvantages of more or less fragmentation, integration, or centralization of institutional complexes. In particular, there is no evidence that the emergence of a division of labor depends on a high level of centralization or integration. Nor have the contributions to this volume identified centralization as an influential driving force. We may hypothesize that it might affect the speed and kind of a division of labor, more than its emergence as such. Keohane and Victor (2010) suggest that decentralization of an institutional complex may have advantages. Further research can assess the performance and potential of less or more centralized institutional complexes under varying conditions—including the number of preexisting institutions, the extent of cross-institutional knowledge, and the levels of malignancy and political saliency, which contributors to this volume have identified as influencing the success of interplay management (see also Biermann, Pattberg, et al. 2009).

Stability and Change

Much like individual institutions themselves, interinstitutional divisions of labor do not reflect an erratically changing balance of power, but appear relatively stable. They enjoy relative stability because those operating the institutions that form a complex, whether competitive or complementary, have limited room or incentives for challenging and modifying an established division of competence. Should they do so, that might endanger the effectiveness of all institutions involved, including the one they favor (see also Gehring and Oberthür 2006, 338–339). A similar conclusion derives from the logic of institutional niches: once an institution has established itself in a functional niche within the overall governance system, those operating it are unlikely to jeopardize the institution's survival insurance or to invest heavily in trying to capture territory already occupied by others.

We may thus conceive of the emerging divisions of labor as "interlocking structures" (Underdal and Young 2004b, 374–375)—a meta-institution of a higher order. The term "structures" clearly involves a concept of stability. The structures are interlocking because the collective decision making in the interacting institutions—and the related behavior of actors in the implementation of the relevant institutions—constantly reproduces the division of labor. Much like customary law, the reproduction of a stable division of labor in the decisions of the elemental institutions of the complex creates and stabilizes the actors' mutual expectations that future decisions will also follow the established division of labor. The elemental institutions thus interlock to create a structure that takes the form of an informal institution of a higher order (see also Gehring in this volume).

The resulting interlocking structures of institutions remain susceptible to change. Because of the relative stability of an established interinstitutional division of work, such change will require more than marginal shifts in the underlying balance of power, however. As open social systems, institutions are exposed to scientific, technological, socioeconomic, and political developments (DiMaggio 1986; Scott and Davis 2007). Especially in environmental governance, their robustness or resilience—that is, their ability to survive and shape actor behavior—depends on their flexibility and capacity to adapt (Gehring 1994; Young et al. 1999/2005; Young 2010). Incremental changes have repercussions on other elements of an institutional complex but typically leave the basic division of work unchallenged. In contrast, new scientific, technological, socioeconomic, and political developments may induce more fundamental changes in the underlying balance of power, changes that can unsettle the existing equilibrium and trigger the search for a new balance.

The contributors to this volume provide ample evidence of such challenges and subsequent changes. Thus, the new balance between institutions in the areas of trade and the environment resulted from the challenge that certain MEAs posed to the WTO's regulatory authority concerning environmentally motivated trade restrictions, by seeking to regulate trade in environmentally harmful products or employing trade restrictions for enforcement purposes (Gehring). With the rise of societal and political concerns about the environment, the environmental constituency managed to create "strategic inconsistency" (Raustiala and Victor 2004, 301) and succeeded in triggering a new interinstitutional balance that is still maturing. In a vertical dimension, Alcock shows how multilateral negotiations and unilateral claims to extended jurisdiction over marine areas, driven by resource rivalry and rapid technological developments, forced a global-level institutional change: sovereign rights among coastal states with respect to resource and environmental management within 200-mile EEZs. In turn, this change in the division of competences between coastal states and others triggered important adaptations in existing national and subnational arrangements for fisheries management.

Achieving change within institutional complexes usually requires considerable time. The interaction between the WTO and MEAs has evolved over two decades, and the new balance that grants MEAs authority to design environmentally motivated trade restrictions within certain limits is still emerging. The mutual accommodation of provider and user concerns that Jungcurt reports in connection with access to and benefit sharing from plant genetic resources applies only to a limited number of crop and forage species found in public gene banks. Issues over other species used in food and agriculture remain unsolved, as do broader controversies regarding property rights to genetic resources, despite more than two decades of international discussion. Similarly, Stokke shows that calls from environmental organizations, Arctic parliamentarians, and, most recently the European Parliament for the building of new, hard-law institutions for environmental regulations in the Arctic encounter potent resistance from states and others who argue that the existing frameworks are adequate. The balance within institutional complexes is relatively stable, not merely because of the "stickiness" of their component institutions (Young 2008, 8; see also Karlsson-Vinkhuyzen and Kok in this volume) but also because those institutions tend to interlock.

The long time required to change an interinstitutional balance can be problematic when it comes to achieving environmental objectives. The stickiness of institutional complexes may serve to protect environmental achievements in global governance. Yet, more often than not, ensuring appropriate environmental protection requires change rather than preserving the status quo. The pressures of global environmental change are so dramatic that substantial change in the landscape of international institutions may be necessary to prevent or at least limit irreversible damage. From an environmental perspective, the long times required for establishing or changing interinstitutional divisions of labor to enhance the contribution of institutional complexes to solving environmental problems and achieving sustainable development constitute a significant challenge.

Given the current "status quo bias" of institutional complexes, the lack of clear guidance in prioritizing environmental concerns constitutes another obstacle to the appropriate integration of environmental concerns into international institutions. There is nothing to indicate that existing mechanisms for achieving interinstitutional equilibria—which usually fall short of "rational" and coordinated interplay management— would inherently or structurally drive institutional complexes to accord greater priority to environmental concerns (or any other analytical standard such as sustainable development). On the contrary, since most environmental institutions are relatively new, they face an uphill battle when trying to balance the first-mover advantage of existing institutions. Over the past decades, the major driving force in that battle, which has resulted in important advances, has been the rising public concern about and political saliency of environmental issues. However, these assets have not been sufficient to "green" institutional complexes, nor can their sustained support be taken for granted. More targeted, structural prioritization of environmental concerns among international institutions may thus be required. While a strengthened environmental arm of the UN may not by itself be able to achieve this goal, other options include establishing a principled priority for environmental protection requirements enshrined in international institutions under general international law, and the introduction of related procedural requirements for nonenvironmental institutions (see Oberthür 2009).

Research Frontiers

Together with the progress of relevant research since the mid-1990s, this volume offers fertile ground for future studies on institutional interplay in global environmental governance. Here we focus on identifying core areas for future research on the core themes of this volume, interplay management and institutional complexes. For a broader discussion of the research agenda on institutional interaction, see Gehring and Oberthür (2008, 220–223).

A logical next step in research on institutional complexes would be to identify categories and types of institutional complexes. One potentially fruitful dimension here is the degree of fragmentation, integration, or centralization of institutional complexes (see, e.g., Biermann, Pattberg, et al. 2009; Keohane and Victor 2010). This involves addressing nontrivial problems of the measurement of fragmentation and the determination of the boundaries of institutional complexes. Similarly, the findings presented in this volume should enable further progress in the systematic analysis of the logics and dynamics of functional divisions of labor within institutional complexes. Eventually, this may allow us to identify specific forms and patterns of such divisions of labor as a basis for distinguishing theory-driven types of institutional complexes. Such forms and patterns of interinstitutional divisions of labor could then be seen in terms of varying degrees of fragmentation and centralization of institutional complexes. This line of research might include the exploration of the ways in which more basic norms and principles of the international social order shape the dynamics of institutional complexes (Underdal 2008, 57). Progress toward a more fully fledged theory of institutional interplay, including the identification of conditions under which institutions tend to influence each other's normative development or effectiveness, could provide an important underpinning for this exploration of institutional complexes.

The exploration of the effects of institutional complexes also deserves continued scholarly attention. First of all, exploring the varying effects of different categories and types of institutional complexes, and related divisions of labor, seems a logical and integral part of the investigation of such categories and types envisaged above. In this context, future studies may systematically bring into focus, and distinguish between, impacts on individual institutions, on the governance of relevant issue areas, or on international environmental governance at large, including the more basic social orders on which governance rests (see also Biermann, Betsill, et al. 2009; Underdal 2008, 57).

Let us now turn to our second core theme, interplay management. Interplay management and the manageability of institutional complexes can be considered a research topic of high priority. Actors are increasingly aware of the significance of institutional interplay and institutional complexes, and have already begun attempting to employ and shape interinstitutional complexity purposefully. This raises the question of how and to what extent the institutional complexes that have so far largely emerged and evolved "spontaneously" become subject to, and can be made subject to, collective interplay management efforts.

The current volume provides a firm basis for efforts to broaden our understanding of existing interplay management, its performance. and conditions for success in several ways (be it with respect to institutional complexes or "simpler" interinstitutional relationships). First, extending empirical studies of institutional interaction and interplay management beyond the established focal areas of trade and the environment, climate governance, and ocean governance (Oberthür and Gehring in this volume) may assist in advancing relevant knowledge. Such an extension of the empirical field of study could include transnational institutions involving private actors and cases of noninteraction—that is, of situations in which an interaction did not materialize despite the presence of favorable conditions. Second, distinguishing systematically between different kinds of actors (governments, nongovernmental organizations, international secretariats, partnerships, etc.) may fruitfully link interplay management research to research on agency in global environmental governance (Biermann, Betsill, et al. 2009). Third, the elaboration of tools for more precise and comparative assessment of interaction effects could provide important inputs to our thinking about interplay management. Finally, greater attention should be paid to the politics of interplay management, including the question of the conditions under which actors choose to pursue problem-solving interplay management aiming to enhance global environmental governance, as opposed to strategic interplay management to advance their own agendas (see also Young 2002, 111–138).

Broadening our understanding of interplay management and institutional complexes should also be an important input to our thinking about policy options for enhancing synergy, mitigating conflict, and enhancing environmental governance. By identifying the conditions for the successful implementation of these policy options, it may be possible to clarify how various actors can best advance interplay management under different circumstances, including various types of institutional complexes. Such research promises to provide valuable input into ongoing debates about the reform and development of global environmental governance (see also Oberthür 2009; Biermann 2008, 287–290; Biermann and Bauer 2005; Chambers and Green 2005).

Concluding Remarks

The chapters in this book have examined two core themes on the agenda of research on institutional interaction, interplay management and institutional complexes, in a broad range of policy areas. The cases presented do not necessarily constitute a representative sample of international environmental governance, so some caution is advised regarding generalizability. All the same, they do allow us to generate more general conjectures that may guide future research. In concluding this chapter and volume, let us single out three key insights from our analysis for particular mention.

First, interplay management efforts aimed at maximizing synergies, avoiding conflict, and enhancing global environmental governance tend to be decentralized, with low levels of crossinstitutional coordination. Most of these efforts involve states or others acting individually (*autonomous interplay management*) or, more frequently, acting collectively but unilaterally within the established institutional boundaries (*unilateral interplay management*). Existing structures for joint and overarching interplay management transcending the institutions involved, including general principles of international law and overarching attempts to coordinate among several institutions, provide a basis and framing for decentralized interplay management efforts. However, they have rarely played lead roles in shaping cross-institutional relations.

Second, over time, divisions of labor tend to emerge among the elemental regimes of broader institutional complexes or "global governance architectures" (Biermann, Pattberg, et al. 2009). As these divisions of labor are reproduced through practice, they shape mutual expectations of actors, enjoy relative stability, and provide for interinstitutional order that constrains the choices available even for those who have not explicitly approved this division of labor. While specific mechanisms related to interest maximization, normative frameworks, and processes of diffusion and learning drive and shape the emergence of interinstitutional divisions of labor, the latter are the outcome of an essentially political process and remain susceptible to change in response to major shakings of the interinstitutional equilibrium.

Third, the environmental achievements of interplay management in these evolving interinstitutional orders have been mixed. On the one hand, emerging divisions of labor, such as the one between the WTO and MEAs, may constitute significant progress for global environmental governance. On the other hand, this progress is likely to be insufficient and too slow to prevent irreversible damage to natural ecosystems and natural life-support systems; from an environmental perspective, it may be a case of too little, too late. That in turn gives rise to the question of how to facilitate and expedite interinstitutional equilibria that reflect the integration of environmental objectives.

Strengthening environmental policy integration in institutional complexes may eventually be a matter of political will rather than of institutional design. It is unclear whether the main existing proposals for reforming and developing global environmental governance would serve to enhance its effectiveness. The very limited success of moderate attempts at joint and overarching interplay management does not bode well for proposals for a World Environment Organization or other ways of far-reaching centralization or coordination. Also, the effectiveness of such proposals in strengthening environmental policy integration across international institutions is uncertain, since they lack a proven potential to address the three key factors identified here as affecting successful interplay management: problem malignancy in terms of compatibility of interests underlying the policy objectives, the political saliency of interplay issues, and cross-institutional knowledge building. And finally, more important than the organizational form and the degree of centralization or fragmentation of global environmental governance may be the international political will to assign principled priority to environmental objectives in the international order at large.

Acknowledgments

We would like to thank Mark Axelrod, Thomas Gehring, Sylvia Karlsson-Vinkhuyzen, Marcel Kok, Harro van Asselt, Oran R. Young, Fariborz Zelli, and three anonymous reviewers for very helpful comments on an earlier version of this chapter.

References

Alter, Karen J., and Sophie Meunier. 2009. The Politics of International Regime Complexity. *Perspectives on Politics* 7 (1): 13–24.

Andresen, Steinar. 2001. Global Environmental Governance: UN Fragmentation and Co-ordination. In *Yearbook of International Co-operation on Environment and Development 2001/2002*, ed. Olav Schram Stokke and Oystein B. Thommessen, 19–26. London: Earthscan.

Biermann, Frank. 2008. Earth System Governance: A Research Agenda. In *Institutions and Environmental Change: Principal Findings, Applications, and Research Frontiers*, ed. Oran R. Young, Leslie A. King, and Heike Schroeder, 277–301. Cambridge, Mass.: MIT Press.

Biermann, Frank, and Steffen Bauer, eds. 2005. *A World Environment Organization: Solution or Threat for International Environmental Governance?* Aldershot, UK: Ashgate.

Biermann, Frank, Michele M. Betsill, Joyeeta Gupta, Norichika Kanie, Louis Lebel, Diana Liverman, Heike Schröder, and Bernd Siebenhüner, with contributions from Ken Conca, Leila da Costa Ferreira, Bharat Desai, Simon Tay, and Ruben Zondervan. 2009. Earth System Governance: People, Places, and the Planet. Science and Implementation Plan of the Earth System Governance Project, Earth System Governance Project Report No. 1.Earth System Governance Report 1, IHDP Report 20. Bonn: International Human Dimensions Programme, Earth System Governance Project. http://www.earthsystemgovernance.org/sites/default/files/publications/files/Earth-System-Governance_Science-Plan.pdf (accessed 7 July 2010).

Biermann, Frank, Olwen Davies, and Nicolien van der Grijp. 2009. Environmental Policy Integration and the Architecture of Global Environmental Governance. *International Environmental Agreements: Politics, Law and Economics* 9 (4): 351–369.

Biermann, Frank, Philipp Pattberg, Harro van Asselt, and Fariborz Zelli. 2009. The Fragmentation of Global Governance Architectures: A Framework for Analysis. *Global Environmental Politics* 9 (4): 14–40.

Brown Weiss, Edith. 1993. International Environmental Issues and the Emergence of a New World Order. *Georgetown Law Journal* 81 (3): 675–710.

Chambers, W. Bradnee. 2008. *Interlinkages and the Effectiveness of Multilateral Environmental Agreements.* Tokyo: United Nations University Press.

Chambers, W. Bradnee, and Jessica F. Green. 2005. Toward an Effective Framework for Sustainable Development. In *Reforming International Environmental Governance: From Institutional Limits to Innovative Reforms*, ed. W. Bradnee Chambers and Jessica F. Green, 1–12. Tokyo: United Nations University Press.

DiMaggio, Paul. 1986. Structural Analysis of Organizational Fields: A Block-model Approach. *Organizational Behavior* 8:335–370.

Drezner, Daniel W. 2009. The Power and Peril of International Regime Complexity. *Perspectives on Politics* 7 (1): 65–70.

Franck, Thomas. 1990. *The Power of Legitimacy among Nations.* Oxford: Oxford University Press.

Gehring, Thomas. 1994. *Dynamic International Regimes: Institutions for International Environmental Governance.* Frankfurt: Peter Lang.

Gehring, Thomas, and Sebastian Oberthür. 2006. Comparative Empirical Analysis and Ideal Types of Institutional Interaction. In *Institutional Interaction in Global Environmental Governance: Synergy and Conflict among International and EU Policies*, ed. Sebastian Oberthür and Thomas Gehring, 307–371. Cambridge, Mass.: MIT Press.

Gehring, Thomas, and Sebastian Oberthür. 2008. Interplay: Exploring Institutional Interaction. In *Institutions and Environmental Change: Principal Findings, Applications, and Research Frontiers*, ed. Oran R. Young, Leslie A. King, and Heike Schroeder, 187–223. Cambridge, Mass.: MIT Press.

Gehring, Thomas, and Sebastian Oberthür. 2009. The Causal Mechanisms of Interaction between International Institutions. *European Journal of International Relations* 15 (1): 125–156.

Haas, Peter M. 1992. Introduction: Epistemic Communities and International Policy Coordination. *International Organization* 46 (1): 1–36.

Ivanova, Maria. 2007. Designing the United Nations Environment Programme: A Story of Compromise and Confrontation. *International Environmental Agreements: Politics, Law and Economics* 7 (3): 337–361.

Keohane, Robert O. 1984. *After Hegemony: Cooperation and Discord in the World Political Economy.* Princeton, N.J.: Princeton University Press.

Keohane, Robert O., and David G. Victor. 2010. The Regime Complex for Climate Change. The Harvard Project on International Climate Agreements, Discussion Paper 10–33 (January). John F. Kennedy School of Government, Harvard University, Cambridge, Mass.

Oberthür, Sebastian. 2009. Interplay Management: Enhancing Environmental Policy Integration among International Institutions. *International Environmental Agreements: Politics, Law and Economics* 9 (4): 371–391.

Oberthür, Sebastian, and Thomas Gehring. 2006. Institutional Interaction in Global Environmental Governance: The Case of the Cartagena Protocol and the World Trade Organization. *Global Environmental Politics* 6 (2): 1–31.

Raustiala, Kal, and David G. Victor. 2004. The Regime Complex for Plant Genetic Resources. *International Organization* 55:277–309.

Rosendal, Kristin. 2001. Impacts of Overlapping International Regimes: The Case of Biodiversity. *Global Governance* 7 (1): 95–117.

Scott, W. Richard, and Gerald F. Davis. 2007. *Organizations and Organizing: Rational, Natural, and Open System Perspectives.* Upper Saddle River, N.J.: Pearson Prentice Hall.

Stokke, Olav Schram. 2004. Trade Measures and Climate Compliance: Interplay between WTO and the Marrakesh Accords. *International Environmental Agreements: Politics, Law and Economics* 4 (4): 339–357.

Stokke, Olav Schram. 2009. Trade Measures and the Combat of IUU Fishing: Institutional Interplay and Effective Governance in the Northeast Atlantic. *Marine Policy* 33 (1): 339–349.

Stokke, Olav Schram, Geir Hønneland, and Peter Johan Schei. 2010. Pollution and Conservation. In *International Cooperation and Arctic Governance: Regime Effectiveness and Northern Region Building* (paperback edition), ed. Olav Schram Stokke and Geir Hønneland, 78–111. London: Routledge.

Underdal, Arid. 2002. One Question, Two Answers. In *Environmental Regime Effectiveness: Confronting Theory with Evidence*, ed. Edward L. Miles, Arild Underdal, Steinar Andresen, Jørgen Wettestad, Jon Birger Skjærseth, and Elaine M. Carlin, 3–45. Cambridge, Mass.: MIT Press.

Underdal, Arild. 2008. Determining the Causal Significance of Institutions: Accomplishments and Challenges. In *Institutions and Environmental Change: Principal Findings, Applications, and Research Frontiers*, ed. Oran R. Young, Leslie A. King, and Heike Schroeder, 49–78. Cambridge, Mass.: MIT Press.

Underdal, Arild, and Oran R. Young, eds. 2004a. *Regime Consequences: Methodological Challenges and Research Strategies.* Dordrecht: Kluwer Academic.

Underdal, Arild, and Oran R. Young. 2004b. Research Strategies for the Future. In *Regime Consequences: Methodological Challenges and Research Strategies*, ed. Arild Underdal and Oran R. Young, 361–380. Dordrecht: Kluwer-Academic.

von Moltke, Konrad. 2005. Clustering International Environmental Agreements as an Alternative to a World Environment Organization. In *A World Environment Organization: Solution or Threat for Effective International Environmental Governance?*, ed. Frank Biermann and Steffen Bauer, 175–204. Aldershot, UK: Ashgate.

Wolfrum, Rüdiger, and Nele Matz. 2003. *Conflicts in International Environmental Law.* Berlin: Springer-Verlag.

Young, Oran R. 2002. *The Institutional Dimensions of Environmental Change: Fit, Interplay, and Scale.* Cambridge, Mass.: MIT Press.

Young, Oran R., with contributions from Arun Agrawal, Leslie A. King, Peter H. Sand, Arild Underdal, and Merrilyn Wasson. 1999/2005. *Institutional Dimensions of Global Environmental Change (IDGEC) Science Plan.* IHDP Report No. 9/16. Bonn: International Human Dimensions Programme on Global Environmental Change.

Young, Oran R. 2008. Institutions and Environmental Change: The Scientific Legacy of a Decade of IDGEC Research. In *Institutions and Environmental Change: Principal Findings, Applications, and Research Frontiers*, ed. Oran R. Young, Leslie A. King, and Heike Schroeder, 3–45. Cambridge, Mass.: MIT Press.

Young, Oran R. 2010. *Institutional Dynamics: Emergent Patterns in International Environmental Governance.* Cambridge, Mass.: MIT Press.

List of Contributors

Frank Alcock   Associate professor of political science, New College of Florida, Sarasota, Florida; director, Marine Policy Institute at Mote Marine Laboratory, Sarasota, Florida, USA.

Harro van Asselt   Marie Curie Fellow, Environmental Change Institute, University of Oxford, United Kingdom, and PhD researcher, Institute for Environmental Studies, Vrije Universiteit Amsterdam, the Netherlands.

Mark Axelrod   Assistant professor, James Madison College and Department of Fisheries & Wildlife, Michigan State University, East Lansing, USA.

Claire Dupont   Research fellow, Institute for European Studies, Vrije Universiteit Brussels, Belgium.

Thomas Gehring   Professor of international politics, Faculty of Social Science, Economics and Management, Otto-Friedrich-University Bamberg, Germany.

Stefan Jungcurt   Researcher, Department of Resource Economics, Humboldt University of Berlin, Germany.

Sylvia I. Karlsson-Vinkhuyzen   Academic research fellow, Finland Futures Research Centre, University of Turku, Finland, and visiting fellow, Department of International Public Law, Leiden University, the Netherlands.

Marcel T.J. Kok   Senior researcher, Netherlands Environmental Assessment Agency (PBL), Amsterdam, the Netherlands.

Yasuko Matsumoto   Associate professor, Graduate School of Global Environmental Studies, Kyoto University, Japan.

Sebastian Oberthür   Academic director of the Institute for European Studies, Vrije Universiteit Brussels, Belgium.

Olav Schram Stokke   Research professor, Fridtjof Nansen Institute, Norway.

Fariborz Zelli   Research fellow, German Development Institute, Bonn, Germany.

Index